PLAY
-BY-
PLAY

Ronald A. Smith

Play-by-Play

Radio, Television,
and Big-Time
College Sport

The Johns Hopkins University Press
Baltimore and London

© 2001 The Johns Hopkins University Press
All rights reserved. Published 2001
Printed in the United States of America on acid-free paper
9 8 7 6 5 4 3 2 1

The Johns Hopkins University Press
2715 North Charles Street
Baltimore, Maryland 21218-4363
www.press.jhu.edu

Library of Congress Cataloging-in-Publication Data
Smith, Ronald A. (Ronald Austin), 1936–
    Play-by-play : radio, television, and big-time college sport /
    Ronald A. Smith.
        p.   cm.
Includes bibliographical references and index.
    ISBN 0-8018-6686-3 (hardcover: alk. paper)
    1. Mass media and sports—United States.   2. College sports—United States.
I. Title.
    GV742 .S64 2001
    796.04'3'0973—dc21

00-011534

A catalog record for this book is available from the British Library.

Contents

Acknowledgments

WHILE I HAVE been involved in writing sport history for more than three decades, I wish to acknowledge three individuals in the Delavan, Wisconsin, public schools who influenced my direction toward both sport and history a half-century ago. First, my "gym" teacher, Webb Schultz, encouraged me as a fifth-grader to be the best that I could be. He later coached me in basketball and baseball, helping me to develop skills that allowed me to pursue those two sports at Northwestern University and play professional baseball for a short time following graduation. A social science teacher, Wally Zimmerman, suggested to me in junior high school that humility was a virtue I should try to cultivate. He may not have been totally successful, though I had the opportunity to practice that and other virtues with him for three years on his football team. Competing on teams was important to me, but the influence of a high school history teacher, Eunice Hahn, sparked an early interest in the study of history. I have had the good fortune to have such mentors and, since the 1960s, to combine interests in sport and history.

Relative to this study, I want to thank two historians who preceded me in producing histories of television and sport, Joan M. Chandler (*Television and National Sport: The United States and Britain,* 1988) and Benjamin G. Rader (*In Its Own Image: How Television Has Transformed Sport,* 1984). Both are members of the North American Society for Sport History, which has been instrumental in promoting the writing of sport history. Two other historians have been particularly helpful in the writing of this volume. Both JoDee Dyreson and John Watterson critiqued the entire manuscript in an early form and provided useful suggestions. Gene Goodwin, a retired professor of communications at Penn State, provided insights from the media point of view. One of my graduate students, Nadine Gelberg, was an especially talented research assistant during the early stages of work on this project.

I also appreciate the gracious help that I have received from universities across America as I have researched radio and television in their archives: Alabama, Arizona State, Brown, Butler, California-Berkeley, Chicago, Clemson, Colorado, Columbia, Cornell, Dartmouth, Drake, Duke, Georgetown, Georgia, Georgia Tech, Harvard, Illinois, Maryland, Michigan, Minnesota, Nebraska, North Carolina, Northwestern, Notre

Dame, Ohio State, Oklahoma, Penn State, Pennsylvania, Princeton, Rutgers, Southern California, Stanford, Tennessee, Tulane, United States Military Academy, West Point, United States Naval Academy, Annapolis, Virginia, William and Mary, Wisconsin, and Yale. Conference collections that were useful included the Eastern College Athletic Conference and the Atlantic Coast Conference. The Library of Congress Manuscript Division was of vital importance relative to the early television network sports leader, the Du Mont Television Network. Probably of greatest value were the vast Walter Byers Papers at the National Collegiate Athletic Association. I was fortunately allowed by the NCAA's Ursula Walsh to wander through the unorganized Walter Byers Payers well before any other researchers had access to them and prior to their becoming part of the NCAA's organized collection.

Finally, I owe much to the Department of Physical Education (later the Department of Exercise and Sport Science and eventually Kinesiology) at Penn State University and its strong graduate program and to my longtime colleagues in sport history, John Lucas and James Thompson. The tradition of quality colleagues and collegiality continues in Penn State's new faculty member, Mark Dyreson. To my scholarly benefit, I was granted four sabbaticals in my twenty-eight years at that fine institution and was given a teaching schedule that allowed time for both researching and writing. Penn State also provided me the benefits of observing the big-time athletics that I enjoy immensely. At the same time, I was able to observe the impact that athletics have on the academic scene, something that requires constant monitoring to protect the academic integrity of the institution. An understanding of intercollegiate athletics' cashing in on radio and television may allow prudent decisions in charting the future course of intercollegiate athletics.

PLAY
-BY-
PLAY

Introduction

"HELL, THAT'S socialism, and we're not in a socialistic state," fumed the University of Michigan athletic director in the midst of the summer of 1975.[1] Don Canham, himself an entrepreneur as well athletic leader at Michigan, was referring to a letter written by the president of California State University–Long Beach. Stephen Horn had just written to all institutional presidents in the National Collegiate Athletic Association asking that the NCAA vote to share the wealth created by NCAA televised football and the NCAA basketball tourney.[2] Horn, a young president, was a staunch Republican who was ironically preaching collectivism. Dividing up the commercial television money among all NCAA institutions was not going to occur in the 1970s any more than it did a generation before or would a generation later. Commercial television was part of the free enterprise system that had been in existence in intercollegiate athletics for well over a century.

Athletic power brokers in the NCAA, including Canham, would not allow the dominant football institutions to receive a lesser amount of money from television than they were already receiving. "Any reductions in the money to the traditional football powers," Canham suggested, "would break up the Association."[3] Cedric Dempsey, athletic director at the University of the Pacific and later executive director of the NCAA, agreed. He wrote then executive director Walter Byers that Horn "rubbed people the wrong way" with his "Robin Hood" plan.[4] When Byers told Horn of the "unacceptability" of his plan, Byers was reflecting big-time football's commercial approach to college athletics.[5] In the months that followed, a new organization of football powers was created, the College Football Association, to protect what big-time football had created. Within a half-dozen years, the CFA challenged the NCAA's TV contract in an attempt to bring even more money to the dominant football-playing institutions. It was a pivotal time in the history of college athletics and an important time in the broadening commercialization of athletics in higher education.

Whoever seeks to understand higher education in America should learn the place of collegiate athletics. Intercollegiate sport has existed since the mid-nineteenth century, and it has been commercialized not just by the introduction of television but from the first contest, an 1852

Harvard-Yale boat race.[6] Not only intercollegiate athletics but also higher education, in many ways, reflects the commercial aspect of America's free enterprise system. In Owen Johnson's successful 1912 novel, *Stover at Yale,* a leading character claims that American universities "are business colleges purely and simply, because we as a nation have only one ideal—the business ideal."[7] The overarching objectives of most institutions, educational or mercantile, are survival first and foremost, then prosperity. Historically, institutions of higher education have survived in America with little federal aid and have prospered, in part, because of their ability to sell themselves to the public.

Intercollegiate athletics, especially big-time college sport, have had remarkable success marketing themselves to the American people. They have done so because they were forced to commercialize themselves in order to maintain a high level of performance rather than slip into mediocrity. College athletics became commercialized well before radio and television contributed to the process. When the University of Michigan was invited to participate in the first Pasadena Tournament of Roses in 1902, the football business manager's response reflected a focus already dominant in intercollegiate athletics: "We desire to make the trip to the Pacific coast during the holidays," asserted Charles Baird, "providing it can be *made to pay.*"[8] Albert Bushnell Hart, the noted historian at Harvard who closely followed athletics from the 1880s through the next half-century, remarked: "The Greeks made it a cult; the English a spectacle; the Americans have made it a business."[9] What big-time athletics did was continue the business tradition by cashing in on the airwaves. The result was an intensification of the commercial spirit surrounding college sport from the 1920s on.

Radio and television, as commercial entities, created symbiotic relationships with intercollegiate athletics nearly from their beginnings in the 1920s and 1930s. Colleges and universities never recommended that nonprofit public radio and television be the vehicle to carry college sport events in an educational medium. Rather, they opted to allow the increase in commercialism to benefit athletics just as intercollegiate sport had increased the visibility of educational institutions among the public. Athletics were further distanced from educational programs even as the institutions used the prestige and sometimes the money brought in by that athletic success. There was never a concerted effort by universities to tie athletics into educational functions by broadcasting games over their own public radio and television stations. Athletics and their long-term commercialization were either too profitable to the universities or not associated clearly enough with educational programs to be included with educational radio and television, as were extension programs or higher culture programs such as classical music, opera, or the reading of literature.

The fact that public radio and television did not carry university games was symbolic of big-time athletics' longtime separation from the academic core of higher education. Yet the use of commercial radio and television in intercollegiate athletics was really in the forefront of the commercialization of all of higher education. Where intercollegiate athletics led, the rest of higher education followed. Corporate sponsorship, campus commercialism, and alumni donations—all were nineteenth-century offerings cultivated by college athletics. Athletics were first developed by students, then taken over by alumni, and finally utilized by the university itself. While big-time athletics have always been part of the American free enterprise system, educational institutions have been less dominated by commercial forces. Private universities took the commercial route first, albeit reluctantly. For instance, Northwestern, presently the only private institution in the Big 10, was in the "real estate, hotel, hospital, and recreation business" prior to World War II.[10] Only later did most universities, especially state-owned institutions, join the business model for survival and prosperity.

Radio and television, while only a part of the commercialism of intercollegiate athletics, were in the forefront by the second half of the twentieth century. At midcentury, the president of Madison Square Garden said that "sports will be to television what music was to radio."[11] Quite possibly true, but radio has also meant a great deal to college sport. Even as late as the 1990s, radio receipts for football powerhouse Nebraska exceeded its income from television.[12] It is valuable to study radio of the 1920s through the 1940s to better understand the place of television in influencing college sport in the second half of the twentieth century.

Leaders of big-time intercollegiate athletics found themselves in a commercial-educational dilemma from the outset. There seemed no easy solution, except for those impractical idealists who have wanted an outright ban on big-time athletics, against the will of most Americans. The dilemma was clearly stated by three NCAA leaders before the advent of commercial radio. In 1919, the year before the first commercial radio station in the nation, Pittsburgh's KDKA, came into existence, an NCAA committee quoted a Brown University professor who pinpointed the educational predicament: "We are told by the college officials that we must conduct our sports . . . along amateur lines but we must finance them along lines that are purely commercial and professional."[13] The early NCAA leaders pointed to the commercial cycle of hiring business managers, now called athletic directors, to be good businessmen, not educators; of paying for high-priced coaches and recruiting teams to win, to fill the stadiums and arenas; of smaller colleges playing larger ones only for the financial payoff; and of big-time institutions scheduling games with weaker ones to produce victories and thus larger gate receipts. The commercial spiral kept deepening as institutions lowered academic standards to maintain high athletic quality, created academic-athletic staffs to keep athletes eligible, increased the number of contests, and scheduled televised sporting events on all days of the week to appease the television networks and increase their own revenues. Because universities were unable or unwilling to pay for athletics out of the general educational budget, the commercial route was taken.

Of the two possible ways out of the dilemma, financing through the educational budget was rejected generations ago for the commercial solution. Critics have been crying foul ever since, especially after radio and television took the commercial approach to a higher level. It has become the commonly accepted model for big-time institutions, and the governing boards and university presidents have not only accepted the model but have also been leaders in promoting the commercial spirit on university campuses across the nation.

This volume was written with an emphasis on firsthand accounts, particularly from sources within colleges and the NCAA. I used internal documents from the archives of nearly fifty colleges, athletic conferences, and the NCAA as primary sources to construct this history of the influence of radio and TV on big-time intercollegiate athletics. While the great contests were being performed in the stadiums and arenas, absorbing the interest of fans across the nation, a lesser-known story of the increased commercialization of college athletics was being played out in the back rooms of individual institutions, the athletic conferences, the NCAA, and the radio and television networks for most of the twentieth century. Very little of the back-room activity falls under the NCAA's basic purpose as defined by its constitution: "To maintain intercollegiate athletics as an integral part of the educational program and the athlete as an integral part of the student body."[14] The primary documents reveal that commercialized athletics were integral to the image of big-time institutions of higher education in America. Radio and television have been a major part of that commercialization, sanctioned by students, alumni, the public, governing boards, athletic departments, and the presidents of universities across the nation. This overwhelming support for big-time athletics has been widespread since the nineteenth century, while opposition has been sporadic and unsuccessful for the same period.

This book is written principally from the viewpoint of the colleges and the NCAA, not from that of radio and TV networks. My interest is not in the media per se but in how colleges and universities have used the media for their own purposes. For over three decades, I have devoted most of my research to better understanding big-time college athletics. After participating in intercollegiate baseball and basketball at Northwestern University in the 1950s, I had the opportunity to play professional baseball in the Chicago White Sox organization for a short time before beginning a teaching career that concluded at Penn State University, which has its own big-time athletic program. My doctoral dissertation at the University of Wisconsin looked at the history of an intercollegiate athletic conference. Since then I have written more than fifty articles and three books on intercollegiate sport. Only when I began researching the beginnings of intercollegiate athletics in what are now Ivy League institutions, Harvard and Yale, did I discover that from the start athletics were permeated with both commercialism and professionalism. When a newly built railroad sponsored the first Harvard-Yale crew meet in 1852, giving athletes from the two premier institutions in America an eight-day paid holiday in the vacation lands of New Hampshire, and when, fourteen years later, Yale hired a professional coach and achieved its first win over Harvard's crew, it was clear that a commercial and professional spirit had invaded college sport.[15] While the private "Ivy League" institutions led the way to commercialization and professionalism, they were outdone in the twentieth century mostly by state-supported institutions and a few sectarian schools.

Radio and, later, television fit well into the commercial model passed on to intercollegiate athletics by the elite Eastern schools. By the time radio came onto the scene in the 1920s, the Midwest, the South, and the West had caught up to the Ivy League institutions in athletics if not in academics. These institutions first began to exploit the airwaves financially through radio in the Depression of the 1930s and almost immediately after World War II, when television became commercially successful. The explosion of television sales around 1950 brought about a deep fear among colleges that a decline in attendance at football, the dominant college sport, might destroy not only football but also the other sports that were dependent upon football gate receipts.

That threat brought about the first successful control measures of any aspect of intercollegiate athletics on a national level, when the NCAA voted overwhelmingly in 1951 to limit the number of football games telecast each Saturday. I devote much of this book to explaining how national control of television came to challenge the traditional "Home Rule," or athletic control by individual institutions and conferences among big-time universities, which had existed since the NCAA was officially formed in 1906.[16] The initial national control, intended to preserve the commercialized stadium attendance, eventually led to added profits from commercial television through the monopolistic NCAA television plan. There was big money to be made from telecasts by the 1970s, and individual institutions began to chip away at the national TV controls, hoping for even greater income. Citing federal antitrust legislation, the College Football Association, comprising a large group of the big-time football powers, challenged the NCAA in court by supporting two of its members, the University of Oklahoma and the University of Georgia, in an antitrust suit. The court case was ultimately decided by the U.S. Supreme Court, which found the NCAA in violation of the Sherman Antitrust Act of 1890, and the NCAA lost its monopoly over television. Eventually the maverick independent football power Notre Dame took over the contracting for telecasts, leading to the demise of the College Football Association. This had repercussions, preventing the NCAA from holding a national tournament to determine a national champion in Division I-A football, the only sport among nearly eighty men's and women's sports that has no "real" champion at season's end.

This history is, then, a story centered on big-time football. Basketball also became an important commercial venture well after midcentury, and its popularity skyrocketed after the networks bought rights and expanded the coverage of the men's basketball tournament in the 1970s. Only big-time football and men's basketball have been significant to commercialized college sport in the past generation or two. No other sports, men's or women's, have been so strongly involved in radio or television. Thus, I do not delve into the world of women's basketball, which had a national television contract worth about one-ninetieth of the men's NCAA tournament at the close of the twentieth century. Nor do I follow the minor televised college sport of men's baseball and other lesser sports from a commercial standpoint. They have been unimportant in the larger picture of commercialization. That could change in the future, however, as women's volleyball or soccer or men's ice hockey could become economic factors if they become more popular and are widely televised in the twenty-first century.

The Media and Early College Sport

"GOOD AFTERNOON, ladies and gentlemen," Bill Stern announced as a hundred or so viewed America's first telecast of a sporting event, a baseball game between Columbia and Princeton universities, May 17, 1939. Stern's introduction of the teams' captains and coaches was seen on a few blurry television screens in New York City. They all appeared to have dark faces, as a result of the sun shining directly in front of the single iconoscope camera, stationed on a wooden platform in the stands between third base and home plate at Baker Field. It was the only remote camera owned by the entire NBC network. When the game started, the players appeared "like white flies" as they raced across the screen, and the ball was seldom seen except on infield plays.[1] That extra-inning game, won by Princeton, was a harbinger of television's impact on college sport development, although television was perhaps no more important than radio, introduced two decades before, or other aspects of the media such as newspaper coverage.

Intercollegiate athletics were "big-time" before the advent of television and radio. In the nineteenth century crowds of 30,000 and 40,000 saw football games and crew meets involving Harvard, Yale, and Princeton. One event, an 1869 crew meet between Harvard and Oxford universities, attracted an estimated crowd of one million, who lined the banks of the Thames River in London to observe a rowing contest between the most elite British and American educational institutions. The newly laid trans-Atlantic cable carried more news of the crew meet back to America than for any other event in the Atlantic cable's early history.[2] That meet, only four years after the American Civil War and at the height of Britain's Imperial power, occurred less than two decades after the first American intercollegiate competition in 1852.[3]

The media covered and promoted intercollegiate athletics from the beginning. The first American intercollegiate contest, a crew meet between Harvard and Yale, was held at Lake Winnipesaukee, New Hampshire, on a "perfect summer day, cloudless, moderately warm, with a light zephyr from the northwest," according to a Boston reporter.[4] Though there was only moderate media coverage, the contest was extremely commercialized. The newly constructed Boston, Concord, and Montreal Railroad paid all expenses on its line for the eight-day excursion for the two crews to the New Hampshire vacation spot. The Boston article pointed out the determined will of the victorious Harvard crew members, decked out their red, white, and blue outfits. The *New York Herald* also noted the two-mile race, saying that intercollegiate sport would "make little stir in a busy world."[5] But college sport would indeed make quite a stir, in large part because of newspapers such as the *Herald.*

Baseball, the second intercollegiate sport introduced, made its debut two years before the Civil War. Two small Massachusetts colleges, Amherst and Williams, played a baseball game in the Berkshire Mountains at Pittsfield after isolated Williamstown had been connected to the rest of Massachusetts by a new rail line. It was a summer contest, with Amherst winning easily, 73-32, under Massachusetts rules. Those rules usually allowed a batter to be called out if a ball was caught either in the air or on the first bounce, but the two teams rejected the "sissy" bouncing-ball rule, allowing only what as called the more "mannish" fly-ball rule. The *Franklin and Hampshire Gazette* noted the "perfect military discipline" of the Amherst men, who prevented the runners from getting "soaked," that is, put out by being hit with the ball between bases.[6] Therein lay a major difference with the New York Knickerbocker rules, which prevented soaking and introduced the concept of being forced out at bases if the ball arrived before the runner. The Massachusetts rules were eventually supplanted by the New York rules, and baseball became the dominant sport for most colleges by the 1860s and 1870s.

The third major sport played by colleges was football, which took two forms: European football, or soccer, and rugby, which was modified into American football. The media took notice of football, seemingly for two reasons. First, there was an element of brutality in both forms. Second, within its first decade of intercollegiate play, football caught the imagination of undergraduates and became a ritualized focus for the community and center for campus esprit de corps. One journalist extolled football's soccer form in 1869, the year of the first intercollegiate contest, for its "bleeding hands, scarred limbs, and clogged breath" and its "rugged path to glory."[7] When Princeton arrived at Rutgers in New Jersey for the first intercollegiate contest, on November 6, 1869, the players displayed "headlong running, wild shouting, and frantic kicking" as Rutgers went on to win the match 6 to 4. At one point players ran headlong into a wooden fence and catapulted spectators seated on top of it to the ground.[8] This turbulent material was prime fodder for media attention, just as was the uproar over a century later when Ohio State's football coach, Woody Hayes, was fired for punching an opposing player in a fit of anger during a bowl game.[9]

The fourth "big-time" sport was track and field, probably the college sport least appealing to the media in the nineteenth century. Track and field first attracted attention when competition began as a side event of the prominent intercollegiate regattas, which were the most publicized college sporting events during the 1870s. For weeks, the media emphasized the rowing contests that usually featured Harvard and Yale against other lesser institutions. A dominating figure in the New York newspaper business, James Gordon Bennett, Jr., owner of the *New York Herald,* offered a prize trophy worth $500 to the winner of a two-mile run in Springfield, Massachusetts, site of the 1873 intercollegiate regatta. Duncan Bowie, a student at McGill University in Montreal, and two other collegians accepted the challenge. Bowie, who had won cash prizes in several other footraces, was allowed to compete despite charges that he was a professional. A professional collegiate runner winning the first intercollegiate track event made for a good story in the midst of the more prestigious crew meet, in which Yale outlasted Harvard before a mass of spectators on the Connecticut River.[10] Headlines in major newspapers and descriptions of the crew meet helped track gain additional status among the big-time intercollegiate sports.

While track and field was an outgrowth of the collegiate regattas, the rowing celebrations themselves were the college media frenzies of the mid-1870s. A series of intercollegiate regattas would not likely have taken place had there not been a dispute between Yale and Harvard over their annual dual crew race in 1870. After Yale broke relations with Harvard over a collision caused by the Yale boat, Harvard started an open regatta for all comers the following year. The newly created Rowing Association of American Colleges soon provided a showcase for colleges to challenge the rowing supremacy of Harvard and Yale and attain the prestige that came with victory.

After the 1873 regatta attracted approximately 30,000 spectators on the Connecticut River in Springfield, Massachusetts, it was moved to a larger body of water at the high-class resort area at Saratoga Lake in New York. Columbia won the Saratoga regatta in 1874, before the largest American crowd yet to witness a college regatta. The *New York World* carried eleven full columns of news of the race, saturating the front page of the paper.[11] Following its victory, the Columbia crew traveled to New York City by rail in a Pullman Palace Car, as newspapers promoted the athletic celebrities.[12] The next year, Harvard and Yale lost again, this time to a "boat load of mechanics from Ithaca," as an elite Harvard student described Cornell's winning crew.[13] Crews from both Harvard and Yale knew that they, not the lesser colleges, brought national acclaim and celebrity status to the regattas, and they soon withdrew to race only against each other again. With their withdrawal, the newspapers and the public in general stopped their support, and the Saratoga regatta died quickly and quietly. The dominant sport weekly of the era, the *Spirit of the Times,* reported "utter apathy among the public regarding the races" in 1876.[14]

At the time when the intercollegiate regattas were losing their hold on the American public, a new phenomenon began to emerge—the Thanksgiving Day football game. The Thanksgiving Day games soon surpassed the crew extravaganzas in popularity with the general public as well as with the socially elite. During the year of the U.S. Centennial, as the Saratoga regatta folded, a small group of select Eastern colleges led by Harvard and Yale decided to play rugby football rather than soccer and to have a championship game to conclude their rugby season. Only the year before, Yale had chosen to play Harvard in a rugby game rather than preserve its own game of soccer. That change forced Princeton to also abandon soccer if it wanted to compete against the more prestigious Harvard and Yale. By the fall of 1876, Princeton had invited Harvard, Yale, and Columbia to form an Intercollegiate Football Association based on rugby rules.[15] The four schools decided to play a championship game on Thanksgiving Day, beginning a football tradition that has lasted well over a century.[16] The first Thanksgiving Day game saw Yale's Walter Camp, the "Father of American Football," receiving the ball out of a rugby scrum (a way of putting the ball in play), racing toward the Princeton goal, and tossing the ball to a teammate who scored the winning touchdown.[17] This was the beginning of fifty years of prominence for Camp, who went on to dominate the rules committee for decades and, in so doing, Americanize rugby football. He, more than anyone else, promoted football through the media in his voluminous newspaper and magazine articles and books, well into the twentieth century. Camp, the sport visionary and entrepreneur, was a major figure in the commercialization of college sport well before radio and television.

The Thanksgiving Day football game became a dominant feature of elite activity in New York City, as it kicked off the winter social season. The first contest, held outside New York City in Hoboken, New Jersey, attracted only about a thousand fans. A dozen years later, 23,000 spectators watched Yale beat Harvard, the largest crowd to witness an event on New York's Polo Grounds. Among the arriving spectators were some of the "shining lights of the social world." These socialites were, according to a New York newspaper, "perched high on gaily decked drags and looking resplendent in beautiful winter costumes."[18]

While massive crowds watched the games at Manhattan Field and the Polo Grounds in the 1880s, the early to mid-1890s were the glory years of the Thanksgiving Day game. Such notables as Cornelius Vanderbilt, the entrepreneur, Mrs. William C. Whitney, the socialite, and John Montgomery Ward, the baseball star and organizer of the first players' union, attended the 1890 game at Eastern Park in Brooklyn.[19] At the 1893 game, Princeton won a 6-0 game over Yale as a crowd of more than 40,000 overflowed Manhattan Field. With prominent multimillionaires looking on, members of the media scribbled notes to feed the eager readers of the daily newspapers. Box seats at the games cost over ten times the ticket price to major league baseball games.[20] The extravagance, fueled by the media, brought complaints from those who opposed the expanded commercialization of the Thanksgiving Day football frenzy, both in New York City and, increasingly, across the nation. The president of Lafayette College in Pennsylvania complained that the Thanksgiving Day game was an "extravagant affair leading to costly uniforms, travelling in special cars, staying at expensive hotels, and hiring professional coaches." He noted the Yale-Princeton game revenue was greater than the cost of running a small college with twenty-five professors.[21] A professor at Stanford University protested after the Stanford-California Thanksgiving Day game in San Francisco that "nobody eats a Thanksgiving dinner any more, or even stays in Palo Alto on that day. Thanksgiving has lost every vestige of its original character."[22] Similar sentiments were stated a century later when millions of Thanksgiving dinners were preempted by televised football.

Commenting on the national popularity of the Thanksgiving Day game, the *Chicago Tribune* estimated in 1896 that 120,000 players competed in 5,000 Thanksgiving Day games that year. One was an indoor game at the Chicago Coliseum, between the University of Chicago, coached by the legendary Amos Alonzo Stagg, and the University of Michigan, already a powerhouse in the Midwest.[23] The traditional game was bringing wealth to athletic departments of the big-time institutions, from the East Coast "Ivy League" schools to the West Coast elites, Stanford and California. Stanford's athletic manager, Herbert Hoover, later

President of the United States during the Depression, collected gate receipts of $30,000 in grain bags for Stanford's game with California in San Francisco.[24]

The height of the Thanksgiving Day game was occurring at the same time that the 21-year-old son of an Irish-Italian couple, Guglielmo Marconi, sent a series of telegraphic signals through the air, the first use of the wireless radio. Coincidentally, that was more than a decade after a German, Paul Nipkow, had patented a disc-scanning system that sent pictures by way of a radio transmitter, a forerunner of television. So at the same time the Thanksgiving Day intercollegiate football game was at its peak, radio and television were introduced in their most primitive stages. In less than two decades, a football game would be broadcast.

Before radio and television, big-time intercollegiate athletics were still highly commercialized, garnering business sponsorship and gigantic gate receipts, and professionalized, with paid coaches and subsidized athletes. What radio and television eventually did was not to commercialize or professionalize college sport but rather to intensify the process that had been in existence well before the invention of either media form. The intensification of the big-time professional and commercial model using new forms of media did not begin in earnest until the 1920s, when, after a period of experimentation with Marconi's new wireless invention, radio became a commercial success.

2 — Marconi, the Wireless, and Early Sports Broadcasting

GUGLIELMO MARCONI was born in 1874, the year Harvard accepted rugby football for its own game and changed the nature of American football forever. As a youth, Marconi often isolated himself in his third-floor room on his parents' estate near Bologna, Italy, experimenting with electrical "Hertzian waves" activated by a spark jumping across a gap. He was successful at ringing a bell using wireless telegraphy, first from across a room and eventually over distances outside, using Morse code to send messages. After the Italian government showed no interest in his experiments, Marconi took his invention to the British Isles. Britain, mistress of the oceans, could utilize wireless telegraphic communications to hold together her domination of the seas. Marconi's distance tests on the Plains of Salisbury reached nine miles, and his invention soon gained financial backing.[1]

Much of the industrialized world, including James Gordon Bennett, Jr., owner of the *New York Herald,* soon learned of the amazing invention, especially after Marconi used his wireless telegraph to send an account of the 1898 Kingstown Regatta to the *Dublin Daily Express.* Bennett, who had promoted intercollegiate athletics for a generation, wanted to use the wireless to sell his New York newspaper and in the process promote sport. The America's Cup race, the premier yachting event, was set for October 1899 between the U.S. entry *Columbia* and tea baron Sir Thomas Lipton's Irish-owned *Shamrock.* Only four years after the invention of the wireless, Bennett offered Marconi $5,000 to cover the America's Cup competition for the *New York Herald.* The commercialization of American sport using this new technology began with the best of five races off Sandy Hook, New Jersey; the *Herald*'s owner hoped this advantage would help his paper compete against William Randolph Hearst's *New York Journal* and Joseph Pulitzer's *New York World.*[2] Bennett, who three decades earlier had sponsored Henry Morton Stanley's search for David Livingston in the depths of Africa to increase *Herald* sales, knew that a newspaper coup could be achieved if he could have the results of the America's Cup race in print before the ships returned to port. The wireless telegraph, carrying a signal fifteen to twenty miles, worked as Marconi expected. During the first race between the eventual American victor *Columbia* and Lipton's British challenger *Shamrock,* Marconi successfully dispatched over 2,000 words to the *Herald* office. Only three or four words needed to be repeated. "It worked," according to Marconi, "very well, indeed."[3] The promotion of the wireless was intensified.

As valuable as the telegraphic wireless technology was to oceangoing vessels, it would be truly successful on land only when the series or burst of dots and dashes of the wireless current could be replaced by a continuous wave on which the human voice would be carried. What was needed was the way to transform Marconi's wireless telegraph into our common conception of the radio. Experimentation with this end in mind occurred in private labs and in universities. One of the experimenters was Reginald Fessenden, who was first successful in voice transmissions at the turn of the century, using crystal detectors, commonly known as crystal sets. Lee de Forest soon invented the Audion tube, which could detect and amplify radio waves.[4] College professors in engineering and physics experimented with radio in the late nineteenth and early twentieth centuries at state institutions like Arkansas and Nebraska, at private colleges like Tufts, Tulane, and Wittenberg, and even at a Roman Catholic school, Notre Dame.[5] Notre Dame is a curious case, for one would not have expected strong scientific study at an institution dedicated principally to the promotion of the Catholic religion in a predominantly Protestant nation. Nevertheless, Professor Jerome Green was transmitting messages from one room of the science hall at Notre Dame to another building at the same time that Marconi was first transmitting wireless messages across the English Channel.[6] Notre Dame, which eventually became the institution most successful at using radio and television of football to further its image, was, indeed, an early advocate of broadcasting.

The use of wireless telegraphy to broadcast college sporting events, however, evidently first occurred not at Notre Dame but at the University of Minnesota, in the same year as the sinking of the *Titanic*. The year 1912 was significant in radio for two reasons: the first precedent-setting federal regulations required a license for anyone transmitting radio signals, and a tragic sea accident raised the public's interest in radio. The 1912 law was largely ignored, and thus only the sinking of the SS *Titanic* made a great impact. A 21-year-old operator of a Marconi wireless receiver, David Sarnoff, heard weak signals in a New York Wanamaker store from the *Titanic* as it was sinking. Sarnoff, a Russian-born immigrant, gave information to the press, alerted ships, and received information about deaths and those who had been saved from history's most famous boat tragedy. Sarnoff's name became instantly recognizable, well before he became general manager of the Radio Corporation of America at age 30. Four years after the *Titanic* incident, Sarnoff wrote: "I have in mind a plan of development which would make radio a 'household utility' in the same sense as the piano or phonograph." Sarnoff continued, "The 'Radio Music Box' can be supplied with amplifying tubes and a loudspeaking telephone, all of which can be neatly mounted in one box."[7]

As Sarnoff proclaimed this, investigators at the University of Minnesota were still experimenting with a spark transmitter using regular telegraph signals. In 1912, Professor F. W. Springer and a young instructor, H. M. Turner, began an experimental radio station with the call numbers 9X1-WLB. As part of their investigation, Springer and Turner broadcast accounts of Minnesota's home football games to a sparse audience.[8] The efforts at the University of Minnesota preceded the first commercial station in the country, KDKA of Pittsburgh, by broadcasting a football game nearly a decade before the "first station in the nation" was founded. Minnesota's game broadcasts also predated what is generally, and incorrectly, recognized as the first wireless broadcast of a football game, that of a 1920 game at College Station between Texas A & M and Texas.[9]

A major reason why a period of eight years existed between the Minnesota broadcasts and the Texas A&M radio play-by-play was the impact of World War I. As soon as the United States declared war against Germany in early 1917, the Navy took over commercial wireless stations and amateur radio was shut down for the duration of the war. Following the war, a national debate ensued as to whether radio should continue to be governmentally controlled, as was the case in many countries, or free enterprise should rule airwave communication. A Congressional bill was proposed to "secure for all time to the Navy Department the control of radio in the United States."[10] Had the bill passed, the Navy monopoly would have allowed one branch of the military to control America's airwaves, possibly allowing no sports broadcasts except for the annual Army-Navy football game.

After the bill failed, the Navy Department backed a private proposal instigated by General Electric to form the Radio Corporation of America (RCA) in 1919 and to "force" American Marconi, a British-held firm, to transfer all its assets and operations to the new company. As all land wireless stations were in the Navy's hands, American Marconi had little choice but to accept the transfer. Within months, General Electric was joined by American Telephone and Telegraph, Westinghouse, and United Fruit Company (with its armada of fruit boats roaming the Western Hemisphere).[11] At the beginning of the 1920s, there seemed to be a radio monopoly created by the RCA cartel of GE, AT&T, Westinghouse, and United Fruit.

Only the amateur group of radio fanatics and possible antitrust action stood in the way of a successful monopoly. The amateurs who had begun by assembling their own radio receiving units became entrepreneurs themselves, purchasing parts from producers such as GE, Westinghouse, and AT&T, then building sets and marketing them. They also began building transmitters, and new stations grew rapidly in 1921 and 1922.[12] The cartel's anticipated control of broadcasting and sale of radio receivers never materialized. Not only did the amateurs become professionals themselves, but the cartel members also began having internal squabbles over the sale of equipment and control of telephone lines for distant radio control. AT&T, for instance, created the first long-distance broadcast of a football game, an October 1922 Princeton-Chicago contest at Chicago's Stagg Field, carried on AT&T lines to AT&T's station, WEAF, in New York City.[13]

WEAF was the prime force in creating "commercials" to make radio profitable.[14] Before commercials, many radio stations broadcast music and other programs in order to sell their own radio equipment.[15] Possibly the best example of early radio equipment marketing was done by KDKA, a Westinghouse station in Pittsburgh. So successful was KDKA that Westinghouse created other stations: WJZ in Newark, New Jersey, WBZ in Springfield, Massachusetts, and KYW in Chicago. General Electric opened WGY in Schenectady, New York, KGO in San Francisco, and KOA in Denver. RCA started WJY in Jersey City and WRC in Washington, D.C.[16] Commercials, not just the sales of radios by radio stations, soon became the lifeblood of radio. A business would buy a block of time to sponsor an entire program. Eventually radio, and later television, would become so expensive that businesses would buy a minute, thirty seconds, or less to sponsor events such as college sports.[17]

The 1912 Minnesota radio experiment was soon forgotten, and the 1920 Texas A & M game, located in the Texas outback, had little impact on the development of radio itself, which had its greatest growth in the industrial Northeast. The 1922 Princeton-Chicago game was, though, a breakthrough for college broadcasting. Princeton was part of the original Harvard-Yale-Princeton triad and, for the previous half-century, had been central to the development of big-time football in America. The University of Chicago had borrowed significantly from Yale, the "jock" school of America for the previous fifty years. Chicago's professional coach was the legendary Amos Alonzo Stagg, a Yale alumnus and one of the winningest coaches since being hired to promote the university through athletics in 1892. However, Chicago or any Big 10 institution had never been visited by an Ivy League team in football. To accomplish this scheduling coup, Stagg dropped the traditional Michigan game and, in doing so, caused a storm of controversy. Stagg said that the series of games scheduled with Princeton would be "the most important intersectional athletic contests that have ever been held in the country."[18] That was probably true.

Following Chicago's 1921 defeat of Princeton, 9-0, at Princeton, in what had been headlined as "Western Football's Greatest Triumph," the game in Chicago the following year was called the "greatest game of the century." It may have been. There were more than 100,000 ticket requests, more than enough to fill the Chicago stadium three-fold. Scalpers were getting as much as a hundred dollars for a three-dollar ticket. With this type of excitement, AT&T's station, WEAF, decided to broadcast the game at Stagg Field back to New York using long-distance telephone lines, radio broadcasting, and a public-address system. The excitement of the Princeton comeback victory from an 18-7 deficit in the fourth quarter was transmitted instantaneously beyond the football stadium via telephone lines to WEAF in New York City, and then on to fans with radios on the East Coast. WEAF provided a truck on New York's Park Row with a radio receiving set that operated a public-address system from which street crowds could listen to the game. A crowd in front of the Tribune Building "jammed the thoroughfare and ran well into the thousands" to hear the radio report of the game. The "clearly reproduced" cheering of the throng at Stagg Field was heard nearly a thousand miles away as Princeton stopped Chicago two feet from the goal line to preserve a 21-18 victory.[19]

The Princeton-Chicago broadcast was the first of a number of interregional games that were used to promote college football and bring financial rewards to radio stations and networks. Football could be employed to sell not only all kinds of advertising but radio equipment as well. Since college sport had been commercial from the beginning, commercial radio fit well into the business end of college athletics. What the radio did was intensify intercollegiate athletic commercialism, drawing athletics even farther from an educational model.

With the beginning of the 1922 Princeton-Chicago game, radio had made itself an integral part of the nationalization of football, by making interregional competition immediately available to masses through the airwaves. The impact of college football broadcasting was not immediately known. Would radio bring the message of higher education to the masses? Would universities use their own educational stations, such as WHA at the University of Wisconsin, to further educational ideals through the popularity of football? Would broadcasting games lead to greater corruption of higher education by the process of commercialization? Would radio increase the interest in football and increase gate receipts through greater attendance? Or would the broadcasts contribute to people staying at home and not paying to see the game at the stadium? Over the next decade, many of these questions would be answered. The excitement of football on radio would push the commercial broadcasting route rather than that of public radio controlled by the educational institutions themselves, and sports announcers on commercial radio would soon come to the fore.

3 The Broadcasters

COMMERCIAL SPORTS announcing began at the first commercial station in the nation, Pittsburgh's KDKA, only months after KDKA had been established to sell Westinghouse radio equipment. On November 2, 1920, the Pittsburgh station, the only licensed commercial station in America that year, created a sensation by broadcasting Warren G. Harding's presidential election win over Democratic challenger James M. Cox. Less than a half year later KDKA did a remote broadcast of a soon-forgotten prizefight. Westinghouse's KDKA had surpassed RCA's radio efforts in both politics and sports broadcasting. The New York area and David Sarnoff, who five years before had predicted almost exactly what radio could do in America, were, nevertheless, not to be outdone. Sarnoff, by now age 30 and general manager of RCA, decided to broadcast the heavyweight championship fight between champion Jack Dempsey and France's Georges Carpentier in July of 1921. This international fight put RCA and Sarnoff in the limelight and produced the first recognizable sports announcer.

Sports announcers needed to be created. The most logical individuals to announce games were sportswriters from the print media or knowledgeable station announcers in the new radio medium. Major Andrew J. White was the first major sports broadcaster, brought into the field to cover a significant event in radio history. At the time White was chosen to announce the Jack Dempsey–Georges Carpentier match from Boyle's Thirty Acres in Jersey City, he was employed as publisher of RCA's journal, the *Wireless Age,* and also acting president of the National Amateur Wireless Association. Sarnoff arranged for White's voice to be carried to a transmitter owned by the U.S. Navy. Franklin Delano Roosevelt, then Navy Undersecretary, ordered a radio-telephone transmitter be placed at the Lackawanna Railroad terminal in Hoboken, more than two miles from the the the temporary stadium in which about 90,000 people crowded to watch the fight. Telephone lines were run from the fight venue to the railroad terminal. There, an associate of Major White, J. O. Smith, repeated White's description of the four-round match to a listening audience.[1]

Knowing that the fight was of historical significance, Sarnoff created a kind of network, originating at the Newark station, WJY, and carrying

White's commentary on the fight to sixty-one cities. Fight promoter Tex Rickard arranged for radio sets and loudspeakers to be located in theaters, halls, auditoriums, ballrooms, and barns throughout the East. Admission fees were collected in the radio halls and used to aid victims of World War I in France and to erect facilities for American Navy and Marine Corp veterans.[2] Ironically, in the fourth round, Dempsey, labeled a World War I draft-dodger, knocked out Carpentier, a twice-decorated French war hero. However, the fight reaped rewards for the development of sports broadcasting and for boxing thanks to RCA's humanitarian gesture.[3] The Dempsey-Carpentier fight broadcast can be seen as one of two key events in the development of sports broadcasting. The other milestone, a generation later, was the national telecast of the 1958 National Football League championship game, in which the Baltimore Colts defeated the New York Giants.[4]

In the fall of 1921, WJZ expanded sports broadcasting by sending that year's World Series, between the New York Yankees and the New York Giants, over the airwaves. The baseball play-by-play was done by Sandy Hunt, a reporter for the *Newark Sunday Call*. Hunt, who had suggested the broadcast in the first place, announced the games while stationed in a box seat. A telephone line carried his words to the station in Newark, where Tommy Cowan repeated the words over the air to the public, in much the same way that Major White and J. O. Smith had broadcast the Dempsey-Carpentier fight. The broadcast of America's national pastime was so popular that the station received 4,000 pieces of mail in response.[5]

KDKA, not to be outdone by RCA's WJZ, began broadcasting college football that fall. Harold W. Arlin, a pioneer broadcaster at KDKA, gave the play-by-play for at least two games in the fall of 1921, the first of which was the Pittsburgh–West Virginia contest. Arlin used a microphone that looked like a "tomato can with a felt lining," something he called the "mushophone." Arlin's second game was the Pitt-Nebraska contest. After a Pitt score, Arlin yelled so loudly into the microphone that the modulation meter needle was knocked off and the game went off the air for several minutes.[6]

KDKA was technologically far ahead of the broadcasting technique of the University of Nebraska, which also put football on the air that fall. Nebraska, a major football broadcaster through the twentieth century, began broadcasting in 1921 with a student announcer, J. A. Brooks. The station, 9YY, formed in 1920, was initially only an experiment. Brooks used a telephone and relayed the play-by-play to two engineering students, who translated his message into a spark transmitter. The next year, the University of Nebraska was given its first standard broadcast license, for WFAV, a 100-watt station.[7] Nebraska and other university stations fell behind the commercial stations in most areas of broadcasting, though, as the free enterprise system outstripped government-supported radio.

Commercial stations such as KDKA in Pittsburgh became the leaders when it came to turning out innovative sports broadcasters. Ted Husing, one of the early greats, told a story of KDKA broadcasting a University of Pittsburgh game in 1922. In this particular game, a Pitt sophomore who happened to have a bet on the game served as the announcer. To provide the play-by-play, the student announcer decided to carry the mike up and down the field, using a trailing wire that occasionally got tangled up by the players on the sidelines. The young announcer had a $100 bet on the Pittsburgh team, which was losing by a point late in the game but threatening to score. He commented:

> Thirty seconds left to play, ladies and gentlemen, but it's enough. Only inches to go. One buck by Big Jack Hoozis and it'll be all over. Old Jack Hoozis will be the hero on Pitt campus tonight, all right. Time in—they're coming out of of the huddle—they're lining up— double wing-back formation, and Hoozis will take it. Signal—here comes the play—Hoozis has his arms out for it—the ball's passed— and . . . O-o-oh! the goddam bonehead fumbled it.

It was too late once the announcer realized what he had said; he dropped the mike and was never again heard on KDKA.[8]

Other inexperienced broadcasters joined the field, some reluctantly. One was Grantland Rice, sportswriter for the *New York Tribune*. Rice was a logical choice to be a sportswriter-turned-broadcaster. He had graduated Phi Beta Kappa at Vanderbilt, where he had played football and baseball while majoring in Greek and Latin. He was probably the best-known sportswriter of his time, but he was also an early broadcaster of baseball's World Series. In 1921, KDKA's sister station in the New York area, WJZ in Newark, had become the first to broadcast a World Series game, carrying it back to the station in Newark, where Tommy Cowan repeated Sandy Hunt's words to a listening audience.[9] The following year, Grantland Rice was asked to do the direct play-by-play from a box seat near the New York Yankee dugout for the second consecutive "subway series," between the Babe Ruth–led Yankees and the Giants, managed by John McGraw. The WJZ signal carried 300 miles, and an estimated 1.5 million fans listened to the series broadcast. Rice was not quite sure how to translate the action to the fans, as he had so effectively done in the newspaper business. After the crack of the bat, he would wait for the shout of the crowd, hesitate a few moments, and then describe what had happened. Wrote one listener, "I would hear the crowd let out a terrific roar and it would seem ages before I knew whether it was a single or a three-bagger that had been made or whether the side had been retired." Rice, who never felt comfortable behind the mike, said that the broadcasting officials wanted him to keep talking, but, he admitted: "I didn't know what to say."[10] He did know what to write, and he found that broadcasting interfered with his exemplary sports reporting.

That same fall of 1922, WJZ continued, without Rice, to broadcast college football games as radio stations and radio sales expanded. W. S. Flitcraft, a sports editor, announced a game of the week from the Polo Grounds. WJZ was part of the vast expansion of college sports broadcasting heard across the country. The number of both radio stations and receivers was growing exponentially. In 1921, there were only five stations licensed by the U.S. Department of Commerce. In just the first six months of 1922, nearly 400 stations came into existence.[11] Radio set sales lagged only slightly. That year there were an estimated 400,000 sets, and the number tripled by 1923 and tripled again the next year.[12]

Sports announcers, unlike football coaches, were not hired by universities to publicize and bring prestige to the many publicly owned institutions of higher learning. In the 1920s, many public institutions paid their football coach more than full professors and, in a few cases, more than the university president.[13] This was true of both small and large institutions, with smaller institutions surprisingly paying a higher percentage difference to the football coaches than to full professors.[14] The same institutions, especially the larger ones, were actively engaged in the growth of radio. In a number of cases, the radio stations on campus were broadcasting news, music, market reports, and lectures. They were also broadcasting football games, but the practice did not effectively continue. While commercial radio expanded, university-owned stations showed a similar growth. By 1922 there were seventy-two university and school licenses among the 500 stations in existence.[15] If, as athletic officials and university administrators often claimed, college athletics were an integral part of higher education, why didn't universities continue to use their own radio stations to broadcast football games and gain control of the promotion and publicity coming from intercollegiate athletics? Probably the best answer is that, despite what officials and administrators said, college athletics, for well over a half-century, had not been considered educational and did not seem to belong in the academic realm.

The use of commercial radio broadcasting rather than educational radio was merely reflecting the common practice in intercollegiate athletics from the nineteenth century. Harvard may not have been the first, but it was early in dismissing any close connection between athletics and education. A Harvard faculty committee in the 1880s voted to prohibit intercollegiate athletics only if athletics interfered with "College work."[16] At the University of Chicago, only four years after its founding in 1892, coach Amos Alonzo Stagg attempted to separate athletes from the rest of the student body. Stagg arranged for an athletic dorm and a training table facility, removing his athletes from the general student population and providing them with special meals.[17] At nearby Northwestern University, President Thomas Holgate stated in his annual report that "athletics are the by-play of students and should largely be self-supporting." Yet, at the same, time he opposed their "objectionable commercial aspects."[18] As president, he had no plan to make athletics both self-supporting and noncommercial. When radio came into existence, it may have seemed obvious to educational leaders that educational radio should stay noncommercial and not be used to financially-support intercollegiate athletics.

Educational leaders distanced themselves from the broadcasting of athletics because athletics did not meet their educational objectives. Commercial radio soon filled the vacuum, not for the purposes of education but for money. The position for commercial radio was no better stated than by Harold Lafount, a Utah manufacturer and member of the Federal Radio Commission, in 1927: "Commercialism is the heart of broadcasting in the United States. What has education contributed to radio? Not one thing. What has commercialism contributed? Everything."[19] Within a few years, stations such as WEAF and WJZ in the New York area, WMAQ and WDAP (later WGN) in Chicago, KDKA in Pittsburgh, and WWJ in Detroit moved into collegiate sports broadcasting and reaped the profits that it could produce.

Commercial radio station managers put some of their best announcers on the air to cover football broadcasts. Quin Ryan joined what became WGN ("World's Greatest Newspaper") radio and announced the 1924 Illinois-Michigan game featuring Red Grange. In that game, Ryan announced Grange's four touchdowns and gain of about 250 yards in the first twelve minutes of play against an undefeated Michigan team.[20] (The same Quin Ryan, a couple of years later, broadcast the famous Scopes Trial on evolution from Dayton, Tennessee, back to Chicago.) Ty Tyson broadcast the first Michigan game for WWJ in Detroit. In 1925, Sigmund Spaeth announced the Rose Bowl game between Stanford and Notre Dame for WGBS, which was carried by wire from Pasadena to New York City.[21] While broadcasters across the nation were gaining local name recognition, the most famous announcers, now known as sports broadcasters, emerged in New York City, the communications center of America. There, the two greatest sports announcers of the 1920s and 1930s were Graham McNamee and Ted Husing.

Graham McNamee and Ted Husing Dominate the Airwaves

4

THE TWO best-known sports broadcasters of the 1920s and 1930s, Graham McNamee and Ted Husing, came along just as radio began expanding in the early 1920s. In 1922, there were less than a half-million radio sets in use in America. The next year the sale of radios rose threefold, and then it increased threefold again the following year. After 1924, sales increased by nearly 2 million sets each year for the next decade.[1] These substantial radio sales created greater value for commercial radio and raised the place of sport in that market setting.

AT&T took a leadership role in promoting commercial radio by selling broadcast time over its telephone lines to stations, called "toll stations," which formed a network. The stations supported themselves by advertising a variety of products rather than only radio equipment, as Westinghouse was doing through KDKA in Pittsburgh. In toll broadcasting, companies such as Goodrich tires, Lucky Strike cigarettes, or Eveready batteries provided the money for producing the program content and worked with advertising agencies to put the program on the air. AT&T contended that toll stations allowed any individual or company to broadcast rather than limiting the medium to special-interest stations such as Westinghouse's KDKA. AT&T could easily connect a variety of stations thorough its telephone lines, such as the 1922 Chicago-Princeton game, which was broadcast back to AT&T's New York station, WEAF, from Chicago. A month later, the Harvard-Yale game was broadcast using

AT&T's long-distance lines, even attracting about 500 Princeton students who jammed into the space of one auditorium set up specifically to hear their perceived educational superiors play football.[2]

AT&T, using WEAF as its lead station in New York City, had plans for a multistation hookup. AT&T had a coast-to-coast network by the end of 1924, comprising twenty-six stations. Were it not for antitrust legislation, such as the Sherman Antitrust Act of 1890, AT&T might have gained a virtual monopoly of network broadcasting, as it controlled the only long-distance telephone communication system capable of connecting the network stations. The federal government soon began an investigation into monopoly complaints, and eventually AT&T withdrew from direct broadcasting and sold its New York City station, WEAF, to RCA. RCA, in turn, created a new company, the National Broadcasting Corporation (NBC), in 1926, which would soon become the national network leader. NBC, not AT&T, brought the first coast-to-coast broadcast to America, the Stanford-Alabama Rose Bowl football contest on January 1, 1927.[3]

By that time, the format of radio was, to a great extent, set. There would be nationwide broadcasts, financially supported by company sponsors and provided free of charge to a growing listening populace. The broadcast of collegiate sporting events, especially football, would eventually be part of that format. Educational radio was easily outdistanced by commercial radio, with its silver-tongued announcers. Soon New Yorkers Graham McNamee and Ted Husing would be to sports broadcasting what H. V. Kalternborn and Edward R. Murrow were to radio newscasting.

Graham McNamee burst on to the sports announcing scene in 1923, soon after being hired by WEAF as an announcer and baritone soloist. Raised in Minneapolis, he had been taken to New York City when he was 19 by his mother to study music and train his voice.[4] McNamee had enjoyed a successful music career, singing in an Aoelian Hall concert, giving solos in New York City churches, and performing in a Broadway musical before being hired by WEAF.[5] He had also played baseball and hockey, so his sports experience, combined with a quality voice and musical background, was attractive to WEAF. Working as a general announcer, McNamee was asked to cover the Harry Greb–Johnny Wilson middleweight boxing championship match from New York's Polo Grounds. As McNamee had also done some amateur boxing, he was familiar with details like hooks, jabs, roundhouses, feinting, ducking, and clinching. The "infectious excitement" of his announcing was considered a success from the first broadcast.[6] A couple of months later, Mc-Namee joined Grantland Rice, of the *New York Tribune,* in broadcasting the 1923 World Series.

McNamee was thrown into the limelight when he announced at the subway series between the Yankees and Giants, the second World Series broadcast in history. Grantland Rice had been the first play-by-play announcer carried live on radio when he served as principal announcer in the 1922 World Series. The next year, Rice was again behind the mike reporting the World Series between the repeat league champions, Giants and Yankees. This time, however, Rice was on WEAF, assisted by Graham McNamee. In the fourth inning of the third game, Rice suddenly retired from the broadcast box and returned to his full-time job as a newspaper writer. Rice believed that in sports announcing everything went right through his head and directly to his mouth, and it was detracting from his newspaper reporting. The task of completing the Series was given to McNamee.[7] Unlike Rice, McNamee was able to fill the slow spots in the broadcast by discussing the batter's mannerisms, the manager's moves, or the actions of the spectators. Following McNamee's World Series success, WEAF received 1,700 pieces of mail.[8] Two years later, after his World Series broadcast, that number had grown to 50,000 responses, and McNamee received an inscribed cup from *Radio Digest* voting him the most popular radio announcer, thanks in part to his expanded sports broadcasting.[9]

Following the 1925 World Series, in which the Pittsburgh Pirates defeated the Washington Senators, McNamee was asked to broadcast intersectional football games. McNamee teamed with Phil Carlin, whom McNamee called his "radio twin," to do the Army–Notre Dame and the Pennsylvania-Chicago games. Football, according to McNamee, took two individuals, a "pointer," who could use field glasses to identify the players, and the announcer, who caught the action and named the principal players. The pointer used a little card that listed all the players' numbers, and he pointed out or whispered the name to the announcer.[10] McNamee and Carlin teamed up to do the Rose Bowl game between Alabama and Stanford in 1927, as mentioned earlier, the first coast-to-coast broadcast on the new NBC network. According to Red Barber, later considered one of the great radio sports announcers, McNamee was the "greatest." Another contemporary, writer Heywood Broun, said that McNamee was "able to take a new medium of expression and through it transmit himself—to give out vividly a sense of movement and of feeling."[11] McNamee's fame grew as he became nationally known. By the 1930s, he was generally considered the best sports announcer in the nation, possibly challenged only by Ted Husing.

Husing was about a dozen years younger than Graham McNamee, but he got into broadcasting only a year later than McNamee. Husing, like McNamee, had been an athlete in high school and participated in semi-pro football for a few years. He never graduated from Stuyvesant High School in New York and was, according to his own account, a "hellion."[12] He quit school and went West, bumming on the railroad and taking odd jobs, working as a hired hand in Kansas wheat fields, a shiller at a street carnival, and a Broadway barker. When World War I came, he joined the army, giving a false name because he was underage. Still unsettled after the war, he finished high school and attended Columbia University for a couple of years. In 1924, Husing applied for a position as a radio announcer, saying that he was a college graduate and knew something about music. Lying on both accounts, he got the job at WJZ and signed with RCA's David Sarnoff for $45 a week.[13]

Major Andrew White, who had broadcast the Dempsey-Carpentier fight, became Husing's mentor in sports broadcasting. Husing's career began with the World Series of 1925, which WJZ broadcast in the studio using ticker tape reports from the field of action. Actual on-site play-by-play started with the University of Pennsylvania–Cornell game in 1925 at Franklin Field in Philadelphia. For the pregame show, Husing climbed onto the unfinished upper deck of Franklin Field and crawled under a tarpaulin thrown over a scaffold to protect him and White from the rain. Because White did not show up in time for the pregame show, Husing took over, discussing the weather, crowd, cheerleaders, and band. By game time, White had arrived to do the play-by-play while Husing helped by holding up scraps of paper for White to read. Only between quarters did Husing do any commentary.[14]

Husing left WJZ and New York, only to return and gain prominence in sports announcing. After Husing had been promoted by WJZ to radio salesman, a position deemed more important than that of an announcer, Husing tired of the job and left New York for a short time. He took a job with a Boston station, WBET, announcing Boston Braves games,[15] but quickly returned to New York when WHN was established. He then gained additional sports experience by announcing Columbia University football games in 1927. A radio critic from the *New York Herald Tribune* compared Husing's coverage to the announcing of the McNamee-Carlin duo:

Husing has given more complete information, more accurate and prompt news of the changing position of the ball and acute observations as to place, possibilities and potentialities of the teams and individual players on the field before him than have either of the more noted announcers. . . . Husing is likely to become radio's most appreciated football describer, unless, of course, Mr. McNamee and Mr. Carlin come close to realize that the primary purpose of a football broadcast is not to furnish verbal entertainment but to provide immediate news of what the twenty-two football players are doing.[16]

General consensus was probably on the side of McNamee and Carlin, though Husing early on showed a dramatic, clear, fast-talking, staccato but resonant voice.[17]

Husing's biggest break came when he joined the Columbia Phonograph Broadcasting System (later CBS), which had been formed in September 1927. Husing signed with the three-month-old CBS following the 1927 football season at WHN. He rejoined Major Andrew White and would remain with CBS for the next two decades. In the fall of 1928, Husing, then an office manager for CBS, was sent to broadcast a Chicago football game in place of Major White, who was ill. According to William S. Paley, then the 26-year-old head of CBS, that game helped move Husing toward being the "most famous sportscaster in the country."[18]

Ted Husing's invention, the annunciator board, helped him to broadcast college football games more efficiently than Graham McNamee or anyone else. Husing experimented in the mid-1920s with the mechanical device, operated by an assistant, to identify key players during games. It may have been used first in a Princeton-Navy football game at Princeton's Palmer Stadium in 1926.[19] Husing's assistant peered through binoculars and pressed buttons according to the number of the ball carrier or the tackler, and the names lit up on Husing's board. Previously, he had been given this information by an assistant who wrote names on a piece of paper or whispered to him.

By 1929, when Les Quailey joined Husing in announcing games across the nation, the annunciator board had been developed so that the assistant had a separate keyboard with numbers that corresponded to names on a glass board. Les Quailey used high-power Zeiss binoculars to identify jersey numbers, entered those numbers on keyboard, and the player's name flashed on for Husing. Quailey, a former quarterback at Alfred University, was able to tap the buttons without having to take his eyes off the game action.[20] Using the Annunciator Board, Husing re-

ported on the Penn State-Lafayette game played only days before the
stock market crash of 1929, a game he later claimed was "without par-
allel in football annals." Lafayette was leading 3-0 with only five seconds
to play when it punted to Penn State. Husing described Cooper French
and Frankie Dietrich waiting to receive the kick. French received the ball
on his own forty-yard line. He streaked to the right, eluded a couple of
tacklers, and lateraled the ball to Dietrich just as he was about to be tackled. Dietrich cut behind interference and dashed in for a victory touchdown after the time had run out. That game remained in Husing's memory as the greatest until the famed 1935 comeback victory of Notre Dame
over Ohio State, 18-13, known by many as the "Game of the Century,"
the most exciting game that Husing had ever broadcast.[21] The CBS team
of Husing and Quailey was, in some ways, superior to that of NBC's Mc-
Namee and Carlin. Husing would continue sports announcing until after
World War II, winning best sports broadcaster of the year awards in the
1930s.[22] Radio broadcasting of college football would, however, have to
overcome those who perceived it as a threat in the early 1930s for Mc-
Namee and Carlin to continue to thrive as radio announcers of intercollegiate sport.

5   The Radio Threat to College Football Attendance

AT THE TIME the stock market crashed, ushering in the Great Depression, the idea of colleges generating significant income from selling radio
rights to their football games was considered a remote possibility. During the 1920s, many college football games were aired on what were
termed "sustaining broadcasts." That is, the radio station put the games
on the air at no charge to the college and gained no income from advertising. There were many such broadcasts, such as a President Calvin
Coolidge's address, the reception of Charles A. Lindbergh after his 1927
nonstop solo flight from New York to Paris, or the *National Grand Opera
Company Hour*. This differed from "sponsored" programs, in which a
business put up money and received advertising in exchange for sponsoring a particular program. For instance, in 1926, programming on
AT&T's station WEAF consisted of about half "sustaining" and half
"sponsored" programs, with "sponsored" or "commercial" radio time

costing between $150 and $600 per hour.[1] Colleges usually did not ask for compensation from radio stations providing sustaining programs, knowing that they were receiving free promotion from the football game broadcast and that the radio station was making no money directly from the event. Free publicity was appreciated, and it remained that way well into the 1930s.

As the Depression wore on and income from football gate receipts decreased, however, colleges began to see radio broadcasting as a possible revenue source. Yet, at the same time, many believed that sustaining radio or even sponsored radio, in which a portion of the advertisement revenue might go to the college, could have a negative impact upon overall revenue. Fans might stay home to listen to the game rather than pay to attend the game in person. How this played out had an impact during the Depression and would influence how colleges looked at the television situation a generation later.

"The combination of depression and radio is threatening football receipts," a Stanford University Board of Athletic Control official wrote in 1931.[2] The same year, a radio station administrator complained to the Stanford University president that barring free radio broadcasts would be essentially un-American.[3] The stage was set for a battle over the propriety of broadcasting college football games, not only at Stanford and the Pacific Coast Conference but across America. The Eastern Intercollegiate Association, which included the so-called Ivy League institutions and a few others such as Army, Navy, Penn State, and Syracuse, voted to disallow radio for the 1932 season. The Southern Conference of twenty-three institutions banned broadcasting the same year, and the Southwest Conference did likewise as the Depression hit its depths.[4] The question was also being debated by the Big 10, the Big 6 (now the Big 12), and the Pacific Coast Conference. It came to a head at a special NCAA meeting in the summer of 1932.

The NCAA members decided to have a special meeting in Pasadena just before the 1932 Los Angeles Olympics.[5] Not only could college officials discuss the impact of radio on college football, but they could also get their ways paid to the second Summer Olympics Games held in America. Yet the NCAA was only able to discuss the matter; it could not take action because the national organization had a policy from its beginning, in 1906, to be neither a legislative nor an enforcement arm of college athletics. The individual colleges of the NCAA agreed collectively to act individually. Under that policy, which came to be known as "Home Rule," it was up to each institution, individually or collectively through conferences, to legislate and enforce legislation. Thus when Major John L. Griffith, commissioner of the Big 10 Conference, opened the discussions in Pasadena, everyone knew that the NCAA would not set national policy. Only after World War II, when television entered the picture, would policymaking become a function of the NCAA.

Two major arguments were used against broadcasting college football. The dominant one was that gate receipts might plummet, especially on inclement days when people would rather stay home and listen to the game. Lynn St. John, athletic director at Ohio State, believed that a home radio party with the game's progress diagrammed on a blackboard "was almost as good . . . as being at the game."[6] The second negative was that big-time programs on the radio, particularly broadcasts of the important games, might have an even greater impact on football attendance at smaller colleges.[7] Those who might have gone to a Miami of Ohio–Oberlin game would stay home instead to hear the Ohio State–Michigan game on the air. "It seems to me," commented L. C. Boles of the College of Wooster, "that the smaller colleges are a little in the same position as the independent groceries with the chain stores."[8] The point was not lost on those attending the NCAA meeting, for small colleges were constantly in fear of being swallowed up by the large institutions.

Using radio to generate money for colleges, however, was not a major point in discussing the positives of radio broadcasting. The University of Minnesota, for example, had received only $500 from the commercial station WCCO in 1931 for the rights to broadcast all of its home games.[9] Although there was little research to support the claim, a number of NCAA participants believed that football broadcasting would stimulate new interest in football and, in the long run, increase gate receipt revenues. Even if radio revenues did not offset gate receipt declines, many persisted in the opinion that radio publicity would benefit the institution as a whole.[10]

Most athletic officials recognized that they were caught in a radio dilemma. If they allowed radio broadcasts, gate receipts would drop; if they banned radio, public sentiment would turn against the institution, as free radio already had been part of college football for nearly a decade. Dana X. Bible, football coach at Nebraska, maintained that "we need broadcasting to keep the good-will of the people."[11] Ralph Aigler, professor of law and longtime faculty representative from Michigan, concurred. "After people are accustomed to listening to games over the radio and then it [is taken] away," Aigler commented, "I wonder whether there has been sufficient weight given to the ill will which is going to develop from the disappointment on the part of these people."[12] That disappointment might even be registered in the state legislature when appropriations were debated for the University of Michigan or any state institution. In addition, offending the alumni and general public might hurt the larger efforts to raise money for the institution.[13]

Some thought that football broadcasts at state universities, such as most Big 10 institutions, belonged to the people of the state. Officials at the University of Iowa considered the university property of the state of Iowa, and therefore thought the people of Iowa were entitled to football broadcasts.[14] During the 1932 season, Iowa fans enjoyed that entitlement, listening to accounts on station WOC in Davenport by a $5-per-broadcast announcer. At the end of the season, that announcer, Ronald Reagan, was given a raise to $10 per contest to do the play-by-play.[15] A half-century later Reagan was leading the nation, often in a style reminiscent of the way he, as a sports announcer, had carried the color of a game over the airwaves. At the University of Illinois, radio rights were not sold, even though certain games, such as the Army-Illinois game, were broadcast nationally.[16] Michigan also did not sell its game rights. Michigan officials believed that "people do not care to hear about toothpaste and cereals and beauty preparations along with touchdowns or fifty yard runs."[17] So while Reagan sang the praises of Maytag Washing Machines to Iowa listeners, Michigan residents got advertising-free football games.

Though the 1932 special NCAA meeting participants had no intention of voting to control radio broadcasting on a national basis, a straw vote showed that nearly 90 percent of those voting believed that radio hindered football revenue.[18] Major Griffith, who had presided over the roundtable discussion on broadcasting, closed the discussion with a sage remark: "I am surprised no one suggested looking into the future as to the possible effect of the college games when television is perfected," Griffith projected. "We will have television in a few years, and it will be possible for a man to sit at home and not only listen to the account of the game, but to see the action."[19] In less than two decades, the NCAA would be forced to deal with television in a more emphatic way than just in discussion.

The NCAA convention noted only one athletic conference that had a definite policy to broadcast games. The Pacific Coast Conference had voted only two days before the Pasadena meeting to pursue broadcasting on a conference basis. The Pacific Coast Conference made an agreement with NBC, the Don Lee–Columbia Broadcasting System, and the Hearst Radio Service to broadcast by geographical zones so that big games would not be aired in certain areas. The only big game to be broadcast on the entire West Coast was the Stanford-California game, played on a Saturday when no other conference games were played.[20] This reflected the supposition that prohibiting the broadcasting of, say, a prominent Stanford-Southern California contest along the entire West Coast might help the attendance of less prominent games such as the Oregon State–Washington State contest.

The Pacific Coast Conference agreement provided a feature to increase interest in college football and boost stadium attendance. NBC agreed to air two West Coast programs during the week designed to help excite audiences about college football, *Pigskin Romances* and *Football Rally*. *Pigskin Romances* was an idea borrowed from the radio promotion of Broadway theater, namely a program called *The First Nighter,* which enticed the theater-going crowd. "Pigskin Romances" pictured the colorful side of the collegiate activities revolving around football and was broadcast every Thursday evening for twelve weeks during the fall. *Football Rally* was another half-hour program, featuring one of the PCC institutions each week and providing interviews with coaches and college music by a fifteen-piece orchestra and a male quartet. The seventeen installments of this program were designed to help colleges sell football tickets and radio stations sell advertising. The Hearst Radio Service pledged it would coordinate the Hearst newspaper sports page, radio column, and radio broadcasting to achieve maximum football interest. The Don Lee–Columbia Broadcasting System provided services similar to those of NBC to help colleges sell seats in the stadiums.[21]

By the mid-1930s, the Pacific Coast Conference was receiving $100,000 from radio broadcasts of about 100 games each year. Before that, few American institutions had been making significant money from radio broadcasts.[22] Most of the colleges were not charging for radio rights, though Kenneth "Tug" Wilson, athletic director at Northwestern University, believed that in the future Northwestern might receive some of the $5,000 in advertising accruing to stations from just one of its game broadcasts. "It was too bad for [stations]," the future Big 10 commissioner said, "to get all the money."[23] Two years after the Pacific Coast Conference contract, which had been made possible by money from the Associated Oil Company, a Big 10 official stated that the conference was making "good money" from radio fees, what amounted to about $1,000 per broadcast.[24] Few schools were so fortunate. Even Notre Dame still had to pay NBC $600 to have its games broadcast by WJZ in the New York City area.[25]

As the Depression wore on and football attendance bottomed out, there was an increasing belief among college authorities that they should profit from "sponsored" radio broadcasts of football. Fewer institutions were willing to give their rights away free of charge. The Big 10 and Ivy League institutions, the two leaders in college sport, wrestled with the problem in the mid-1930s. Increasingly, conferences abandoned ideas of collective action in controlling radio rights and moved toward institutional control. The Big 10 had discussed the possible need for control of radio from about 1930. In 1935, the athletic directors of the Big 10 raised the question of selling exclusive broadcasting rights for football, as the Pacific Coast Conference had done three years before. For these rights, the Conference would ask for $100,000. When the proposal was turned down by Minnesota and Chicago, however, it died. A similar proposal was discussed the following year, but it also came to naught.[26]

At least one Big 10 institution found that it could strike its own deal for sponsored radio and bring in more than one-tenth of the proposed $100,000 total conference fee. Michigan sold its football radio rights to Detroit station WWJ in 1934 for $20,000, put up by the Chevrolet auto company.[27] The next year, Ohio State received $10,000 from the Ohio Oil Company, while Northwestern failed to attain the $10,000 that it wanted from station WGN in Chicago and Illinois received only $1,650.[28] Nevertheless, colleges were increasingly broadcasting their games. A survey of the Nebraska State Journal showed that thirty-seven of seventy-two major institutions broadcast games, and twenty-four of those thirty-seven had sold their rights.[29] The Big 10 was probably leading those institutions that were moving toward "sponsored" broadcasts and away from "sustaining" radio.

The Ivy League institutions, which had at first collectively banned radio broadcasts, soon decided to take the laissez-faire approach and bargain individually for radio income. Yale broke tradition in a big way in 1936 by signing an agreement with the Atlantic Refining Company that provided the school with $20,000 for broadcasting its football games. The amount, as large as the earlier, unannounced Michigan contract, made national news in Time magazine.[30] The University of Pennsylvania also signed with Atlantic Refining for just over $10,000.[31] There was no unanimity among other Ivy institutions. Harvard and Princeton, in particular, opposed the sponsored radio broadcasts. President Harold Dodds of Princeton stated the position effectively. "I view the sale of radio broadcasts as further surrender to the commercial atmosphere," Dodds emphasized, "which already surrounds intercollegiate athletics to a troublesome degree." The Yale action, he said, was "most unfortunate."[32] Commercial athletics, which had been initiated by Yale and Harvard over eight decades before, was not to be denied by a minority of college presidents.

Harvard held out, but not for long. President James Conant strongly opposed commercialized radio broadcasts of Harvard games, but William Bingham, the athletic director, believed that "sponsored" broadcasts would not only increase good will among the alumni but also increase athletic revenues.[33] Socony Oil Company, in 1937, offered Harvard the same financial deal that it was offering Yale, $35,000 for one year or $65,000 for two years. Socony would broadcast ads, no longer than one and one-half minutes, before the game, between periods, and after the game, but not during the game. President Conant fought with Bingham and his athletic governing board over the issue, as Conant sided with Princeton's President Dodds in preserving sustained radio. Conant went so far as to make a proposal to both NBC and CBS to see if one or both would carry Harvard games in nonsponsored broadcasts. In this way, Conant believed, "the alumni pressure or commercialization would automatically disappear" and allow Harvard to stay off the "road of overemphasis."[34] Many radio stations were no longer willing to carry games on a sustaining, noncommercial basis. The two presidents lost the battle over commercialism, but their universities gained additional athletic revenue from radio. Ironically, at the same time, NBC officials invited Conant and Dodds to a demonstration of television, to which Dodds replied: "I am looking forward to the television demonstration with much pleasure."[35] That new medium would dramatically increase the commercial impact on college sport within a decade, but not before Notre Dame went through its own struggle of conscience over whether or not to commercialize its football broadcasts.

6 In the Image of Rockne: Notre Dame and Radio Policy

AS THE twentieth century came to a close, Notre Dame was the only university to ever have a coast-to-coast television network, NBC, carry all of its football games. In the mid-1930s, NBC wanted to carry Notre Dame games exclusively to a national radio audience but was denied that opportunity by Notre Dame officials.[1] Notre Dame, like Harvard, Princeton, and a number of other institutions, attempted to keep a sustaining policy, allowing anyone who wished to broadcast its games do so at no charge to the broadcasters. That policy began to form during the middle of Knute Rockne's thirteen years as head coach at Notre Dame, and the extensive broadcasting of Notre Dame games may have contributed to the success that Rockne and Notre Dame football achieved—and even to the success of the institution itself.

Rockne, coach from 1918 through 1930, knew the value of publicity through all forms of media, and he used it to his own and Notre Dame's benefit. Radio came to Notre Dame football in 1924, when WGN, the *Chicago Tribune* station, aired the game against Nebraska. That game, a 34-6 Notre Dame victory preserving an unbeaten string at Cartier Field in South Bend dating back to 1905, was played before the largest home crowd, 22,500 spectators, against what Rockne described as the "dirtiest team we played" and one of the most anti-Catholic.[2] Rockne believed the publicity gained through broadcasting as well as print media was good for Notre Dame. When WGN asked permission in 1926 to broadcast the Penn State–Notre Dame game, Rockne replied: "We will be very tickled to have your broadcast."[3] Several years later Rockne was laid up by an attack of phlebitis and a blood clot in his right leg, which kept him from making the trip with his team to New York City to play the Army team. Rockne stayed home and listened to his team's 7-0 victory in a sold-out stadium game to which 300,000 people had tried to get tickets. Notre Dame's popularity would continue to increase because of its nonexclusive radio policy.[4] There was an irony in the fact that Rockne was a leader in commercializing himself and Notre Dame football for financial profit, while the official radio policy was to maximize publicity, not financial returns for athletics.

While other colleges moved toward selling exclusive, commercial broadcast rights to radio stations, Notre Dame kept its nonexclusive policy. Even at the depths of the Depression, the traditional Army–Notre Dame game in New York City was a sellout, with scalpers getting as much as $25 a ticket. President-elect Franklin Roosevelt was in attendance for the 1932 game Army–Notre Dame contest. The game was broadcast nationally on both networks, CBS and NBC, with Graham McNamee serving as one of the announcers. Notre Dame could have sold its broadcast rights for large sums, but the school continued its sustaining policy throughout the 1930s. Reflecting on that policy in the 1940s, Vice President John Murphy said that Notre Dame had "been passing up several hundred thousand dollars a year for the past decade or more—dollars that could have been ours had we handled radio differently—if we didn't believe whole-heartedly" in a nonexclusive policy.[5] So dedicated was Notre Dame to this policy that it actually paid NBC $600 to carry the broadcast of the Southern California game from the West Coast to the East Coast in 1934.[6] In one way, Notre Dame could afford to do this to gain publicity for the Catholic school. Its athletic program was in good financial condition thanks to football gate receipts. From World War I to 1934, football revenue had provided about $4 million to build such campus structures as the Schools of Engineering and Commercial Law, two campus dormitories, and the football stadium, which still stands on the campus.[7]

Notre Dame was willing to continue the nonexclusive broadcasting policy, providing game attendance remained high and *good* publicity was gained from the broadcasts. Yet good publicity did not always result. In 1936, announcer Ted Husing interviewed New York's mayor, Jimmy Walker, during the halftime of the Army–Notre Dame football game. Walker voiced some remarks that were uncomplimentary to the Roman Catholic Church, promting Hugh O'Donnell, Notre Dame vice president, to complain to CBS president William Paley. Paley, the son of a Russian Jewish immigrant and wealthy manufacturer of La Palina Cigars, apologized to O'Donnell, indicating that Ted Husing had been informed that his interview had been distasteful. "I am very confident," the CBS head wrote, "that Mr. Husing will take fully into consideration your viewpoint in this matter in further selections of persons for presentation between the halves of any games in which Notre Dame is a participant."[8]

After the mid-1930s, there was increasing financial advantage to selling exclusive rights to radio broadcasts. Yale's and Michigan's $20,000 contracts were evidence of this trend. Notre Dame was enticed but did not succumb, at least not at first. James McCarthy, dean of the Commerce School at Notre Dame and head of the Faculty Board in Control of Athletics, asked several individuals in 1937 about the advisability of selling radio rights. One was Warren Brown, longtime writer for the *Chicago Herald Examiner*. Brown advised McCarthy that "unless there was a really worthwhile amount of money forthcoming, I'd hesitate about going commercial, even though everybody else is doing it." The newspaperman observed, "It will not be the first time that Notre Dame has stood alone. . . . My Jewish acquaintances have taught me that, by the very fact that Notre Dame is hard to get, the time will come when you can make a much better deal than now."[9] Another writer and one-time student at Notre Dame, Arch Ward of the *Chicago Tribune,* gave additional guidance. Ward, in the 1930s, had created both the annual College All-Star Football Game, featuring future NFL stars in a game against the NFL champions, and the Major League Baseball All-Star Game. He told Mc-Carthy that he hoped his former school would be able to "take the lead in preserving the amateurism of college football and at the same time to check the chiselers who like to capitalize on your reputation." Ward did advise that if Notre Dame were to sell its broadcasting privileges, the sponsor should "engage a national hook-up."[10]

Others were divided on the question of selling Notre Dame's radio rights. One New York writer figured that if the regents of Yale and other universities felt no ethical pangs from selling their broadcast rights, Notre Dame could do the same.[11] M. H. Miller, a Du Pont lawyer from Wilmington, Delaware, counseled McCarthy to keep the present policy, in light of the publicity and goodwill that had developed. There are "things of greater value than money," he said. "Notre Dame belongs to the public," Miller believed, much the same way that the two military academies did.[12] A Chicago native suggested that if Notre Dame did sell its rights, at least the halftimes should be used to sell the "University of Notre Dame as something other than an adjunct to a football stadium."[13] This is exactly what Notre Dame officials wanted—a way to publicize the university nationally and internationally and bring it greater renown as an educational institution.

After several months of discussion, the Notre Dame authorities decided to continue allowing any network or station to broadcast games, but only upon a sustaining, noncommercial basis. They made this decision knowing that NBC was willing to give Notre Dame national visibility by broadcasting all its home games without advertisers.[14] NBC did continue its policy of carrying all Notre Dame home games but vacillated somewhat several years later. During a lackluster, low-scoring season, after a loss to Iowa and a near-loss to Southern Methodist, NBC questioned broadcasting Notre Dame's final 1939 games against Northwestern and Southern California. Clearly, Notre Dame football under Elmer Layden lacked a dynamic element that NBC believed was necessary to continue the broadcasts. Notre Dame, now accustomed to national radio exposure, began to look elsewhere for that visibility.[15]

Just before America's entry into World War II, Notre Dame wavered on its radio policy and concocted a plan for both commercial and non-commercial broadcasting. It would allow individual stations, but not networks, to broadcast on a commercial basis with sponsors. President John Cavanaugh suggested Notre Dame collect a fee from individual stations for "non-exclusive commercial broadcast," but continue its sustaining, noncommercial relationship with networks such as NBC. Notre Dame wanted to gain the financial benefits of commercial radio while maintaining a large exposure from sustaining broadcasts. As one Notre Dame official reasoned: "The permitting of sponsored broadcasts would increase our coverage, beyond any question of doubt, and would add to our revenues."[16] They would win both ways, Notre Dame administrators reasoned. Notre Dame also wanted to control the content of any advertising, banning ads for alcohol, patent medicines, and laxatives.[17] Tobacco and political advertising were later added to its list of banned advertisers.

Income from this arrangement was not significant at first because Notre Dame did not want exclusive contracts. During its first season of the new policy in 1941, radio revenue from the four home games totaled only $1,000, while NBC and several other stations continued broadcasts on a sustaining basis. That was less than 10 percent of Michigan's radio take the same season.[18] The next season, less than a year after the Japanese attack on Pearl Harbor, Notre Dame's radio income grew to more than $10,000, but a third of that came from one game against Michigan. In 1943, Notre Dame received less than $3,000, but then collected over $12,000 in 1944. That year, Notre Dame games were carried on as many as eighty-five stations on the CBS network, all on a sustaining basis. Thus, the Notre Dame policy of "maximum radio coverage consistent with the dignity and general welfare of the University" was carried through the war years and after.[19]

Radio income for Notre Dame football did not rise dramatically after World War II as the nonexclusive radio rights policy was continued. In 1946 and 1947, the radio receipts were only about $15,000.[20] At that time, television was beginning to emerge as an economically viable medium and the nonexclusive policy was again challenged at Notre Dame. For one thing, Notre Dame had thirteen radio booths at its stadium. As each TV station needed three booths, a nonexclusive policy would have stretched the facilities beyond their capacity. The desire to televise Notre Dame football and the indications that television rights could be a strong revenue source for the institution placed pressure on officials to change their policy and allow exclusive contracts in both radio and television. Vice President John Murphy, in charge of the Faculty Board in Control of Athletics, stated prior to the 1948 football season: "Our position [is] that after this season we do not know whether we should go exclusive, or stick to our non-exclusive radio policy, carrying that over into television."[21]

The next season, Notre Dame moved to exclusivity in both radio and television. An "Irish Football Network" of twelve radio stations was created, while the fourth television network, Du Mont, won exclusive rights to Notre Dame football and carried games to the East Coast on the newly laid coaxial cable from the Midwest. From 1949 on, the "Irish Football Network" expanded rapidly to forty-nine radio stations in 1951 and 115 stations in thirty-one states and Alaska in 1953.[22] Radio, though, was not to dictate policy for Notre Dame despite its rapid expansion in the late 1940s and into the 1950s. Television would emerge as the most powerful force. As Notre Dame's Vice President commented in 1949: "My head is swimming from all of this television business."[23]

Notre Dame was in the position it wanted. It had winning football, with three straight undefeated teams under Frank Leahy, the most successful coach since Rockne. It had its own expanding radio network. Notre Dame had more television visibility than any other institution, just two years before the NCAA decided to limit television exposure. "No other university will be on so many stations so often during 1949," stated WGN-TV's Paul Fogarty. The unsuccessful bidder for the exclusive TV rights to Notre Dame football, RCA (bidding for NBC), had even offered to purchase TV sets for the Sisters' Convent and Knute Rockne's widow, Bonnie Rockne.[24] All this just as a new and energetic vice president was chosen to lead Notre Dame in athletics—Father Theodore Hesburgh. Hesburgh could see in 1949, as he saw more than four decades later, how the money in radio and television could benefit his university. Television, Hesburgh emphasized, "might well be a great financial boon to the school, and we can certainly use it at this time with so many ideas of progress and development."[25] Notre Dame was belatedly on the road to the commercialized athletic radio and television riches, and Hesburgh would be in a leadership role for nearly a half-century.

Radio Goes "Bowling": The Rose Bowl Leads the Way

7

WHILE NOTRE DAME administrators struggled with the question of commercial or noncommercial broadcasts in the 1930s, there was little doubt in the minds of three newly founded football bowl game committees that they were, from the first, commercial entities. Three major postseason bowl games were created in Southern regions to bring added revenues to their communities: the Cotton Bowl in Dallas, Texas, the Sugar Bowl in New Orleans, Louisiana, and the Orange Bowl in Miami, Florida. They were Depression additions to the "Granddaddy of Them All," the Rose Bowl, created decades before. Some college administrators questioned the commercialism of the new bowl games, even if this was of little concern to others. It was not just administrators from Notre Dame who worried about the commercial aspects of football broadcasts, some other college presidents had similar concerns. For instance, Frank Graham, president of the University of North Carolina, opposed commercial broadcasts of football games because he believed intercollegiate athletics "should be under educational control and less under outside and commercial control."[1] Yet intercollegiate history had been on a commercial path from the beginning, and bowl games continued the process.

After it had surveyed 400 institutions, the NCAA declared at its annual meeting in 1936 that it was "entirely ethical for colleges and universities to sell broadcast rights."[2] It was not unexpected that Yale would sell its radio rights to the Atlantic Refining Company; Michigan would sign a radio agreement with Kelloggs Corn Flakes; Ohio State University would market exclusive rights to the Ohio Oil Company; and Iowa would make an agreement with the Maytag Washing Machine Company.[3] Bowl committees had even less hesitation about increasing the commercialization of football, straying farther away from the educational model desired by President Graham of North Carolina. If most presidents had been opposed to creeping commercialism, they would have fought hard not only to keep game broadcasts noncommercial but also to ban bowl games. For the most part, presidents were often silently accepting, if not advocating, commercialism while speaking out for higher educational goals. Then and now, college presidents have not been immune to commercial hypocrisy.

The origin of the bowl game is not entirely clear, although most claim that the first was the Rose Bowl game of 1902 in Pasadena, California. This can be easily challenged, however, for there was a New Year's Day football clash in New Orleans on January 1, 1890. Thomas L. Bayne, who played football for Yale in 1884, came up with the idea. He was a lawyer and realtor in New Orleans, as well as president of the Yale Alumni Association of Louisiana, and he wanted to introduce the eastern game to southerners. Because most Southern institutions had not taken up

American football by 1890, Bayne created two teams, mostly of northern players from Ivy League institutions, to play a game in the deep South. While players had come from institutions as varied as the Massachusetts Institution of Technology, Virginia, Notre Dame, and Tulane, Bayne called the two teams "Yale" and "Princeton," the two traditionally strongest teams in America. It was the first intercollegiate football game in New Orleans and ended with "Yale" beating "Princeton" 6-0. The grandstand at Sportsman's Park was, as the *New Orleans Daily Picayune* noted, "filled with the choicest flowers of New Orleans society."[4] This bowl game was in the vanguard of the growth of deep South football.

The University of Chicago, led by its football coach, Amos Alonzo Stagg, could also claim to be an innovator in bowl games. Stagg, who had organized the first indoor football game at Madison Square Garden in 1891 when he was a coach of the Springfield College football team, introduced an indoor New Year's Day contest three years later in Chicago. There, Stagg invited the unbeaten Notre Dame team to play his Chicago Maroons. Competing on a floor of tanbark (broken pieces of tree bark used in tanning leather) at Tattersall's Riding Academy in Chicago, Stagg's team won 8-0 on a short 110-by-60-foot field. Two thousand fans saw coach Stagg, the former All-American at Yale, actually play the entire game at right halfback and score a touchdown.[5] The following fall, the year Marconi invented the wireless telegraph, Stagg took his team to sunny California. The trip was part of a larger plan by University of Chicago's president, William Rainey Harper, to bring prestige to his new university by beating opponents throughout the nation. As Harper wrote to Stagg at his hiring, he wanted Stagg "to develop teams which we can send around the country and knock out all the colleges. We will give them a palace car and a vacation too."[6] Stagg delivered, beating Stanford on Christmas Day and defeating the San Francisco Reliance Athletic Club on New Year's Day of 1895.[7] While the postseason games of the 1890s were not titled "bowl games," the precedent certainly had been set before the 1902 Rose Bowl game.

On the day New Orleans hosted the so-called Yale-Princeton game on January 1, 1890, an auspicious event transpired in Pasadena, California. The elite Pasadena Hunt Club held a Tournament of Roses, a day of fun and games with a small parade and medieval tournament. There was still no thought of a football contest, but the next year a marching band was added to the parade of flower-bedecked horses and carriages. By 1895, a Tournament of Roses Association had been formed, and soon the tradition of floats, queens, and grand marshals was created.[8]

By the turn of the century, discussion of an East-West football contest on New Year's Day was underway. Michigan, under Fielding H. Yost, was asked to participate in the first Tournament of Roses game (1902) against Stanford, the team Yost had previously coached. Commercialism prevailed from the beginning. The Michigan Athletic Association maintained it would accept the invitation only if the Pasadena Tournament of Roses Association would provide all expenses for traveling first-class tourist in a sleeping car on a route providing scenery of the West, generous food expenses, staying at a first-class hotel, and returning through New Orleans.[9] After the contest, Yost reflected upon the game: "We left a snowstorm in Michigan, went to California, played eleven men at ninety degrees and beat Stanford 49-0." Michigan's "point-a-minute" team, led by All-American halfback Willie Heston, crushed Stanford so badly that the contest was shortened to prevent further western humiliation by the East. Otherwise, the Rose Bowl festivities and contest were a success, with an estimated 50,000 people attending the parade and about 8,000 spectators paying 50 cents for general admission and $2.00 for box seats to the game.[10] The West, however, was not ready to challenge the East for football supremacy immediately, and the next game was not held until just before America's entry into World War I, well over a decade later.

In 1916, four years before KDKA began radio operations in Pittsburgh and a half-dozen years before the first intersectional Chicago-Princeton football broadcast, Brown University traveled to Pasadena to take on Washington State in the second Tournament of Roses game. This time the West won 14-0. The Rose Bowl then became an annual contest throughout the twentieth century, taking place even during the 1918 influenza epidemic of the First World War and, a generation later, despite the perceived threat of a Japanese invasion of the West Coast following the bombing of Pearl Harbor. Early on, controversy erupted among NCAA members over the advisability of postseason games.

The first major conflict over an Eastern team traveling 3,000 miles to play a single football game occurred when Harvard was asked to play in the 1920 New Year's Day game. The NCAA had voted in principle, without legislative or administrative power, to oppose several commercial-professional activities primarily associated with football. These included the hiring of seasonal coaches, scouting of opponents, elaborate training tables, summer training camps, and postseason games.[11] Colleges across the nation were wrestling with the commercialization of football following World War I, and the Tournament of Roses game was a focal point of attention for Harvard, which was attempting to raise funds from the alumni, including those on the Pacific Coast. The West Coast Harvard alumni believed that if Harvard accepted the invitation to play in the Pasadena game, the trip would help the "Endowment Fund on this Coast more than anything else we can do." They lobbied Harvard President A. Lawrence Lowell to allow Harvard to compete against Oregon. Yet a majority of the Harvard faculty opposed what they considered a frivolous contest that would prevent the players from attending one day of classes.[12]

The Harvard faculty voted 37-16 to oppose the football team's trip to the Rose Bowl after the Harvard Athletic Committee had voted to accept the invitation, and a power struggle erupted between the faculty and the athletic committee. With this, the increasingly apparent commercial-educational struggle in higher education became even more visible. Dean of Harvard College and chairman of the athletic committee, LeBaron B. R. Briggs, led the campaign to participate in the game against the desires of his faculty. "The general interests of Harvard in the West, and in particular the alumni of the West, who have been giving their work and their money for the intellectual interests of the University" wrote Briggs to President Lowell, "care intensely for such student life as is represented by the team."[13]

Commercialism and money won out over educational interests. The Rose Bowl income for the two previous East Coast teams, Brown and Pennsylvania, had been nearly double the cost of traveling to the West Coast. The Harvard Athletic Committee, knowing this, had unanimously passed a motion to go to Pasadena, "in case the players want to go."[14] The Harvard Club of Southern California and California's Governor William Stephenson, who knew the commercial and prestige value of entertaining Harvard in California, supported the action.[15] The faculty backed down and voted to allow the athletic committee to carry out its earlier decision to attend the game—but with the understanding that "there would be no time wasted after returning in getting back to the serious work of the class room."[16] The Rose Bowl would become increasingly commercialized, a process that came to include radio broadcasts. Although Harvard's 7-6 victory over Oregon in 1920 was not broadcast, radio would be added within a few years.

By 1925, when the Rose Bowl was first commercially broadcast, the Eastern Big 3, Harvard, Yale, and Princeton, had voted that there should be "no post-season contests, or contests for the purpose of settling sectional or other championships, or involving long and expensive trips or extended absence from the university."[17] The Stanford University Faculty Committee on Athletics had also taken a stand opposed to postseason games.[18] The Big 3 kept its promise, but Stanford did not. Stanford, in 1924, hired Glenn "Pop" Warner, successful coach of the University of Pittsburgh, for a salary of $7,500 and $2,500 for expenses. The contract, influenced by the commercial Rose Bowl event, stated that if Warner took Stanford to the Rose Bowl game, he would receive another $2,500, a 25 percent bonus.[19] In his first season at Stanford, Warner led his team to a 7-1-1 record and secured a trip to the 1925 Rose Bowl to meet Notre Dame.

This was one of the most famous Rose Bowl games, broadcast on station WGBS by announcer Sigmund Spaeth and carried by wire to New York City.[20] Spaeth had all the elements of great drama before him. The famous "Four Horsemen" backfield of Harry Stuhldreher, Don Miller, Jim Crowley, and Elmer Layden led Knute Rockne's Notre Dame team. Earlier that year, Rockne had almost lost the chance to again coach his "Four Horsemen" when he signed a three-year contract with the University of Iowa, only to break it and sign a ten-year contract at $10,000 a year to remain at Notre Dame.[21] "Pop" Warner's star fullback was Ernie Nevers, who only ten days before the game had had casts removed from two broken ankles. Nevertheless, Nevers played the entire game on offense and defense, carrying the ball thirty-four times for 114 yards and helping Stanford outgain Notre Dame by 119 yards. It wasn't enough, as Notre Dame capitalized on Stanford mistakes and won 27-10.[22]

This was the first and last commercial bowl game for nearly a half-century for Notre Dame. Rockne, who was not adverse to bowl games, decided to cash in on the commercial aspect of the game after an Irish supporter from New Orleans had made arrangements for Knute and Bonnie Rockne to vacation free at San Diego's Coronado Hotel and have the use of an automobile.[23] Notre Dame later decided not to participate in Bowl games and declined future offers. This decision was made, evidently, as an attempt by Notre Dame administrators to try to help preserve the precarious health of Rockne, who, between attacks of phlebitis or severe nervous strain, seldom made it through a season without a serious illness.[24] Only in 1970 did Notre Dame again accept a bowl bid, when it played Texas in the Cotton Bowl. Four decades after Rockne's death, Notre Dame felt that to remain competitive in recruiting, to maintain national rankings, and win national championships, it needed to participate in bowl games. These considerations were evidently more important than financial gains, including television and radio revenues.[25] Without Notre Dame, other schools had a greater opportunity to visit sunny Southern California and the Rose Bowl.

Some Southern schools wanted to replace the Northern and Eastern teams participating in the Rose Bowl. In 1927, less than two months after the debut of NBC radio, the first coast-to-coast network broadcast of a Rose Bowl game took place, between "Pop" Warner's Stanford and Alabama, coached by Wallace Wade. Before Alabama went West, the Southern Conference had voted to waive its rule against intersectional games.[26] Alabama, the first Southern school invited to the Rose Bowl in 1926, lost that game but was given a second opportunity the next year. Alabama's first Rose Bowl victory, a 20-19 win over Washington, gave Alabama and the South a great boost in state and regional pride. The national radio broadcast of the second Rose Bowl game against Stanford increased Southern prestige in intercollegiate football, as Alabama held the perennially powerful "Pop" Warner team to a 7-7 tie.[27] Graham McNamee and his "twin" broadcaster, Phil Carlin, did the play-by-play.

Graham McNamee continued to broadcast the Rose Bowl games. The annual Rose Bowl game may not have been as popular as radio's most successful offering, the minstrel show *Amos 'n' Andy,* but it gained the attention of the nation. In 1927, McNamee broadcast not only the Stanford-Pittsburgh game, won by Stanford 7-6, but also the Rose Bowl Parade.[28] The following year, McNamee shared the radio booth with Bill Munday, the first Southern announcer on any network. They were at the mike, broadcasting to a nation with some 8 million radio sets, when one of the most memorable plays in college football history took place. Undefeated Georgia Tech was playing California in 1929 when California's Roy Riegels picked up a fumble, reversed directions, and began running toward his own goal line. The play resulted in an eventual safety, providing the two points needed to allow Georgia Tech to eke out an 8-7 victory. "Wrong Way Riegels" has remained the single most remembered "goof-up" in Rose Bowl history if not intercollegiate history. About fifteen years after the sensational wrong-way run, Riegels had a reunion with his teammate, Benny Lom, who had caught and stopped Riegels on the one-yard line. Lom played a phonograph album of Graham McNamee describing Riegel's run, a memory that became the signature event of his life.[29]

The Rose Bowl, NBC, and Graham McNamee were established pioneers of college football broadcasting by the time the stock market crashed in 1929. In the early 1930s, as the Depression wore on, there was a call for postseason charity games to help the needy. The Shriners in

San Francisco decided to have an East-West game in 1933. By the mid-1930s, the commercial success of the Rose Bowl had led other Southern cities to host their own bowl games on the first day of the year. Despite numerous protests by college presidents, such as Minnesota's Lotus Coffman, that "post-season games meant an exploitation of their institutions, an exploitation of the game, and an exploitation of the students," the commercial bowl games increased.[30]

The Orange Bowl began in 1935, when Pennsylvania's Bucknell University beat hometown Miami 26-0. The next year, the Orange Bowl paid CBS $500 to put in a telephone line to broadcast Catholic University's 20-19 victory over Mississippi. Ted Husing became the voice of the Orange Bowl that year. From his modest beginnings, Husing helped popularize the Orange Bowl in the 1930s just as McNamee had done for the Rose Bowl in the 1920s.[31] Only the previous fall, CBS had chosen Husing to announce the nationally broadcast "Game of the Century" between Notre Dame and Ohio State. Husing had been able to tell a national audience how two quick touchdowns in the last quarter and a final "Hail Mary" pass into the end zone brought Notre Dame the victory. That account was certainly more satisfying to Husing than his broadcast of a regular season Harvard-Dartmouth game, in which Husing inadvisably made disparaging remarks about Harvard's golden-boy quarterback, Barry Wood, during the game. His comment that Wood was "playing a putrid game" brought the enmity of Harvard officials, who banned Husing for life from announcing at Harvard stadium.[32] Orange Bowl officials felt more affection for Husing and continued to use his play-by-play for a decade.

In addition to the Orange Bowl, a number of other bowl games and postseason charity games were created in the 1930s, though radio became important to only a few of them. Between 1930 and 1934, there were possibly 100 postseason charity games played in numerous cities north and south, generally in December. The Dixie Classic, a bowl game in Dallas, was renewed in 1934 after a couple of starts in the 1920s, but it only lasted a year. The following year, the Sugar Bowl debuted at Tulane Stadium in New Orleans, where Tulane beat Temple 20-14. The Sun Bowl in El Paso, Texas, began with a tie between Hardin-Simmons and New Mexico State in 1936, and has continued to the present, reflecting commercial sponsorship in its name. The next year, Dallas inaugurated the Cotton Bowl with a Texas Christian victory over Marquette University.

The proliferation of bowl games held away from college campuses merely increased some educators' opposition to the heightened commercialization of football and its connection with commercial radio. William Bingham, athletic director at Harvard, told his president, James B. Conant, that "'bowl' games are becoming a nuisance."[33] The chairman of the Big 10 Faculty Representatives believed that commercial aspects of bowl games, the Rose Bowl in particular, increased the "target for opponents of football to shoot at."[34] The outcry became louder after World War II than it had been during the Depression. To many Americans, however, the bowl games, like the World Series, were important contests, not frivolous or negative commercial events. In the midst of World War II, historian Dennis Brogan made this case in his book *The American Character*. "The Rose Bowl, the Cotton Bowl, the other intersectional games— these are instruments of national unity," Brogan believed, "a religious exercise of a kind [an Ancient] Greek would have understood."[35] Only two days after the massive Japanese bombing at Pearl Harbor, which precipitated the U.S. entry into World War II, a spokesman of the Orange Bowl placed the bowl games in perspective for many Americans. Only hours after the declaration of war on Japan, E. E. Seiler remarked: "I think the public will raise hell this New Year's Day and then get down to business."[36]

Pearl Harbor raised the threat of a Japanese invasion of the West Coast. Almost immediately, Rose Bowl organizers sought a new temporary home away from Pasadena. Less than a month after the Pearl Harbor disaster, Duke University, hosted and lost 20-16 to Oregon State, in a Rose Bowl held in Durham, North Carolina, before 56,000 spectators. It was, as were all Rose Bowl games since 1925, broadcast on radio. Broadcasting had brought bowl games to the national consciousness, something that only newspapers had done before. In the future, though, television would raise the commercial ante and national awareness far beyond that created by radio.

Sport and the New Medium of Television   8

WHILE RADIO was in its commercial infancy during the Roaring Twenties, a newer medium was being developed both in America and abroad. Three countries were in the forefront of television, sometimes known as "visual wireless" or "visual radio." Some aspects of television technology actually preceded those of radio. The German Paul Nipkow patented a disc-scanning system for sending pictures via a radio transmitter in 1884. Two decades later, another German transmitted photos over telephone wire from Munich to Nuremberg. A Russian émigré in America, Vladimir Zworykin, patented an Iconoscope ("electronic eye") television system for Westinghouse only three years after Westinghouse's KDKA began operation as the first commercial radio station in America. In England, John Logie Baird produced the first successful television demonstration in 1926. A year later, Bell Telephone Labs provided the initial public television demonstration in America, transmitting Herbert Hoover's image from Washington, D.C., to New York City. Shortly after, there was enough interest in television for a magazine titled *Television* to begin publication, at almost the same time that the first talking picture, *The Jazz Singer,* came to the silver screen. These advancements prompted *New York Times* sportswriter John Kieran to comment at the second Jack Dempsey–Gene Tunney heavyweight fight that many of the 140,000 spectators at Soldier Field in Chicago "will probably stay home and see the next battle of the century by television."[1] Nevertheless, radio became the moneymaker in the 1920s and 1930s, and television progress was slowed.

Even as American researchers like Philo T. Farnsworth of Philco, Vladimir Zworykin of RCA, and Allen B. Du Mont of Du Mont Laboratories developed television with a reasonable image quality by the mid-1930s, Germany took the lead in telecasting to the public. After Adolph Hitler grabbed power in 1933, the Nazi regime realized that television could be a major means of carrying propaganda. The 1936 Berlin Summer Olympics were the first showcase for German television. Because the Nazi government favored a mass viewing environment over home viewing, twenty-eight halls in Berlin, Potsdam, and Leipzig were furnished with television sets for the Summer games. During the Berlin games, more than 150,000 individuals saw the daily three- to eight-hour programs from the Olympics.[2] Germany claimed a victory in having the first public television in the world just as it easily won the most gold medals in the 1936 Olympics, turning the event into a propoganda triumph.[3]

Britain and America were not far behind in the television race. The elite British Wimbledon tennis tournament was telecast to about 3,000 homes by the British Broadcasting Corporation for the first time in 1937, when Don Budge beat Frank Parker for the title. The following year the BBC telecast a women's field hockey contest.[4] Meanwhile, American technology, especially that of RCA, was being used by both the Germans and the British as they moved into programming. The Americans, lacking the governmental support found in the German and Britain state-controlled television monopolies, were delayed in their programming. As the Federal Communications Commission stated in 1938: "Television is not ready for standardization or commercial use by the general public."[5] In America, manufacturers in the free enterprise system, funded by private capital, were fearful of selling TV sets to the public that would become obsolete and aggravate the new owners. Each television equipment manufacturer created its own standard, and the FCC delayed setting universal standards. The FCC also authorized only limited commercial operation, further delaying the development of TV.[6]

In the spring of 1939, RCA was determined to debut commercial television at the New York World's Fair. On April 30, President Franklin D. Roosevelt became the first president of the United States to appear live on television when he opened the fair. NBC transmitted the proceedings on Long Island across the East River to a small TV audience eight miles away in Manhattan's Radio City. RCA television sets, with 5-inch and 9-inch picture tubes and priced from about $200 to $600, picked up the activity. The summer's 45 million fair-goers could see television for the first time, along with the introduction, for most of them, to both fluorescent lights and plastics.[7]

Less than three weeks after the opening of the world's fair, the first telecast of an American sporting event took place, a college baseball game with Bill Stern behind the microphone. Only a half-decade before, Stern had been given the opportunity to broadcast the Army-Illinois football game on NBC radio. He had asked his friends and relatives to send telegrams to the network praising his work, but some arrived two days before the contest. As a result, NBC fired Stern.[8] Five years later, and after he had lost a leg in an auto accident, NBC rehired Stern and gave him the opportunity to be the first television sports announcer on May 17, 1939. NBC's experimental station W2XBS set up one camera in the stands on the third-base side, about fifty feet from home plate, at Columbia's Baker Field. There, not far from the camera, Bill Stern gave the play-by-play while the operator of unwieldy RCA Iconoscope camera attempted to pick up the action. Even before the game, when Stern introduced the captains and coaches, they could hardly be recognized on blurry television screens, as their faces appeared dark owing to the sun passing directly in front of the camera.[9]

The image of the game itself, between Columbia and Princeton, was no better and probably worse. As dramatic as was the voice of Bill Stern, the limitations of one camera angle and the poor quality of the picture on snowy screens detracted from the scene. Only by listening to the announcer could one follow the action. The cameraman focused on the pitcher during the windup and attempted to follow the ball to the plate. Whenever the ball was hit, Stern would describe the flight of the ball, but the cameraman had difficulty following it. According to Stern, he kept glancing behind to look at the bulky camera: "I had no monitor. I had no idea where the damned thing was pointing. I never knew whether the thing could keep up with the play or not."[10] The *New York Times* reported that "the players were best described by observers as appearing 'like white flies' running across the screen. . . . The ball was seldom seen except on bunts and infield plays comparatively close to the camera."[11] Said Stern: "We got so we were actually praying for all the batters to strike out. . . . That was one thing we knew the camera could record."[12] But the camera did catch Princeton's steal of home in their 2-1 extra-inning victory, as Princeton climbed into fourth place in the Ivy League.[13]

Princeton and Columbia—and baseball itself—would not again be important players in the development of televised college sport, but college sport was to be part of the formula for the success of television. Newspaper writer Thomas Hutchinson was right when he wrote just prior to the Columbia-Princeton game that "outdoor sports will furnish much of the most interesting material we could televise."[14] When a radio showman was asked to suggest a successful formula for television, he said: "Sex appeal, newsreels, sporting events and drama!"[15] It was not evident at the time that sports would be to television what music was to radio.[16]

A flurry of sports telecasting in New York City, both professional and college, followed the Columbia-Princeton baseball game. Boxing, unlike baseball, was a nearly perfect sport for telecasting, as all the close-up action could be captured. Two weeks after the baseball telecast, the heavyweight Max Baer–Lou Nova fight in Yankee Stadium was telecast on W2XBS in New York to a few hundred homes with television. The contrast to radio is revealing. The year before, the famous two minute, four second knockout of the German Max Schmeling by Joe Louis had taken place. For the Louis-Schmeling fight, about 23 million radios had been tuned to the fight, nearly two-thirds of all radios in America and twice as many as had listened to any of President Franklin Roosevelt's famous fireside chats.[17] It would be more than a decade before television would reach such an audience.

The city of New York also hosted the first major league baseball game, an August match-up between the Cincinnati Reds and the Brooklyn Dodgers. Red Barber, who had signed to broadcast Dodgers games on radio, did the announcing on TV as ultrashortwaves were transmitted from Ebbets Field to the main station atop the Empire State Building. This time, two cameras were used, as well as a new telephoto lens. Both cameras were on the third-base side, one by the visitors' dugout, the other in the upper deck, where Barber sat surrounded by fans while he did the play-by-play. There was no TV monitor for Barber, no real communication with the director in a truck outside the park, no assistant, and no broadcasting booth. Nevertheless, within three months of the first sports telecast, there had been a vast improvement in the quality of the product.[18] By then, the first commercials were being offered by Barber. For one of the more famous ads, Barber opened a box of Wheaties, shook out a bowlful, sliced a banana, added a spoonful of sugar, poured on milk, and said: "That's a Breakfast of Champions."[19]

Only two weeks after Hitler invaded Poland, igniting World War II, American college football telecasting began, first as scrimmages and then as full-blown intercollegiate contests. Testing out the new medium, NBC, with Bill Stern at the microphone, telecast a Fordham University scrimmage early in the season of 1939. A few weeks later a Long Island University football practice was also telecast. These were preliminary to the first football game ever telecast, in which Fordham University beat Waynesburg College of Pennsylvania 34-7 on September 20, 1939. Bill Stern did the play-by-play from Triboro Stadium on Randall's Island in New York's East River. One Iconoscope camera was set up on a tripod on the forty-yard line before a crowd of 9,000, possibly four or five times the number of people watching the game on TV. The views of the game that were transmitted were generally static shots of moving players, who appeared minuscule when they were across the field and gigantic when they neared the camera. This partially successful telecast was followed by Manhattan–St. Bonaventure and City College of New York–Scranton games in October.[20]

College football telecasting preceded the professional football games of the National Football League by less than a month. The Brooklyn Dodger football team played the Philadelphia Eagles in Ebbets Field before 13,000 spectators in October as NBC carried the 23-14 Brooklyn victory to fewer than 1000 TV sets in the New York City area. Allen "Skip" Walz, a former Golden Gloves champion and New York University football star, was the announcer. This time two Iconoscope cameras were used, one near Walz, who sat in the mezzanine with the camera over his

shoulder, and another on the fifty-yard line. While there was no monitor in the telecasting box, Potsy Clark, the Brooklyn coach, used one as
an experiment to get a better view of the game. Because it was a cloudy
day, the picture got darker and darker as the game progressed, and, according to Walz, it eventually went "completely blank and we reverted
to a radio broadcast."[21]

Playing for the Philadelphia Eagles in that contest was Franny Murray, an individual who would become a significant figure in opposing
NCAA control of college football telecasting in the early 1950s. In the
first professional football game telecast, Murray ran and passed well,
scoring a touchdown. A University of Pennsylvania All-American in
1936, Murray eventually returned to his alma mater as the athletic director in 1950, following a career as a radio and television commentator,
a promotional executive for professional sports, and a special agent for
the Department of Justice during World War II.[22]

The University of Pennsylvania became the educational institution
most involved in the use of television in America well before Francis
Murray came onto the scene as athletic director. The Philco Radio and
Television Corporation agreed to telecast all the Penn home football
games in 1940 using an experimental license, station W3XE. While the
telecasts were not considered by the university to be commercial, they
were sponsored by the Atlantic Refining Company and the N. W. Ayres
Advertising Agency.[23] The pioneering telecasts emanated from Franklin
Field, only a stone's throw from the plot of ground on which Eadweard
Muybridge had perfected his classic photography of humans and other
animals in motion in the mid-1880s.[24] The Philco experiment put the
University of Pennsylvania in the forefront of telecasting for more than
a decade.

Philco used two cameras, one on each twenty-five-yard line, while announcer Bill Slater covered the game for both radio and TV. One camera, with a telescopic lens, did close-up shots, while the other was used
for general action. A new type of camera called the Orthocon gave a
clearer picture, with better contrast between light and dark areas, than
the previous Iconoscopes. Signals were sent by shortwave from an aerial on top of Convention Hall to the Philco plant. There, from a higher
aerial, signals were sent to the Philadelphia area, including a major
pickup area in the Warwick Hotel. At the hotel, a special press showing
of the game was offered. One student reporter noted, "Watching the
game by television was almost as good as being there." Probably psy-

chologically high from his experience of watching Penn destroy Maryland 51-0, he exulted, "Television is here to stay!"[25]

For the next decade, Penn telecast all its home football games, with the exception of those during one year of World War II. While most of the nation virtually forgot about television during the war, the University of Pennsylvania, along with corporations such as RCA, Philco, and Du Mont, continued to do research and development as they anticipated the end of the war effort.

Even before the University of Pennsylvania began telecasting its games, television was introduced into the festivities of the Rose Bowl. The Rose Bowl football game, which began in 1902 and became regularized in 1916, was predated by the Rose Bowl Parade. The tradition of flower-bedecked horses and carriages had begun in 1890 and continued through the years. By the time the January 1, 1940, Rose Bowl Parade arrived, precedent had been set years before for the parade theme, float sweepstakes winner, tournament queen, and grand marshal.

The parade's tradition and general appeal made the idea of telecasting it interesting to Don Lee, an early West Coast pioneer in television. Lee began regular Los Angeles telecasts on station W6XAO as early as January 1939, when he carried programming to four Los Angeles schools. He soon moved outdoors with portable equipment, telecasting Hollywood Park professional baseball contests. He placed two cameras along the first-base side, one with a telephoto lens and, just above it in the grandstand, one with a wide angle lens. The few people who owned home television sets expressed pleasure at Lee's results. If he could have telecast the 1939 Rose Bowl parade, he would have been able to show the child motion picture star, Shirley Temple, who was Grand Marshal of the Rose Parade. Instead he had to settle for the first wooden marshal, Charlie McCarthy, and his ventriloquist, Edgar Bergen, on New Year's Day in 1940.[26] Lee's camera was stationed on top of the balcony of the Elk's Club, where it could effectively survey the flower-covered floats and marching bands and relay the signals to several hundred home TV's.[27]

Prior to World War II, then, television had made a small mark on college sport and its surrounding festivities. Telecasting remained experimental, and there was no commercialism at first on the part of the colleges. There is no available evidence to show that colleges were paid any fees for telecasts, unlike commercial radio, the fees for which were growing rapidly in the 1930s. That would change soon after World War II, as the rapid growth of television put dollar signs in the eyes of both television networks and the institutions of higher education. Television, like radio, would conform to the same commercial spirit that had dominated intercollegiate athletics from a period before the invention of either radio or television.

9 Networks, Coaxial Cable, Commercialism, and Concern

WITH THE DEFEAT of Germany in the Spring of 1945 and the capitulation of Japan three months later, players in the American economy, including makers of television sets, prepared for an economic boom. Following the war, television manufacturers were able to go into full production, and by 1946 television sets were being mass produced. Coaxial cable, produced by AT&T, was first laid on the East Coast in 1946 and spread to the Midwest shortly after, clearing the way for television network success.[1] The heavyweight championship fight between Joe Louis and Billy Conn not only achieved the highest radio rating in history on ABC's network of 195 radio stations, but it was also telecast on the new NBC network to a few thousand homes in New York, Schenectady, Philadelphia, and Washington, D.C. The Louis-Conn fight was described in 1946 by one television executive as "the most important event in the history of television.[2] Following the successful telecast, *Business Week* predicted that sport would create a new public acceptance of TV.[3] Television did that just as it sold shaving equipment for the Gillette Razor Company and other manufacturers' products.

By 1947 there were two major networks, NBC and CBS, and two more that were growing rapidly, ABC and Du Mont. ABC was created in 1943 after antitrust action forced NBC to divest itself of one of its two radio networks. Du Mont was founded by Allen B. Du Mont, a scientist in the business of manufacturing high-quality television equipment. In 1946, Du Mont broadcast all the New York Yankee home games (with Mel Allen behind the microphone), the home football games of the New York Giants, and a number of other contests in Washington, D.C., Philadelphia, and Boston. The Du Mont Television Network also telecast the 1946 Army-Duke football game, probably the first telecast of a Southern team.[4] By the fall of 1947, eight cities in the United States had TV stations: New York, Schenectady, Philadelphia, Washington, Detroit, Chicago, St. Louis, and Los Angeles. Boston and Baltimore were also eager to enter the market. There were only about 50,000 television sets in the entire country at the time.[5] The TV networks were about to play the commercial game with colleges, institutions that were ready to financially capitalize on the rapidly growing popularity of sports, especially football.

Sporting events became a principal factor, possibly the main factor, in enticing people to buy television sets. The glamourous events on TV included contests such as the Joe Louis–Billy Conn fight, the baseball World Series, beginning in 1947, and the Army-Navy football game the same year. Not surprisingly, neighborhood taverns were often the first to buy television sets, allowing the decidedly male patronage to both drink and watch sports. The Catholic Church in the Chicago area was aware of young men's attraction to the bars and tried to woo them back from the taverns by purchasing television receivers for the parish churches, particularly after Notre Dame football began to be telecast.[6]

Television station managers obviously knew of the Notre Dame attraction and made overtures to telecast all its home games, while Notre Dame extended its radio policy of nonexclusive rights to include television. In 1947, the three Notre Dame home games were carried by WBKB to an estimated audience of 165,000 per game in the Chicago area. Transmitting the signal seventy-five miles to Chicago required three multiple relays in New Carlisle, Michigan City, and Chicago. The engineering was successful, as the picture and the voice of play-by-play announcer Joe Wilson came through clearly. It was an expensive venture for WBKB, and Notre Dame's nonexclusive rights policy was an indication that the university expected little income from television. As Vice President John Murphy noted at the close of the season, "We realized . . . that we were cutting off a very, very large source of income. . . . Good will is much more important to us."[7] The first telecast showed the famed Golden Dome of Notre Dame as announcers commented that Notre Dame was famed for scientific research, for cultivation of the arts, and for humanity to mankind, giving the Catholic school what it wanted—good publicity. To ensure that advertising was kept positive and in good taste, Notre Dame retained the right to approve television advertising, as it had in radio, strictly forbidding ads for alcohol, cigarettes, patent medicine, and laxatives.[8]

The nonexclusive rights would last only one more season, as Notre Dame officials realized "how important getting Notre Dame can be to these people in television."[9] For exclusive television rights to Notre Dame football in 1948, RCA offered $10,000 while WBKB in Chicago offered $5,000 or 25 percent of gross sales, whichever was greater. There was also potential money to be made if coaxial cable could connect Chicago (and also Notre Dame) with the East Coast and if the theater television concept could be put in place.[10] Rejecting both exclusive rights offers, Notre Dame accepted the nonexclusive rights of Television Productions, which paid the Irish $350 per game or $1,400 for the season, a far cry from what the exclusive rights were worth.[11] A single game, played in Baltimore against Navy, brought Notre Dame an additional television income of $6,600.[12]

Two major networks, NBC and Du Mont, bid for Notre Dame football telecast rights in 1949, and there was additional interest among WGN and WBKB in Chicago, Admiral Corporation, RCA, ABC, and CBS. While professional football teams were receiving an average of about $3,000 per game and major league baseball teams were accepting $1,000 per game, RCA offered $50,000 to broadcast five Notre Dame games.[13] The Du Mont Television Network, a New York City concern and major player in early television, bid a minimum of $36,000 for rights to telecast to an eight-station network, with $2,150 for each additional station that it could recruit. Notre Dame accepted Du Mont's network contract for 1949, with Chevrolet as the commercial sponsor.[14] After the signing, an executive of WGN-TV in Chicago wrote of Notre Dame: "Certainly no other university will be on so many stations so often during 1949."[15] That was to be true for the next half-century. The network coverage only added to Notre Dame's football revenue, and Notre Dame officials recommended "a pronouncement to the effect that television had not cut down on our attendance this year."[16]

Though Notre Dame, as *the* Catholic football institution, was able to push its way to the television forefront because of its national visibility, the University of Pennsylvania could press forward because of its interests in both experimental and commercial television. The University of Pennsylvania had been telecasting its football games since 1940, and in 1949, a Penn graduate student, Jerry Jordan, began a study of the impact television had on in-stadium sporting event attendance. Jordan, a Phi Beta Kappa from Princeton and the son of an advertising executive involved in sports, was probably biased toward commercial broadcasting of college football. Not surprisingly, his initial research suggested that television had no adverse effect upon gate receipts.[17] Penn, with a decade of television experience, was, however, losing football attendance. Season ticket sales from 1947 to 1949 had dropped 30 percent, and they dropped another 14 percent the following year. While this could be attributed to the impact of television, there is also evidence that Penn fans were becoming increasingly reluctant to come to Ivy League games.[18] As the number of home Ivy opponents doubled, game attendance was cut nearly in half.[19] Penn officials concluded that scheduling games against non-Ivy League teams such as Army, Navy, and Penn State would do more to increase attendance than would cutting back on TV coverage.

As an undergradute, Jerry Jordan had won an award for original scientific research at Princeton's Department of Psychology with his paper "The Effect of Television on Living Habits." He had been a member of Princeton's 150-pound football team and continued to cultivate his love of football by serving as assistant coach of Penn's 150-pound team in 1949. Although Jordan's research ran counter to the experience of many athletic officials across the nation, the youthful Jordan was asked to speak before the NCAA convention in January of 1950. He told the athletic officials what they were prone to disbelieve. Once the novelty of television had worn off, Jordan told them, "TV does not hurt attendance and may account for part of this increase" in attendance.[20]

Of the major football powers, only the University of Pennsylvania and Notre Dame agreed with Jordan's findings. Penn could claim substantial TV revenues, more than any other university in 1950 with the possible exception of Notre Dame. ABC gained the rights to telecast Penn football in 1950 for $75,000, a much higher price tag than any institution other than Notre Dame could command.[21] Penn, under its youthful president Harold Stassen, pushed hard for increasing the TV revenues. Stassen may have had political motives for pushing Penn higher into big-time football visibility. Coming to the University of Pennsylvania after having served as governor of Minnesota, Stassen had higher political ambitions, as evidenced by his run for the presidency in 1952 and his participation in a number of political campaigns over the next two decades. Stassen knew that joining with Notre Dame for national TV promotion could enhance his reputation. When Penn and Notre Dame agreed to a series of football games, it seemed to confirm Penn's movement toward the big-time and away from the Ivy League. For whatever reasons, Penn's and Notre Dame's desire to attract commercial TV revenues for their individual institutions, against a growing NCAA collectivist sentiment to cooperatively limit football telecasts, resulted in a sharp conflict in the early 1950s among NCAA institutions.

From 1949 to 1951, the drive by Penn and Notre Dame to secure greater TV revenues was on a collision course with those who feared TV's harmful effect upon gate receipts. The earliest opposition to unrestricted commercial TV broadcasts by individual collegiate institutions evidently began in the East. Ivy League football attendance showed a marked 25 percent, decline from 1947 to 1950. In contrast, the Southeast Conference declined only 1 percent, the Pacific Coast Conference declined 7 percent, and the Big 10 actually gained 2 percent in those years.[22]

Even at the postwar height of college football growth, from 1945 to 1948, there was enough concern among institutions of the NCAA to hold a special 1948 roundtable" session on the future of television in college sport.[23] A major speaker at the meeting was William Eddy of WBKB in Chicago, the station that had carried Notre Dame for one year and Northwestern University games for the two previous years. "Television will not hurt the gate," Eddy tried to assure NCAA delegates. "In the case of television, I am positive, that radio's experience will be duplicated. . . . It is a fact," Eddy may have overstated, "that many colleges exist because of the publicity . . . various teams receive, and in this respect, the television industry is opening the gate to a new type of promotion."[24] With WBKB devoting 55 percent of its programming to sports, Eddy had much to gain by trying to convince the NCAA representatives that television would benefit, not diminish, college football interest and finances.

The athletic director of Northwestern, Ted Payseur, was a good choice to follow Eddy's presentation. For two years Northwestern, a leader along with the University of Pennsylvania in allowing its games to be telecast, had offered TV rights to WBKB. "I feel that Northwestern has not been hurt in the last two years," Payseur told the gathering. "I do think it is a problem we are going to have to meet as individual schools, conferences, or the NCAA."[25] Northwestern may not have been hurt, but financially it had gained little from its early TV exposure. For the first year, WBKB only paid Northwestern for the construction of stadium TV booths. For the second year of TV rights, Payseur only received the same small amount that the school charged for radio.

A third presentation at the NCAA convention got to the root of a problem that would only be settled after the NCAA faced a major drop in football attendance by the early 1950s. Namely, should the NCAA collectively control television? Don Spencer, CEO of a company that wanted to represent the NCAA in future television negotiations with networks and advertising agencies, was the speaker. He urged the NCAA to create a television committee and to approve an official national representative (his organization) to work with the committee to form a collective national football television policy.[26] Spencer's proposal went against four decades of NCAA history, in which it had exercised no legislative, regulatory, or administrative power. The NCAA had only used the persuasive power of individual institutions or conferences acting for what they considered the good of intercollegiate athletics. In short, Spencer was asking the NCAA to end its policy of "Home Rule," in which individual institutions acted in their own self-interest, and instead give itself the authority to act for the interest of all.

Chairman of the roundtable meeting, T. P. Heard of Louisiana State University, spoke for the tradition of the NCAA when he reacted to Spencer's suggestion. "There is no intention at this time," Heard said, "to set up any regulatory body to handle this matter."[27] Heard probably did not detect the irony of his own comments. A day later, the NCAA voted to change its constitution and, for the first time, implement a national policy, the "Sanity Code," to limit recruiting and scholarships for athletes. The new regulatory body set up to enforce the national policy was the Compliance Committee. This committee could recommend removing from the NCAA any institution that gave athletic scholarships or recruited athletes with the promise of financial aid.[28] The greatest success of the NCAA as a regulatory body, forming a TV cartel, would not come into existence for three more years.

For the moment, the NCAA would defer to individual institutions and conferences when it came to the development of television. In the East, the Eastern College Athletic Conference, at its first annual meeting only a month before the NCAA roundtable discussion, had displayed great concern for the negative impact television had on eastern football attendance. Of the ECAC's fifty-four institutions, less than one-fifth had any games shown on TV in the fall of 1947. Asa Bushnell, commissioner of the ECAC, warned: "If you gentlemen are not worried about television, I think you should be." Bushnell believed that "television is the scientific method which has been developed to consign all athletic directors to the Smithsonian Institute and to make football stadiums of interest only to archaeologists." Bushnell's alarm, however, was not universally shared at the meeting. The University of Pennsylvania's athletic director, who had the most experience in televising football, was not convinced. "Whether television will increase general interest and have a stimulating effect on the game," Jamison Swarts stated, "I don't know."[29] Neither did others. It didn't take long, however, for many to make up their minds.

Table 1   **Dollars Spent on College Football Admissions**

1943	$26 million (mid-World War II)
1946	78 million (1st post-war football TV)
1949	106 million (1st intersectional TV)
1950	99 million (call for NCAA TV control)

Source: Jerry N. Jordan, "Sports Met TV's First Big Threat in 1950," Speech at the College Physical Education Association meeting, 29 December 1950, Series 5/21/7, Box 1, University of Wisconsin Archives.

The East's concern mounted, and the ECAC exerted pressure on the NCAA to place limits on television. A survey was called for, and the NCAA contracted an independent agency to conduct a study of 1948 football attendance along the East Coast from Connecticut to Maryland, where most of the stations and television sets were found. The findings showed increased television and decreased game attendance.[30] A new motto resulted: "Radio aroused curiosity and television satisfied it." When Notre Dame, with its string of three undefeated seasons, announced that its games would be telecast into the East for the 1949 season, it caught the attention of a group of Eastern colleges. "Television of those Notre Dame games," an alarmed Asa Bushnell stated, "is bound to hurt attendance in all areas covered. . . . How many people are going to want to attend a small college game if they can sit home and watch Notre Dame instead?"[31] As attendance at Ivy League and other Eastern football games dropped, many concluded that television was the major culprit. Indeed, in 1949 money collected from football admissions was at an all-time high, but the East was already feeling a downturn that would have an impact on the rest of the nation by the early 1950s. To punctuate the concern of the East, Columbia's athletic director and chairman of the new ECAC TV Committee remarked: "I am very much afraid that unless the East carries the ball on this television picture," Ralph Furey emphasized, "some of the people in other parts of the country, who just don't understand the picture, are just going to let it go by the wayside." Furey noted with some incredulity that the chairman of the NCAA Television Committee had never even seen a football game on television.[32]

At midcentury, while institutions in the East raised the question of television's negative impact on gate receipts, two institutions, the University of Pennsylvania and a Midwestern giant, Notre Dame, pushed for institutional freedom in developing college sports telecasting. Both institutions appeared more assured than did Stanford's representative to the NCAA, Alfred Masters, who said: "I feel like a little boy who got a very elaborate mechanical toy for Christmas and who does not know what to do with it."[33] With seemingly no fear of the new medium, Notre Dame and the University of Pennsylvania moved to benefit financially by individually going the commercial route.

Notre Dame Chooses Commercial TV

AT THE SAME time that the University of Notre Dame decided to "go commercial" with its television plan by selling its rights exclusively to Du Mont Television, Bill Fay, a writer for *Collier's,* made several forecasts about the television revolution. Fay predicted that, because of television, minor league baseball would collapse, major leagues would expand to Los Angeles and San Francisco, games would be played mostly at night, indoor fields would be built to accommodate TV, basketball would become the number-one world spectator sport, and colleges would have empty football stadiums.[1] Though Fay's crystal ball was often clear, attendance in college football stadiums, while it fell significantly, didn't reach the crisis stage he foresaw.

Among those few institutions that saw no attendance decline was Notre Dame, and apparently the leaders of the Catholic school had no fear of TV. One of the most fearless was the new executive vice president, Theodore Hesburgh, a 32-year-old priest who had attended Notre Dame only four years after Knute Rockne's untimely death in a plane crash. Though Notre Dame had an athletic director, Hesburgh was essentially in control of athletics in his position of executive vice president, the position that has traditionally ruled Notre Dame athletics. He became involved in the TV business from the start and would continue to remain actively involved after he became president in 1952, continuing even as president emeritus after his retirement in 1987. A strong case could be made for Hesburgh being the most important individual in televised college sports during his four decades of leadership at Notre Dame.

Following another undefeated football season at Notre Dame in 1948, during which time stadium sellouts and exclusive TV rights brought in less than $10,000, Theodore Hesburgh attended his first NCAA meeting, along with President John Cavanaugh and athletic director Edward "Moose" Krause. They were present at the TV roundtable discussion and heard the Eastern College Athletic Conference Television Committee chairman Ralph Furey claim that "television is a potential threat to the financial structure of intercollegiate athletics."[2] They listened to the University of Pittsburgh's athletic director, Tom Hamilton, criticize Notre Dame for announcing that it would telecast games into Pittsburgh during four Pitt home games the following year.[3] Father Hesburgh was then called upon by Kenneth "Tug" Wilson, chair of the meeting and commissioner of the Big 10, for his ideas on television. Hesburgh conjured up a biblical analogy and applied it to television: "If it is from God, we can't stop it; if it is not, it will die of its own accord."[4] Clearly Hesburgh could see that both God and mammon were on his side. He reserved his thoughts of television riches, however, for private conversations, revealing nothing to NCAA members.

Two months before the NCAA convention, Hesburgh had been advised that the NCAA had the intent of "throwing cold water on the idea of televising of football games, on the plea that it is hurting attendance." At the same time, he was counseled not to take the advice of RCA of Chicago to tell the NCAA that despite TV, ticket sales were positive at Notre Dame. There were negative attitudes toward Notre Dame, Hesburgh was reminded, both because it was Catholic and because it had been successful in expanding its television coverage. Any Notre Dame push for greater TV coverage might not be well received by other NCAA institutions.[5] Hesburgh was well advised, and he did not show Notre Dame's hand in television negotiations. Those ongoing negotiations included theater telecasts during games, postgame showings, television highlight features, and network telecasts.[6] During the 1949 football season, Hesburgh was apprised that Fighting Irish football theater television alone could bring in over $1 million for just two games.[7] That figure was questionable, but Notre Dame football was a much greater attraction than any other university team in America.

Hesburgh was aware that money from football could be used to build up the university, not just athletics, as was the practice at a number of other institutions. Robert Dunne of San Francisco even suggested that a movie about Notre Dame could be produced, with actor and singer Bing Crosby playing Hesburgh and without "the damned love element." The story, Dunne said, could be built around Hesburgh's "fight to build an independent university without tax-funds."[8] Hesburgh thought that "the movie idea is good, if it were done the right way so as to give the complete picture of Notre Dame." Television money, too, "might well be a great financial boon to the school, and we can certainly use it at this time with so many ideas of progress and development."[9] The commercialization of Notre Dame, then, could help build the university into a greater institution. Of course, Dunne advised, to make money "you must win!"[10]

Father Theodore Hesburgh's and other officials' goal, when Notre Dame asked for bids for the 1950 TV contract, was to enhance the greater development of Notre Dame with the television "money ball." Though the Big 10 had advised Hesburgh that it was seriously considering banning football telecasts for the 1950 season, Hesburgh considered hiring a full-time television expert versed in promoting Notre Dame through football telecasting.[11] Hesburgh was straying from his statement at the January 1950 NCAA meeting that in television policy "we want to benefit the whole of sports because what is good for sports is good for the country at large."[12] The actuality was more like what is good for Notre Dame football is good for the institution at large. That is essentially the philosophy other institutions of higher learning would have taken had they possessed the national image of Notre Dame football. In the highly individualistic nature of higher education in America, self-serving interests came first and cooperation for the larger good was a far second, even among a Big 10 conference that feared Notre Dame's dominance in football and in television.

Hesburgh's special working relationship with Leslie Arries, Director of Sports and Special Events at the Du Mont Television Network, helped Du Mont obtain exclusive rights to Notre Dame football for the 1950 season. Arries and Du Mont had enjoyed the benefit of telecasting Notre Dame games the previous two years. Notre Dame and Du Mont had developed such a chummy relationship that just before the letters went out for open bids, Hesburgh asked Arries to suggest whether the pregame, postgame, and movie rights should be bid at the same time as the live game rights.[13]

Three networks, NBC, ABC, and Du Mont, were asked to bid for the 1950 rights. Hesburgh had been advised by Edgar Kobak of New York, former head of the Mutual Broadcasting System, to set a minimum price of $100,000 for rights to telecast five Notre Dame games. This was half what the Major Leagues had received in 1949 for the television rights to the World Series and considerably more than any other university, including the other major television power, the University of Pennsylvania, had received from football telecasts.[14]

When Hesburgh indicated to an adviser that "we would probably do the best with DuMont and Chevrolet," he revealed his desire to retain Du Mont because, in his words, that network "really goes out to make the finest presentation possible."[15] Yet NBC opened its bidding with an offer of $110,000 for the TV rights to broadcast over its forty-four NBC stations and affiliates to an estimated audience of 6.5 million for each game. Notre Dame, knowing that NBC had the largest network by far, asked NBC to make a supplementary bid. NBC raised the ante $40,000, to a total of $150,000.[16] ABC offered $145,000 for the five-game schedule, the highest amount ABC had ever offered for a sports event.[17] Du Mont, however, jumped over both bids with an offer of $185,000, which was accepted by Notre Dame.[18]

The Notre Dame television network contract in 1950 was criticized, just as Notre Dame came under attack four decades later when NBC gained the rights to telecast its games nationally. Big 10 schools were probably most upset, for Notre Dame telecasts would directly affect their Midwest games. The day Notre Dame received its offer from NBC, Big 10 commissioner "Tug" Wilson asked Notre Dame to hold off making contractual arrangements so that Notre Dame could meet with the Big 10 about the control of television. Wilson, trying to convince Notre Dame that his conference was taking the ethical high ground, said that the Big 10 "must consider what is good for college athletics overall and college football in particular."[19] At the time, support was growing among Big 10 institutions to ban the telecasts of conference games for 1950, and indeed that action was taken.[20] Yet when Notre Dame refused to be involved in the Big 10 ban, the conference voted to allow a major theater chain to show Michigan football in Detroit and Northwestern and Illinois games in Chicago with only a thirty-second delay in the live broadcast. It was an obvious effort to impact the Catholic school, as Chicago and Detroit were the major metropolitan areas closest to the University of Notre Dame. Notre Dame, in fact, had good cause aside from financial gain to go ahead with its television plans. The school could well have been retaliating against three Big 10 institutions for dropping Notre Dame from their football schedules.[21]

Notre Dame's success in gaining a network TV contract alarmed a number of institutions nationally and triggered collective action on the television issue. The 1950 NCAA Convention began the process, somewhat belatedly, by appointing its first NCAA Television Committee, made up of Ralph Furey of Columbia, Tom Hamilton of Pittsburgh, and Willis Hunter of the University of Southern California, to study the problem of television. Within a year the committee helped bring about what, in many ways, was the most important piece of legislation in NCAA history.

The collective TV plan of the NCAA radically changed the function of the NCAA from primarily a debating society to a well-financed legislative and administrative organization. Abandoning "Home Rule" for collective NCAA action had begun with the 1948 Sanity Code, but that code, calling for the national control of financial aid and recruitment, had lasted only a couple of years before it was judged inoperative and abandoned. Just at that point, the NCAA decided that individual action regarding TV by institutions such as Notre Dame jeopardized the financial stability of football and thus of all intercollegiate athletics. Individual action, or Home Rule, in existence since the formation of the NCAA in 1906, was abandoned again for an experimental NCAA television plan for 1951. With that action, Notre Dame's dominant financial advantage from television was lost for the next four decades.

Notre Dame lost its lucrative television network contract, but not before it had quietly worked to introduce a "Super Conference" for football. Less than a month after the NCAA had called for collective national control of television, President John Cavanaugh of Notre Dame suggested a Super Conference of football powers. Cavanaugh asked more than a dozen other institutions to join together to reform college athletics on such issues as financial aid to athletes, long-term coaching contracts, and television. "Rather than having one school like ourselves for the whole network," Cavanaugh suggested to his potential Super Conference members, "we could have the network consider all the games within the schools in our association, and leave it to the network, the sponsors, and perhaps, a core of sportswriters and telecasters who would know the public interest, to select the game which would be most in public demand on any particular Saturday." Cavanaugh believed that members of the association "could impose upon ourselves whatever controls would seem necessary in the interest of other schools." Cavanaugh's insights, though not accepted in 1951, eventually were put into practice by the College Football Association in 1984 and by some of the major conferences in the 1990s.[22]

A national Super Conference, Cavanaugh believed, would be based on two technological developments that brought colleges closer together for national rather than regional contests. Convenient air travel and mass communications, especially television, had led him to propose a national conference.[23] Testing the waters for a Super Conference with television control failed to attract the interest of other presidents, however. Cavanaugh's suggestions were gracefully but coolly received by institutions such as the University of Southern California, Southern Methodist, Army, and Navy.[24] Few could see the financial or educational potential of television for the colleges as had the leaders of Notre Dame. Cavanaugh, unlike other college presidents, saw that Notre Dame "could introduce our athletic events as one phase of our over-all education endeavor" on a year-long basis, not just during the football season.[25]

Notre Dame, rebuffed in an attempt at founding a Super Conference that could control its own television rights, continued with its desire to retain Home Rule over its own telecasts. It persisted with little support from other institutions, except the University of Pennsylvania. Notre Dame and Pennsylvania hoped that the U.S. Department of Justice, specifically its antitrust division, could get involved. Notre Dame suggested, with legal logic, that the NCAA's control of television was a restraint of free trade under antitrust laws. Vice President Theodore Hesburgh met with lawyers for Notre Dame and contacted the U.S. Department of Justice soon after the NCAA decision to experiment with the control of TV in January 1951.[26] The lawyers, agreeing with Hesburgh, advised that "the individual freedom of contract and of trade by the *individual colleges* who desire to televise their football games on Saturdays . . . is interfered with and, therefore, an unreasonable control over live television industry is perpetrated."[27] They also advised that if Notre Dame took independent action in opposition to the NCAA plan, it might cause one of two negative reactions for Notre Dame: expulsion from the NCAA or a boycott from athletic contests by other members of the NCAA. Both threats were real.[28]

Besides the University of Pennsylvania, Notre Dame had few allies in its quest to restore Home Rule on the television issue. As the NCAA's experimental plan was being readied for the 1951 football season, the University of Pennsylvania had its own problems with the large Eastern College Athletic Conference and fellow Ivy League members. Notre Dame more or less quietly resisted, watching for the reactions of other institutions to the more aggressive Penn officials. Notre Dame's desire for television money and exposure would have to wait until the matter was taken up by the other players of the game—the University of Pennsylvania, the NCAA, and the courts.

11 Penn Challenges the NCAA and the Ivy League

THE UNIVERSITY of Michigan, under athletic director Fritz Crisler, called for the NCAA to begin a two-year ban on college football telecasting in 1950, but even if the NCAA had wanted to ban telecasts it was not easy to break nearly a half-century NCAA tradition of Home Rule. When the NCAA was formed after the contentious 1905 football season, the new organization proclaimed the doctrine of Home Rule, that is, each member of the NCAA retained institutional autonomy over its own athletic program. At the original meeting of what became the NCAA, the group resolved that the academic authorities at the individual colleges and universities were "ultimately responsible for the conduct of athletics within their own respective institutions."[1] This concept would apply to such areas as eligibility rules, coaching salaries, stadium building, ticket sales, and, had they been in existence, radio and television contracts. The first NCAA president, Palmer Pierce of West Point, wrote to Princeton University president and future U.S. president, Woodrow Wilson, that the NCAA had "decided to give the greatest independence to institutions."[2] The message from the earliest time was that the NCAA would only make recommendations and serve as an advisory body. Therefore it was up to individual institutions or athletic conferences to act honorably while serving their own self-interests.

Home Rule was to guide the NCAA until after World War II. Postwar times saw the emergence of frequent airplane travel and numerous interregional contests. At the same time, the late 1940s was a time of rapid expansion of television in college sport. There was a need for national eligibility rules to ensure fairer competition and to successfully incorporate the recent phenomenon of television into college sport. In 1948, the NCAA broke with Home Rule and began implementing its national rules for the recruitment and subsidization of athletes, known as the Sanity Code. The code was founded on the principle that student athletes must be admitted to college based on standards similar to nonathletes, standards that hadn't worked before in big-time athletics, didn't work then, and haven't worked since.[3]

Two years later, the NCAA funded a study to determine whether or not there was a need to control the telecasting of football games nationally to preserve gate attendance.[4] The conclusion was that TV did hurt gate receipts, indicating that national controls were logical and needed and that the NCAA should amend its constitution "in order that television be properly controlled."[5] An overwhelming number of NCAA institutions agreed that controls were needed, but they took no action to amend the constitution. Then, voting 161-7 to create an experimental TV plan, members cast aside the tradition of Home Rule among NCAA institutions. The NCAA was on its way toward national control and reining in a future dominant financial entity.[6]

The elimination of Home Rule in television, while passed by 96 percent of NCAA institutions, was challenged by Notre Dame and the University of Pennsylvania. By 1950 Pennsylvania was the leading institution in football telecasting, which had begun a decade before. In that
year, President Harold Stassen of the University of Pennsylvania appointed Francis Murray as athletic director. Murray, the 1936 Penn All-
American halfback and former National Football League player, had
been a special agent for the U.S. Department of Justice during World War
II. Following the war, he worked in radio and television—as a media promoter, not an educator. Hiring Murray was an indication of the commercial route President Stassen wanted Penn athletics to take, a different path from the publicly proclaimed, but never entirely embraced,
educational position of Ivy League institutions.[7]

Murray and Stassen knew that there was a large amount money, as
well as promotion, in telecasting Penn games. Penn had sold its rights
to Philco broadcasting company on an exclusive basis for the previous
three years. When ABC offered $100,000 for the network rights to Penn's
home games in 1950, President Stassen dropped Philco's $52,500 con-
tract for exclusive rights and accepted the ABC proposal.[8] Notre Dame
was the only other school that could attract that kind of income. In comparison, the University of Oklahoma was paid a paltry $3,000 to telecast
all of its home games in 1950, the year after Oklahoma went undefeated
and Bud Wilkinson was voted coach of the year.[9] With the increased TV
exposure and revenue, Stassen could build Penn (and himself) into a national power, a goal reflected in his new slogan, "Victory with Honor."[10]

To other Ivy League institutions, "Victory with Honor" meant big-time
football and a series of football games with Notre Dame. To that, a critic
of Stassen wrote to the Penn Board of Trustees: "Mr. Stassen is having
difficulty in subduing his political tendencies and wishes to ingratiate
himself with the Roman Catholics."[11] Penn's competing against Notre
Dame, playing against a big-time Catholic school, and dominating the
eastern TV market alarmed Penn's traditional rivals in the Ivy League.
At an Ivy League eligibility committee meeting at the conclusion of the
1950 football season, a statement was made implying that if Penn considered itself strong enough to meet Notre Dame, "it was too strong to be
met by the other teams" of the Ivy League.[12] It was true that Penn's coach,
George Munger, had a record of forty-five wins, six losses, and three ties
against Ivy institutions. In his thirteen years with the school, only Cornell and Princeton had beaten Penn. The increased tension over Penn's
momentum as a football power came at a time when most of the other

Ivy League institutions were not only questioning the impact of television on gate receipts but also moving away from big-time football in the post–World War II era.

Nevertheless, Penn charged on with its individualistic and commercialized TV policy, with little regard for either the Ivy League or the NCAA. Shortly after the NCAA's decision to control telecasting, the Du Mont Television Network's Les Arries reported to Father Hesburgh at Notre Dame that "there is no question about President Stassen's intentions to televise his schedule."[13] In 1951, Penn, after having asked for a three-year bid of at least $1.5 million, received an $850,000 offer from the Du Mont Television Network to telecast its twenty-three home football games for the next three years. While the NCAA was drawing up TV policies for its experimental year, Notre Dame, according to Hesburgh, was "still on the fence" about televising in 1951.[14] Notre Dame wished to follow "the reactions to Pennsylvania's move," not wanting to "act hastily in the matter."[15] Penn, however, went ahead with its own plan to televise its eight-game home schedule, including contests with California and both major military academies and home games against Notre Dame the following two years.[16]

Penn's scheduling a game against Notre Dame, and especially Penn's telecasting of that game, further angered both the Eastern College Athletic Conference and the Ivy League institutions. The ECAC urged all its members, including the University of Pennsylvania, to give their full support and complete compliance to the NCAA experimental TV plan.[17] "If two or three institutions can nationally televise this fall," Robert Hall of Yale concluded at an ECAC meeting, "there can't be any intelligent experimentation."[18] Colonel Blaik, coach of the U.S. Military Academy, raised the question of canceling games with Penn, effectively boycotting the school, if it did not follow the new NCAA policy.[19]

Evidently not deterred at first by the possibility of a boycott by Eastern opponents or by potential expulsion from the NCAA, the University of Pennsylvania notified the NCAA in June that it would not participate in the organization's experimental plan for controlled TV but would independently telecast its home football games in 1951. Immediately, Asa Bushnell, commissioner of the ECAC, asked its members to compete only against those institutions that would support the NCAA's TV plan.[20] That threat probably held greater force than Penn's argument that the NCAA plan was not within the constitutional authority of the NCAA and, more importantly, was a violation of the Sherman Antitrust Act of 1890. The Sherman Act specifically forbade conspiracies in restraint of trade, and there was no question in President Stassen's mind that the NCAA policy was restraining free trade in television.[21] Stassen would be proven legally correct three decades later, but in 1951 his opinion seemed to matter little, as the NCAA Council had labeled Penn a "member not in good standing" and planned to vote on terminating its membership at the next annual meeting.[22]

Stassen had support where he thought it was important, in his board of trustees, but outside pressure in the form of a boycott was paramount. Stassen kept his board well informed on the TV question in the spring and summer of 1951. The board, after a full discussion, resolved to authorize Stassen to enter into a football TV contract for 1951.[23] Newspaper critics gave Stassen less support. Arthur Daley of the *New York Times* called the actions of Stassen "selfish" and suggested that Penn would likely find that it had no one to play.[24] He was right. Four Ivy institutions—Cornell, Columbia, Dartmouth, and Princeton—almost immediately dropped Penn from their schedules, as did the University of California.[25]

A group boycott by Ivy institutions, the ECAC, or the NCAA was illegal under the Sherman Antitrust Act, but Penn did not test the actions in court. Under the Sherman Act, every combination or conspiracy that restrained competition was illegal. President Cavanaugh of Notre Dame believed that the NCAA Television Committee was asking members of the NCAA "not to play a university which televises its games," and he soon received a "veiled threat" from the Big 10 commissioner, "Tug" Wilson, that his school would also be boycotted.[26] The ECAC made it clear that it did not want its members to compete against Penn, and individual members of the Ivy group followed that instruction. The prospective Penn boycotters never took seriously a threat of legal action against them for violating federal law. What they were concerned with was whether TV might ruin intercollegiate sport.

After half of Penn's future opponents indicated that they would not continue to compete against Penn, President Stassen and his Board of Trustees had to reconsider their independent policy.[27] Despite the assurance from the chairman of the trustees that the "action of the N.C.A.A. was wrong" and that "it should be challenged,"[28] the efforts by opponents to destroy Penn's schedule and pressure from Penn alumni and friends of President Stassen to continue to participate in Ivy League contests won out. One alumnus told Stassen that the TV question was not a matter of Penn's freedom to pursue its own policies but "an effort on your part to promote your political aspirations."[29] Another individual wrote Stassen that he had "offended the most intelligent section of public opinion [bringing] discredit to yourself. If you do not believe that the common good is more important than the private gain of any individual (or college), we had better give up the hope that you will ever hold high public office."[30] That statement, probably more than anything else, cut Stassen to the quick.

The NCAA was unwilling to go along with Penn's request that the U.S. Attorney General give a ruling on the legality of the NCAA plan.[31] Assistant Attorney General in the Department of Justice Antitrust Division, H. Graham Morison, likely a friend of University of Pennsylvania's Francis Murray, told Murray that the Department of Justice had "instituted a full investigation" into the legality of the NCAA TV plan.[32] At the time there were three other governmental probes underway to see if there were antitrust violations in professional sports and their television policies.[33] Both Penn and Notre Dame were making overtures to friends in the Department of Justice to suggest that the NCAA TV plan was a conspiracy in restraint of trade, a question that took over three decades to finally decide in a Supreme Court case.

While Penn was waiting for an opinion from the Department of Justice, Harold Stassen decided to present a suggestion to revise the NCAA's TV plan. The Penn proposal called for local institutions, not the NCAA, to act as the TV contracting agents. Individual institutions would voluntarily refrain from telecasting nationally on two Saturdays and locally on two Saturdays during the fall football season. On each of the other five playing dates, individual institutions would be free to telecast. This, Stassen believed, would allow for the experiment the NCAA desired and at the same time relieve the NCAA of antitrust violations.[34]

Penn, though, received no support for its plan, not even that of Notre Dame's Theodore Hesburgh, who had plans of his own. Notre Dame reluctantly went along with the NCAA plan, one that would give Notre Dame a nationally televised game against Southern Methodist University and a regional game with Michigan State. More importantly, Hesburgh believed that after the NCAA experiment had concluded, his institution might get a big payoff of possibly $120,000 for telecasting the Southern Cal game in December, which would be bid on by the four networks, ABC, CBS, NBC, and Du Mont. Hesburgh's proposal would include not only the game telecast but pregame and postgame coverage, kinescopic reproductions on other days, theater TV (big-screen TV with an admission charge), and other types of live, pay-per-view TV, including skiatron and phonovision.[35] Skiatron was a system of scrambled TV signals that required a 50-cent or $1.00 charge to unscramble the game, while phonovision required a fee to a telephone company to receive the TV game. Notre Dame was obviously shying away from the bad publicity Penn was receiving for being so blatantly against the NCAA.

Standing alone, Penn had little recourse but to abandon its individualistic policy, refund its $80,000 advance from ABC, and look to "further opportunities" in the future.[36] Penn, unlike Notre Dame, refused to accept any TV games under the NCAA plan, stating that it did not want to be a part of any action in violation of the Sherman Antitrust Act. Staking a claim for future contracts, Francis Murray quoted H. Graham Morison, Assistant Attorney General of the Department of Justice Antitrust Division. "If the colleges commercialize football," Morison claimed, "they must expect commercial rules to be applied to them. If they compete for gate receipts, they should expect to be governed by the laws of free competition." At least, in the Department of Justice, Penn had one friend on its side.[37]

As the first year of the NCAA experimental plan came to a close, Murray charged privately that the NCAA and its TV Committee were "making capital of the Hitler philosophy of the big lie."[38] Publicly, he asked the ECAC to again support institutional control to alleviate adverse public reaction experienced from the 1951 NCAA plan. Murray believed this would conform to the historic institutional control of radio, prevent the U.S. Attorney General from bringing an antitrust suit against the NCAA, and end the "centralized national control" that was contrary to the "basic principles of free institutions." He quoted from newspapers that opposed the NCAA plan. "Commercialism," the *Indianapolis Star* charged, "is the motivating force behind the NCAA's niggardly parceling of games to televiewers." Murray's pleas were for naught, as the ECAC voted with only one dissenting vote (Penn's) to recommend future control of TV by the NCAA.[39] Meanwhile, the NCAA had to study the 1951 experiment to see how the organization might control television in the future.

12 The NCAA Experimental Year

WHILE THE University of Pennsylvania and Notre Dame fought a losing battle to preserve individual institutional control over football television contracts, the NCAA experimented with the first national controls during the 1951 season. The overwhelming 96 percent vote of NCAA member institutions to experiment with national controls had given the NCAA Television Committee confidence to do what it thought was best to protect the financial welfare of individual members and still provide the public with limited entertainment. Revenue, surprisingly, was not a major concern for the NCAA Television Committee when it opened the bidding for sponsorship. Yet, even though money was not an uppermost consideration, evidently no thought was given to telecasting on the educational TV that was beginning to be introduced across the nation.[1]

The NCAA chose to go the commercial route, and the first NCAA TV plan attracted sponsor considerations from Westinghouse Electric Corporation, Chevrolet, Atlantic Refining Company, and two networks, Du Mont and NBC. The networks originally warned that several planned experimental blackouts were financially risky and technically unfeasible. The networks wanted unrestricted live television, not a nationally controlled NCAA strategy with experimental variables. Nevertheless, when it became clear that NCAA members wanted a controlled program with blackouts, the networks and national sponsors showed increased interest.[2] The high bid came from Westinghouse, which offered a minimum payment of two and a half times the station's advertising rates. That minimum payment itself was over half a million dollars, but Westinghouse eventually paid the NCAA $679,800 in rights fees. As there were twenty games telecast during the 1951 season, the average rights fee came to about $34,000, a little less than Penn would have received from ABC for each one of its games, had they been telecast. One of the reasons why the NCAA received so little money was that the NCAA plan allowed all networks and independent stations to carry games on a sustaining, non-advertising, basis if they chose to do so. Networks, on the other hand, wanted exclusive rights and were willing to pay for them. As it turned out, only station WOR-TV in New York carried NCAA games on a sustaining basis. Westinghouse, as sponsor, chose NBC and its fifty-two-station network, representing a market of 87 million people linked by coaxial cable. A majority of all television stations in the United States were NBC affiliates, and, because of the wide coverage, an estimated 35 million Americans saw at least some of the games.[3]

The NCAA plan, announced in the spring of 1951, was a compromise between Notre Dame's and Penn's calls for unlimited television and the Big 10, Eastern, Southern, Southwestern, and Pacific Coast conferences' previous bans on all football telecasting. Under NCAA control, no college would be telecast more than once at home and once as a visiting team. There would be one telecast for each region on most Saturdays, with three coast-to-coast TV games during the entire fall. On two Saturdays, each region would be blacked out and have no football telecast, testing the theory that the lack of television coverage would increase gate receipts. There would be additional experiments with color TV, three types of pay-per-view TV (phonevision, skiatron, and theater), and postgame motion picture showings.[4]

The original NCAA plan called for a division of television dollars in which the NCAA would receive 60 percent of receipts and 40 percent would go to the colleges being televised. A major complaint came from Notre Dame and a few other institutions regarding the 60-40 division of revenues. Notre Dame, reluctantly cooperating with the NCAA plan, would not accept an "arbitrary tax of 60% of proceeds," that would bring over $400,000 to the NCAA treasury.[5] As the estimated cost to the NCAA of running the TV program was less than $100,000, Notre Dame suggested that NCAA's share of the profits should cover only the expenses of the NCAA Television Committee. Enough pressure was brought to bear by other institutions that the assessment was reduced to 18 percent. Even then, when the Notre Dame–Southern Methodist University game was telecast to the largest TV crowd of the year, estimated at over seven million viewers, Notre Dame complained that it was assessed nearly one-third of the total NCAA TV budget for the year. Later on in the season, when the Notre Dame–University of Southern California game was picked to be telecast, Notre Dame could not understand why its game was being assessed at the same time the Army-Navy game was exempted by the NCAA Television Committee. Further, Notre Dame officials complained that bowl games, which Notre Dame traditionally had bypassed, would not have a TV assessment.[6] Despite Notre Dame's protests, the NCAA plan with Westinghouse was carried out, although not without major problems.

Even before the NCAA plan was put into action, several states, including Oklahoma, had considered forcing state institutions to telecast their games. An Oklahoma state legislator, George Miskovsky, authored a bill to make telecasting of all Oklahoma and Oklahoma A & M football home games mandatory. Miskovsky was appealing to his district supporters who especially wanted to see Oklahoma games. He called the NCAA action "high-handed and arbitrary."[7] Oklahoma was having phenomenal success under coach Bud Wilkinson, concluding a thirty-one-game winning streak during the 1950 season before losing in the Sugar Bowl to Kentucky, coached by Paul "Bear" Bryant. All of Oklahoma's home games had been telecast for a mere $3,000, but Miskovsky likely was less interested in the financial return to the University of Oklahoma than he was in gaining votes in his next election. Oklahoma president George Cross, who later wrote a book, *Presidents Can't Punt,* asked both the Big 7 Conference (predecessor to the Big 8 and Big 12) and the NCAA what would happen to his institution if Oklahoma passed the mandatory telecasting law. The Big 7 predicted that each of the universities would cancel football games with Oklahoma if it telecast all its games, a reaction similar to that of Ivy League institutions to Penn's threats. An NCAA Executive Council member told Cross that Oklahoma would be asked to resign from the NCAA.[8]

Officials at Oklahoma convinced enough of the state legislators that it was not in the best interest of Oklahoma football to pass the required television legislation, and the bill died. Senator Miskovsky did win one prize: whereas Miskovsky had held football seats in the end zone the previous season, President Cross directed the athletic business manager to make sure Senator Miskovsky received "seats as nearly on the 50-yard line as possible during the coming season."[9] President Cross was not the first and certainly not the last to choose the pragmatic, if not ethical, position on athletics in higher education by soliciting the goodwill of the power brokers with a bribe or special perk. To Miskovsky's credit, the premium tickets changed his position only in the stadium, not toward telecasting Oklahoma games.

Other states considering actions similar to Oklahoma's were Nebraska, Minnesota, and Illinois. In Nebraska, the state legislature passed a bill requiring that Nebraska football games be televised but allowed the mandatory telecasts to be on a delayed basis. This was acceptable to Big 7 faculty representatives, who agreed to sell delayed telecasts of Big 7 football in 1951 for $28,000.[10] Two states with Big 10 institutions, Illinois and Minnesota, also had bills presented during the winter and spring of 1951 that would force institutions to telecast their games. The Big 10 institutions had banned all TV for the 1950 season, and the following year they opposed state legislation to open up telecasting that they believed would be unfavorable to the financial welfare of athletic departments.[11] Neither the Big 10 nor the NCAA had to deal with any state making live football telecasts mandatory, but the NCAA Television Committee was forced to make some controversial calls during that first year of controls.

The NCAA Television Committee had flexibility to experiment by blacking out certain areas and carrying particular games to various regions while at the same time allowing institutions to make requests of the committee. Notre Dame again became intricately involved in disputes over TV policy. When the Southern Methodist–Notre Dame game was chosen for a national broadcast, the committee decided to black out the game in the Syracuse, New York, area, presumably to test whether this would influence game attendance at the Illinois-Syracuse game. Because Illinois was undefeated and ranked in the top ten nationally, Notre Dame claimed that the blackout would have no impact on what would be a sellout contest whether the telecast of the SMU–Notre Dame game was shown or not. Notre Dame officials believed that the members of the Television Committee were "picking the spot that would be most beneficial to their argument that the televising of outstanding games would be detrimental to the local games."[12] In other words, the blackout, the NCAA could later claim, contributed to the full attendance in Syracuse. Because of Notre Dame's opposition to any NCAA TV control, it was not unexpected that the NCAA Television Committee might exhibit a bias against Notre Dame.

The Television Committee later slighted the Catholic university again in a regional game, Notre Dame at Michigan State. President Theodore Hesburgh was angered that the Television Committee did not allow the Michigan State game to be televised in South Bend, even though, as Hesburgh said, "there were no other games to compete with."[13] Yet, shortly before the game, the NCAA made a special exception for Detroit. Because of a technical transmission problem at Detroit's WWJ in attempting to handle both audiovisual signals of the originally scheduled Navy-Maryland game and the MSU–Notre Dame game, station WWJ asked for and received a special waiver to carry just the Michigan State game in Detroit in place of the Navy-Maryland game. So thanks to this special favor, Detroit fans got the opportunity to see the Notre Dame–Michigan State game, although the game was blacked out in other Michigan cities and nearby South Bend.[14]

In a more politically motivated action by the NCAA, the Television Committee changed the date of a scheduled blackout in the Washington, D.C., area, allowing a Michigan State–Notre Dame game to be telecast.[15] Ralph Furey, NCAA Television Committee chairman, tried to explain the exception by saying "it was purely a local problem."[16] Chances are that it was purely a local *political* problem. It was not likely a mere coincidence that the only blackout waiver given for the entire schedule was for an area where members of the Department of Justice's Antitrust Division were living, giving them the opportunity to see one of the most anticipated games of the 1951 season. The NCAA and the Television Committee were alert to the legal dangers of restraint of trade allegations in the first year of controls, just as they were three decades later when the NCAA TV contract was made illegal because of antitrust violations.[17]

The NCAA did not give in when the Governor of Kentucky requested that the Kentucky-Tennessee game be telecast in the scheduled blackout area of Louisville. The last game of the season was a sellout, and WHAS-TV and the *Louisville Courier Journal* put pressure on state and national politicians and on the NCAA to allow the telecast. Head of the NCAA Television Committee, Ralph Furey, received about 400 telegrams and innumerable letters asking him to make an exception and telecast the Kentucky-Tennessee rivalry.[18] When the committee voted unanimously not to cave in to the pressure, Kentucky's Governor Lawrence Wetherby and a member of Congress asked the U.S. Department of Justice to order the NCAA to remove its ban. This request came on the heels of the Department of Justice's decision to file a suit against the National Football League for its broadcast restrictions.[19] At the time, the NFL restricted both radio broadcasting and telecasting in the home territory of its teams. Like the NCAA plan, the NFL's policy was a clear restriction on free trade.[20] Officials at the Department of Justice took no outward action on Governor Wetherby's request, as they decided to await the results of the department's antitrust action against the NFL before taking on the colleges. That was to be more than a two-year wait.

Once the season had ended, the NCAA membership evaluated the impact of television on football attendance during the 1951 experimental year. Paid attendance kept dropping, at an even greater rate, which could be interpreted in several ways. If attendance had dropped only 3.2 percent with no national TV regulations in 1950 and had dropped 5.9 percent with a national plan of limited television in 1951, one could argue that the plan was ineffective. The drop in attendance, however, might have been far greater if Notre Dame, Penn, and other institutions had instituted their own network plans or if networks had bid for special contests to be telecast and had paid individual institutions large sums for the most publicized events. Since the number of television sets had quintupled in the two years after 1949, the resulting loss of stadium attendance could be considered minimal.[21] That is, unless you were an athletic director who counted on football ticket sales to generate revenue for your entire athletic program.

The consensus of NCAA institutions at the end of the season was that continued national controls were needed. The Big 10 was probably rep-

Table 2   **Paid Attendance in College Football (1947–51)**

Year	Paid Attendance	Change from previous year
1947–48 (average)	15,248,000	—
1949	15,675,000	up 2.8%
1950	15,172,000	down 3.2%
1951	14,272,000	down 5.9%

Source: Figures are from "Report of the NCAA 1955 Television Committee to the Fiftieth Annual Convention of the NCAA," January 10–11, 1956, Records of the Office of the President, 1949–56, Box 16, Folder "NCAA Television Plan, 1954–55," Georgia Tech Archives. Attendance continued to deteriorate for the next two years, but not at the rate for 1951. It took a decade for gate attendance to reach the late-1940s levels.

resentative of the general feeling of institutions across the nation when it voted unanimously that live TV coverage of football needed to be controlled in the future, with eight of the ten schools wanting control at the national rather than conference level.[22] The Big 10, of all conferences, should have been pleased with the number of its conference games (five) broadcast on TV that fall. Only the Ivy League, with three games, came close to that total.[23] When the NCAA meeting convened in January 1952, the membership again voted overwhelmingly, 171-8, to continue the NCAA TV controls.

From a legal standpoint, the NCAA could afford to continue in the path it had taken the previous year because the Department of Justice was still involved in action against the NFL. The Department of Justice made it clear that the civil suit against professional football was a "test" case, indicating that it would take no action against other sports, such as NCAA football, until the courts had ruled on the NFL case. The NCAA Television Committee believed that the 1951 plan and "any similar plan was and is completely lawful."[24]

Reassured by the delay in the NFL case and by another overwhelming vote by members of the NCAA, the Television Committee could rebuff the University of Pennsylvania's Fran Murray. The Penn athletic director commented at the end of the 1951 season: "I can't conceive of the N.C.A.A. trying to impose the same restrictions another year."[25] The committee, however, further restricted its telecasting policy for 1952, allowing only eleven games to be telecast, down from twenty the previous year. The NCAA would continue its control over college football telecasting for the next three decades, but not without challenges from both inside and outside. The next such challenge would come from the Du Mont Television Network.

Networks:
The Du Mont Challenge

13

UNTIL NOVEMBER 1953, when federal Judge Allen Grim's ruled in favor of allowing professional football to have a monopoly in telecasting, there was good reason to believe that the NCAA TV cartel would be deemed an illegal restraint of trade. The possibility of an antitrust ruling had given hope to nonconformist institutions such as Notre Dame and Pennsylvania as they continued their efforts to do away with the NCAA TV plan. There was even greater reason for a major network, Du Mont, to fight the NCAA's control. Du Mont was a maverick in telecasting, as it was the only network that had not grown out of radio broadcasting in the 1930s and 1940s. NBC, CBS, and, to a lesser extent, ABC had millions of dollars of radio money behind their television efforts, along with a large group of affiliate radio stations. Du Mont, unlike the others, was a manufacturing corporation headed by a cantankerous scientist, Allen B. Du Mont. He had established the Du Mont Laboratories in 1931, early in the Depression, and later developed the cathode-ray TV tube. Within a half-dozen years, Allen Du Mont produced the first all-electronic television receiver. To experiment with his inventions, he established an experimental TV station in 1938, W2XVT, in Passaic, New Jersey. A year after that, Allen Du Mont was demonstrating the all-electronic television receiver at the New York World's Fair, ready for sale to the public. Although World War II slowed the effort to expand television, a month before the 1944 allied D-Day attack against the Nazis in Normandy, France, Du Mont initiated station W2XAB in New York City and in two years established the first permanent network, linking New York through Philadelphia to Washington, D.C.[1]

Television was not a money-making proposition during the first years after the war, but Du Mont knew that television programming could help sell his TV receivers and that sports would be a major factor in the growth of such programming. At the close of World War II, there were only six television outlets—NBC had two, in New York City and Philadelphia; CBS had two, in New York City and Chicago; Du Mont had one, in New York City (WABD); and Don Lee had one, in Los Angeles, the station that had broadcast the Rose Bowl Parade in 1940.[2] Despite

Table 3 **Du Mont TV Revenues versus Costs (1946–1949)**

Year	Income	Expenses	Net Loss
1946	$71,184	—	($704,051)
1947	218,702	$1,113,809	(895,104)
1948	1,011,336	2,435,428	(1,424,088)
1949	2,435,966	5,000,457	(2,564,491)

Source: "Harvard Business School Study of Allen B. Du Mont Laboratories, Inc., 1951," Du Mont Laboratories, Box 16, Folder "H, 1950–51," Manuscript Division, Library of Congress.

the rapid sales growth of home TV sets that followed the war, all TV networks were still operating at a loss as late as 1951.

Du Mont's net losses kept increasing, but sports telecasting, including college football, was continued to be seen as a major avenue for developing profits. Du Mont began sports telecasting early, by showing all New York Yankee home games in 1946 with Mel Allen behind the mike. Seven New York Giants home games in the National Football League and eleven other contests played in Boston, Philadelphia, and Washington, D.C., were covered by the Du Mont Television Network the same year.[3] By the end of 1947, the Du Mont Television Network could carry sporting events to four stations. Within another year, the network consisted of sixteen stations in the Midwest and on the East coast, linked by AT&T's newly laid coaxial cable.[4]

Du Mont TV continued challenging the other three networks in sports telecasting as it moved on to college football in 1949, with Notre Dame high on its list. That year, Du Mont was able to approach Notre Dame after the East-Midwest coaxial cable was extended to South Bend, Indiana, and the Notre Dame stadium. Competition among the four TV networks to cover Notre Dame football was bound to raise the interest of Notre Dame officials. The previous year's TV bounty, according to one Notre Dame administrator, would look like "'peanuts' this fall."[5] Notre Dame officials knew that among the interested parties were WGN and WBKB in Chicago, CBS, ABC, NBC, and Du Mont.

Notre Dame accepted Du Mont's telecasting proposition, which provided the school with a minimum of $36,000 if eight stations were connected for the four home games and the North Carolina–Notre Dame game at Yankee Stadium in New York. A maximum of $51,000 would be paid if more stations were added. In addition, Notre Dame would get 25 percent of gross admission charged or a minimum of $500 for each theater setup offering simultaneous, large-screen telecasts of its games. Both the Chevrolet-sponsored home telecasts and the theater showings were successful. Twenty cities received the telecasts, and theaters—especially those in Irish-dominated Boston—were filled with enthusiastic fans who enjoyed excellent pictures of the games.[6]

The next year, all four networks began a bidding war to carry the Notre Dame games. CBS was least interested because it had already begun to court NFL teams; by 1950, CBS had nine of them under contract.[7] Notre Dame was quite satisfied with the work Du Mont had done in 1949, but it nevertheless opened up the bidding to all the networks. As Notre Dame's Theodore Hesburgh was advised by Edgar Kobak, a major communications player from New York City, "Du Mont and Chevrolet should be given every opportunity to meet anybody else's offer or bid." Kobak believed that Notre Dame should have a minimum price more than double that of the previous year, at least half of the $200,000 that baseball's World Series had received in 1949.[8] Notre Dame was not entirely convinced that Du Mont had the best network, as NBC was larger, with more affiliate stations. NBC in 1950 had eleven of the top twenty shows on TV, with the highest average rating (26.8) and the highest average number of stations per program (30). Du Mont lagged behind the other three networks in all categories.[9] Notre Dame wanted the greatest exposure as well as the most revenue from the live game, pregame and postgame, newsreels, and highlight films, along with movie and theater rights.[10] Notre Dame allowed NBC to give an additional bid after Du Mont, but it came up short.

In justifying the choice of Du Mont over NBC, Vice President Theodore Hesburgh told an adviser that Du Mont made the strongest presentation. Indeed, Du Mont did just that. Du Mont's TV network director, Mortimer Loewi, bragged to Allen Du Mont following the season that telecasting "the Notre Dame games brought about not only the clearance of the largest network in the history of television but also substantial profitable billings, plus, most important, a nationwide acceptance of the Du Mont Television Network as a service organization."[11] Du Mont TV could be proud to have Notre Dame football, and it certainly was one of the most successful programs in Du Mont's decade of telecasting. Du Mont's other few successes included Ted Mack's *The Original Amateur Hour,* begun in 1948, and the first *Jackie Gleason Show,* soon to be bought out by CBS.[12] Du Mont's success with Notre Dame, however, ended up being short lived, as the NCAA soon took over telecasting of Saturday afternoon football.

There is no question that Du Mont was a major player in sports and college football telecasting the year the NCAA took control. Following the overwhelming NCAA vote in January 1951 to limit football telecasting, Notre Dame was reluctant to challenge the NCAA outright by allowing Du Mont or any other network to telecast its games that year. After receiving little support to set up a Super Conference with its own television policy, Notre Dame "sat on the fence" and let the University of Pennsylvania challenge the NCAA.[13] Du Mont could not wait for fence-straddling Notre Dame, and it instead offered Pennsylvania a three-year, $850,000 contract, which Penn accepted. Had the Ivy League, the Eastern College Athletic Conference, and the NCAA not threatened Penn with sanctions and a boycott if it allowed Du Mont to telecast its games, Du Mont would have remained in the "big leagues" of football telecasting.

Du Mont TV was given a chance to continue in college sport when the NCAA opened bidding for telecasting rights. Westinghouse Electric outbid the networks for the contract and chose NBC, not Du Mont, to carry the 1951 NCAA football schedule on NBC's fifty-two-station network.[14] Du Mont was being outflanked by NBC and CBS in most aspects of telecasting in the early 1950s, and it seriously considered going to court to break up the NCAA football telecasting monopoly. Refusing to bid on the 1952 NCAA contract, Du Mont spent a significant amount lobbying college presidents, governing boards, state legislatures, and the U.S. Congress to break up the NCAA monopoly. The NCAA Television Committee chairman, Robert Hall of Yale, and Director of the NCAA TV Program, Asa Bushnell of the Eastern College Athletic Conference chided: "We are amazed that the Du Mont Network should endeavor to break down a program with which the Network . . . had a chance to bid before the program went into operation."[15] It is, however, not surprising that networks wanted to make money, just as colleges thought they needed to protect their income by limiting television.

Allen Du Mont began a public crusade condemning the NCAA monopoly. Speaking before the New York Football Writer's Association in 1952, Du Mont called the NCAA TV football plan "a restraint of trade inappropriately disguised by an academic cap and gown." The NCAA plan, he said, "is violating federal antitrust laws by acting in combination to restrain the telecasting of college games." The colleges, he believed, had collectively voted away the property rights held by individual colleges.[16] Du Mont hired a Washington, D.C., law firm, which wrote a nineteen-page memorandum balancing the pros and cons of whether Du Mont should sue the NCAA over its football telecasting monopoly.

The firm reasoned that the monopolistic control of the NCAA violated the Sherman Antitrust Act, no matter what were the aims of the NCAA.

The legal recommendation was to take action against the NCAA, but the Du Mont Television Network needed to balance two competing goals. On the one hand, Du Mont needed sports such as college football to secure station affiliation to its network, which now spread from the East Coast to Omaha, Nebraska. As NBC, the television leader, had purchased exclusive rights to telecast the NCAA contests and General Motors had exclusive rights to advertise, Du Mont had been shut out of a market that was crucial to its tenuous existence. Yet, if Du Mont challenged the NCAA in court, it would raise a serious public relations question. "Du Mont would be placed in the undesirable position," the legal advisors noted, "of preferring profits to the welfare of athletics."[17] What Du Mont needed was for important colleges such as Notre Dame and Pennsylvania to join in any legal action. This did not occur, and Du Mont dropped out of the college telecasting scene.

After Du Mont decided not to challenge the NCAA monopoly in court, the network appeared to make a sound move by contracting in 1953 to televise forty-eight NFL games on Saturday nights and Sunday afternoons. The NFL games were garnering high Nielsen ratings at the same time professional football gate attendance was increasing.[18] The same fall, the *United States v National Football League* antitrust case was decided in favor of the NFL, permitting the monopolistic NFL practice of protecting home teams from outside telecasts of other games.[19] This decision gave most NCAA officials confidence that the Department of Justice would not attack the NCAA television plan as a restraint of trade.

In the long run, Du Mont was unsuccessful in telecasting at both the college and professional level. Though Du Mont was the first network to have a full schedule of NFL telecasting, the network could not remain competitive, as CBS—with greater financial backing and more affiliated stations—was able to outbid it. Du Mont made one last effort to get back into the college game, but that too was a losing battle. In 1953, the same year that Du Mont contracted for many of the NFL games, it made overtures to some NCAA members about breaking away from the organization's television policy. One such offer was to Jim Tatum, successful coach at the University of Maryland. Tatum had considered forming a TV network with "fellow dissidents," and Du Mont followed up by having discussions with Tatum.[20] Du Mont knew that Notre Dame would be in the vanguard of the rebellion if other schools would consider forming a television pact outside the NCAA. A press release coming out of Theodore Hesburgh's office in 1953 called the NCAA plan "socialistic, a removal of incentive to excellence and a premium placed on mediocrity . . . where poorer programs are being kept alive by subsidies from the better programs."[21]

Du Mont also was aware that Harvard was opposed to the restrictive NCAA television policy. Expressing strong feelings coming down the chain of command from President James B. Conant, the Harvard Athletic Committee proclaimed that "Harvard reserves the right to make its own independent decisions as to whether and at what times its athletic events will be televised."[22] Yet, Du Mont officials concluded that they should "not expect much in way of support from Harvard. . . . Its action is purely Harvardian, [displaying] Harvard's independence."[23] While there were those who questioned the NCAA plan, they were too few and not organized to give support to the Du Mont Television Network to form another television scheme.

The Du Mont Television Network wanted to play with the big boys—NBC, CBS, and, to a lesser extent, ABC—but it lacked the financial resources and possibly the willpower to be successful. When ABC merged with United Paramount Theatres in 1953, it reduced Du Mont's chance to be even the third major network. Du Mont was further hindered by the fact that it was largely owned by Paramount Pictures (not to be confused with United Paramount Theaters) owing to a sale of stock and loans to Du Mont in the late 1930s; Paramount Pictures believed TV was a threat to movie attendance and thus hindered Du Mont's expansion. The Du Mont Television Network continued to ring up losses during the rest of its existence, though sports brought it some prestige. A last hope for Du Mont appeared in 1954, when merger talks with ABC were held. The proposed ABC–Du Mont network would have been a formidable competitor to NBC and CBS, but the merger effort fell through.[24] The little-remembered Du Mont Television Network played an important role in the early history of college football telecasting, but it died in 1955. The NCAA continued to rule over telecasting for the next three decades, contracting with NBC, ABC, and CBS at different times, but it did not always operate in peace and harmony with either networks or individual institutions and conferences. The Big 10 and Pacific Coast Conference would next challenge the restrictive NCAA television pact.

Regional Conferences Challenge
a National Policy

14

BY THE TIME the national policy for television was put into place by the NCAA institutions, intercollegiate athletics had been part of college life for a century. In those hundred years, from the very first intercollegiate contest between Yale and Harvard, the competitive emphasis had been principally on conference-based or regional rivalries. In the mid-twentieth century, these close interstate, or nearby intrastate, contests remained the major attractions in college sport. Harvard and Yale still played "The Game" in East Coast football, just as California and Stanford fought "The Big Game" on the West Coast. The Michigan–Ohio State game in the Midwest, the Alabama-Auburn contest in the South, and the Oklahoma-Texas battle in the Southwest serve as similar examples. Interest for intraregional contests almost always eclipsed that for national contests, unless a national championship was on the line. One illustration to the contrary was the traditional Notre Dame–Southern California football game, begun in the 1920s and continued for the remainder of the century. But then, Notre Dame was the only nonmilitary institution of higher education in the twentieth century that had a true national following—in part owing to a sense of identity among a large but minority religion in America. Notre Dame was the exception to the rule of conference and regional loyalties.

Since conference or regional contests dominated the public interest, it was only natural that some institutions would challenge the NCAA policy. It took little time for some universities to realize the possibilities of telecasting a number of the more desirable regional games, achieving higher TV ratings, increasing profits, and gaining prestige. Ratings, profits, and prestige were not originally the major concern of NCAA members—protection of gate receipts had been foremost on their minds. By the mid-1950s, though, the decline of attendance at college football games had abated. By 1954 and 1955, there were moderate gains in attendance for the first time since the 1940s, raising overall attendance to just above the 1951 level, when TV controls first had been mandated by the NCAA. Nevertheless, attendance was 700,000 below what were considered the pretelevision years of 1947-48. Television had seemed to

Table 4   **College Football Attendance, 1947–1955**

Year	Paid Attendance	Change from Previous Year
1947–48 (average)	15,248,000	—
1949	15,675,000	up 2.8%
1950	15,172,000	down 3.2%
1951	14,272,000	down 5.9%
1952	14,196,000	down 0.5%
1953	13,754,000	down 3.1%
1954	14,091,000	up 2.4%
1955	14,556,000	up 3.3%

Source: "Report of the NCAA 1955 Television Committee to the Fiftieth Annual Convention of the NCAA," 10–11 January 1956, Records of the Office of the President, 1949–1966, Box 16, Folder "NCAA Television Plan, 1954–55, Georgia Tech Archives.

threaten the collective demise of football, but when that apparent threat diminished, colleges became more concerned with their individual or conference desires relative to television policy.

After the experimental 1951 year, in which there were only three coast-to-coast telecasts, the NCAA decided to eliminate the more popular regional games and conduct only one national "Game of the Week." Attendance at games facing regional telecasts, the NCAA leaders quickly learned, was "hurt more than those played against non-regional telecasts."[1] The NCAA thus reduced the number of televised games from twenty to twelve and the number of colleges participating from thirty to twenty-four.[2] As the number of television appearances by any institution was reduced to one per year, the quality of the Game of the Week was also diminished. Lindsey Nelson, the first announcer of the series, sarcastically commented on the opener of the 1952 season: "Roll the drums and sound the trumpets! It is: TCU versus Kansas from Lawrence, Kansas. Yeah, well."[3] Nelson had hoped to broadcast the opener from the Notre Dame stadium or the Yale Bowl. The NCAA leaders' rationale behind the weakened schedule was that one national college football telecast each week would mollify enough of the public to prevent the seeking of legislative or judicial relief from the state or federal government. By providing minimal telecasting, the institutions of the NCAA believed they could fend off major public complaints and governmental action.

Internally, the NCAA originally had wanted to dilute the amount of television money going to the big-time institutions that dominated the TV market. Thus, the few institutions to be telecast would surrender a large portion of TV revenues, as much as a proposed 60 percent, to support all NCAA institutions, not just those fortunate enough to be chosen for the Game of the Week. As head of the NCAA Television Committee, Thomas Hamilton reasoned in 1951: "Institutions participating in television . . . should share those receipts generously with the other NCAA member schools who are making this experiment possible."[4] After complaints by the big-time schools, especially Notre Dame, the television money going to the NCAA was reduced from the proposed 60 percent to 18 percent in the first year of the NCAA plan, and within a few years cut even more, to less than 5 percent.[5] The original "Robin Hood" proposal to take from the rich and give to the poor could not withstand the pressures of the football elite.[6]

Likewise, the NCAA's policy of reducing the number of games telecast, demanded at first by both the large and small institutions alike, eventually came in conflict with big-time football schools. Certain conferences wanted greater exposure of their institutions than one national game a week could provide. Pressure mounted, especially within the Big 10 Conference and the Pacific Coast Conference. These conferences, two of the most prominent in the 1950s, wanted more regional games so they could increase the number of their telecasts.[7] The collectivist beginnings of the NCAA TV policy were about to be challenged.

By the mid-1950s, the Big 10, with attendance more than 20 percent greater than that of any other football conference, could tolerate increased television coverage without risking a decrease in gate receipts. This was in marked contrast to the 1950 season, the year before NCAA control, when the Big 10 had banned live television coverage of its games.[8] The Big 10's prerogative also differed from that of the majority of NCAA institutions, which still feared the growth of TV. The NCAA did continue to experiment with its TV plan by allowing telecasting of sold out games if the telecast would likely not have negative effect upon other games in the locality. The NCAA also allowed small colleges to telecast their games, having little fear that their audience would be large enough to challenge attendance at the big-time schools.

In 1953, the NCAA decided to experiment on a regional basis by telecasting parts of four games during the same day. This was allowed, according to the NCAA Television Committee chair, because parts of games would not "satisfy the interest of the real football fan who might otherwise attend the contest in person." The committee hoped that the panorama of football action would "stimulate the interest of fans in attending the games themselves without satisfying that interest by the presentation of the full contest."[9] The four-game partial telecasting experiment was a technical success but a major disappointment to those who watched. The parts of the four games telecast from Princeton, New Jersey, Champaign, Illinois, Iowa City, Iowa, and Memphis, Tennessee, received many comments from NBC viewers, 90 percent of which were unfavorable. Key plays were generally missed, there was no continuity of action, and placing advertising proved difficult, making the advertiser, General Motors, unhappy.[10]

A slate of regional games, however, appeared to many NCAA members to be a threat to gate receipts. A member of the NCAA Television Committee, J. Shober Barr of Pennsylvania's small Franklin and Marshall College, spoke out against a change in policy at the annual NCAA convention. "Regional television," Barr said, "would mean electric chair death to our kind of football."[11] Asa Bushnell, commissioner of the Eastern College Athletic Conference, which included Ivy League schools, concurred. "The most difficult television competition for the games to meet," Bushnell believed, "is the competition provided by the attractive games in the local area."[12]

Opinions on the harmful effect of regional TV were reinforced by research conducted for the NCAA by the National Opinion Research Center (NORC) survey. For 1953, the NORC report showed that football fans wanted what the NCAA was not giving them—televised regional games and a full slate of big-time teams. The NORC survey concluded that "two factors—regional vs. non-regional and overall attractiveness of the game—appear to account for almost all the variation in the size of the television audience." In other words, "when the game is very attractive and is also played nearby, the TV audience is largest."[13]

The Big 10 and the Pacific Coast Conference now felt that they were popular enough to have both large gate attendance and increased revenue and exposure from telecasting of their games. They began putting pressure on the NCAA Television Committee to change its policy of limiting regional games. The Big 10 Television Committee opposed the NCAA's 1954 TV plan, which would provide no more than three games originating from any one NCAA district. The NCAA opposed the proposal that Big 10 institutions had unanimously endorsed for incorporating regional telecasts. The Big 10 said it was not threatening the NCAA, that its proposal "would not imply any prospective unilateral action by the Conference, independent of NCAA controls and policies." Nevertheless, breaking with the NCAA policy was clearly one of the Big 10's options, as future action would show.[14]

At the 1954 NCAA convention, the vote was 172-9 to pass the NCAA's

TV plan, but when it came to the more important spring referendum on the TV plan, which was more fully developed, there were an additional 17 negative votes cast. This brought the percentage of NCAA institutions voting for the plan to less than 90 percent for the first time, as a group of big-time athletic powers began to resist the restrictive legislation on regional telecasts.[15] Certainly the Big 10 schools and, presumably, those of the Pacific Coast Conference were the major protesters of the NCAA plan. After the annual NCAA meeting, the Big 10 asked the television committee for regional TV, but their request was rejected.[16] The NCAA used its spring report on TV's effect on football attendance to justify its conservative plan. "There can be little doubt that if the NCAA program were to show only regional games to the fans in all parts of the country, and if the fans knew they could count on such a schedule," the report read, "the adverse TV effects that we have shown in this report would be very much greater."[17]

The greatest fear of regional TV came from the South, for the Dixie states were late in the spread of television and were only beginning to feel the negative effects of the medium on gate receipts. The Southeastern Conference, especially, feared television regionalization and the Big 10 influence. James Corbett, athletic director at Louisiana State University and NCAA television liaison officer, wanted monetary interests of television to be secondary to concerns for gate receipts. Corbett was afraid that the Big 10's move would lead to the "rich getting richer" if regional selections were made part of the TV plan.[18] Corbett got support from Cornell's Robert Kane, a member of the NCAA Television Committee. Kane wrote about the dominant conference: "The Big 10's attitude on this is entirely a selfish one."[19] And of course it was selfish. It reflected not only the picture of intercollegiate athletics over its history but also the historic nature of higher education in America, which first began in what became the Ivy League institutions. Individual institutions and later conferences did what was best for themselves. When Yale had accepted a very large amount for its radio broadcasts in 1936, against the wishes of both Harvard and Princeton, it had been looking out for its special interests rather than the collective welfare of its chief competitors.[20] Survival was any institution's first concern, and growth seemed no less important. If the Big 10 could get additional exposure and revenue from television at the expense of other conferences, it was no less a calculated move than a business outdoing its competitors in America's free enterprise system. The Darwinian motto "survival of the fittest" echoed throughout the football television drama as if it were a contest for the national championship. The Big 10 and the Pacific Coast Conference were the leading conferences, and as such they continued to push their own agendas despite the NCAA's resistence.

The Big 10 and Pacific Coast Conference were not successful in dramatically changing NCAA TV policy in 1954, but they prevailed the next year. Fritz Crisler, Michigan's athletic director, complained in early 1955 that the 1954 TV plan "was more restrictive than any of its predecessors." Increasingly, state legislatures in the seven-state region of the Big 10, according to Crisler, were introducing resolutions or bills mandating greater TV exposure of Big 10 football games. Political pressures combined with what Crisler called the desire of institutions for "prestige . . . and revenue" were driving the Big 10 toward some form of regional television.[21] The Pacific Coast Conference, which had already aligned itself with the Big 10 in yearly Rose Bowl participation, again sided with the Big 10 by strongly favoring regional telecasts. At the same time, the majority of NCAA members, in a straw vote, expressed their preference for a national Game of the Week rather than regional telecasts, with 86 percent rating the protection of gate receipts as being most important.[22] Yet this same majority was put in a difficult position if it voted for a continued restrictive policy, as it risked having both of the leading conferences leave the NCAA and form their own television contract. The athletic director at the University of Illinois, Doug Mills, commented that the Big 10 "may be divorced" from the NCAA over the issue.[23] The threat was not greatly veiled.

The NCAA Television Committee felt the pressure to accommodate the Pacific Coast and Big 10 conferences. The plans of the previous four years, designed to "protect gate attendance," were running headlong into a desire by the favored few to expand the use of television. The TV committee, with the authority to adopt a "best" plan, decided to move toward regionalism. The campaign by the Big 10 and the Pacific Coast conferences was successful in that the new plan called for five weekends of regional TV, with the remaining eight weekends scheduled for a national Game of the Week. The compromise was enough for the two conferences to remain within the NCAA plan, and both sides could claim partial victory. The Big 10 and Pacific Coast conferences had their regionalization plan recognized, while the majority of the NCAA members who favored a Game of the Week were guaranteed that format in eight of the thirteen playing dates.

The South, late in being affected negatively by television, was relieved that protection of gate receipts had not been forgotten when the new NCAA TV plan was formed. Jeff Coleman, a former member of the NCAA Television Committee, attended deliberations and represented southern views opposing regional TV. Coleman told the committee that "a regional television program would be very injurious to some member institutions" of the Southeastern Conference.[24] There was a strong belief that "the televising of a game like Notre Dame each Saturday or a game out of the Big 10 each Saturday would have a very deteriorating influence on the gate receipts" in the South.[25] A University of Tennessee faculty representative to the Southeastern Conference expressed a common Southern belief: "We in the South are very anxious to keep the control of television under a national agency rather than to make it a regional activity."[26] There was irony in the South favoring national control, since historically states' rights or regional solidarity had dominated thinking in the former Confederate area. There was further irony in that only five years before, the Southeastern Conference, along with the Southern Conference and the Southwest Conference, had threatened to break away from the NCAA over compliance with the national NCAA Sanity Code, which restricted athletic scholarships and recruitment of athletes. Only after states' rights had won out, with the defeat of the Sanity Code, did the three southern conferences agree to stay in the NCAA.[27]

The adoption of the 1955 compromise TV plan had the effect of "holding the membership together," according to Alabama's Dean A. B. Moore. He nevertheless cautioned the NCAA's Executive Director, Walter Byers: "It is possible that it may prove to be the end of national control."[28] Notre Dame, meanwhile, continued to be vocal in its long campaign for ending national control by the NCAA. Edmund Joyce, vice president of Notre Dame, continued to call the NCAA plan reactionary, arbitrary, and artificial while castigating the NCAA Television Committee's decision to prevent the telecast of the Notre Dame–Iowa game from South Bend that fall.[29] Notre Dame notwithstanding, for more than two decades the new NCAA TV plan accommodated a vast majority of NCAA institutions. Big-time institutions began to reap the financial harvest that television could offer, and smaller institutions benefited from the set percentage of television receipts that went to the NCAA headquarters to finance programs helpful to all institutions, large and small. The NCAA was eventually financed principally with TV funds, first with those from football and later with the massive payload from the NCAA basketball tournament. The compromise of 1955 appeased most of the big-time institutions for years to come and created a steady stream of wealth for the NCAA. It did not, however, solve the problem created by the tremendous growth of professional football in the 1950s and 1960s, which provided direct competition for college football. The encroachment of the NFL on the collegiate domain demanded attention.

15   TV and the Threat of Professional Football

COLLEGES HAD *the* game of football in America until more than a decade after World War II.[1] Some perceived televised football as a threat to live attendance around 1950, but telecasting had a greater impact on the sports of baseball and boxing than on college football. Major League baseball attendance fell by over 30 percent, and a majority of minor leagues ceased to exist. Boxing at the club level declined precipitously. Other forms of entertainment also felt the impact of TV, especially movie theaters, which saw a 40 percent drop in box office receipts in less than three years.[2]

Professional football, unlike college football, baseball, or boxing, possibly had less to fear from television in the early 1950s. Major networks had little interest in telecasting the games because pro football had only a small national following. From the beginning of pro football, in the late nineteenth and early twentieth century, the professionals were located principally in small northern towns west of the Appalachian mountains toward the Mississippi River. With games primarily on Sunday afternoons, often using college players who competed under assumed names to protect their amateur status, professional football lacked widespread radio exposure and garnered little interest from television executives in the 1940s.[3]

Following World War II, however, professional football teams expanded to larger cities and attracted more and more fans to their games. As late as 1952, pro football still averaged less than 30,000 spectators to its games, which represented record attendance for pro football.[4] The upstart Du Mont Television Network telecast five National Football League games in 1951, as well as the championship All-American Football Conference, in which coach Paul Brown's Cleveland Browns triumphed over the New York Yankees, 14-9. Those watching the game on TV could see Otto Graham throw to Max Speedie and Dante Lavelli and hand the ball off to Marion Motley and Lou "The Toe" Groza attempt field goals. All five had been college players before the arrival of regular pro gridiron telecasts. In 1953, Du Mont telecast, for the first time, a full NFL schedule.[5] NFL telecasting, though, did not raise enough advertising revenues for Du Mont, hastening the collapse of the Du Mont Television Network.

Until NFL football entered the picture, Sunday afternoon television had been reserved principally for serious culture—classical concerts, drama, and special news programs. When Du Mont's pro football telecasts captured over a third of the Sunday afternoon television audience in 1954, other networks and collegiate administrators took notice. Television had effectively promoted the professional game. By 1956, CBS recognized the newly created audience and purchased NFL TV rights, posing a challenge to NBC, which had just paid $1.25 million for rights to the NCAA's "Game of the Week." Previous to NBC's acquisition, the NCAA rights were held for one disastrous year by ABC, which had overbid for them and lost nearly $2 million.[6] Actually, CBS also wanted the rights to NCAA telecasts but had been outbid by NBC. At the time, Bill MacPhail of CBS Sports believed that college football had more pizzazz, with its school spirit, coeds, and tradition. "My God, was I wrong," MacPhail said later. "The NFL turned out to be the whole backbone of our sports operation."[7] Indeed, the rapid growth of the NFL and its increased drawing power on TV placed the preeminence of NCAA telecasts in jeopardy, drawing the ire of NCAA officials.

Even from the beginning of the NFL in 1921, college leaders showed some fear of the pros. The American Football Coaches Association, a college coaches' group, was formed following the inaugural NFL season and immediately became an approved organization of the NCAA. Pro football was obviously on the coaches' minds, as the group passed a resolution accusing pro football of being "detrimental to the best interest of American football and American youth." The Big 10 had previously voted to take varsity letters away from those who played pro ball and not allow anyone who played the professional game to officiate Big 10 games.[8] Four years later the colleges experienced what they believed was an even greater threat to their game. The greatest name in college football, Red Grange, using a sports agent, signed a professional football contract one day after his last Big 10 game with Illinois. College officials had reason to fear an improved pro game: possibly the most glamorous college football star of the twentieth century was now playing for the Chicago Bears. Grange's turning pro, Big 10 commissioner Major John L. Griffith said, "will certainly hurt the amateur sport, just as I am confident that it will help the professional game."[9] Griffith, without official action by the Big 10 faculty representatives, ruled that the Big 10 regulation banning amateur status in all sports for anyone playing pro baseball was now applicable to any football player who signed a pro contract.[10] Grange, playing in a Chicago Bear's uniform on Thanksgiving Day of 1925, only days after completing his career at Illinois, drew an overflow crowd of 39,000 at Cubs Park, the largest crowd ever to see a pro football game.[11] The American Football Coaches Association again criticized the pro game and voted, without authority to enforce its action, to prohibit anyone who "plays, officiates, or coaches in pro football" from coaching in the colleges.[12] It is likely that Grange's move to the pros was the greatest threat to college football until the television peril of the 1950s.

Grange's impact on professional gate attendance was not long-lasting, but one result of his pro signing did have repercussions that lasted over a half-century. In a concession to the colleges, the NFL agreed not to sign any future collegian until his class had graduated. Rather than protecting the rights of student-athletes to pursue their best interests, the pros and colleges colluded to protect the college football commercial investment. From 1926 until the 1980s, the agreement held and was not challenged in the courts. Only when Herschel Walker, the great University of Georgia player, decided to test the "Grange Rule" in 1983 did the illegal, but never challenged, collusion of the pros and colleges break down. By then the pros threatened colleges not only by signing their best (and still eligible) players but also by capitalizing on the expansion of television.

From the 1930s to the 1950s, the college game had little to fear from the languishing pros, but that would soon change. With the coming of television, the pro game was elevated, and would eventually outstrip the college game in national interest. In part, this was because the NFL, with fewer areas to protect from TV overexposure, was able to show all league teams on TV. The NCAA, wishing to protect the gate receipts of numerous big-time teams as well as small colleges, allowed only limited television coverage, broadcasting only a small percentage of its games each year. The result, according to Asa Bushnell of the NCAA Television Committee, was that it appeared to the American people that "the pros are performing a public service while the colleges are depriving the public of its just due."[13] Notre Dame President Theodore Hesburgh argued for a greater acceptance of the broader, more laissez faire, telecasting model of the pros. "One has only to see how professional football, through the use of television," wrote Hesburgh, "has built up a great following."[14] True enough, by the mid-1950s, the colleges were looking over their shoulders at the NFL's increasing interest and TV ratings, while their own TV ratings declined. The Big 10, fearful of the five NFL franchises in their geographical area, asked college game broadcasters to bar pro game discussions on their game telecasts.[15] They could not, obviously, prevent telecasting of NFL games in Cleveland, Chicago, or Detroit. The Big 10 was less interested in developments in New York City, though they and other colleges probably should have been.

The New York Giants won their first NFL title in almost two decades in 1956, and the communications center of the world made the Giants the first important media team in the NFL. Not only was New York the media axis of America, but the Giants also had a media star, similar to Red Grange a generation earlier. Frank Gifford, the Giants' star halfback, had a radio and television show, a newspaper column, and movie potential. When the Giants, two years later, played the Baltimore Colts, with quarterback Johnny Unitas, in the NFL championship game in New York, the television audience numbered about 30 million. The "greatest game in NFL history" ended in a sudden-death overtime as Unitas handed off to Alan Ameche, a Heisman Trophy winner four years before at the University of Wisconsin, for the game-winning touchdown. The Baltimore–New York game pushed NFL football into the limelight, especially after Tex Maule of *Sports Illustrated* claimed it was the greatest football game ever played. The NFL's skyrocketing image gave college football concern for its position in the media competition.[16]

The threat of televised pro football became a federal issue in Congress when, in 1959, Senator Estes Kefauver of Tennessee said that he would introduce legislation to prevent professional football from telecasting at the same time college football games were being played. While the NFL traditionally competed on Sunday, a new league, the American Football League, was considering playing games on Saturday.[17] Though that threat to the college game did not materialize at the time, a key congressional act was passed in 1961, exempting the NFL and other professional sports from antitrust suits involving television.

The Sports Broadcasting Act of 1961 had been initiated by the NFL's decision that year to sell its television rights as a league package rather than allowing individual clubs to continue to sell their rights. Newly elected 33-year-old "boy" NFL commissioner Alvin "Pete" Rozelle was the chief negotiator for the new NFL contract. The agreement eliminated television competition among NFL teams and, instead, divided television income equally among league members. Almost immediately, Federal Judge Alan K. Grim ruled that the NFL was in violation of antitrust laws and voided the contract.[18] The NFL quickly appealed to Congress for legislation to negate Judge Grim's antitrust ruling. Wasting little time, a cooperative Congress constructed a bill to exempt the professional sports teams in football, baseball, basketball, and hockey from antitrust action. The Sports Broadcasting Act of 1961, passed by a voice vote and signed by President John F. Kennedy, created a legal television monopoly for professional football; at the same time, it gave colleges limited protection from the encroachment of the NFL's and the newly organized American Football League's telecasts.[19]

The momentous Sports Broadcasting Act, a financially defining piece of legislation written for the benefit of pro football, prohibited the pros from playing on Friday night and Saturday afternoon, the traditional times for college football. "I think this legislation will go a long way," stated William Flynn, Chairman of the Eastern College Athletic Conference Television Committee, "in helping football, college football, keep its interest with the public."[20] While the NCAA, and college sports in general, were not included in the antitrust exemption to allow pooling of TV rights, the act protected colleges from the growing professional football interest in telecasting when traditional college games were played.[21]

The protection suddenly seemed illusory when, in 1964, the NFL announced that ABC would telecast five of its games on Friday nights. Foul, cried the NCAA. Even though the NFL would not telecast within seventy-five miles of any college games, it would legally telecast at a time when upwards of 10,000 high school games were being played weekly.[22] Alarmed, Walter Byers, Executive Director of the NCAA, contacted a number of senators and the powerful Congressman Emanuel Celler, chairman of the House of Representatives Committee on the Judiciary. Byers stated that while the 1961 act did not specifically ban the pros from telecasting on Friday nights during high school games, doing so "certainly violates the spirit of the agreement."[23] Sundays were for the pros, Saturdays were for the colleges, and Fridays were for the high schools, the NCAA maintained. The colleges' desire to protect the high schools from the pros was not exactly altruistic, for the high schools were the feeder system for college football talent. Paradoxically, less than a decade before, the NCAA had strongly considered telecasting on Friday nights, to the consternation of not only high schools but also some small colleges that played their games on Fridays.[24] Yet keeping high school football programs healthy, if not those of small colleges, was important for the success of the historic commercial model in the colleges.

While it was unthinkable for colleges to condemn pro basketball or pro baseball for playing on Fridays or Saturdays, there was something almost sacred about the days on which football was played. Those dates were considered sacrosanct because football was the sport that drove the financial train in many high schools and most big-time colleges. The days were inviolable enough so that congressmen and senators listened when the NCAA spoke. Through the efforts of college and high school leaders who reached legislators such as Celler, Senate minority leader Everett Dirkson, and Senator Edward M. Kennedy, pressure was exerted on commissioner Pete Rozelle and the NFL to change their plans for Friday night telecasts. The congressional threat to reevaluate the Sports Broadcasting Act of 1961 and possibly eliminate the NFL monopoly over telecasting its games was a factor in altering the NFL's plan.[25] There had never been a clearer case demonstrating the NCAA's fear of the pros and the commercial threat that they posed.

The phobic action of the NCAA did not lessen once congressional pressure had limited pro football telecasting. The NCAA Television Committee soon demanded that NBC make "no mention of professional football" during any segments of future NCAA football telecasts.[26] This, according to the NCAA's Executive Director, Walter Byers, might have been an NCAA retaliation to the NFL's effort to challenge the legality of the NCAA TV plan. The NFL, through its law firm, had questioned the legitimacy of the NCAA's own TV contract, a plan that, when challenged two decades later, would turn out to be in violation of antitrust laws.[27] But the restriction was more likely due to continued NCAA paranoia of the NFL. That anxiety became so great that the 1965 NCAA Television Committee came within one vote of also asking NBC to discontinue promotion of its own NCAA football on any professional American Football League telecast.[28] Furthermore, NBC was not even given an opportunity to bid on the next NCAA football contract. Instead, without any open bidding, ABC, which did not have a contract with either the NFL or the AFL, was given a four-year contract by the NCAA. NBC's Carl Lindemann angrily telegraphed the NCAA: "I could not be more shocked at the shoddy treatment . . . by the National Collegiate Athletic Association."[29] Broadcaster Lindsey Nelson explained the reasoning behind such shoddy treatment: "The NCAA had an abiding fear that the college game would somehow be relegated to a secondary role [to the NFL]."[30] The colleges's fear of the pros had helped advance ABC in its move toward an eventual dominance of sports telecasting.

In another case of professional football anxiety, the NCAA contacted congress in an attempt to legally disallow professional football teams from drafting college football players until after the athlete's fourth year, following his matriculation. The NCAA hoped such an action would prevent star collegians from leaving for the professional ranks, diluting the college game. The argument college officials posed, however, was that college football players should not be seduced away from a college degree by the lure of professional football. This educational argument simply veiled the college athletic departments' attempt to preserve their own commercial interest in their players. Though the Senate considered a bill to outlaw early signing with pro football teams, nothing came out of the Senate Judiciary Committee activity.[31]

The expanding threat of professional football and its growing TV audience had a strong impact upon another longtime controversial issue in college football: the advisability of two-platoon, or free-substitution, football. Colleges had been adverse to player substitutions from football's beginning, in the 1870s. After all, a competitor should be able to play an entire manly game without the need for a substitute. Not until the war mobilization, just before the United States' entry into World War II, did a liberalization of the substitution rule occur. In 1941, the rules committee decided that the severe loss of athletes to the military required a change to a "free-substitution" rule.[32]

Despite unlimited substitution being allowed under the rules, there was little innovation among the conservative coaching profession until Michigan's coach, Fritz Crisler, had to meet the great Army team shortly after the end of World War II. In playing the number-one team in the nation, Crisler believed that he might effectively use eight players on defense who were different from those playing on offense. He thought the fresh players might be able to hold down the lopsided scores that the veteran players of Army were enjoying against weaker opposition. Indeed, the score remained tied until the end of the third quarter, when Army erupted for a 28-7 win. Army's coach, Earle "Red" Blaik, was so impressed with Michigan's two units that he called them "platoons."[33] Crisler's two-platoon system changed football, but not without a fight between the old guard and the new guard of the coaching profession.

The two-platoon system of football created more excitement for the fans, as both the skill level and energy level rose. It had a negative effect in that larger teams became more expensive to sponsor and the era of the all-around player came to an end. Specialists, such as skillful passers or specially trained field goal kickers, could play even if their blocking and tackling skills were lacking. While the majority of coaches favored the liberalized substitution rules, the Football Rules Committee

became stacked with traditionalists while economy-conscious administrators moved to cut the costs of football. In 1953, the free-substitution
rule was voted out by the committee.[34]

So as the threat of pro football, with its liberal substitution rules and
more exciting game, intensified by the 1960s, colleges continued to play
traditional, if less thrilling, two-way football. The tradition-bound college Football Rules Committee continued two-way football longer than
the situation dictated, in part because of Tennessee's former great coach
and then athletic director General Robert Neyland, chairman of the committee. At the 1960 rules meeting, Neyland was trying to avoid a vote on
unlimited substitution when coach Frank Howard of Clemson forced the
question. With a recent change in committee structure, there was now
an overwhelming majority in favor of free substitution. Cornered, Neyland asked for all those opposed to two-platoon football to raise their
hands. Neyland immediately grasped the hand of David Nelson, who
was sitting at the head of the table with him, and raised it along with his
own. He then declared: "There doesn't seem to be any sentiment to return to that chicken-shit football. Meeting is adjourned," and walked
out.[35] Neyland's influence could not last forever. For the next five years,
the Football Rules Committee moved closer to unlimited substitution,
finally losing the rear-guard battle over requiring players to both block
and tackle in 1965. "Chicken-shit" to some, but exciting, free-substitution football allowed the colleges to meet one more challenge of professional football. Dan Devine, who coached both professional and college
football, recalled: "Two-platoon football enabled college football to compete with professional football for fan interest."[36] He was right, but the
threat of pro football still did not diminish.

Professional football, with innovative commissioner Pete Rozelle,
continued to beat the colleges in promoting its brand of football. There
was no question that the NFL was less constrained because it never tried
to represent itself as being anything other than a commercial venture.
Since college football claimed that it was a vital part of the colleges' educational programs, it needed to appear to the public to be concerned
about the educational mission. As an example, colleges were hesitant to
advertise alcohol on commercial telecasts, but they eventually caved in
to the lure of money by the end of the 1960s.[37] Despite the colleges' mission, money from TV revenues proved more important than the ethical
issue involved. Disparities between pro and college television revenues
became more pronounced when the NFL attracted additional attention
from networks, which in turn could sell advertisements during NFL

telecasts for a greater price than those shown during college football.[38] In an attempt to slow the growth of pro football popularity, the NCAA included in its TV contracts provisions prohibiting football announcers from discussing pro football. For instance, the NCAA announcers knew from the TV committee they were not to say: "That boy has the moves to make a great pro."[39] Advertisements during NCAA games could not even show pictures of pro athletes. The NCAA Television Committee at one point voted unanimously to oppose commercials using the great running back and Heisman Trophy Winner O. J. Simpson in his pro football uniform. The NCAA did not want Simpson to "publicize or promote professional football either directly or indirectly."[40] In addition, the NCAA banned any announcers who had had strong connections with professional football in the past.[41] Star NFL quarterbacks John Lujack and Frank Albert were unanimously rejected for broadcasting assignments because of their "close affiliation with professional football."[42] The NCAA's fear of the pros even reached the level of the college marching bands. When several college bands performed at televised pro games, the TV committee worried that the exposure would "enhance professional football game telecasts" and discouraged the bands' appearances at future NFL games.[43]

As the 1960s came to a close, the NCAA–pro tension was exacerbated by the NFL's decision to expand beyond Sunday afternoon contests into prime-time *Monday Night Football*. ABC, which for the past few years had been telecasting only college football, decided to get into the pro game. *Monday Night Football* combined the promotional expertise of both NFL commissioner Pete Rozelle and ABC's talented Roone Arledge,[44] but the colleges did not give the proposed new Monday telecasts much credit. The NCAA's television guru, Asa Bushnell, hoped that "Houdini Rozelle's reach will finally exceed his grasp."[45] NCAA executive director Walter Byers agreed, but he was still concerned about the attractiveness of NFL games and the difficulty of keeping NCAA football telecasts unique, relative to the pro game.[46]

Arledge, on the other hand, saw both college and pro football as pure entertainment. As probably the most creative mind in the history of televised sports producing, Arledge had already begun to improve college football telecasts by what he often stated as "taking the fan to the game, not the game to the fan." Arledge increased the number of cameras, placing them on the field, in cranes, in blimps, and in helicopters. No aspect of the game environment escaped the Arledge eye, for the television viewer could now hear the crunch of a tackle or a quarterback barking out the signals, see a coach verbally assaulting a player or observe fans screaming at an official, and often—more importantly to ABC—ogle from particular angles thinly clad, well-endowed cheerleaders. In addition, Arledge's innovative slow-motion shots made parts of televised football much better than actually being at the game.

With the successful debut of *Monday Night Football* during the fall of 1970, the NCAA Television Committee asked ABC not to promote NCAA games on Monday nights and certainly not to promote *Monday Night Football* on NCAA telecasts.[47] After ABC had inserted a promotional ad for the NFL during a station break following the Nebraska-Colorado telecast, drawing fire from the NCAA, Roone Arledge defended his network, telling Walter Byers, "If we spend our time picking out isolated little incidents, we are heading down the wrong road and serving the ends of no one." Arledge tried to assure Byers that "our first team is still on Saturday afternoon."[48] Maybe that was the case, but Arledge recognized the new game was pro football, and he wanted ABC to profit from it just as CBS and NBC had done.

Tom Hamilton, an early NCAA leader on the television committee, realized that college football was "losing out in the public interest to . . . the pros who have ruthlessly been gaining the upper hand in the press, radio, and TV." So concerned was Hamilton that he asked the NCAA to support the National Football Foundation's proposal to build a College Football Hall of Fame to compete with pro football's Hall of Fame at Canton, Ohio. The idea had been discussed for a generation, but the success of the pros and the Canton Hall of Fame now generated new interest in continuing the efforts toward a College Hall of Fame. Hamilton proposed a tax on NCAA TV income of one-half percent over six years to fund the building of a hall "in a manner far exceeding the 'pro' Canton establishment."[49]

The proposal to build the hall at Rutgers University, site of the first intercollegiate football game in 1869, was not to be. Unfortunately for promoters of the hall idea, the NCAA was under fiscal stress, having just financed a new NCAA building in Kansas City through TV receipts. Siphoning off TV moneys to pay for an NCAA building was bad enough, but taking money from the televised schools to pay for a Hall of Fame would be worse.[50] Meanwhile, looking for higher immediate TV payoffs during the inflationary period of the Vietnam War, the big-time institutions wanted money to go to their athletic departments, not to a Hall of Fame. There were those who believed, as did the NCAA's Tom Hansen, that the Hall of Fame idea was being sold to them to benefit "the totally eastern flavor of the leadership of the Foundation," that is, the traditional, ivy league elites of the East.[51] In this case, colleges' fear of the pros was less of an influence than was the desire by non-Easterners to reject what they believed was the work of the snobbish Easterners and their second-rate football programs.

Not supporting the elite-led College Football Hall of Fame may have been a poor choice by the NCAA, for the collegians needed any promotion they could gain to compete with the pros for TV ratings and revenue. The NCAA's alarm at the pro's threat was justified by the Nielsen rating changes during the 1960s. When the decade began, NCAA football led the NFL 11.7 to 10.6 on the Nielsen TV ratings system. At the beginning of the 1970s, after the American Football League had joined the NFL, the NCAA had increased to a 13.8 rating, but the NFL's National Football Conference had risen to 17.3 and the NFL's American Football Conference was up to 15.3. The NFL's *Monday Night Football* on ABC, the NCAA football network, had a whopping rating of 18.5.[52] The NFL had won the TV ratings war with college football, and the concern about pro football dominance lingered on. Even as late as the 1990s, Walter Byers's successor as executive director of the NCAA, Dick Schultz, continued the litany of fear. This time, Schultz made his remarks relative to the declining television interest in the bowl games concluding the NCAA season, and he called for an NCAA playoff system to challenge the NFL playoffs and the Super Bowl. "The National Football League," Schultz groaned, "is slowly strangling college football."[53] Nevertheless, as the NCAA and college football fought to remain clear of the shadow of professional football, they would work effectively with network television, especially ABC.

 ## 16 Roone Arledge and the Influence of ABC-TV

WHILE LEADERS of college football remained nervous about professional football for a half-century or more, they had lost much of their fear of television by the time Roone Arledge and ABC-TV gained the preeminent position in college football telecasting. While colleges were still apprehensive about TV, they had much to love about the networks and telecasting as one of the most dominating commercial businesses in the twentieth century. Colleges had already made the choice to broadcast football through the commercial rather than the educational avenue.

Once that decision had been made, colleges reinforced their nineteenth-century decision to make athletic departments commercial entities rather than integral components of education. The desire to obtain money for athletics was often in the minds and hearts of those running college sports, and the negotiations with networks simply intensified the commercial spirit of college athletics. ABC's Roone Arledge, a programming whiz, was more adept at programming college athletics as entertainment than were his staid CBS and NBC network competitors, and he helped ABC create increased wealth for big-time college athletics.

ABC, after a financially disastrous one-year stint with college football in 1954, reentered the NCAA bidding war at the beginning of the next decade. ABC was a distant third place in the NBC-CBS-ABC triad of networks when it bid just over $3 million and became the network of the NCAA in 1960. That was the year the pudgy redhead, Roone Arledge, moved from NBC, where he had won an Emmy Award for producing Shari Lewis' puppet show, *Hi Mom*. The 29-year-old Arledge became the producer of ABC's college football series after presenting ABC with a bold plan for covering the NCAA Game of the Week.

How ABC won the 1960 bidding contest with NBC and then hired Arledge is worth recalling, for quirks of the past often determine future direction. After its football fiasco in 1954, ABC, with the financial backing of the Gillette Safety Razor Company, decided to again enter the football fray six years later. NBC itself had reentered NCAA football in 1955 by purchasing the rights for nearly half of what ABC had paid the previous year. It took another five years for the football rights fees to climb to ABC's 1954 purchase price.[1] ABC's resulting reluctance to get into the bidding war with CBS and NBC, ironically, helped get the NCAA contract into ABC's hands in 1960. Almost no one expected ABC to challenge once again.

A fortuitous event developed for ABC as it entered the bidding for the 1960 TV contract against incumbent NBC. Gillette, television's foremost sports advertiser, found its longstanding Friday Night Fights being dropped by NBC. The until-recently highly successful Friday night show had been displaying a slow drop in Nielsen ratings. Gillette, however, wanted to continue sponsoring the spectacle, for Gillette sales had risen in direct proportion to its sports telecast advertising. Gillette had increased its market share in shaving products from 16 percent to over 60 percent after advertising over the air first on radio and then on television.[2] Through its advertising agency, Gillette contacted ABC with an offer the struggling network could not refuse. If ABC would carry the weekly fights, Gillette promised $8.5 million in advertising, more money than ABC had received for sports advertising in its entire history.[3] Gillette's underwriting had just made ABC a big-time sports network, allowing the network to compete for the NCAA football telecasts. First, though, it had to outwit and outbid NBC.

Tom Gallery, a bulky and gregarious Irishman, had been head of NBC Sports since 1952, when NBC acquired its first NCAA contract. According to the NCAA's Walter Byers, Gallery made NBC the dominant sports network for a decade and a half.[4] But Gallery was outsmarted in 1960 by Edgar J. Scherick, who plotted with ABC to snare the contract from NBC. With the exception of ABC's one failed year, NBC had been the sole network carrying NCAA football from the beginning of the NCAA's national control of big-time football telecasts. Scherick, who owned Sports Programs, Inc., predecessor to ABC's sports department, convinced Tom Moore, head of the ABC television network, that with Gillette's backing ABC should bid again on the NCAA contract.

Meeting with the NCAA in New York City, NBC's Tom Gallery brought with him two, or possibly three, contract bids in separate envelopes. If Gallery felt there were no other serious bids, he planned on submitting the lower bid. As CBS was strongly involved in telecasting NFL games, Gallery sensed that CBS would not be a player in the college contract. He looked around the room and saw no one from ABC or CBS, leading him to believe that his lower bid would surely win. Yet Scherick knew of Gallery's traditional tactics and had sent into the meeting an unknown and innocuous-looking employee from ABC's business department, Stan Frankle. Frankle was over six feet tall, but he was a young, skinny, and balding individual with stoop shoulders and horn-rimmed glasses. Acting the part of an espionage agent and looking as inconspicuous as he could, Frankle waited for Gallery to submit NBC's bid. Gallery looked around and, seeing no competitor, deposited his low bid with the NCAA. Frankle then walked up to the NCAA's chief TV negotiator, Asa Bushnell, and submitted the lowest of two ABC bids.[5] ABC won with a two-year, $6,251,114 bid, projecting that NBC would only offer its usual 10 percent over the previous contract. The $1,114 was added to the $6.25 million bid "to give the bid character," according to Scherick.[6] This shrewd move began ABC's rise in becoming the world's leading sports network.

With the NCAA contract in hand, ABC soon hired a group of telecasters to take on the new responsibility of college football and, in less than a year, ABC's *Wide World of Sports*. Among the newcomers hired were Jim Spence, Chuck Howard, Chet Simmons, and Roone Arledge. Arledge, who would go on to become the icon of televised sports, was paid $10,000 to join ABC.[7] With its new hires, ABC was poised to make an impact in sports telecasting. Because ABC was in a distant last place among the three major networks, with the least number of affiliate stations, it could afford to be more radical in its programming, knowing that it would be difficult to sink lower. As Leonard Goldenson said when he took over ABC in the 1950s: "We had no hit shows, no stars, and nothing in prospect but struggle."[8] Risk-takers such as Roone Arledge were welcome at ABC, just as they were unwelcome at NBC or CBS.

NCAA football under the production of Roone Arledge was indeed a risk to both ABC and the NCAA. Trusting production to someone under thirty years of age was every bit as nerve-racking to the NCAA as ABC's first attempt at telecasting college sports had been in 1954. Walter Byers, the new NCAA executive director, had wanted "to test the competency of ABC and its sports department."[9] In 1960, the NCAA could not know that Arledge would be experimenting with a new concept of sports telecasting.

Shortly after being hired, before ABC began the first college contest of the 1960 season, Arledge sent a memo to Edgar Scherick on his programming scheme.

Heretofore, television has done a remarkable job of bringing the game to the viewer—now we are going to take the viewer to the game!!

We will utilize every production technique . . . to heighten the viewer's feeling of actually sitting in the stands and participating personally in the excitement and color. . . . We must gain and hold the interest of women who are not fanatic followers of the sport. . . . Incidentally, very few men have ever switched channels when a nicely proportioned girl was leaping into the air. . . .

We will have cameras mounted in jeeps, on mike booms, in risers or helicopters, or anything necessary to get the complete story of the game. We will use a 'creepy-peepy' camera to get the impact shots that we cannot get from a fixed camera—a coach's face as a man drops a pass in the clear—a pretty cheerleader just after her hero has scored a touchdown—a co-ed who brings her infant baby to the game in her arms—the referee as he calls a particularly difficult play—a student hawking programs in the stands—two romantic students sharing a blanket late in the game on a cold day. . . . all the excitement, wonder, jubilation and despair that make this America's Number One sport spectacle, and human drama to match bullfights and heavyweight championships in intensity. . . .

In short—we are going to add show business to sports![10]

Arledge wanted his boss to know that ABC would be "setting standards that everyone will be talking about and that others in the industry will spend years trying to equal."[11] He was correct on both scores. Those who worked with Arledge on his first programming venture remembered his composure in the Alabama-Georgia contest featuring legendary coach Bear Bryant of Alabama and a talented Georgia quarterback, Fran Tarkenton. Arledge chose from the bank of monitors in the control truck, producing shots of the crafty coach and the daring quarterback, capturing the crunch of a tackle by increasing the sound, taking panoramic views of the crowd (tending to focus on attractive coeds and cheerleaders), and seizing the emotions of the game better than had ever been done before. The "Roone Revolution" began with NCAA football and later expanded to the Olympics, *Monday Night Football,* and possibly the greatest regular sports show in history, *Wide World of Sports.*[12]

Arledge did not introduce all of his innovations in that first game, but those he did unveil were indications of his future influence on sports telecasting. Before his career was over, Arledge had brought a greater use of technology to sports telecasting while delivering the casual viewer to to the game. Halftime shows of first-half highlights and analysis replaced the previous emphasis on marching bands. Hand-held and isolated cameras and split-screen views were some of Arledge's ideas. He wove shots of the rabid spectators, the excited coaches, and the individualistic style of the players into ABC's coverage. He integrated prerecorded biographical studies and interviews into the contests. Above all, he used what were politely called "honey shots," but referred to as "T & A" in the control room. These views, usually of female cheerleaders and baton twirlers, gave a titillative quality to each telecast.[13] Arledge once remarked about the casual viewers: "If they don't give a damn about the game, they still might enjoy the program."[14]

Yet, for the true football fans, Arledge telecasts provided such features as views of key plays from numerous camera angles, slow-motion shots of decisive plays to enhance each game, and the precursor to instant replays.[15] ABC engineer Bob Trachinger and Arledge created the concept of slow-motion replay while awaiting a game at the Los Angeles Coliseum in the first year of the new ABC-NCAA contract in 1960. The slow-motion replay debuted in the Texas–Texas A & M game, but its first important use occurred in the Boston College–Syracuse contest. Arledge and Trachinger's replay in slow motion of Boston College quarterback Jack Concannon's dramatic seventy-yard touchdown run, as described by Curt Gowdy, was replayed while former quarterback Paul Christman provided the analysis. It was not instant, for the replays had to be taped by machines in ABC's New York studio and, in the case of Concannon's run, the tape was replayed at halftime.[16] Nevertheless, "that moment," Arledge boasted, "changed T.V. sport forever."[17]

Sports and television were changing, but the NCAA was less inclined to change its policy toward strict control of television. Since the beginning of the NCAA football television plan in 1951, the NCAA's major goal had been to protect college football stadium attendance from the invasion of "free" television. As college sport was dependent upon football gate receipts, it was logical for colleges to look at TV as a foe rather than friend. That is, until television money became significant. Then, as ABC's Beano Cook so aptly ruminated as he considered the lure of television money: "Financial situations make us become whores at times."[18] The NCAA was still reluctant to lessen its rigid stance on how many games could be telecast in a season and how many times a successful school could be shown on TV. Nevertheless, as networks began to make money from telecasting college sports and to entice new affiliate stations with the glitter of college football, the colleges were increasingly lured to money's altar. What the colleges wanted was to keep the restrictions on telecasts while still exponentially increasing their TV receipts. This led to conflicts with the networks carrying their games, since networks wanted more flexibility to increase ratings and income.

It made little difference which network won the rights to telecast—they all wanted flexibility from the NCAA in telecasting the games. ABC's initial rights to NCAA football only lasted for two years, for CBS won the two-year bid in 1962 for $10.2 million followed by NBC's 1964–66 contract for just over $13 million. ABC won the 1966 two-year contract for $15.6 million, and it continued on as the NCAA network until the U.S. Supreme Court nullified the NCAA monopoly in 1984.[19] Though ABC remained the NCAA's favored network while it had no pro football telecasts, Roone Arledge consistently campaigned for fewer NCAA restrictions. ABC would have preferred to telecast the best possible match-up each week, with announcers of its choice, unlimited advertising minutes, and no restrictions on who could advertise or what could be contained in the ads. The NCAA, however, attempted to satisfy all of the colleges by maintaining an educational image they believed should be upheld while spreading TV exposure among as many big-time schools as possible. Thus the NCAA would never allow ABC to control telecasts to their fullest commercial extent.

Restrictions on the number of appearances for any one college or whether there should be national or regional telecasts were likely the most debated issues. The original contract in 1951 called for no team to be on the national telecast more than once at home and once at an away game. This was modified with each contract so that by 1962 each of eight NCAA districts had to be represented by at least two different member colleges. There could be no more than fourteen appearances by colleges from one district, and in two years the combined total of appearances could not exceed twenty-seven. Each year, the network had to show at least thirty-seven different member colleges, two of which had not appeared in the preceding five years.[20] This complicated formula diluted the football offerings, lowered the potential ratings, and brought repeated protests from the networks.

Restrictions on appearances got particularly unpopular in 1966 when fans clamored for ABC to televise the Notre Dame–Michigan State game. As the year came to a close, both teams entered the contest with unbeaten records and were rated the top two teams in the nation. They were scheduled to be telecast regionally only, but a storm of letters and telegrams poured in from football fanatics across the nation asking the NCAA and ABC to telecast the game nationally. ABC claimed it received 50,000 letters, including some from nuns in Florida and priests in Connecticut, asking them to telecast the "Game of the Century."[21] The NCAA Television Committee called a special telephone conference to discuss and vote on the proposal to change the programming schedule. In a hotly debated meeting, the final vote was 6-5 to allow the national contest, but chairman Asa Bushnell, who opposed the vote and knew an absent member was also opposed, refused to declare the motion passed. The impasse was broken when Stu Holcomb, Northwestern University athletic director, moved to call upon the Television Administrative Committee to take final action. That motion passed, and the Administrative Committee gave the OK to the national telecast.[22]

While neither football team won, ABC got its greater flexibility and the NCAA triumphed for its controversial decision. The game ended in a 10-10 tie as Notre Dame's coach Ara Parseghian decided to run out the clock before the booing fans at Spartan Stadium rather than risk losing to Michigan State. Nationally, millions saw the game, which featured Bubba Smith, George Webster, and Clint Jones competing against Notre

Dame's Terry Hanratty, who was injured during the contest. It had "sen-sationally high" ratings according to Roone Arledge. While thousands and thousands had stayed away from other college games to watch the contest on TV, NCAA director of public relations Wiles Hallock claimed: "The benefits . . . had overweighed the disadvantages and the damages . . . [and] had served college football well, and the NCAA with it."[23] The 1966 game was remembered for years for the dramatic decision to run out the clock and preserve a tie, but it was also recognized for its impact on NCAA TV policy. ABC's Beano Cook looked back at the game nearly a decade later: "I believe that when Notre Dame is involved in a game for the national title attendance will suffer," Cook recalled, "yet, I be-lieve that only the 1966 game between Notre Dame and Michigan State hurt attendance."[24]

ABC kept up its campaign for greater flexibility and won some con-cessions from the NCAA. "Please don't legislate us into a decline in rat-ings," Roone Arledge kept appealing to NCAA leaders.[25] William Flynn, chair of the NCAA Television Committee, agreed: "The network feels that our rules are far too restrictive and create a great burden on them to produce a good NCAA TV football program."[26] However, as increas-ing NCAA and individual school revenues began to outweigh the threat to gate attendance by TV, the NCAA gradually relaxed its rigid control over its telecasts. ABC was given greater control over choosing teams and was able to decide on telecasts as the season progressed rather than determining the schedule of televised games before the season began. The number of appearances for individual teams kept increasing so that the best teams could be seen more often. Moving games to different times and days also made some headway for network telecasts. The number of ads during each game was increased significantly, and networks were eventually allowed to advertise alcoholic beverages during games. Cig-arettes continued to be advertised in game telecasts until they were fi-nally banned from all of television. One of the longest-standing restric-tions, however, was the NCAA's opposition to professional football players, such as O. J. Simpson, being used in ads shown on NCAA tele-casts.[27]

By the mid-1960s, ABC was the darling of the NCAA, for it did not telecast professional football, a major competitor, the NCAA believed, to college football. When NBC picked up the new American Football League television contract to join CBS and the NFL in telecasting pro-fessional football, ABC was left to telecast college football exclusively. After two-year stints with CBS and then NBC after 1962, the NCAA decided in 1966 to offer ABC the contract without entertaining other competitive bids. The NCAA angered NBC by refusing it the common courtesy of a chance at renewal. However, the NCAA-ABC marriage, which lasted until 1984, nearly had a divorce in the late 1960s as ABC made its decision to enter professional football.

Both Roone Arledge and Pete Rozelle were considering prime-time football telecasts in the mid-1960s, Arledge for ABC and Rozelle for the NFL. The NCAA knew that the NFL and AFL wanted to "maximize exposure and income." Competing for the same TV dollars, the NCAA knew that the pros had been considering telecasting on Monday and Thursday nights as early as 1964. At that time, though, ABC had not wanted to disturb its Monday night programs, *Ben Casey, Cheyenne,* and *The Rifleman,* nor had it wanted to change its winner on Thursday nights, *The Untouchables.*[28] Three years later, though, Arledge urged the NCAA Television Committee to take the lead in bringing about prime-time games for a new two-year deal in 1968. "We feel that in the future," Arledge told the committee, "sports attractions in prime time will become increasingly popular," but the NCAA rejected the suggestion.[29] In the meantime, Pete Rozelle was putting out feelers to see if a major network would consider disrupting its Monday night prime-time shows to put NFL football in their place. Walter Byers, in one of his worst moments of speculation, believed that "a good movie will do better" than Monday night football.[30]

The lingering 1970 ABC-NCAA contract talks and Rozelle's desire for *Monday Night Football* came to a head in 1969. ABC was unwilling to meet the NCAA's demand of $13 million for the next contract, yet ABC needed college football to keep its affiliate stations from jumping to other networks. A major threat to ABC at the time was the upstart Hughes Sports Network, which seemed ready to enter major sports telecasting and take several ABC affiliates with it.[31] In the meantime, the merger of the NFL and AFL was progressing and the NFL's desire for expanding pro football telecasts was increasing. Carl Lindemann of NBC Sports, in its continuing war with other networks, contacted Walter Byers of the NCAA, raising the question of the NCAA's reaction to prime-time football "if ABC aggressively participates in the pro football situation . . . since neither CBS nor NBC has evinced any interest."[32]

The NCAA obviously did not want its collegiate football network, ABC, to join the other two major networks that had already been "tainted" with the professional game. ABC leaders were not overly enthralled with the idea of losing their prime-time Monday night programming, but if the Hughes Sports Network bid on night games, ABC's prime-time affiliate stations might abandon ABC and make the network even weaker. ABC, knowing that it could get a good bargain on rights to telecast the NFL on Monday evenings, chose to counter Hughes, making a successful bid of $8.5 million for a thirteen-game season.[33] The NCAA then had no other viable commercial choice but to deal with a network that was carrying professional football, so ABC continued as the network of college football.

The outward appearance of a love affair between ABC and the NCAA from the 1960s to the 1980s masked volatile discord over telecasting contracts and procedures. This internal warfare, seen generally only by insiders, usually pit the surly and forceful Walter Byers against the opportunistic and cunning Roone Arledge. The conflict between the most powerful person in amateur sport and the leader of sports telecasting became even more heated after ABC had teamed up with the NFL to telecast *Monday Night Football*.[34] According to ABC's Jim Spence, the NCAA believed the NFL "was *the enemy*." Byers and the rest of the NCAA had assumed they had Arledge's word that ABC would not become involved in NFL football. When Arledge bought the Monday night package, Byers insisted that ABC's *Monday Night Football* never be mentioned on ABC's college telecasts.[35] So strong was the bias against pro football that, just as it had done with NBC, the NCAA Television Committee voted to request that ABC not even promote its own NCAA games on *Monday Night Football*.[36]

Contract negotiations between ABC and the NCAA, especially between Arledge and Byers, became skirmishes upon which legends were built. ABC would invariably bring the crying towel to the negotiating table, dripping with supposed financial losses from the previous contract.[37] While there is some truth in statements that networks were losing money in sports telecasting, it would be more accurate to say that if sports were not beneficial in terms of both prestige and money, networks would not continue to spend millions in their contracts with sports leagues or the NCAA. Because networks cannot, owing to antitrust laws, control all of the stations through which they telecast, they must contract with affiliate stations to carry their signal. Affiliate stations demand sports, because their viewers insist on viewing contests and because local advertising on sports events helps produce profits for the stations. Byers and the NCAA Television Committee knew this. They also knew that the profit and loss statements they were shown were shams.

Contract negotiations took place only with ABC in the 1970s. In the contract bargaining for the 1970 ABC-NCAA football contract, Byers felt sure there was enough affiliate pressure on ABC that the network would pay $12 million. Arledge claimed that ABC would lose money if he had to pay over $10 million. "The negotiations are so damned sensitive, so damned bitter," claimed Arledge, "it seems everybody's out for the jugular vein. . . . Statesmen don't exist, especially not in amateur sports."[38] ABC's Beano Cook, observing the contract talks and the battle between Arledge and Byers, called it the "Roone and Walt duel."[39] Byers was such a formidable television negotiator that the NCAA Television Committee generally let him do the negotiating while they looked on—often in admiration, sometimes in horror. In the 1977 rights negotiations, for instance, Byers was determined that a cost-of-living adjustment (COLA) be written into the contract with ABC, as inflation had soared during most of the 1970s. Arledge fought the COLA to the end. In those negotiations, Arledge agreed to $29 million for the first two years and $30 million for the final two years of a four-year contract. Everyone in the tense negotiating room seemed to relax, except for Byers. "And the cost-of-living clause?" Byers prodded. Arledge paused and then said "OK." That clause, probably won solely by the feisty Byers, ended up being worth and extra $2,000,000 to the NCAA.[40]

The battles continued until the last NCAA-ABC contract had been drawn up in 1981, an agreement that was later voided by the U.S. Supreme Court. Jim Spence was then the chief negotiator for ABC and had to face Walter Byers before reporting to Roone Arledge. Spence described Byers as "the loner, austere, very bright, calculating . . . a dictator, and not always a benevolent one."[41] By 1981, the NCAA was in a power struggle with the College Football Association, which had been formed in the mid-1970s by big-time football powers and represented a commercial move to put television revenues in the hands of Division I power schools rather than dividing the money among all NCAA members. The CFA was therefore in the process of creating its own television network as a way of controlling television money. Byers was probably even more intent on wringing the last dollar out of ABC because he wanted to keep as many big-time schools in the NCAA contract as possible. The NCAA had determined to increase football coverage by providing Saturday coverage between two networks—ABC and most likely CBS—but first, Byers had to get a contract with ABC.[42]

After three decades of TV negotiations, contract language as well as the legal staff of both ABC and the NCAA had multiplied greatly. Negotiations in 1981 took place first in Columbus, Ohio, then in San Fran-

cisco, Kansas City, and Denver, before final signatures were attached to
the document in Newport, Rhode Island. The Denver meeting took place
as the formal negotiating period was about to expire, and both sides had
agreed that by midnight on the final day in Denver there would or would
not be a contract. With only minutes to go, Byers was still arguing with
Spence and his second in command, Charlie Lavery. Byers, questioning the veracity of one of Lavery's statements about a previous verbal
agreement, jumped up, stuck a finger in Lavery's face, and nearly created
a brawl with the former Virginia Military Institute running back. Byers,
who himself had been the smallest lineman on the Rice University varsity team four decades before, might have had his last negotiations right
there if things had escalated. The verbal (luckily not physical) battle continued until Spence went to his hotel room to telephone Arledge. By the
time he returned, midnight had passed and Byers was gone.[43]

Though the contract time limit had passed, there was the Denver proposal for a four-year deal for $131,750,000, which both sides agreed to
discuss in Newport, Rhode Island. As the discussion came to a close,
Spence asked Byers if the NCAA would knock off $250,000 from the
final offer, hoping to get a small concession that he could take back to
Arledge. "Walter," Spence asked, "if ABC Sports will commit one hundred and thirty-one and a half million dollars, do we have a deal?" Byers
answered: "You know the number. The number is one thirty-one seven
fifty!" Spence later reported that he looked around the room at the
NCAA committee members, who, with their steely silence, appeared to
be saying "For God's sake, Walter, give it to him. Don't be such a hard-
ass." Byers, as he was wont to do, refused. Spence recollected: "There
would be not one single crumb for me to take back to New York. Strike
one for the cowboy from Kansas City. . . . He had once again stuck it to
the television hotshots from New York."[44]

The rocky partnership between Walter Byers's NCAA and Roone
Arledge's ABC had lasted about two decades. Throughout that time, in
addition haggling over the matter of contract amounts, NCAA leaders
and network executives also debated the question of what should be advertised and how the image of the NCAA and its institutions should be
portrayed. At issue was the problem of whether to advertise such questionable products as tobacco and alcohol. The discussions over advertising alcohol resulted in major controversies in the 1970s, one of which
was the Ohio State Beer Hall incident.

17 Advertising, Image versus Money, and the Beer Hall Incident

BY THE TIME ABC began telecasting college football, institutions of higher learning and their intercollegiate athletic teams had been open to advertising by commercial concerns for over a century. The first crew contest between Harvard and Yale, nearly a decade before the Civil War, had come about when a railroad company paid both schools to row at Lake Winnipesaukee to attract attention and advertise its new railway servicing the New Hampshire vacation site.[1] The image of college students being used to advertise a commercial venture was not likely favorably viewed by either Harvard or Yale administrators. Colleges were educational institutions foremost, not, as they became a century and a half later, the arms of corporate America. In 1852 there were many individual benefactors of colleges, but these supporters lacked the corporate dominance that companies such as Hewlett-Packard, Pepsi-Cola, or Nike enjoyed at the beginning of the twenty-first century. Despite little support or approval of nineteenth-century college administrations, companies continued to sponsor college teams to attract business.

Since institutions of higher education generally refused to bring athletics under the academic model and support teams with the general college budget, sports remained far more prone to develop commercially than did other areas under the auspices of the colleges. Despite college athletics' being peripheral to the educational goals of the colleges, they produced both negative and positive images of higher education itself. From an early time, college regattas held at the commercialized horse-racing and betting mecca at Saratoga Lake in New York brought questionable reputations to the participating colleges while at the same time giving welcome publicity to the participants. The situation was similar for elite Eastern colleges that played football on Thanksgiving Day in New York City: although national publicity brought recognition to institutions such as Princeton and Yale, students acting in undignified ways at those events brought embarrassment to the colleges.[2]

Once radio and television came on the scene in the twentieth century, the commercialism intensified and advertising began to have a greater

impact on the image of the institution. The fact that the media was ben-
efiting financially by selling college sports to business concerns never
seemed to be a problem in free enterprise America. On the other hand,
colleges could not accept money from the media for certain advertisements without creating problems, even if those in athletics would have
gratefully accepted the money. Colleges had an image to preserve, or at
least attempt to preserve, an image that made certain kinds of advertising taboo. Colleges feared the public would get the wrong impression if
their radio broadcasts or television programs carried advertisements
about habit-forming drugs, patent medicines, laxatives, feminine hygiene products, political organizations of any kind, or controversial organizations.[3] Two of the most controversial products were alcohol and
tobacco.

The advertising of tobacco products, unlike that of alcohol, was popular in colleges during the 1920s, when college football broadcasts were
first conducted. Alcohol ads became a moot question. Prohibition followed World War I and continued into the Depression years, so the legal
production and sale of alcohol was not tenable. Tobacco, however, was
an acceptable drug dating back to colonial times. The advertising of tobacco products was a common practice in football game programs and
would soon enter commercial broadcasting. The concern that tobacco
harmed athletes' conditioning as well as the health of other young
people was a major drawback in accepting tobacco money to sponsor
games, even in the 1920s. Notre Dame, for example, had a pre–World
War II policy banning advertising for not only patent medicines, laxatives, and alcoholic beverage but also cigarettes. Illinois had a similar
practice.[4] In the tobacco-growing area of the South, there were different
priorities during the prewar radio broadcasting era. In a discussion of
commercial sponsors for University of North Carolina football, an athletic advisory committee opposed such "harmful products" as alcohol
and proprietary medicines but emphasized that "tobacco should not be
considered in this category."[5]

There was a divided policy on tobacco advertising following World
War II, but tobacco radio advertising during college football games became more common. When Duke University started a football broadcasting network, Chesterfield Cigarettes, made by Liggett and Myers of
Durham, North Carolina, became its principal advertiser.[6] Liggett and
Myers also sponsored televised Big 10 and Notre Dame regional games
in the mid-1950s, under a policy sanctioned by the NCAA that dis-

allowed alcohol ads but yielded to tobacco advertising.[7] The NCAA policy was challenged in the 1960s, when research began to confirm harmful effects from the use of tobacco.[8]

In the midst of the controversial Vietnam War, civil rights battles, and the feminist movement of the 1960s came the first major clash on tobacco use. Just as the inflation caused by involvement in the Vietnam War was beginning to have a negative impact on the cost of running athletics programs, a major source of revenue from TV advertising came under attack by some within the NCAA, governmental officials, and organizations such as the American Cancer Society. Walter Byers, NCAA executive director, may have been one of the first in the movement. He urged the NCAA Television Committee to bar smoking advertisements because he believed there was a greater public awareness of the hazards of smoking, but he was voted down 8-2 by the committee. At the same time, some committee members were attempting to remove the ban on alcohol advertising to increase revenues.[9]

Following an NCAA-ABC contract that allowed the continuance of cigarette advertising for 1968 and 1969, Senators Robert Kennedy and Warren Magnuson and the American Cancer Society asked the NCAA to ban cigarette advertising from college football. Kennedy used the argument that since millions of young people viewed college football, by refusing to advertise cigarettes the NCAA would be setting a good example for the youth of America. The American Cancer Society called on the NCAA as an educational body to "fight this scourge" by removing the advertising. Marcus Plant, NCAA president from the University of Michigan, joined Byers in an unsuccessful attempt to remove this moneymaker from the ABC contract. Plant, a lawyer and significant individual in the history of the NCAA, told Senator Kennedy that he would "use every influence possible to reduce and ultimately eliminate the appearance of such advertising on our programs."[10] The Michigan law professor spoke out so strongly that the R. J. Reynold's Tobacco Company did not renew its sponsorship of the NCAA TV football plan the following year. This obviously angered ABC officials, who then began a fervent campaign to authorize beer sponsorship in order to replace the loss of tobacco advertising.[11]

Within a short time, the federal government came to the aid of those who opposed cigarette advertising. Congress, in 1970, banned cigarette advertising on television beginning on January 2, 1971. Why January 2? Colleges were participating in the major football bowls on New Years Day, and Congress did not want to draw any more fire from the tobacco

industry or hurt the financial take of the bowl games by limiting cigarette advertising for that event. To add to the irony—or, rather, the
hypocrisy—of the situation, the NCAA Television Committee, by a 6-4
vote, decided to allow cigarette advertising for the Fall 1970 season even
though members knew that the federal cigarette ban had been voted to
begin the next January. The committee also voted unanimously to lift restrictions on beer advertising during the game telecasts. Both actions
were taken to appease Roone Arledge and ABC, which had sold only
about three-quarters of the ads for the football series and was about to
lose several million dollars in its NCAA contract.[12] With the negative
image tobacco was quickly gaining, the NCAA moved to accommodate
its football contract by instead casting alcohol advertising in a more positive light.

The negative image of alcohol in education had kept ads for alcoholic
beverages off the airwaves for a lengthy period of time. In a 1936 survey
by the *New York Times,* about two-thirds of schools permitting broadcasts sold their rights commercially, but none, apparently, allowed advertising for alcoholic beverages.[13] For instance, Yale, when it gained an
extraordinarily large sum for its football broadcasts, banned liquor ads.[14]
It was one thing to allow Humble Oil Company or Coca-Cola to sponsor
a game, but it was another to allow the Pabst Blue Ribbon brewery to represent college football to the public. It was even more acceptable to sell
a carton of Camel cigarettes than a case of Budwiser beer. So strong was
antiliquor sentiment in the United States that ten bills were introduced
into Congress from 1934 to 1942 to prohibit liquor advertising on air.
None passed, but the National Association of Broadcasters decided to
ban radio ads for alcohol during World War II.[15]

When television came to American sports in 1939, with the shaky
telecast of the Princeton-Columbia contest, a precedent was set against
the advertising of alcohol over the air. Though commercial television remained unimportant until after World War II, with the rapid growth of
commercial television by the early 1950s, television sports advertising
changed. According to broadcaster Red Barber: "Wheaties dropped out
of it, and, by and large, beer took over."[16] That might have been true of
professional sports, but at the college level there was near unanimous
opposition to advertising alcoholic beverages in 1950. For instance, the
two leading universities in telecasting college football in 1950, Notre
Dame and the University of Pennsylvania, had strict policies. Before
World War II, Notre Dame rejected all ads "not in good taste," including alcoholic beverages. President Harold Stassen of the University of

Pennsylvania advocated no liquor advertising or other products "detrimental to American youth."[17]

The ban on alcohol advertisements continued when the NCAA took control of football telecasts in 1951. That year, Westinghouse Electric Corporation bought the entire rights to NCAA football for $679,800, outbidding two networks, NBC and Du Mont, and two other corporations, Chevrolet and Atlantic Richfield.[18] Therefore Westinghouse Electric of Pittsburgh, not Iron City Beer, provided the advertising pitch. A decade and a half later, there were still no beer ads on Saturday afternoon football telecasts. Yet an exception occurred when the American Football Coaches Association allowed beer commercials in the telecasting of its Coaches All-American Game in Atlanta in 1966.[19] The next year, Tom Hamilton of the NCAA Television Committee suggested that the TV contract allow beer ads in pregame and postgame shows as well as during the game. He withdrew his motion when two Southerners claimed that alcohol ads would be offensive to their section of the country.[20] The new NCAA TV plan would continue to ban all alcoholic beverages, including "intoxicating malt beverages."[21] The NCAA argument was that it should meet the "high standards [for] dignified presentations" and thus make college football "an integral part of the educational program."[22] The NCAA was never shy about making lofty presentations to give the appearance that its institutions were educationally motivated in spite of its clearly demonstrated commercial emphasis.

ABC, the carrying network, however, wanted the greater revenue that could be produced by the beer advertisers. At the time, 10 percent of all TV advertising revenues came from beer ads. The network argued that it was not receiving any of this potential income.[23] ABC asked the NCAA to allow pregame and postgame beer advertising as a one-year experiment to test the reaction of both TV viewers and the NCAA membership. In the spring of 1968, shortly after North Vietnam's successful Tet offensive against South Vietnam and further chaos in the American political scene with the assassination of Martin Luther King, Jr., the NCAA Television Committee agreed with ABC and began negotiating. The committee suggested that no more than 50 percent of the pregame and postgame commercials be related to beer and that the beer commercials must be preceded with the announcement that the ads "originate *away* from the campus and stadium," supposedly distancing beer ads from the university setting. Furthermore, to attempt to protect the image of the NCAA, the beer commercials "must be well removed in time from the on-screen display of the NCAA seal."[24] Nevertheless, strong negative reactions to beer commercials still came from the NCAA council, led by executive director Walter Byers, and beer advertising was delayed for another year.[25]

Financial problems at ABC Sports, though, made the network put pressure on the NCAA to change its antialcohol policy. ABC had paid nearly 25 percent more for its 1968 contract—$10.2 million as opposed to $7.8 million the previous year. It claimed a financial loss of $2 million in the fall of 1968.[26] If, indeed, ABC was losing money on college football telecasts, the trend could have telling effects upon NCAA football, already suffering under the fear that professional football was outstripping the college game. Not only was the NFL getting about 25 percent more for each minute of advertising than college games could command, but the NFL was also about to expand to Monday night telecasts.[27]

A synergy resulted, as ABC wanted beer advertising revenues and NCAA member institutions wanted to obtain larger TV revenues in the future. The moral high ground finally gave way to financial incentive. In a move analogous to states' removing moral restraints during the Depression by allowing pari-mutuel betting at horse races and then taxing those bets, the NCAA in 1969 decided to remove its moral stance against alcoholic advertising.[28] By the spring of 1969, the new contract negotiations with the TV networks called for beer advertising, allowing one beer ad during the game following the statement: "We return to the studio for this message."[29] Thus the NCAA could claim a distance from the questionable beer ads even while it had the smell of hops on its breath.

Almost immediately, ABC called for fewer restrictions on the number of beer ads and their placement within each telecast, and the NCAA Television Committee voted overwhelmingly to comply with ABC's wish.[30] By the early 1970s, Miller Brewing Company was allowed to purchase a special halftime feature for each ABC telecast, with no opposition from the committee.[31] A half-decade later ABC convinced the NCAA Television Committee to permit three sixty-second beer ads in each telecast to prevent a potentially negative "economic impact" on NCAA income.[32] By the time the final NCAA TV contract with ABC and CBS was drawn up in the early 1980s, the number of beer ads had grown to four and one-half minutes because of what the NCAA claimed were "economic realities."[33]

There were a few individuals, such as Arkansas football coach Lou Holtz, who tried to get the NCAA to reverse its new alcohol policy.[34] Resolutions condemning beer ads continued to be presented, but never passed, at the annual NCAA convention. At the end of the 1975 football season, the president of Samford University in Birmingham, Alabama (a Baptist institution), wrote specifically to Ohio State President Harold Enarson asking for his assistance in prohibiting alcohol advertising on NCAA-sponsored telecasts.[35] There is no evidence that Enarson accepted the moral argument or even replied to the request. Yet, when Enarson claimed that an ABC telecast on drinking at his institution reflected poorly on his university, he spoke out with vitriol against the negative image of higher education that ABC was producing.

When the controversy over what came to be known as the Ohio State beer hall incident erupted, the NCAA Television Committee was arguing that any "'referendum on morality' could be very damaging to the economic viability of the NCAA television income."[36] The year 1976 was similar to other college football telecast years in that the NCAA had long since bought into the commercial realm in the interest of its so-called educational function. The NCAA expected only good publicity for higher education, expecting to gain prestige as its student-athletes fought out Saturday gridiron contests for the glory of alma mater and in the name of amateur athletics. Written into television contracts was the statement that the network should add to the dignity of NCAA football by "representing college football as an integral part of the educational program."[37]

In early October 1976, the University of California, Los Angeles, ranked number two in the nation, traveled to Columbus, Ohio, to meet coach Woody Hayes's Ohio State Buckeyes. ABC was in Columbus prior to the national telecast, and producers of the pregame program decided to catch the local flavor of Ohio State students. ABC chose a local beer hall in the middle of the week before the UCLA contest. ABC's Jim Lampley, a recent graduate of the University of North Carolina, had been hired by Roone Arledge as a "youngish, rah-rah type of announcer" to provide sideline color at the games.[38] Being little older than the Ohio State students himself, Lampley reported on the Thursday night beer-drinking students to "capture the mood or pulse-beat" of the Ohio State students. The two and a half minute spot on the pregame show featured indecorous beer-drinking students and ended with announcer Bill Flemming stating: "Well, that's how some of the students spent their Thursday night prior to a big game in Columbus, Ohio."[39]

President Harold Enarson of Ohio State appeared furious and wrote a harsh letter to Elton Rule, President of ABC. "ABC Sports has done it again," Enarson wrote contemptuously. The Ohio State president believed that the year before, Jim Lampley had featured UCLA women as if UCLA were a "farm club" for Playboy centerfolds. Now, Enarson argued, Lampley was making the 55,000 Ohio State students appear to be "football-crazy beer drinkers."[40] Enarson caught ABC just as it attained its new $18 million contract for NCAA football. It was the same season that college football telecasts reached the highest Nielsen rating they had ever attained, 14.1, and as a result ABC executives might have displayed a slight arrogance. (The ABC ratings, however, would deteriorate to under 10 in less than a decade.) Roone Arledge, head of ABC Sports, responded to Enarson, lecturing Enarson that he had "over reacted to what we presented."[41]

In the short run, Enarson, with NCAA backing, may have been successful in forcing ABC television to glorify colleges by showing only positive depictions of football institutions.[42] Yet he did little to raise the moral standard of advertising on TV or to diminish the negative effects of alcohol consumption, which he and the NCAA policy continued to promote through advertising. Strong antidrug programs began in that decade, but few of the NCAA representatives were willing to recognize that alcohol was the most destructive drug in the United States. A resolution was brought to the NCAA convention floor not long after the 1976 beer hall incident. The lengthy resolution began: "Whereas . . . the number one drug problem in the United States . . . is the drug alcohol" and ended with "Now, Therefore, Be It Resolved, that the NCAA Television Committee be directed to cease its present practice and . . . eliminate in its next contracts with television networks the promotion of the drug, alcohol, on NCAA telecasts."[43]

The resolution's backers believed the NCAA "should be honest about its stand on drugs," eliminate the hypocrisy in its TV advertising actions, and revert to an earlier policy. Despite his earlier fervor, there is no evidence that President Enarson took the high ground on this issue and supported the antialcohol resolution. A member of the TV committee spoke against the resolution at the convention, noting that beer and wine advertising had brought to member institutions, including Ohio State, a total of $3,954,545 from football TV advertising the previous year and additional $648,571 from the basketball championship TV revenues. The NCAA voted down the antialcohol resolution.[44]

The Ohio State University beer hall incident was symbolic of the paradoxes and hypocrisies in the advertising policies of intercollegiate athletics. The last NCAA TV football contract was signed for the 1982–85 seasons, just prior to its being voided as an antitrust violation.[45]

In that contract, allowances for beer and wine advertising were increased, not diminished.[46] The "economic realities" of NCAA advertising policies, as Walter Byers called them, were really sanctioned by university presidents. The NCAA was largely directed by presidents of member institutions, such as Harold Enarson. Presidents, nearly universally, personally appointed the faculty representatives who voted at NCAA meetings, and thus those representatives generally represented the presidents, not the faculties. This was another confirmation that college presidents had accepted the commercial model, using commercial telecasts in an attempt to raise the image of their own institutions. Enarson was caught in his own contradiction. He was representative of those who had chosen to use commercial television rather than educational television for the promotion of institutional prestige, yet he was among the first to criticize the commercial medium when the image of his own institution was tarnished.[47]

Presidents, such as Ohio State's Enarson, clearly favored the commercial athletic model just as long as the telecasts paid the athletic bills and positive things were said about their own institutions. That certain aspects of the commercialization of football, specifically alcohol advertising, improved the quality of higher education is debatable. What is less debatable is that presidential hypocrisy occurred over the issue of commercialism in the name of supposed educational outcomes. Over two decades later, the issue of alcohol advertising had still not entirely gone away. On his retirement as coach of the famed University of North Carolina basketball team in 1997, Dean Smith declared that it was hypocritical for college athletics "to have student-athletes tell young people they should say no to drugs when we say yes to beer ads."[48] Though controversy over advertising would continue, there was little question that the money from advertising strengthened the policy of promoting the business of athletics over educational values. An important part of the business of promoting came from the television announcers.

 ## The Television Announcer's Role in Football Promotion

RADIO AND television announcers for college athletics played the publicity game much as did college presidents—principally glorifying the positive aspects of the game and ignoring the negative ones. College football often was thought to be the apex for an announcer's career. The college game, after all, was played by amateur student-athletes on bucolic Saturday afternoons among teams of friendly strife. Announcers, first on radio and then on television, were expected to depict that scene. For the most part, the golden voices did just that. From Bill Stern to Lindsey Nelson to Keith Jackson, the announcers promoted a rosy picture of college sport to a receptive American public.

Bill Stern began his career in broadcasting when he was allowed to do two minutes of a football game on the radio with Graham McNamee in 1935.[1] Stern's smooth voice, chatty presence, and knack for pulling out the right anecdote were far more suited to radio than television. Stern also appeared more interested in telling a good story than in precise reporting, something more favorably received in radio, where listeners could not see if Stern was accurately describing the game. Rising rapidly with NBC from the mid-1930s, Stern was chosen to do a running commentary when NBC telecast the first baseball game in the spring of 1939, and he was also assigned to the initial football contest the following fall. Stern and NBC practiced for the first intercollegiate football telecast during two scrimmages, one at Fordham College and the other at Long Island University. The results were promising.[2]

The initial football telecast with Stern in the announcer's chair was between Fordham and Waynesburg College of Pennsylvania on September 30, 1939. A newspaper account waxed eloquently about the sharpness of the picture, questioning why a viewer would leave the comfort of the home "to watch a gridiron battle in a sea of mud on a chilly autumnal afternoon." Stern, according to this account, was "calm and factual." There was "nothing emotional about his tongue" and the "excitement is left to the audience."[3] There is stronger evidence, however, that Stern was seldom calm and often stretched the facts to fit his needs.

Stern may have been quieter than usual during his first football telecast, but he was generally anything but nonemotional. According to broadcast historian Ray Poindexter, Stern's "glib, dramatic style would be a vocal trademark for a long time."[4] Confirming this assessment is a story told by announcer Harold Grams, who was broadcasting a game at Evanston between Illinois and Northwestern. In the booth next to Grams was Ted Husing for CBS, and next to him was Bill Stern of NBC. Husing was yelling so loudly into his microphone that his voice penetrated Grams's booth. After the game Husing apologized to Grams: "I had to talk as loud as I did because I had that Bill Stern on the other side of me, and I couldn't let his voice feed into my microphone."[5] Besides being loud, Stern's factual faux pas were legendary. In a Notre Dame–Army game, after the military academy had kicked off and Terry Brennan received the ball, Stern mistakenly said that Emil Sitko had received it. When Stern realized his mistake and saw that Brennan was about to score, he yelled: "Sitko laterals to Terry Brennan who goes for the touchdown."[6] Sterns did the same thing in another game, saying Army's legendary Doc Blanchard had lateraled to Glenn Davis. Famed horse-race announcer Clem McCarthy advised Stern not to take up announcing horse races: "Remember, Bill you can't lateral a horse."[7]

Stern's television firsts did not lead to a high-profile career in telecasting, and he returned to radio announcing, where he was more comfortable. He led NBC, rivaling CBS's Ted Husing as the nation's leading sportscaster in the 1940s.[8] Apart from his mistakes, which were more apparent on television, Stern was like a number of announcers who tried to move from radio to television. According to historian Mary O'Connell, the radio men were used to talking a lot and "they refused to subjugate themselves to pictures which told the story better than their words. They wanted to remain the stars they had been in radio."[9]

Like Stern, Lindsey Nelson began his career in radio. But unlike Stern, Nelson achieved great success in the television booth. As a boy in rural Columbia, Tennessee, he had become interested in radio and sport by listening to the legendary Graham McNamee and Ted Husing broadcasting big games in the East—Yale, Harvard, Columbia, and Army. Hearing Graham McNamee's 1927 description of the second ("long-count") Jack Dempsey–Gene Tunney heavyweight championship from Chicago's Soldier Field and eavesdropping on Lou Gehrig's World Series exploits while in his high school history class added to Nelson's determination to become involved in radio.[10] Nelson attended the University of Tennessee during the late 1930s, where he worked with local broadcasters as a spotter and he observed both Ted Husing and Bill Stern as they broadcast Tennessee games. Stern asked Nelson to help out as a spotter for Tennessee's undefeated and unscored-upon team in the 1939 Rose Bowl game. Following the game, Stern gave Nelson his spotter's board, used to identify players' numbers. It consisted of two pieces of soft wood, cut into boards about one foot by six inches, on which material such as the line-up could be tacked. Stern was pleased with Nelson's performance and told him, "You are my idea of the best spotter in the U.S."[11]

Within a decade, Lindsey Nelson had set up the "Vol Network" under Tennessee football coach General Robert Neyland. That was somewhat surprising, since Nelson's first encounter with Neyland had nearly been his last. As an undergraduate, Neyland had worked as a stringer for the Knoxville *Journal,* obtaining information on the upcoming Alabama game that could be beneficial to its major rival. The autocratic Neyland demanded that Nelson report to his office, and the first words out of the general's mouth were "Nelson, I'm gonna hang you by the balls!" Damaging information being passed around by people in the media was dangerous to Tennessee football, Neyland told him, and it was to stop.[12] Neyland "got my complete attention," Nelson remembered, and he learned a valuable lesson in media survival as he moved on to an outstanding career in announcing.

Nelson made his name in radio during the postwar years before moving into television. He broadcast local Tennessee games for several years and gained national exposure broadcasting for Gordon McLendon, who had built up a multistation network specializing in sports programming.[13] Nelson did live broadcasts and re-creations of contemporary and historic contests, becoming McLendon's leading voice. NBC hired Nelson in 1952, after the famed Tom Gallery moved from Du Mont to become NBC's director of sports. (This was also just before NBC gained rights to the NCAA football series.) Nelson was given the task not of announcing but of supervising the NCAA telecasts. While Nelson directed, Mel Allen, who had formerly done Notre Dame telecasts for the Du Mont Television Network, provided play-by-play for NBC's first season of NCAA football telecasts. Allen was paid $750 per game, while Bill Henry of the *Los Angeles Times,* color commentator at a number of Rose Bowls, was paid $1000 per game to provide commentary.[14]

During this season, NBC discovered the commercial need for game officials to call timeouts for specific time limits so that General Motors could get in its allotment of advertisements. The NCAA Television Committee cooperated, devising a system in which a man on the sidelines with a red hat and white gloves would signal the white-capped referee when play could be resumed following the timeout.[15] Nelson was a savvy producer, who was able to control the ads himself. During a Notre Dame game, he chose not to cut to a commercial after being told to do so. When the NBC game director called to "cue the commercial," Nelson declined. When given the order in stronger language to cut to the commercial, Nelson again refused, reasoning that "one does not cut to a commercial in the middle of 'Cheer, Cheer, for Old Notre Dame.'"[16] He was right. Early in his career, Nelson discovered the power of Irish football.

Despite his success in directing and producing football telecasts,

Lindsey Nelson yearned to be a sportscaster. Following his first season with NBC, a meeting was called with General Motors, the NCAA football sponsor, to discuss possible color announcers to accompany Mel Allen's play-by-play. Lindsey Nelson's name was suggested, and Nelson very willingly moved from producer to color man. He even had the opportunity to be the play-by-play announcer for a regional game with Bill Munday, who had done the "Wrong-Way Roy Riegels" Rose Bowl of 1929 with Graham McNamee but later succumbed to alcoholism. Nelson was on his way to doing what he wanted, and he eventually became the leading sports telecaster of his day.[17] His career in NCAA telecasting, though, was delayed a year when ABC gained rights for the 1954 season, during which Jack Drees and Tom Harmon did the telecasts. That was, as has been noted, a financially disastrous year for ABC. Yet ABC's loss became fortunate for Nelson and NBC.

The next year, when NBC regained the rights, Lindsey Nelson became the head announcer, but before that he had been asked to do the Cotton Bowl game at the end of the 1954 season. NBC had the Cotton Bowl contract that year for the Alabama-Rice game in Dallas. Seated along side Nelson as color man for the event was Red Grange, the great Illinois runner from the twenties. Grange, who had been doing broadcasting since the 1930s, was chosen by Tom Gallery to assist the youthful Nelson. It was the start of one of the great TV partnerships, Nelson and Grange, who would share the announcer's booth for the next five years. The night before the Alabama-Rice game, the two were discussing improbable actions that might occur on the field. Grange asked Nelson if he knew the ruling if anyone came off the bench to make a tackle. Nelson did not. Grange declared that this was one of few cases in which points might be awarded for the infraction rather than having yards penalized. The following day, after Rice had recovered a fumble by Alabama's Bart Starr, Dickie Moegle took a handoff and raced up the sideline going for a touchdown. To the announcers' amazement, as Moegle ran in front of the Alabama bench, Tommy Lewis jumped onto the field to down him. Nelson quickly announced that if, in the judgment of the referee, the runner would have scored, the officials could grant him a touchdown. Just then, the referee raised his arms upwards—a score for Nelson in his first national telecast. Within a month, Red Grange sent a copy of his new autobiography to Nelson with the inscription: "You are the first guy who knows the rules."[18]

The insightful Red Grange was a fine partner to the eloquent Lindsey Nelson. Grange had worked for CBS radio in the 1930s, earning the princely sum of $7,000 in 1937 for doing three weekly shows during the football season. Soon after World War II, Grange did both play-by-play and color duties. He teamed with Chicago's Bob Elson in telecasting Big 10 and Notre Dame football games in 1947, as well as working Chicago Bear games. He was low-keyed, unlike many announcers of his time, gaining a reputation for sound analysis.[19] Nelson had almost a reverence for Grange's work and said that "no more modest hero than Red Grange ever lived."[20] Their teamwork resulted in NCAA Football receiving the *Look* magazine sports award, which was presented on Ed Sullivan's *Toast of the Town* show after the 1956 season.[21] The NCAA Television Committee was ecstatic over the Nelson-Grange team, and they continued using the duo until Ed Scherick and ABC pulled off a trick in 1960, purchasing the NCAA football package away from unsuspecting NBC. Though ABC soon hired Curt Gowdy and Paul Christman to do the games, Nelson was honored by his colleagues, who voted him the top sports broadcaster that year.[22] The five years with Grange was the longest Nelson ever worked with one analyst.

Red Grange was finished with NCAA national football telecasts after 1960, but Lindsey Nelson was not. When CBS acquired the NCAA rights in 1962, Nelson once again was asked to do the play-by-play, this time with analyst Terry Brennan, the former coach of Notre Dame. Two years later, when NBC bought the series, Nelson followed the rights. With the next contract, won by ABC, the NCAA put pressure on Roone Arledge to retain Nelson, but Arledge had signed Chris Schenkel to a lucrative sports announcing contract. As college football began to recognize the increasing threat of pro football, the NCAA Television Committee felt it was important "to maintain the college image with which Lindsey Nelson has come to be closely identified."[23] The ensuing confrontation between Arledge and Jim Corbett, Louisiana State University athletic director and head of the NCAA Television Committee, was won by Arledge. Nelson was out of NCAA telecasts for the next sixteen years as ABC continued the football series.[24] In 1982 Nelson returned, when the NCAA decided to expand its television opportunities by telecasting on a split-network setup, using ABC, CBS, and the Turner Broadcasting System. Three decades after Lindsey Nelson had begun doing NCAA games with NBC, he returned to broadcasting, staying with CBS for another three years. "Lindsey Nelson," wrote William Taaffe of *Sports Illustrated*, "is the class of the CBS speakers bureau." By that time, however, a new name, Keith Jackson, had long become associated in the nation's mind with college football telecasting. Taaffe could state with his particular authority: "No one can compete with ABC's Keith Jackson and Frank Broyles."[25]

Keith Jackson, with or without Frank Broyles, was a success behind the mike just as was Lindsey Nelson, independent of Red Grange. Jackson, like Nelson, had been born on a farm in the rural South (near Carrollton, Georgia). After a stint in the Marines following World War II and a degree in political science from Washington State University, Jackson began work at KOMO-TV in Seattle while freelancing with ABC. He had assignments with ABC's *Wide World of Sports,* covered baseball's "Game of the Week, and was made the original announcer in 1970 of *Monday Night Football,* teaming up with the brash Howard Cosell and former Dallas quarterback Don Meredith. But Jackson was replaced on *Monday Night Football* after one year by Roone Arledge's favorite celebrity and former pro football star, Frank Gifford. Gifford, it appears, had been Arledge's first choice from the beginning but was tied up for a year in a CBS contract. Once free, Gifford was brought in and Jackson became expendable.[26]

The exit from *Monday Night Football* proved to be a blessing in disguise for Jackson. In 1974, Jackson was chosen by Arledge to replace Chris Schenkel as the primary NCAA football announcer. This decision was most satisfactory to the NCAA, for, just as the organization had preferred Lidsey Nelson to Schenkel eight years earlier, it preferred Jackson to Schenkel. A generation later, it was clear that the Jackson–NCAA football match had been made in gridiron heaven. Jackson's down-home folksiness combined with his nearly faultless preparedness and reluctance to criticize anything about college football endeared himself to the NCAA leadership and to many fans. Favoring the positive over the negative aspects of the game, Jackson once said that he did not "believe a 20-year old kid should be criticized for making a mistake."[27]

Jackson's own telecasting view was that the announcer should "amplify, clarify, punctuate and then get out of the way." This approach served him well for a generation, as he became the individual most closely identified with college football telecasting. Viewers could identify with the rural imagery he used to described the players and the games: "Big uglies down in the trenches," "laid a few licks on folks," "gully washer," "tail draggers," and "hay bales at the rodeo." One writer parodied Jackson's favorite expression "Whoa, Nellie, I'm gonna tell ya" with his own Jacksonian description: "When the feathers git to flyin' and they start a-knockin' heads and rubbin' the paint off their helmets, there ain't nobody more colorful in that big ol' TV booth."[28]

All of this endeared Keith Jackson to his sporting audience, but he did not exist for three decades as a leader in college football broadcasting without his share of controversy and criticism. One of the greatest controversies arose during the telecasting of the Clemson–Ohio State Gator Bowl in 1978. Ohio State was led by Woody Hayes, the 65-year-old coach with the second-best career win record among active coaches, outdone only by Bear Bryant at Alabama. Still, Hayes's 1978 team had a mediocre record of 7-3-1 and was fourth place in the Big 10 when it met Clemson. It was quite a disappointment for Hayes to be relegated to the Gator Bowl when he had made six Rose Bowl appearances in the past decade. Yet, beating seventh-ranked Clemson could be somewhat redemptive.

At a luncheon the day before the contest, Keith Jackson presented Hayes with a pair of boxing gloves, the Gator Bowl's idea of a joke based on the coach's pugnacious past during his twenty-eight years at Ohio State. Some of the coach's past exploits included throwing the yard markers onto the field to protest an official's decision in a Michigan game, firing a metal film case at a player who refused to go to classes, pushing a photographer's camera into his face, and, only the year before, punching an ABC cameraman.[29] Hayes did not appear amused at Jackson's presentation. The next night, at the game, another "boxing gloves" incident by Hayes cast aspersions upon Keith Jackson's honesty in his reporting and terminated Hayes's coaching career at Ohio State.

With less than two minutes to play, Ohio State was losing. Freshman quarterback Art Schlichter only moments before had led an Ohio State comeback, leaving his team only two points behind, 17-15. Clemson soon lost the ball, and Ohio State was driving toward victory. With Jackson reporting, Schlichter dropped back to pass to his tailback, Ron Springs. Clemson middle guard Charlie Bauman dropped back into pass defense, jumped in front of Springs, intercepted the ball—snuffing out any chance for an Ohio State win—and returned it before being tackled at the feet of the Ohio State bench and Woody Hayes. Before a nationwide television audience, Hayes lashed out and landed a fist to Bauman's neck, just below the face mask.[30] While the TV fans saw the action, Jackson apparently did not. He said nothing about Hayes's detestable conduct. When the producer kept asking Jackson to comment on the slugging incident, Jackson refused because he did not see the blow. Had this had been a major bowl game, there would have been a special replay machine for the announcer to see, but ABC did not want to expend the extra money to have such replays at the Gator Bowl. Therefore Jackson could not see what the entire audience had viewed.

Critics of Jackson claimed that he had been covering up the incident to protect college football and Woody Hayes. This would not have been unusual, for the NCAA had from the beginning of its televised football package asked its networks and announcers to give only a positive representation of the college game. In defense of Jackson, however, it seems that Woody Hayes was not among Jackson's favorite coaches—men such as Frank Broyles, Bear Bryant, Fritz Crisler, Duffy Daugherty, Ara Parseghian, Joe Paterno, Bo Schembechler, and Amos Alonzo Stagg.[31] Jackson would have been less likely to cover up for Hayes than for one of his more favored coaches. Two decades after the incident, Jackson was still trying to explain that he had not covered up and had in fact simply not seen the incident. "The irony of the thing," Jackson said, "was Woody Hayes and I never really did get along with each other. I sure wasn't protecting him." Jackson, like many politicians and celebrities over the years, blamed the media. The media, Jackson wailed, "dumped the whole bucket of crap on me."[32]

Jackson survived the affair; Hayes did not. Ohio State President Enarson, who for the previous two years had castigated ABC for not promoting the college game for the benefit all of higher education, was placed in the uncomfortable position of either not firing Hayes for his transgression against the game and being hypocritical once again in his actions or firing Hayes and incurring the hostility of the Ohio State fans. When Hayes was asked to resign, he replied: "No, goddammit, you bastards are going to have to fire me." Enarson, the pragmatist, let his athletic director, Hugh Hindman, do the deed.[33] The whole episode was one of the low points in the lives of both Woody Hayes and Keith Jackson. Jackson, however, braved the incident to become probably the best-known college football telecaster since the medium's origin.

The NCAA and its member institutions, for obvious reasons, disliked controversies such as the Woody Hayes slugging episode. Leaders worked behind the scenes to reduce any dissonance created by the announcers, the networks, or circumstances surrounding the games. It often appeared as if the TV broadcasters were barkers for a circus as they promoted the college pastime. Rather than "telling it like it is," as Howard Cosell proclaimed he did on the NFL's *Monday Night Football,* college sportscasters for the most part told it like the NCAA wanted it told. That is, if they were allowed to work for the network in the first place. As noted, the NCAA had a policy ruling that individuals who were associated too strongly with professional football were *persona non grata* to broadcast college games. Former pro players were often rejected as color announcers. Included in the list of shunned NFL stars were Johnny Lujack, Frank Albert, and Paul Hornung in the 1960s, when the fear of professional football overtaking the college game was at its apex.[34] Yet others, such as Red Grange, Paul Christman, and Tom Harmon, all of whom had played professional football, were apparently not tainted with the same brush and became color commentators for NCAA games.

Regardless of a telecaster's background, controversial issues of the times made it very difficult for the colleges to create an image of football appropriate to the unblemished view of America they hoped to project. Generally the purveyors of college football increased their positive comments on virile football and its pristine autumns and colorful marching bands playing the national anthem at the very moments social controversy was taking place in American society or an unsettled international situation existed. Two examples come readily to mind, incidents surrounding the Vietnam War and the Arab-Israel Sadat affair.

No event had a more troubling effect upon American society in the second half of the twentieth century than U.S. involvement in the Vietnam War, which even overshadowed the civil rights movement. The fact that Vietnam and civil rights protests came together in the 1960s made this decade as troubled a time for America as any since World War II and the Depression. College athletics, especially football, could not escape the controversy that America was experiencing in both crises. College football games, like other major sports events, were symbolic of national unity and what was good about America; where else among special events in American life was playing the national anthem considered nearly a sacred national obligation? It would have been considered a national desecration to not play the national anthem at a football game, while no one expected to hear the anthem before a similarly sized audience at a rock concert or horse race. So when a college band protested the Vietnam War by not following a "patriotic" theme, as did the University of Buffalo band, it caused a stir among athletic administrators as well as ABC officials.

In the midst of the longest war in U.S. history, the University of Buffalo band joined student demonstrations across America and turned "antiwar" during Buffalo's game with Holy Cross. The halftime show, titled "Give Peace a Chance," was to be part of the ABC-televised game in 1970. The situation in America was extremely tense, as only the spring before, devastating killings of college protesters had occurred on two college campuses, Jackson State and Kent State. Knowing that campuses had become tinderboxes, the NCAA Television Committee met with ABC's Roone Arledge, Chuck Howard, Barry Frank, Beano Cook, and Geoff Mason at the beginning of the season in an attempt to contain the potential for demonstrations and riots during televised football games. Roone Arledge believed that it was "hard to define when a demonstration was a bona fide news story or just another attempt to get on TV." Both ABC and the NCAA agreed, though, to "attempt in every way possible not to encourage demonstrations." ABC, likely fearful that ignoring a game demonstration would be looked at as opposing freedom of the media, asked that ABC-NCAA discussion be "kept confidential."[35] Not covering a game disturbance would also jeopardize TV ratings at ABC. This would be unfortunate at any time, but at the close of the 1960s, ABC was experiencing a downturn in ratings after its meteoric rise only a few years before, when it had gained equity with NBC and CBS. ABC then became the butt of an oft-mentioned cruel joke about its prime time shows: "If you want to stop the Vietnam War, put it on ABC— it'll be over in 13 weeks."[36]

The Buffalo band's halftime performance not only sarcastically looked at the war, but in its performance it also commented on racism and pollution. ABC, however, chose to turn its camera away from the political controversies, instead panning traffic, elm trees, and cloudy skies before switching back to headquarters in New York City for eight minutes of scores.[37] As the Vietnam War was tearing America apart, ABC and the NCAA decided to play the patriotic game in 1970. That year became what Jerry Izenberg has called the "first full-fledged 'God Bless America Season.'"[38] Patriotic songs at football games would back America's involvement in Vietnam. Such tunes as "The Battle Hymn of the Republic," "America the Beautiful" and "This Is My Country" were heard wherever NCAA games were played and ABC television cameras were placed.

This was not a new phenomenon in 1970, for the NCAA had been asking television networks since early in the Vietnam War and civil rights movement to turn its cameras away from any political demonstrations or related disturbances.[39] Soon, the NCAA counsel George Gangwere prepared with "tender care" a provision to be written into future NCAA TV contracts. The provision provided that the network "will not telecast such disturbance . . . caused by a protest group, civil rights group, or similar organization of social dissent."[40] Little had changed since the time television had become commercially viable and networks had to weigh the need for open and honest expression against their desire for profits and fear of antagonizing the advertisers and other moneyed interests.

In such struggles, the greed of money managers generally triumphs over free and open expression, as it did in the Buffalo band affair.[41]

Several years later, the NCAA, again thinking like a money manager, raised a ruckus over ABC's coverage of Egyptian President Anwar Sadat's landing on Israeli soil, a historic first. It was a political event of worldwide importance that led to a permanent peace accord between an Arab nation and a Jewish one. Unfortunately for the NCAA, the landing took place during the Michigan–Ohio State football game, one of a couple games important for Nielsen ratings of NCAA telecasts that season. Lower ratings could affect future NCAA TV earnings. Walter Byers was furious with Roone Arledge and ABC for interrupting the game for the historic landing. "The NCAA . . . has been seriously damaged by ABC's action," Byers wrote Arledge, because the Sadat trip "was no 'event,' important or otherwise, to be televised." The arrival of Sadat's plane in Tel Aviv, Byers complained, "could not in and of itself reasonably be construed as 'an event of overwhelming public importance,'" as the NCAA-ABC contract read.[42]

Nearly two decades later, Walter Byers changed his mind about the importance of the Sadat trip. Finally realizing that some events are more important than a football game, Byers recognized that the peace initiatives between Egypt and Israel had resolved three decades of continuing conflict and war between two Middle Eastern countries. Of the millions of television viewers that day, only a few rabid alumni and trivia buffs would remember the 14-6 Michigan victory over Ohio State. As Byers later revealed: "We were after exposure and Nielsen ratings for college football; I was as competitive and combative as a football coach."[43] Competitive actions like this by Byers and the NCAA made a statement about the commercial nature of big-time college sport as a whole.

Indeed, in attempting to bring in as many dollars as possible to the organization and to the institutions, the NCAA was as competitive as the teams were on the field of play. The announcers contributed to the publicity and profitability of the college game by being part of the boosterism that surrounded intercollegiate athletics, especially football. Announcing for the networks fit nicely into the free enterprise system that had developed in intercollegiate athletics well before the advent of either radio or television. The colleges, through the NCAA, used the networks and the announcers' ability to promote the positive aspects of the game and cash in on the popularity of football. Cable television, however, would soon challenge the network monopoly of college football.

19 The Cable Television Dilemma:
More May Be Less

BY THE 1970s and 1980s, NCAA institutions were learning that more television, especially the proliferation of cable TV, might dilute the market and mean less income to them. Cable TV came into existence in the late 1940s, as a means of bringing television signals to remote areas, and was first set up in Astoria, Oregon, and the mountainous regions of Pennsylvania.[1] It was then called CATV, for Community Antenna Television, because an antenna might be placed on high ground to catch a signal from an urban area and bring it via cable to small communities that previously had been inaccessible to signals.

Cable has long since lost the CATV label and, with it, its original reason for being. At first, cable was looked upon favorably by the networks, for it brought a larger audience to network programs and thus helped generate greater advertising revenues. Free, over-the-air telecasts by networks continued to dominate telecasting in the 1950s and 1960s, while experimental pay-cable generally lacked financial stability. Most people refused to pay for cable television if they could freely receive the offerings of the major networks, ABC, CBS, NBC, and the short-lived Du Mont TV.[2] Cable, or CATV, however, was not regulated by the Federal Communications Commission initially because the signal was not transmitted over the air but merely relayed over cable. Thus cable was able to develop until the mid-1960s without government interference.

Free from FCC regulation, cable operators were able, eventually, to bring in signals from distant cities, challenging local stations for an audience and advertising revenues. This ability increased once satellites were used to transmit signals in the 1960s and 1970s. Sports programs and popular movies were siphoned off or imported from distant signals and used by local cable systems free of charge. Networks and local stations began to look at cable operators as rivals with an unfair competitive advantage because of the FCC's laissez-faire attitude. Protests from the National Association of Broadcasters fell on deaf ears at the FCC until the mid-1960s, by which time there were more than one million cable subscribers among the 1,325 cable systems. The FCC first took regulatory action in 1966, in response to the newfound belief that cable TV "will destroy or seriously degrade the service offered by a television broadcaster."[3] Cable operators in the 100 top markets were prohibited by the FCC from importing signals from other markets, and the siphoning off of such desired programs as college and professional football and popular movies was severely restricted. By that time, the NCAA had spent a number of years experimenting with cable, closed circuit, and pay television.

NCAA leaders were not oblivious to the potential windfall from cable and pay television. For example, during the NCAA's first year under a $2.6 million contract with NBC for a Game of the Week telecast in 1952, the NCAA was negotiating for a $50 million pay-as-you-view contract with International Telemeter Corporation, a subsidiary of Hollywood's Paramount Pictures Corporation. Under this never-completed contract, a scrambled signal was to be transmitted by regular commercial TV stations. An "unscrambler box" installed in homes would then unscramble the picture when fed with coins. For instance, if 10 million homes paid 50 cents per game, one NCAA game would gross nearly double the entire year's NBC contract.[4]

The grandiose telemeter scheme was not instituted, but a much smaller experiment was conducted the next year in Palm Springs, California. In the first ever football pay-per-view contest, the University of Southern California–Notre Dame game was brought to the coin-operated telemeter boxes of seventy Palm Springs homes. Each homeowner paid one dollar to see Notre Dame's 48-14 victory over USC, bringing Frank Leahy his last "away" triumph in an illustrious career as Notre Dame's second-most successful coach.[5] Paul MacNamara of International Telemeter Corporation boasted that his telemeter pay-per-view system could "gross several million dollars" for a Notre Dame–USC national game.[6] This may have been true, but at the time the NCAA was more interested in controlling television than in promoting it for the benefit of a couple institutions, and Notre Dame's popularity was considered far more of a threat than a benefit to other NCAA members.

Notre Dame, meanwhile, consistently wanted to open up television of all types, cable, over-the-air, and pay-per-view, to the consternation of most other NCAA members. The NCAA did not restrict closed-circuit television through most of the 1950s, and Notre Dame took advantage of the NCAA's inaction. In 1955, Notre Dame had all ten of its games telecast on closed-circuit television. Notre Dame contracted with the Sheraton Hotel Corporation to telecast a number of games in Sheraton's hotel chain, in thirteen cities including Chicago, New York, Boston, Philadel-

phia, Washington, D.C., and St. Louis. Admission was a costly four dollars, and, according to Father Edmund Joyce, Notre Dame's vice president, the project "barely broke even."[7] If the wildly popular Notre Dame
had trouble producing revenue from cable telecasting, other institutions
were likely to have even more difficulty.

Experiments continued with the tacit approval of the NCAA as long
as they caused "no appreciable damage to any other concurrent games"
played in the area of the telecasts. The important Hartford Experiment
in Connecticut began in 1962 as the first experimental broadcast subscription channel. It commenced with four hours per day of decoded
prime-time TV, paid for by subscribers on a monthly basis. Among other
programs emanating from Hartford were the Floyd Patterson–Sonny Lis-
ton heavyweight boxing championship, the Bolshoi Ballet, and college
football. The Yale-Cornell football game in New Haven, Connecticut,
opened the college sport offerings on October 20, 1962. The Hartford Experiment lasted seven years before it surrendered to financial failure.[8]
While the experiment was not a monetary success, it led to the FCC's decision in 1968 to permit broadcast pay-TV on a commercial basis.

The liberation of commercial cable TV in the free-market economy
caused the NCAA to reevaluate some of its longstanding policies. The
NCAA allowed any game sellout to be telecast at the home institution,
and it allowed away games to be broadcast back to the visiting team's
home area if the game was at least 400 miles away and did "no appreciable damage" to other college games within the broadcast area. "Exception telecasts," as they were called, were introduced in part because
the NCAA was "placating the Justice Department," according to NCAA
TV head Asa Bushnell. The Justice Department in the early years had
kept a watchful eye on the restrictive NCAA TV policy—which had become what Bushnell conceded was a "benevolent monopoly."[9] Cable, or
CATV, allowed stations to expand upon the exception telecasts by picking up the signals of a local cable station and broadcasting them virtually anywhere, thus placing in jeopardy the exclusivity contract with the
network carrying the NCAA Game of the Week. In other words, a local
commercial station was generally denied the right to broadcast a game
under NCAA policy, but that same local station could find the game
being carried via local cable. Despite the rule that allowed for exception
telecasts, with cable becoming prominent there was "appreciable damage" being done to the network contract. The 400-mile rule allowed a
sellout to be telecast to the visiting team's home market over one station or cablecast over one or more systems. The flooding of the market

with cable football was again placing NCAA controls and network exclusivity in danger.[10]

The NCAA was caught in a dilemma. If it placed greater restrictions
on cable transmissions and exception telecasts, it would jeopardize its
"benevolent monopoly" status with the Antitrust Division of the Department of Justice; if it allowed greater use of cable and exception telecasts, it would face a challenge by the carrying network for breaking the
exclusivity contract while possibly saturating the market with football
and lowering game attendance. Knowing that Notre Dame and possibly
a few other colleges could benefit from the loosening of NCAA policy,
the NCAA Television Committee in 1969 allowed games to be cablecast
on subscription TV if the broadcast was deemed "to be beneficial to intercollegiate football." This policy, of course, was subject to a wide range
of interpretation on what was considered beneficial. In 1970, when Notre
Dame's WNDU-TV was allowed to broadcast all of its home games,
Michigan's athletic director, Don Canham, protested. Not only would
this, according to Canham, appreciably damage the ABC telecasts, but
he could also "visualize Notre Dame selling games on a national network
of CATV."[11] The NCAA kept a close eye on Notre Dame and also on the
expansion of cable TV, limiting use of closed-circuit television only to
the campus.[12]

The NCAA listened closely, however, when the Management Television Systems (MTS) proposed a closed-circuit television football championship playoff in 1971. The year before, MTS had created the first
color, closed-circuit television network in order to broadcast the Joe Frazier–Jimmy Ellis heavyweight championship. MTS decided that a championship game between the two top-rated football teams could yield a
multimillion-dollar payoff, probably grossing at least $15 million to be
divided among MTS, the NCAA, and the competing institutions. MTS
estimated that the "Poll Bowl," based on newspaper ranking, would
reach up to 4 million spectators, who would watch the event on giant-
screen, closed-circuit television. In an attempt to mollify the organizers
of strong end-of-the-season bowl games, MTS said that it would telecast
the championship game before the bowl games took place and thus reduce the threat to those games.[13]

After debating the issue, the NCAA Television Committee voted 8-4
in favor of the "Poll Bowl," but there were too many other forces arguing against the idea.[14] Besides the major threat to the traditional bowl
games, the choice of the two teams would be arbitrary, based on the end-
of-the-season poll (hence the bowl's nickname). In addition, there was

already a growing movement within the NCAA to "share the wealth" from television among all NCAA members, not just the elite football schools. Then, too, there was the NCAA Football Championship Committee, which had been disbanded because of opposition to any type of big-time college football championship.[15] So, despite any effort to "try to make more money for the colleges at a time when they badly need it," according to Asa Bushnell, the NCAA turned down the MTS proposal. Walter Byers, NCAA Executive Director, simply stated to MTS that "NCAA legislation currently prohibits appearances in any such season-ending playoff."[16] That ended the short-lived excitement for either national closed-circuit college telecasting or for a championship in big-time football.

A few years later, Home Box Office (HBO) made overtures to the NCAA, hoping to offer NCAA football and gain new subscribers to HBO's services. HBO began telecasting in 1972 when it relayed a live hockey match and a film from New York City to 385 pay-cable subscribers in Wilkes-Barre, Pennsylvania. In less than a year, HBO was able to lease a satellite and begin beaming its programs across the country, first carrying the Jimmy Ellis–Ernie Shavers championship bout from Madison Square Garden to Disneyland. In 1975, HBO brought the Muhammad Ali–Joe Frazier fight, dubbed the "Thrilla in Manila," from the Philippines to its nearly half-million subscribers.[17] The following year, HBO approached the NCAA with an offer of $10,000 per game even though HBO was paying an estimated $70,000 or more for feature movies. Michigan's Athletic Director, Don Canham, complained that the offer amounted to only about one penny per subscriber, and, more importantly, it was not an experiment but "a violation of the NCAA contract with ABC." The NCAA's Walter Byers disagreed, claiming that the proposed twelve game cablecasts featured teams not on the ABC schedule and the NCAA would find out how valuable the "second echelon" of big-time schools could be to the NCAA and its institutions.[18] The 1976 HBO proposal was rejected, but the next year, over the protest of ABC, the NCAA Television Committee authorized HBO to telecast a maximum of three games at $50,000 per game for a one-year experiment.[19]

The use of cable television persisted, placing the NCAA's TV policy in a difficult position regarding the limiting of football television exposure to protect gate attendance and the financial structure of college sport. The NCAA continued to discuss the problems of cable TV throughout the 1970s, complaining that uncontrolled cable companies were carrying games that local television stations were prohibited from broadcasting, while at the same time regional telecasts were carried by cable outside the regional boundaries. The NCAA even considered banning all regional telecasts and returning to one national Game of the Week, something it threatened to do when it appealed to the FCC to put greater restrictions on cable transmissions of sporting events.[20] The NCAA also appealed specifically to Notre Dame to not allow its TV exemptions to be cablecast by unauthorized companies outside of its area. If the games were pirated, the NCAA warned, Notre Dame might lose future network regional telecasts.[21]

The threat posed to the NCAA by Notre Dame's exceptions, however, may not have been as great as that which developed at Ohio State in the 1970s.[22] In Columbus, the home of Ohio State University, Warner Communications in 1977 set up an interactive cable system in which subscribers could do such things as buy products, summon the police or fire company, or get pay-per-view movies or sports events with the press of a button. It was called QUBE. In its first year, QUBE asked the NCAA Television Committee for permission to cablecast Ohio State football games at the same time ABC was telecasting its NCAA games. ABC claimed this would violate its exclusive 1977 contract with the NCAA even though the contract stated that "a closed circuit telecast . . . may be authorized by the committee upon request of a member institution."[23] If QUBE was allowed to telecast Ohio State games, it would obviously compete with ABC's affiliate station in the Columbus market. This was the first instance in which a cable company, and not a local station, was willing to broadcast an exception game during a network telecast. Earlier that year, the NCAA had granted Ohio State's TV station permission to present its four home games to four branch campuses of Ohio State— a decision probably influenced by ABC's embarrassing "beer hall incident" of the previous Fall, which had angered Ohio State president Harold Enarson and placed ABC in a defensive position relative to the NCAA.[24] ABC said little about Ohio State telecasting the games to its branch campuses, but the QUBE intrusion bothered ABC more, as the network saw the commercial cable invasion as a vital precedent that would lead to future diminished advertising profits.[25]

The NCAA Television Committee originally considered the QUBE telecasts to be experimental and legal under the ABC-NCAA contract. The committee then vacillated, disallowing one game QUBE desired and allowing others that ABC opposed.[26] Both organizations were at odds: ABC opposed any game being shown by QUBE, while QUBE opposed any restrictions on its telecasting. The NCAA was caught in the middle not only of the QUBE-ABC argument but of an investigation by Congress into television practices and sports programming. A Communications Subcommittee of the House of Representatives Interstate and Foreign Commerce Committee was beginning a probe of network antitrust implications in the control of sports activities, such as the choice of network for the Moscow Olympics, professional boxing championship tournaments, and the exclusivity provision of the NCAA football telecasts. Adding to the NCAA's troubles, the Internal Revenue Service was claiming that network arrangements with the colleges were not related to educational purposes of higher education and therefore should be taxed.[27] With the Congressional inquiry on the horizon and the IRS breathing down the necks of institutions of higher education, its was not surprising that the normally steadfast NCAA vacillated in its policy toward QUBE and commercial cable telecasting.

When ABC, with the help of the NCAA, prevented QUBE from telecasting Ohio State games against Illinois and Indiana, Warner Cable challenged ABC and the NCAA in court. The significance of Warner Cable's suit was that it challenged the NCAA television plan was a violation of federal antitrust statues. The suit was settled out of court in the summer of 1978, to the benefit of Warner's QUBE. Warner was allowed to telecast up to five Ohio State games per year in 1978 and 1979. Warner, in return, would provide the NCAA and ABC with copies of all research data related to the Ohio State cablecasts.[28] The decision would benefit ABC little, but QUBE and the NCAA could live effectively with the settlement. Leaders of the NCAA believed they could look forward to a longer period of relief from antitrust action. Walter Byers penciled in notes before the settlement meeting with Warner and ABC: "WHAT WE DO HERE," Byers emphasized, "MUST STAND AS A PATTERN ELSEWHERE."[29] Byers was correct in his perception of the importance of the settlement, but he was wrong if he thought the antitrust cease-fire would last well into the future.

Even before the conditions of the settlement had been implemented, the commercial cable movement was making further invasions into the NCAA-ABC monopoly over big-time college football. Within a month of the Warner settlement, the director of Pay Television, Charles Morris, suggested to the NCAA that a subscription pay-TV plan would produce greater income than QUBE's pay-per-program system. Morris indicated, rightly, that subscription TV would outperform per-program viewing because 95 percent of TV subscribers favored monthly payments over the QUBE system. At the same time, individual institutions other than Notre

Dame were being queried about cable rights. Michigan was offered hundreds of thousands of dollars for a four-year contract by a Los Angeles–based company, National Subscription Television, partly owned by the famed TV producer Norman Lear.[30] The Entertainment and Sports Programming Network (ESPN), incorporated in July of 1978, was also poised to benefit from cablecasting of college football.[31]

When, in 1979, the NCAA proposed expanding cable and satellite telecasting, ABC again protested and suggested that the NCAA instead seek an antitrust exemption from Congress. The federal government had specifically exempted professional team sports television contracts from antitrust laws under the Sports Broadcasting Act of 1961. ABC's Jim Spence urged the NCAA to request "congressional protection" to prevent the Warner QUBE experiment from infecting the entire cable industry and ruining ABC's football TV exclusivity. Walter Byers responded sharply: "Whether the NCAA needs an exemption from the antitrust laws . . . is a question for the NCAA to determine." As ABC had refused earlier to face the possibility of "suits from cable interests in other cities," Byers was not entirely sympathetic to ABC's problem now that there was money to be made for the NCAA by expanding into cable.[32]

Yet, when the Warner-QUBE two-year agreement allowing telecasting in Columbus of Ohio State games came to a close in 1980, ABC and the NCAA both decided not to allow QUBE to cablecast games that were not otherwise televised by ABC unless QUBE purchased all remaining tickets of all college games within its cablecasting area. This time, QUBE would come out the loser in the first legal decision challenging the NCAA football telecasting policy. QUBE's request for a court injunction to allow telecasting of Ohio State games not telecast on ABC was disallowed, the judge ruling that this telecasting would potentially threaten the financial stability of the NCAA and its member institutions. The judge determined that QUBE had an alternative; it could have chosen to buy out conflicting college games within the cablecast territory.[33]

Almost as soon as the Warner-QUBE case had been resolved, the NCAA decided to broaden its one-network contract with ABC to include two networks and a "superstation." Throughout the 1970s, the NCAA had been driven by the strength of the big-time football powers to expand television opportunities and increase television revenues. While the NCAA Television Committee had discussed expanding to TV doubleheaders in the 1960s, in the mid-1970s a group of big-time football schools formed the College Football Association, principally to put pressure on the NCAA to provide for their needs.[34] Increased television receipts going to the big-time institutions was a major goal according to Michigan's president Robben Fleming. "The purpose of the CFA is money," Fleming told his colleagues from the Big 10, who, along with those from the Pacific Coast Conference, were reluctant to join the CFA.[35]

The CFA, without either the Big 10 or the Pacific Athletic Conference in its fold, decided to form its own TV committee in 1979 to evaluate the NCAA TV plan and to reverse the decreased percentage of TV fees going to its members. Those members included the Southeastern, Southwest, Big 8, and Atlantic Coast Conferences as well as independents such as Notre Dame and Penn State.[36] The pressure of the CFA to increase TV wealth for its institutions created great tension within the NCAA over increasing receipts from its football telecasting. A logical method was to increase the number of networks telecasting NCAA football to two. The NFL had three networks in the 1970s: CBS and NBC on Sunday afternoons and ABC on Monday nights. Robert James, commissioner of the Atlantic Coast Conference, had suggested a second network in 1976, and CBS had made a second-network proposal to the NCAA the following year. The members of the NCAA, though, had not yet been ready for a plan that a majority believed would damage stadium attendance.[37] Nevertheless, in 1979 the NCAA membership granted the NCAA Television Committee the authority for the first time to negotiate with one or more TV networks in future plans.[38]

As the CFA continued its attempts to change TV policy in its favor, the NCAA reacted by expanding television coverage and reorganizing the divisional structure of the organization to give the big-time schools more power.[39] This meant that the powerful schools would have more freedom to direct their own affairs, including control over television. The three-year television plan, beginning in 1982, called for two networks and a supplementary series to be offered on Saturday evenings. CBS joined ABC, the longtime NCAA network, in a contract that nearly doubled the NCAA's income from the 1980–81 contract with ABC. The supplementary series went to Ted Turner's Atlanta-based national superstation, WTBS, which was more a cable service than a broadcasting station.

Ted Turner's operation, the most widely distributed cable network in America, paid $17.5 million for the supplementary series, an amount that exceeded other bids by $10 million and brought a windfall to the NCAA. It was understood by ABC and CBS that the series would be carried over cable or pay over-the-air television.[40] Turner, however, decided not to use cable or pay over-the-air TV, but rather to utilize free satellite on his UHF television station in Atlanta, WTBS. The NCAA accepted Turner's bid and completed the contract before ABC and the NCAA had finalized their contract, which ABC believed would outlaw free local noncable broadcasts. The disagreement led to a court case in which ABC and Cox Broadcasting, its affiliate in Atlanta, challenged the NCAA and Turner's free over-the-air Atlanta broadcasts. The case was decided in favor of Turner and the NCAA by the Georgia Supreme Court. Earlier, CBS had been "coerced into accepting [an] addendum" to its contract allowing the free arrangement between Turner and the NCAA.[41]

By the time the ABC–Cox Broadcasting case had been decided in 1982, the NCAA was embroiled in a fight for its life over the question of who owned the property rights to telecast college football games, the NCAA or the individual institutions. This fight was led by the University of Oklahoma and the University of Georgia, but these leaders had the financial backing of conferences and individual institutions within the CFA. This final battle for TV rights would change the direction that college football and college athletics would take from the 1980s on. In many ways the saga came to define college sport in the last two decades of the twentieth century.

TV Money, Robin Hood, and the Birth of the CFA

FROM THE commencement of the NCAA's control of football telecasting in 1951, the NCAA had operated from one principal source of income, the NCAA basketball tournament, which began in 1939. Membership dues were a distant second source of income.[1] In 1960, for instance, proceeds from the men's basketball tourney accounted for nearly 60 percent of the entire operating budget for the NCAA, and the event's earnings continued to cover over 60 percent of the NCAA operating expenses for many years to come. Football TV assessments, meanwhile, were accounted for separately and considered outside the general income of the organization from their origin, a situation that continued for more than two decades.[2] As expenses to run the NCAA football TV plan never reached the level of TV income, a rather large surplus developed from football television receipts. From early on, this source of easy money became a target for various interests within the NCAA that had little to do with big-time football. How the television money was spent, both the assessment that went to the NCAA and that which went to the competing schools, contributed to a near breakup of the NCAA. More than one "Robin Hood," out to grab NCAA football TV revenues and distribute them among poorer schools, arose in the three decades of the NCAA television plan.

Robin Hood, the twelfth-century robber who stole from the rich to give to the poor, had twentieth-century parallels in college sport. From the NCAA's beginning, there was a clear-cut difference between the small and the large colleges—between those that had big-time athletic programs and those that did not. Not until after World War II, when the NCAA instituted its Sanity Code—a policy of control and enforcement of recruiting and eligibility—and expanded into the control of football telecasting, did the differences between large and small colleges lead to questions of money distribution. Until the basketball tourney and the football television incomes reached significant proportions in the 1950s and 1960s, the NCAA eked out a meager existence on its small membership fees. No Robin Hoods emerged, for there were not yet riches to plunder and distribute among the poor.

From 1941, the basketball tourney profits were divided evenly,[3] that is, half went to the NCAA to run its programs and the participating teams received the other half. Yet, the small schools benefitted by the increase in NCAA programs that the money funded. In 1951 the NCAA received $52,500, and the sixteen competing teams averaged just over $3,000 each for their share of the basketball championship income. A decade later the NCAA received $177,800, and teams received that same amount to divide. By the 1970s, the NCAA was receiving a half million dollars and the competing teams were apportioned the same amount.[4] There was never a major controversy over the distribution of funds from the NCAA basketball tournament, but the football money was another story.

In its first year, 1951, the NCAA Television Committee suggested that 60 percent of the football TV revenue go to the NCAA and 40 percent to the participating schools. It reasoned that "those institutions participating in television . . . should share those receipts generously with the other NCAA member schools."[5] Yale's athletic director, Robert Hall, who certainly realized Yale was no longer the number-one draw in collegiate football, suggested that relative to television revenues it was "high time that our colleges adopted a point of view that is unselfish and do what is best for the common good."[6] This was a 180-degree turn from the individualistic view Yale had held fifteen years earlier, when it had the biggest radio contract and never offered to share its booty with the NCAA or Ivy League neighbors on its football schedule. Notre Dame's Theodore Hesburgh, on the other hand, was no socialist. President Hesburgh, who opposed any NCAA TV control, was strongly against the 60-40 deal, calling it part of the "socialistic tendency" in the country. Hesburgh and his right-hand man Edmund Joyce maintained that this "share-the-wealth" inclination would be similar to Notre Dame having to share its endowments and patent rights with all other colleges.[7] Hesburgh was Robin Hood's antithesis, for he was trying, unsuccessfully, to create a Super Conference to put control of television money solely in the hands of the big-time power schools.[8]

Twelve years after the first NCAA TV plan and a dozen years before a California State University president would be christened the new "Robin Hood," the NCAA Television Committee debated the need for a plan to distribute revenues more widely. As a new TV network plan was up for bid, the TV chair and commissioner of the Western Athletic Conference, Paul Brechler, said that any acceptable plan must be good for the entire membership, providing "broad protection even at the cost of lessened fee payments." Surprisingly, two of the representatives of powerful football schools and conferences, Howard Grubbs of the Southwest Conference and James J. Corbett, athletic director of Louisiana State University, agreed. Grubbs was concerned that the "large will eat the small," and Corbett suggested a plan in which colleges hurt by TV could collect damages from a pool of television money. Walter Byers, playing to both sides, as his position as NCAA executive director required, did not want to subsidize smaller colleges with receipts from major college football. Nevertheless, he suggested that the large colleges should find an undefined but "respectable means of repaying their debt to college football."[9]

Sharing the wealth was on the minds of many college athletic officials across the nation. One responded to a Midwesterner survey: "I have yet to learn what the dangers of a 'share the wealth' program are. . . . If the NCAA is really concerned about athletics in all member colleges . . . efforts would be made to equate the wealth and thereby aid in establishing good athletic programs around the country."[10] The TV committee took the middle course, allowing most of the telecasting money to continue to go to those schools chosen to be on TV and, at the same time, demanding that the network spread its coverage among a number of institutions rather than sticking to those with the best record or the greatest potential Nielsen ratings. In addition, the committee got ABC to telecast the new College Division championship games and use NCAA TV revenue to conduct the College Division playoffs. The NCAA sanctioned four bowls to conduct the College Division playoffs: the Grantland Rice, Camellia, Pecan, and Tangerine Bowls.[11] These playoffs were one way for the NCAA to satisfy small colleges, probably a gesture to ensure that the less powerful colleges would continue to vote for the network TV plan even though it principally benefitted the big-time football schools.

The mid-1960s also saw the NCAA Executive Committee apportioning significant amounts of the largess to nonfootball purposes. A postgraduate scholarship fund of $50,000 was created and added to each year in an effort to promote the idea of athletics as educational and raise the image of intercollegiate sport. The $80,000 cost of the NCAA statistical service for various sports was taken out of football TV funds and placed under a renamed National Collegiate Sports Services Bureau, located in New York City, the communications capital of America. The promotion of all intercollegiate sports from TV revenues was the result of this grant.

The NCAA Executive Committee also decided to use football television revenue to fight the Amateur Athletic Union's control of important amateur sports. The NCAA created a special reserve fund to support the newly initiated U.S. federations, which were independent of the AAU control, in basketball, gymnastics, track and field, and wrestling. Support for fighting the AAU increased to the point that in 1968, more TV money was being spent on supporting the federations than was used for the combined operation of the TV committee, underwriting of the TV Contingency Fund, and the promotion of football.[12] In 1970, the fees from the ABC network contract, which amounted to over $500,000, were divided among twelve different NCAA functions, only two of which were directly related to football or television.[13] Within two years, the NCAA assessment on the TV contract was raised in order to pay for the construction of a new NCAA headquarters near Kansas City. Opposing this continued encroachment on football receipts, Don Canham, athletic director at Michigan, complained: "My real fear, of course, is that when we are faced with another cash situation (perhaps women's intercollegiate athletics) we will again tap the television money."[14] One can understand Canham's antagonism later on when others, including a college president, entered the scene as the Robin Hoods of the mid-1970s.

By that time, there had been a quarter century of calls for dividing the increase in football television money more equitably, both the share received by the NCAA and that given to individual institutions that participated in the telecasts. Each time the wealth grew, there was a call to share it with all NCAA institutions, not just those who were generating it. This was a major reason why the large institutions called for the NCAA to be divided into three divisions—I, II, and III—in 1973, so that similar institutions could better control their own affairs. Two years after the reorganization, the president of a California college raised the intensity of discourse on sharing NCAA football TV wealth. Stephen Horn managed to escalate the cold war between the small and large institutions to a hot war.

Stephen Horn was one of the few college presidents to attend annual NCAA meetings in the 1970s. Horn was an honors graduate of Stanford with a Masters in Public Administration from Harvard and a Ph.D. in Political Science from Stanford. Actively engaged in Republican politics, with previous involvement as a legislative assistant to California's Senator Thomas Kuchel, Horn came to the NCAA with a strong interest in governance in education.[15] Horn's active participation in the NCAA came only after his own institution, California State University, Long Beach, was found guilty in 1974 of NCAA violations in both the basketball program, led by coach Jerry Tarkanian, and football. The NCAA penalties included a two-year banishment from the national basketball tourney and loss of television appearances for both programs.[16] Horn's knowledge of NCAA governance, however, was greater than the diplomacy he displayed. In his very first NCAA meeting, he insulted the 1974 delegates by calling for presidents "to appoint intelligent delegates next year" and saying that anyone who believes "there is nothing wrong in his [athletic] program is . . . either naive, a fool or stupid . . . maybe all three."[17] Soon after the convention he wrote to a number of college presidents about the need for presidential control of athletics with the observation that "university and college presidents are not sufficiently familiar with what is going on in their own intercollegiate athletic programs."[18] With his initial year of involvement in the NCAA, he began a crusade to reform the NCAA.

Of major concern was cost-cutting reform. A rare special convention was called in the summer of 1975 to discuss a variety of methods for cutting athletic costs. Stephen Horn was in the middle of this effort. He particularly wanted to cut the number of athletic scholarships in football, a most controversial move. The colleges had already agreed in 1973 to limit the number of football grants-in-aid to 105, but there was strong pressure to make a greater reduction.[19] While the NCAA Council recommended the maximum number be ninety-five, Horn called for dropping it to sixty-five: "I still think the fans of Michigan, Ohio State, USC, Alabama and Stanford . . . would go out to see 65 grants-in-aid play." Since only forty-eight players could suit up for away games, Horn asked if the difference between forty-eight and ninety-five was only "raw meat for practice all week."[20] One can imagine the antagonism toward President Horn as Division I voted to turn down Horn's proposal.

Horn, though, had already created a horde of enemies thanks to his Robin Hood proposal for the television revenues. In mid-July, only a month before the special cost-cutting convention, Horn sent a memo to all presidents of NCAA institutions outlining his scheme for distributing income from the next NCAA football television plan. Instead of nearly all of the income being divided among the participating Division I schools who dominated the network coverage, he suggested that Division II and III schools receive half the earnings and Division I receive the other half. To further anger Division I schools, Horn proposed that 25 percent of the money from postseason football contests should be given to Division II and III institutions, 25 percent divided equally among all Division I football institutions, and only 50 percent divided among the institutions playing the games, out of which those teams would have to pay their own travel expenses.[21]

Those who opposed Horn's plan called him many names, the kindest of which was "Robin Hood." Commissioners of the major football conferences met soon after Horn had released his plan. They were upset that a major change in the division of money was proposed and acknowledged that the acceptance of such a plan would jeopardize the entire structure of the NCAA. The presidents of the Big 10 met at a special meeting with Wayne Duke, Big 10 commissioner. Duke indicated that the plan might even lead to the "breakup of the NCAA organization."[22] Don Canham, a NCAA Television Committee member from Michigan, had earlier stated that "any reductions in money to the traditional football powers would break up the Association."[23] Walter Byers, meanwhile, told Horn that "the unacceptability of your approach" was manifest.[24]

Others worked to discredit Horn. When it was learned that Horn was on a panel for an event titled "The Crisis in Intercollegiate Athletics: Presidential Participation," under the auspices of the American Council on Education, another president on the panel, Harry Philpott, was asked to undermine Horn's credibility. The commissioner of the Atlantic Coast Conference, Robert James, sent a letter to Byers with proposed comments that might be used by President Harry Philpott of Auburn to undercut

Horn. In it were charges that Horn's institution wanted a greater share of the TV money because Long Beach had recently joined Division I in 1973 and had collected only $576 in football gate receipts from its own students that season. Long Beach State might "consider membership in Division II where the limitations approved at the NCAA Special Convention will assist it in saving money," the sarcastic suggestions continued. The cold war tactic of charging Horn with seeking to "turn the NCAA into a socialistic government" was another piece of advice that the letter suggested might be used to embarrass Horn.[25]

Horn only exacerbated the situation when he accused representatives of a number of big-time conferences with "secretly planning a 'super' division either within or without the framework of the NCAA."[26] Walter Byers felt constrained when he responded to Horn about the secret planning of member institutions but did suggest that Horn might better manage Long Beach's football program by being "consistent with its traditions and resources." That, one might surmise, meant returning to Division II football, where Long Beach belonged. To this, Marcus Plant, a past president of the NCAA from Michigan, agreed. "Long Beach State is not in financial difficulty because of the lack of concern of the NCAA," Plant remarked, "it is in difficulty because of its misdirected ambitions. . . . There is a place within the NCAA for Long Beach to solve its problem. That place is not Division I." In the meantime, Byers told Horn that he should send his TV proposal to the TV committee rather than trying to write a plan on the NCAA convention floor.[27] When Horn declined that stratagem, the NCAA Council maneuvered around Horn at the 1976 Convention by pointing out that, according to their constitution, Horn's Robin Hood TV proposals, like any TV proposal, would need a two-thirds vote. To this Horn responded: "I congratulate them on their ingenuity."[28] As the NCAA had always been powered by the largest institutions, there was little doubt that they would never allow Horn to be successful in his endeavor. Horn's share-the-wealth proposals were defeated by voice vote at the 1976 convention.[29]

President Horn stimulated a growing movement to split the big-time football powers away from others in the NCAA. Michigan's Marcus Plant was clear on this issue. "If this present divisional alignment does not work," he wrote, "the next step will be a federation of autonomous divisions and after that will be separate organizations."[30] Reorganization into three divisions "did not decide the issue of television controls," Walter Byers lamented.[31] The lack of Division I control for a football television plan did not lead to the breakup of the NCAA, but just such a breakup loomed closer with the creation of a big-time football organization, the College Football Association.

President Horn's July 1975 letter outlining his television division legislative proposals brought an almost immediate reaction. The commissioners of seven big-time conferences—the Atlantic Coast, Big 8, Big 10, Pacific 8, Southeastern, Southwest, and Western Athletic Conferences—met to discuss the ramifications of Horn's proposals.[32] Television was the key issue in the formation of a steering committee, predecessor to the CFA, despite later CFA Congressional testimony that the problems that had led to the CFA "did not center on television."[33] The CFA's original stated objective was to "maintain high quality of competition . . . consistent with academic goals," but it was clear that the CFA was first concerned with money from TV contracts.[34] Following the hurried July meeting, twenty-five individuals representing the seven conferences and independents Notre Dame and Penn State met in mid-October. They agreed that another reorganization of the NCAA was needed to provide greater control by Division I members over such things as television. The steering committee of nine was formed with representatives of the seven conferences and Notre Dame and Penn State.[35] The proposed reorganization of Division I into I and I-A was not carried out by the annual NCAA convention in January 1976, further frustrating the steering committee. In April 1976, the committee met in Dallas to draft criteria for Division I membership in football so that the big-time schools would not be outvoted by the less prominent schools like Horn's Long Beach State.[36]

By July 1976, the steering committee was coming closer to becoming a formal organization when twenty-three individuals met in Denver and voted unanimously to explore forming the CFA. At the organizational meeting in Dallas on December 20, 1976, members accepted the CFA's Articles of Association. Instead of separating from the NCAA, they agreed to "become a forum through which the major football programs might refine and sponsor points of view consistent with their needs *within* the NCAA."[37] The next year, the CFA, without both the Big 10 and the PAC-8, held its first annual meeting of sixty institutions. The absence of these two conferences was significant, as the CFA would have been extremely powerful if the Big 10 and PAC-8 (which soon became PAC-10) had joined. The Big 10 athletic directors and NCAA faculty representatives favored joining the CFA, but a majority of the presidents opposed the action.[38] According to Notre Dame's Edmund Joyce, the presidents feared that the CFA "wanted to eliminate all restraints from the sport of football" or, as Michigan's president Robben Fleming (who once said the only issue was money) stated, that the Big 10 presidents' "principal concern is one of overemphasis upon football." They also feared the CFA's possible withdrawal from the NCAA.[39]

The CFA quickly developed a white paper to support an NCAA reorganization plan and the creation of Divisions I-A and I-AA, a clear attempt to separate the big-time Division I schools from the less significant ones. The CFA believed that there were about eighty or so big-time football schools, not including Division I schools such as the Ivy League. The criteria for Division I-A, CFA organizers believed, should be based on strength of schedule, stadium capacity, and gate attendance. However, at the January 1978 NCAA convention, a motion known as the Ivy Amendment was passed, which eliminated the need to meet schedule, stadium, and gate requirements—requirements that most Ivy institutions could not meet. The amendment allowed Division I institutions that sponsored twelve or more sports (which Ivy League schools did) to be in the top division with the football powers. The extremely close votes angered CFA member institutions in what one participant described as the convention with the most divisive issues in his memory over the past two decades.[40]

The CFA found that it was difficult operating without an executive director and promptly hired Chuck Neinas. Commissioner of the Big 8 and former executive of the NCAA under Walter Byers, Neinas was, at the time, chair of the CFA Television Study Committee. Neinas, with a $65,000 salary, began his CFA leadership in the spring of 1980, but he had a clouded past with respect to the administration of the NCAA TV plan.[41] Neinas had been a member of the NCAA Television Committee in 1976 when he was censured for attempting to influence ABC to carry more Big 8 football games. As an NCAA Television Committee member, he met with ABC affiliates at a breakfast sponsored by the Big 8 Conference in an effort to influence their selections, according to other members of the committee. This violated a 1973 policy that prohibited committee members from contacting the carrying network in an attempt to obtain more appearances for an institution or conference. Neinas's former boss, Walter Byers, had recommended Neinas for the position of commissioner of the Big 10 five years before the incident. Now, however, Byers condemned Neinas's actions as "not appropriate for a member of the NCAA Television Committee. . . . I think it crucial that the Committee conduct its affairs without even the appearance of impropriety."[42]

The specter of revenge may have entered the plot, regardless of whether Neinas is considered the antagonist or the protagonist in the struggle for TV dollars. Five years before his censure, Neinas had lost the elite Big 10 commissioner's position to Big 8 commissioner Wayne Duke because he had been unable to define his philosophy of intercollegiate athletics in an interview before the selection committee. As a result, Neinas lowered his sights, applying for, and becoming, the next commissioner of the Big 8 instead. There, according to Walter Byers, who knew both Neinas and Wayne Duke very well, Neinas told Duke that "he would show those Big 10 people."[43] Neinas had a number of opportunities to do just that. First, when he was Big 8 commissioner, he tried to get ABC to give more television appearances to the Big 8 even though it meant going against NCAA TV policy. Second, he was able to show up the Big 10 by becoming executive director of the CFA. Third, he would eventually lead the CFA to separate itself from the NCAA television plan by creating a competing CFA plan. Whether or not there was vengeance in his heart, the scenario lends itself to this motive.

With Chuck Neinas as CFA executive director, and with his longtime experience with television, the CFA was poised to challenge the NCAA's television monopoly. The leadership would come not only from Neinas but also from Oklahoma, a Big 8 school that felt it had been slighted in television revenues; from an outspoken president of the University of Georgia; and from an individual who was behind all of them, President Hesburgh and the University of Notre Dame, who for three decades had opposed the NCAA's football television controls.

21 TV Property Rights and a
CFA Challenge to the NCAA

FOR NEARLY the first half century of the NCAA's existence, there was little need for litigious action either from within or from without the organization. Lawsuits were unnecessary, for the NCAA neither passed legislation nor enforced it—there was little to challenge. By the 1960s and 1970s, however, the NCAA had expanded both its legislative and executive duties. With this expansion, the NCAA also became the target of lawsuits, reflecting, perhaps, society's larger distress as the nation went through the strife of the civil rights and women's rights movements and the Vietnam War. Individuals and institutions within the NCAA increasingly took the NCAA to court, but they generally lost. The NCAA claimed that it had won twenty-nine of the thirty court cases brought against it from 1971 to 1976.[1] Nearly all cases had been initiated by either an NCAA member institution or by an individual within an NCAA institution.[2]

Television policy was a major irritant to a number of institutions. The University of Oklahoma, in particular, was aggravated at the NCAA's enforcement of legislation, including television sanctions. In the early 1970s, the NCAA penalized Oklahoma after a football staff member falsified a high school football player's transcript. As part of its punishment, Oklahoma was forbidden from telecasting its games for two years. Oklahoma argued that the TV ban was a violation of the Sherman Antitrust Act. Among other arguments, the NCAA claimed that it had no commercial objectives and that the Sherman Act was aimed at "combinations having commercial objectives."[3] The courts accepted the claim that football was part of the educational objectives, not commercial objectives, of an institution.

Not long after this ruling, the University of Oklahoma backed the University of Alabama in the Hennessey lawsuit, taking the NCAA to court, this time to reverse a cost-cutting NCAA measure that reduced the size of football coaching staffs. Oklahoma's football coach, Barry Switzer, opposed the rule, and he was joined by two Alabama assistants under coach Bear Bryant. They asserted that the NCAA, as a voluntary organization, did not have the right to interfere with contracts between an employee and employer. The NCAA action, they believed, was a violation of the Taft-Hartley Act and the Sherman Antitrust Act.[4] However, in the 1976 Hennessey case the courts determined that the NCAA had the right to limit the number of coaching positions as a reasonable restraint of trade.[5] Again, Oklahoma, along with Alabama, lost the court battle to the NCAA, but they did not give up their war over antitrust contentions. It would not be the last, nor the most important, attempt by institutions, including Oklahoma, to overturn NCAA action involving property rights and restraint of trade. Although the NCAA won the Hennessey case, NCAA legal counsel George Gangwere predicted that discussion of antitrust issues would likely "encourage other anti-trust cases."[6]

Oklahoma was certainly not alone in its litigation against the NCAA. Two important cases involved the University of Minnesota. Both appeared to have little to do with telecasting, but they set precedents that would impact the NCAA and television. In 1976, two players from the University of Minnesota basketball team were involved in an on-court fight during a game with Ohio State. Without going through the due process of a hearing for the players as demanded by the Fourteenth Amendment to the Constitution, they were summarily suspended for the season by the Big 10 Conference. The lack of due process to protect the players in this case was important for emphasizing the need to protect both individual and institutional property rights from infringement by conferences or a national body such as the NCAA.[7]

Four years later, as University of California, Long Beach, president Stephen Horn was attempting to take television money from the rich to divide among the poor, the University of Minnesota challenged the NCAA in a property rights case. In an institutional case against the NCAA, Minnesota refused to accept the NCAA's decision to declare several Minnesota athletes ineligible for competition for breaking the NCAA's rule against accepting financial favors. The institution had punished the wrongdoers, but the penalty was not severe enough for the NCAA. The NCAA further penalized the University of Minnesota with three years probation and a two-year ban on television and postseason competition. In the lower court rulings, Minnesota argued successfully that intercollegiate athletics were property rights entitled to due-process guarantees. The opportunity to participate in college sport, Minnesota argued, was an important part of the athletes' educational experience. The NCAA had, Minnesota maintained, deprived the athletes of due process over a property right guaranteed by the Constitution. The judge agreed, saying that "the opportunity to play intercollegiate basketball . . . is a property right entitled to due process because it may . . . lead to a very remunerative career in professional basketball."[8] A higher level court overturned the ruling, however, citing that minimum due process was given and siding with the NCAA's sanction.[9]

Property rights, although not always upheld by the courts, became more of an issue to both institutions and individuals within the NCAA. In the 1970s, the broadcasting property rights of institutions were of central importance to both the NCAA football television package and the CFA and its institutions. Around this time, a significant educational court ruling, though not specifically related to sport, created a climate in which institutions could argue effectively against the monopolistic TV policy of the NCAA. In the 1975 case *Goldfarb v. Virginia State Bar,* the court ruled that educational institutions were not entitled to the blanket immunity from antitrust laws that they had previously enjoyed. Carl Reisner of the *Yale Law Review* wrote: "After Goldfarb the NCAA's anticompetitive practices are susceptible to antitrust attack."[10] Following the Goldfarb ruling, the NCAA, being an organization of educational institutions, could no longer feel sure that it was exempt from prosecution under the Sherman Antitrust Act of 1890. "In the past," confided NCAA general council George Gangwere, "we have always confidently maintained that educational endeavors were in general exempt from anti-trust proscriptions." That position, Gangwere continued, "has been somewhat eroded."[11] If anything, that was an understatement.

Throughout this time, as property rights became paramount, the CFA spoke to a number of other issues, including educational ones. Education was normally not what mattered most to the big-time football schools: the CFA, after all, had been formally organized in December 1976 after the NCAA had failed to allow big-time football powers to have a greater say in Division I legislation, including control of television.[12] The CFA was cast in a negative light for having organized principally to increase television revenue among its ranks. To improve its image, therefore, the CFA moved to reclaim standards recently lost when the NCAA took collective action to lower academic requirements for athletes.[13] The CFA board of directors created three committees, two of which would emphasize academic standards and ethics.[14] Penn State's head football coach, Joe Paterno, was asked to head the new CFA coaches' committee, with the suggestion that the CFA could "re-establish a SAT floor of the 1.6 rule" for athletic eligibility.[15] President Robben Fleming of the University of Michigan scoffed at the CFA academic show, calling it "window dressing" to the real purpose of the CFA, which was to increase revenues to the big-time schools.[16] He was probably right; a football coach, Tom Osborne of CFA institution Nebraska, soon complained about the coaches' committee academic recommendations. Osborne said that the "triple option" CFA recommendation for freshman eligibility—a high school 2.25 grade point average, a 750 SAT test score, or a 17 ACT test score—had been passed simply "in order to enhance the 'respectability' of the CFA."[17]

It was still television, not academics, that drove the CFA to action. Chuck Neinas, before becoming executive director of the CFA, proposed a CFA Television Committee in 1979 to examine the NCAA football TV plan. The committee should "determine if CFA institutions have relinquished the television rights to their own football games."[18] Speaking on the impact of the NCAA TV plan on the CFA, Neinas questioned the TV fees being redistributed to expenses such as payments to schools participating in championships in all NCAA sports, proposed payment of major medical insurance for all NCAA athletes, and possible sponsor-

Table 5   **NCAA TV Plan Appearances**

Year	CFA Appearances	Big Ten–PAC-10 Appearances	Other Appearances
1976	66%	17%	17%
1977	67%	19.5%	13.5%
1978	56%	21.5%	22.5%
1979	55%	20%	25%

TV Nielsen Ratings of NCAA Football

Year	TV Ratings
1976	14.1
1977	13.2
1978	12.0
1979	11.4

Source: "Report of CFA Television Study Committee," 22 May 1980, President Banowsky Papers, Box 74, Folder 13, University of Oklahoma Archives.

ship of women's championships. The Robin Hood scheme President Horn had championed four years before had not gone away, Neinas believed. At that meeting, Neinas became chair of a CFA Television Study Committee, which would report at the next annual CFA meeting.

The aggressive work of Neinas's committee produced a report that verified what many CFA member institutions already believed: the number of appearances of CFA members in the NCAA TV plan was consistently diminishing. At the same time, there was a steady decline in the TV Nielsen ratings. The CFA Television Study Committee concluded that "it is the caliber of programs sponsored by the CFA membership (plus Big 10 and PAC-10) that attracts the networks, and subsequently the sponsors." Because ratings would determine future TV fees for rights, the CFA wanted a different NCAA plan, one that would telecast more CFA games. At this time, the CFA decided to continue working with the NCAA TV plan but wanted to "preserve its options, rather than be bound by a future possibly unacceptable NCAA Football Television Plan."[19]

The CFA board of directors instructed the Television Study Committee to interpret the data and develop a football TV plan that would be more beneficial to its members. The network sharks, smelling blood, began discussions with the CFA about the future of college football telecasting. The CFA felt that it was in a good position to persuade the NCAA to consider a two-network approach, check the potential for cable television, limit the amount of television dollars used for nonfootball purposes, and, if these did not work, to go ahead with its own TV plan.[20]

The CFA retained Philip Hochberg as legal counsel to help its TV committee. Hochberg was a young lawyer from the nation's capital who had worked with both the National Hockey League and two National Basketball Association teams. He had also been a special consultant to the Communications Subcommittee of the House Interstate and Foreign Commerce Committee, which in 1977 investigated possible monopolistic action by television networks, including ABC's dealings with the NCAA. Hochberg, who had an interest in football and had been the press box announcer for both the University of Maryland and Washington Redskin football games, was particularly knowledgeable about cable television. He made a special point of reminding the CFA of the "growing awareness of property rights" and citing litigation that supported "property right theory."[21] He was a significant participant in the CFA's eventual efforts to challenge the NCAA TV plan.

The CFA felt increasingly confident as the NCAA saw its traditional legal invincibility weakened. The CFA sensed that if all else failed in reclaiming a greater share of income from television, it could attack the NCAA TV plan legally. Even Walter Byers was forced to admit that "educational institutions and organizations are not as free to enter into so-called [TV] pooling arrangements now as they formerly were."[22] The NCAA position on pooling became so weak that the organization abandoned action to combine its basketball tourney TV plan with an in season basketball package. "A basketball television plan," NCAA general counsel George Gangwere strongly advised, "would . . . be almost solely designed . . . to increase revenues by the elimination of competition."[23] The proposed basketball plan was a clear violation of antitrust laws, Gangwere warned. Phil Hochberg, Chuck Neinas, and the CFA sensed the same might be true with the NCAA football plan.

While the NCAA was battling on a number of legal fronts and Walter Byers was warning that the NCAA was liable to be "blind-sided with antitrust charges," the CFA was pouring its efforts into creating a TV plan with which it would feel comfortable.[24] The CFA Television Study Committee members had met with representatives of the three major networks and ESPN in April of 1980 to discuss their feelings about a TV plan involving two networks. Not surprisingly, only ABC, the network that had carried the colleges for the past decade and a half, favored continuing with a single-network plan. CBS's Kevin O'Malley suggested that two networks would bring additional promotion to the series and increase regional appearances, thus gaining higher ratings and greater advertising revenues. ESPN's Chet Simmons, as expected, spoke out for the flexibility that a cable TV station would be able to offer, for instance, by providing prime-time telecasts.[25]

The meeting between the CFA and networks, along with a previous CFA memorandum, received keen attention from the NCAA Television Committee, and the NCAA invited the CFA Television Study Committee and ABC to make presentations at its next meeting. Discussion of the CFA's written response to the NCAA TV policy monopolized much of the meeting. The CFA, with Chuck Neinas as its major spokesman, demanded that the CFA receive a greater share of income from future telecasts, increased regionalization of telecasts, and a reorganization of Division I to eliminate non-big-time institutions such as the Ivy League schools. Neinas also recommended that strong consideration be given to having two networks carry NCAA football. He closed with a statement that the CFA institutions wanted to remain within the NCAA structure, but the threat of its withdrawal from the NCAA remained.[26]

The outspoken CFA Television Study Committee surveyed CFA membership to find out the level of support for changes in the NCAA TV plan. There was nearly unanimous response to the survey, but members held differing opinions as to future directions. Less than one-third of CFA members wanted to increase the total number of football TV appearances, and, surprisingly, only a little more than half called for allowing only Division I football schools to vote on the NCAA TV plan. About four out of five institutions favored investigating a two-network plan. As far as reversing the trend of utilizing TV football revenue for other NCAA related projects, a major concern of the Television Study Committee, consensus was lacking. While 70 percent of respondents approved cutting back on these expenditures, there was support for spending TV money on NCAA enforcement, championship travel in all sports, and postgraduate scholarships. The least-favored expenditures were expenses for women's championships, if the NCAA were to sponsor women's sports, and construction of a NCAA building. Despite the recommendations of the CFA Television Study Committee, only 27 percent of CFA schools favored the development of a separate CFA TV plan. Those who did favor one cited the expenditure of TV money on non-football projects as a major reason.[27] The CFA itself, unlike its Television Study Committee, was far from united in its opposition to the NCAA TV plan, and so it had to proceed more slowly in its efforts to gain greater money for CFA institutions.

While the CFA lacked power of unanimity among its big-time member institutions and had been unsuccessful in enlisting any Big 10 or PAC-10 schools into membership, it believed it had the power of law over institutional TV property rights. Nearly three decades before, a Georgia Tech alumnus worried over handing rights to the NCAA had written: "To lose your right to televise football in Atlanta could destroy a very valuable asset."[28] The property right to telecast intercollegiate football, the NCAA assumed, had been granted to the NCAA since 1951. The CFA challenged this assumption beginning in early 1981, and within the year a court case would be brought to test it.

By March 1981, the CFA board of directors had determined that it would ask member institutions to withhold their votes on the proposed 1982–85 NCAA TV plan and to consider one proposed by the CFA. Chairman of the CFA board, President Fred Davison of the University of Georgia, asked each CFA institution to "maintain its options" by withholding its vote. Davison, advised by legal counsel, believed that an alternative CFA television plan would not be in violation of the NCAA constitution. The CFA plan would ensure greater income to CFA members while providing the NCAA with a hefty 8 percent of the TV receipts.[29] The plan, nevertheless, was a direct challenge to NCAA control.

The NCAA council was clearly upset and met the following month, adding an official bylaw interpretation that "the Association shall control all forms of televising of the intercollegiate football games of member institutions during the traditional football season." That action, the CFA retorted, was "a direct usurpation of the right of each member institution to control its own property." Television rights, the CFA maintained, were "no less institutional than control over gate receipts. . . . Property rights must not be relinquished by innuendo and the [NCAA's] past practices and customs."[30] The CFA, in other words, was challenging the NCAA's assumption that institutions relinquished their property rights when they became members of the NCAA. "The principle of institutional control of institutional property," a CFA position paper declared, "must be sacrosanct."[31] The battle began.

NCAA leaders decided to use a power play, in part based on the membership's 220-6 vote to accept the NCAA TV plan, even though they knew that a number of CFA members had withheld their votes. Division I-A had voted 60-1 for the plan with 26 abstentions.[32] With NCAA council backing, President James Frank threatened university presidents who did not accept the NCAA TV plan with "several penalties," including probation or possible expulsion and having their institutions cited as members not in good standing.[33] NCAA officials knew that there was no unanimous push among CFA institutions to have their own TV contract, and they also knew that if the CFA members left the NCAA or were removed from it, they would be losing a very lucrative $48 million three-year TV contract for the NCAA basketball tournament.[34] Football was no longer the only driving force among big-time institutions, though it was still the most important for the majority of the schools. With the Big 10 and PAC-10 on the side of the NCAA and with the NCAA basketball tourney as part of the power equation, there was no clear sense of who would win the fight for control of football telecasts. Nor was it clear whether institutional property rights could be relinquished to the NCAA by a vote of the majority of the members. The CFA, working with NBC, quickly developed its own TV plan and prepared for legal action.

The CFA joined forces with NBC, who, after twelve years of telecasting the NCAA basketball tourney, had only recently lost a bitter battle to CBS for the tournament contract. The competitiveness and vindictiveness among networks was well known, and this atmosphere was combined with Chuck Neinas's animosity toward both the Big 10's Wayne Duke and his former boss at the NCAA, Walter Byers.[35] This led to the most volatile situation in the NCAA since the fight over the Sanity Code and the failed expellant vote in 1950. NBC let it be known that it would pay big dollars for a CFA football contract, as a kind of retaliation against CBS for grabbing the Final Four tourney. The CFA knew that it had to bring in more money to its members than would be generated by the NCAA contract, and only in June had the CFA board of directors authorized a CFA TV plan for football. At that June meeting, CFA legal counsel Philip Hochberg had advised the leaders being harried from the outside: "You are not troublemakers; you are not rabble-rousers; you are not insurgents trying to tear down the fabric of collegiate athletics; . . . you are seeking to get your fair share."[36] The CFA by then had the comfort of knowing that NBC would share expenses in any lawsuit between the CFA and the NCAA over television rights.[37]

While the NCAA worked out a four-year agreement with ABC, CBS, and Turner Broadcasting, the CFA reached a deal with NBC. Whereas the NCAA plan was composed of the entire NCAA membership, including CFA members, the CFA plan embraced only its sixty-three institutions. NBC agreed to a $180 million CFA contract for the 1982–85 football seasons. A week later, ABC and CBS agreed to four-year contracts with the NCAA, for a combined $263.5 million, along with an additional $17.7 million for two years on cable from Turner Broadcasting. Both the NCAA and CFA received exceptionally lucrative contracts, and each group, naturally, claimed that its contract was more beneficial to its constituents than the other.[38] Once the CFA had signed a preliminary agreement with NBC, however, it had to convince individual schools to ratify the deal. Chaos reigned as both the NCAA and the CFA attempted to sell rights to their telecasts but remained unsure if they could deliver the number of institutions necessary for the networks to carry the games.

An initial August vote of CFA members showed that only thirty-three favored the NBC deal while twenty opposed it; several other schools abstained. A final vote was set for September 10, but before it could take place the CFA board decided that the NCAA's threat to penalize CFA institutions was so great that legal action was necessary to protect its members. Thus the University of Oklahoma and the University of Georgia, representing the entire CFA membership, filed a federal class-action suit against the NCAA two days before the final TV vote was to take place. On the same day, the University of Texas brought a similar suit in the Texas State Court and quickly obtained a temporary restraining order against the NCAA.[39]

By then, the Big 8 Conference presidents had called for a special NCAA meeting to once again attempt to reorganize the association. "Reorganization was essential," the presidents concluded, "if the Big 8 is to remain a part of the NCAA."[40] Under this pressure and other big-time demands, the NCAA council agreed to a special convention to reorganize, reducing the number of Division I-A members and increasing the size of Division I-AA. "We want to stay in the NCAA and if an open dialogue leads to a restructuring that is responsive to our legitimate needs, it'll be a big step forward," stated Joe Paterno of Penn State, representing the CFA's view. "But if we're led down the garden path one more time, it may be the last time."[41] The threat of a CFA TV contract or CFA withdrawal from the NCAA caused some institutions that might otherwise have resisted to see that the future of the NCAA was at stake. But not everyone was convinced of the threat. Francis Bonner, vice president of Furman University, called the special convention "a concession to the CFA. . . . It gives them the impression, that the NCAA will go to any ends to keep them in the fold and restore harmony." The CFA ploy, Bonner believed, "was a bluff, and it worked."[42] The call for a special meeting pushed the CFA to delay final acceptance of the NBC contract until mid-December, and the courts also agreed to postpone hearings of the cases brought by the three universities until after the December convention.

Although the special convention had been called for the sole purpose of reorganizing Division I, the CFA wanted to discuss the question of football television rights.[43] Oklahoma's President William Banowsky wrote a strong letter protesting that the convention agenda lacked a discussion of TV property rights. "A special convention agenda limited solely to Division I restructuring without consideration of the football television and cablecasting rights issue," Banowsky told the NCAA president, "cannot lead to amicable resolutions of the legal issues."[44] The NCAA steadfastly refused to broaden the agenda.

The NCAA council, though, was sensitive to the TV issue, and it pushed legislation to provide each Division (I-A, I-AA, II, and III) with control of its own football television policies.[45] Each of the nine NCAA council proposals at the special convention passed, as the NCAA reduced the number of Division I-A members from 137 to 92. This was accomplished by requiring Division I-A football schools to have averaged 17,000 paid spectators per game over the previous four years and to play in stadiums with at least 30,000 seats.[46] All CFA institutions, as well as the Big 10 and PAC-10 schools, met these new Division I-A membership requirements. With the restructuring of Division I-A, the CFA institutions voted to reject the CFA-NBC TV contract. Television could now be controlled by the big-time institutions within the NCAA, but waiting in the federal court was the significant Oklahoma and Georgia lawsuit. Property rights would eventually be settled, but not before three years of court battles.

22 Oklahoma and Georgia Carry the TV Ball for the CFA Team

NOTRE DAME waited three decades for the NCAA television plan to be dismantled. Never far from the action, Notre Dame often stayed in the background, offering moral and financial support when it was not taking a leadership role. Because Notre Dame was the most important football institution and was recognized as such by most other institutions, its support in the CFA's efforts and the Oklahoma-Georgia lawsuit was key.

A couple of months before Oklahoma headed the legal case against the NCAA, the leaders at Oklahoma had to make a decision whether or not to accept the proposed CFA-NBC TV package. Specifically, they wanted to know if Notre Dame intended to sign the NBC offer. If Notre

Dame chose not to sign, it would cause problems for the rest of the CFA institutions.[1] Father Edmund Joyce, Notre Dame's vice president in charge of intercollegiate athletics, confirmed Notre Dame's support. "All the CFA members, including Notre Dame, should stand united behind the plan developed by the CFA Board of Directors." Joyce, while visiting the Vatican in Rome, wrote: "My heart is with the CFA."[2] The words would ring hollow in less than a decade, but in the midst of the TV fight they helped give resolve to other leaders of the CFA to continue their challenge of the NCAA TV policy.

With the support of Notre Dame and some other CFA members, Oklahoma and Georgia carried on the legal struggle. When the CFA voted in December 1981 to drop the CFA-NBC TV plan, Oklahoma and Georgia might well have withdrawn their litigation against the NCAA. In the first three weeks of the lawsuit, Oklahoma ran up legal fees of nearly $20,000 and sent the bill on to the CFA for payment.[3] By early 1982, it was unclear how much assistance could be forthcoming from CFA members. Support was so tenuous that the CFA withdrew from the class-action lawsuit Oklahoma and Georgia had launched against the NCAA.[4] Yet President William Banowsky stood firm for Oklahoma, showing a righteous determination akin to the Christian fundamentalism he displayed as a member of the Church of Christ. College athletics were an important part of Banowsky's life; he said, "I might not have gotten a college education if they hadn't given me a baseball scholarship."[5] Football, television rights, and the University of Oklahoma appeared to be as vital to Banowsky as did his religion. With or without CFA help, he was determined to continue the legal battle.[6]

Oklahoma, the lead institution in the challenge, had requested financial support when the court case began in early September 1981. That support came first from the CFA, as executive director Chuck Neinas promised that the CFA would reimburse the Oklahoma lawyers until the case came up for trial.[7] Neinas believed that the NCAA was attempting to increase legal costs so that "the other side simply cannot afford to maintain the struggle. It has worked for them in the past," Neinas claimed, "and is obviously working for them in this case."[8] Georgia was willing to split litigation costs with Oklahoma, but the two institutions wanted assurance that the CFA or institutions within the CFA would continue to fund the case. Support from individual institutions or conferences within the CFA was critical, for the NCAA had a substantial amount of television money to help fight the case. In 1981 alone, the NCAA spent well over $1 million defending itself in a variety of cases, but it had millions of income from football telecasts and from the basketball tournament to support these heavy costs.[9] The CFA, on the other hand, was running a large deficit as a result of its early commitment to fund the legal costs coming principally from the University of Oklahoma.[10] To help pay these extraordinary expenses, members and conferences of the CFA were asked individually to contribute, as not all institutions supported the legal action. The Southeastern Conference gave $25,000, while Notre Dame and Penn State were the first individual institutions to contribute to the TV Legal Fund of the CFA.[11]

By March of 1982, Oklahoma and Georgia announced they would battle the NCAA only on the issue of antitrust violations; the issue of property rights, so important to them earlier, would be removed from the case.[12] Though the property rights issue did not entirely disappear from future legal decisions, emphasis was placed instead on issues of a NCAA monopoly. As the fall 1982 football season began, Federal Judge Juan Burciaga of the Western District in Oklahoma gave his first ruling on the court case, stating that institutions were entitled to the television property rights and condemning the "presumptuous seizure" and "commandeering" of those rights by the NCAA. Further, he ruled that the NCAA could not prohibit member institutions from selling or assigning their property rights, nor could it require the relinquishing of TV rights as a condition of membership. More importantly, Judge Burciaga concluded that the NCAA contract for 1982–85 with CBS, ABC, and Turner Broadcasting violated sections 1 and 2 of the Sherman Antitrust Act of 1890. The Sherman Act states: "Every contract, combination in the form of trust or otherwise, or conspiracy, in restraint of trade or commerce among the several States, or with foreign nations, is declared to be illegal." The NCAA controls, he said, were "unreasonable, naked restraints on competition" done for "rank greed" and a "lust for power."[13] The NCAA, pointedly, was ruled to be a classic cartel that fixed prices and limited production.

Judge Burciaga used the legal "rule of reason" analysis rather than a "per se" test to determine the antitrust violation. That is, even though the NCAA fixed the price of each telecast without regard to a free-market price and threatened to boycott any institution that would telecast its own games, under the rule of reason these antitrust violations might be found to be reasonable. A per se violation would have to be held to violate the antitrust laws "regardless of any asserted justification or alleged reasonableness."[14] Under the rule of reason, a judge might believe there was an antitrust violation but allow it to exist because it was a reasonable restraint of trade, such as allowing only one television cable system to exist in any particular area. The only NCAA victory, if it could be called that, was the decision of Judge Burciaga to weigh the case under the rule of reason. If the NCAA took the case to a higher court, that court would logically also decide under the rule of reason, and it might turn around and decide that the antitrust violations were reasonable. The NCAA monopoly might be allowed, for instance, if it protected college football telecasting from hurting gate attendance and helped maintain competitive balance in big-time football, as the NCAA argued.[15]

Though Judge Burciaga rejected an NCAA request for a stay or temporary suspension of his ruling, the NCAA got what it wanted from a U.S. Court of Appeals.[16] A stay was granted so that the NCAA TV contract would continue during the 1982 season until the appealed decision was rendered. In the spring of 1983, the U.S. Court of Appeals affirmed the lower court decision in a split 2-1 vote: it agreed that the NCAA TV plan constituted illegal price fixing. This time, however, the Appeals Court made its decision under the harsh per se ruling.[17] The dissenting opinion gave hope to the NCAA, for Judge Barrett believed the NCAA TV restraints, though anticompetitive, were fully justified under the rule of reason. The restrains were, Barrett believed, part of an attempt "to maintain intercollegiate football as amateur competition."[18]

The NCAA then appealed to U.S. Supreme Court Justice Byron R. "Whizzer" White for a stay to allow the NCAA TV plan to continue until the Supreme Court could hear the case. White had been an All-American football player at the University of Colorado in the mid-1930s, a member of the scholastic honorary Phi Beta Kappa, and a Rhodes Scholar. In 1969, he had received the highest NCAA accolade, the Theodore Roosevelt Award. White's sympathies had long been with amateur college athletics, and he believed that the NCAA was upholding amateur ideals when he granted a stay for a second NCAA telecasting season to continue with ABC, CBS, and TBS.[19]

While the U.S. Supreme Court was deciding whether or not it would take the case, a major question arose that involved not only the CFA and NCAA but also higher education in general. The American Council on Education (ACE) was concerned that if the football television case was argued on a per se basis rather than under the rule of reason, it might set a precedent for judging all commercial activities in higher education under the harsher per se analysis.[20] "The failure of the courts to adopt a rule of reason analysis," wrote the ACE counsel, "could subject a multitude of cooperative college and university activities to a vigorous antitrust examination."[21] As universities became increasingly involved in both collective and commercial ventures, a per se decision against the NCAA could have disastrous effects upon higher education. When the ACE offered its brief as amicus curiae to the Supreme Court, it noted the peril of a per se analysis with intercollegiate athletics, which it felt was on "a collision course with broader educational goals." The Sherman Antitrust Act, the ACE stated, was designed for the business world, not higher education.[22]

Even the CFA had good reason to want a rule of reason analysis rather than a per se ruling. If the CFA was victorious through the Oklahoma-Georgia suit against the NCAA TV plan, then the CFA would want to have its *own* TV plan be considered acceptable if a court case ensued.[23] A proposed Supreme Court brief prepared by the CFA but evidently never sent stated that the CFA favored a rule of reason treatment because the CFA "could violate antitrust laws, but still be allowed to contract for a group of colleges." A per se ruling would "threaten the ability of any sports organization . . . to act as a joint sales representative or marketer."[24] Chaos would result. So the NCAA and CFA were in agreement, at least, on the per se–rule of reason issue, though not publicly."[25] The CFA officially submitted a document to the Supreme Court concluding that the NCAA's behavior "mandates a per se analysis."[26] At this point, triumphing over the NCAA apparently had become more important to the CFA than any future CFA TV contracts.

While this legal question was being raised, the NCAA had to make a decision on whether it would seek antitrust exemption from Congress. Even before the Appeals Court decision, the NCAA had been considering "an end run," according to President Banowsky of Oklahoma, by asking for legislation from Congress to do what otherwise was illegal under the Sherman Antitrust Act.[27] Indeed, the NCAA council proposed a resolution for the 1983 NCAA convention to seek from Congress, as a final alternative, "an exemption from the Federal antitrust laws permitting the adoption, performance and carrying out by the Association . . . of a football television plan controlling the televising by member institutions of their games." It was approved by a two-thirds vote of convention delegates despite opposition to any exemption from CFA institutions and some Big 10 and PAC-10 universities.[28]

Almost immediately, the ACE leadership expressed a major concern if football was singled out for a higher education antitrust exemption.[29] The ACE had its own television committee, and its leaders could see the larger picture and the impact upon higher education. Trouble lay ahead if only one small (but visibly significant) realm of education had anti-trust protection while the rest of higher education, and its continually increasing commercial interests, were left unprotected. If football telecasts were exempt and other higher education commercial interests were challenged in the courts, there might be an even greater chance that the new cases would be judged under per se analysis.[30] The ACE worked feverishly to forestall the NCAA's request for Congressional exemption and soon asked the U.S. Supreme Court to decide the TV case by a rule of reason analysis when the case reached the highest court.[31] The ACE got its way, as the Supreme Court case was decided on a rule of reason basis and the NCAA did not request Congressional exemption from anti-trust laws.[32]

The U.S. Supreme Court heard the TV case in March of 1984 and three months later handed down its decision.[33] Its judgment was based on a rule of reason rather than per se analysis, as used by the U.S. Court of Appeals. The Supreme Court voted 7-2 to declare the NCAA TV plans a purely commercial venture in which the universities participated solely for the pursuit of profits. The NCAA had illegally fixed the prices of telecasts, artificially limited the production of televised college football, unlawfully boycotted potential broadcasters, and threatened boy-cotting institutions that diverged from the NCAA TV plan.[34] The NCAA's long-held argument that controlled telecasts would preserve gate receipts was discarded. The NCAA TV plan, the Supreme Court decided, had "evolved in a manner inconsistent with its original design to protect gate attendance." The NCAA, the court reasoned, was telecasting during all hours in which college football games were played across the nation. "The plan simply does not protect live attendance by ensuring that games will not be shown on television at the same time as live events. . . . The greatest flaw in the NCAA's argument," the Supreme Court majority argued, "is that it is manifest that the new plan for foot-ball television does not limit televised football in order to protect gate attendance."[35] It was the first time the Supreme Court had ruled amateur sport to be in violation of antitrust laws.

Two justices dissented from the majority opinion. Justices Byron White and William Rehnquist believed the NCAA television plan had objectives beyond mere profitability and asserted that noncommercial goals played a central role in college sports programs. According to them, the NCAA attempted "to maintain intercollegiate athletics as an integral part of the education program and the athletes as an integral part of the student body and, by so doing, retain a clear line of demarcation between college athletics and professional sports." In short, they believed that the NCAA contributed to keeping college sport amateur and educational "as distinguished from realizing maximum return on it as an entertainment commodity." In a view explicitly not accepted by the other seven members of the court, White and Rehnquist held that the television plan reflected the NCAA's "fundamental policy of preserving amateurism and integrating athletics and education."[36]

Justices White and William Rehnquist notwithstanding, the Supreme Court ruling meant the return of Home Rule for television. Each university could return to standards in the pre-1951 era, when TV property rights unquestionably belonged to individual institutions and conferences. A television free market legally existed again. The apparent winners were the CFA and the television networks and cable systems, not to mention the the fans, who would be treated to a plethora of future games. The CFA appeared to have gained power at the expense of the NCAA. The television networks could probably negotiate contracts for lower prices, while cable systems could negotiate for games previously closed to them. The lawyers on both sides made large sums of money, while those on the winning side gloated.[37]

One could almost hear Notre Dame's president Theodore Hesburgh and his longtime vice president, Edmund Joyce, singing "Cheer, Cheer for Old Notre Dame." Their three-decade fight had been won by a touchdown and an extra point in the U.S. Supreme Court as seven judges agreed with what Notre Dame had been claiming since 1951. The much newer CFA believed their newfound freedom from the yoke of the NCAA would bring financial success through a CFA TV plan. Yet it did not. The freedom of the marketplace brought increased commercialism, but not profits, to the big-time institutions. The Supreme Court's ruling in the Oklahoma-Georgia case reinforced the belief of those who saw big-time college sport as a business entity, not an educational venture. Among them was John Toner, president of the NCAA. Of Oklahoma and Georgia, Toner lamented, "football is a property right to be used as a business tool to make money for their institutions."[38] One thing is clear: the Supreme Court decision reinstated Home Rule for institutions and conferences and created telecasting chaos for the next decade. Nearly all participants, including CFA member institutions, became financial losers after having gained freedom to further commercialize intercollegiate athletics.

TV, Home Rule Anarchy, and
Conference Realignments

FOR THE MONTH or so following the Supreme Court antitrust ruling against the NCAA television policy, the telecasting of big-time football was thrown into frenetic confusion. The day after the Supreme Court decision, the NCAA Division I-A Television Committee conducted hearings in Chicago with conferences, independents, and television networks to determine future actions. Seven of the nine NCAA committee members, ironically, represented CFA member institutions. The purpose of the hearings was to devise a less restrictive NCAA plan to concur with the court's decision to break up the NCAA TV monopoly. Despite a memorandum written by the lawyers for victorious Oklahoma warning that the "NCAA cannot do under a different name what the NCAA is prohibited from doing," the hearings indicated that a large majority of Division I-A favored a NCAA plan.[1]

Within days, the NCAA constructed a new voluntary TV package. The TV committee and NCAA Council quickly endorsed it.[2] Plans of the NCAA called for a three-and-a-half-hour period on Saturdays when individual colleges or groups of colleges could televise football games, and no one school could appear more than four times a year. However, when the 1984 plan was submitted to all Division I-A institutions, it was defeated 66-44 on July 10.[3] All forty-one non-CFA institutions, including those in the Big 10 and PAC-10, voted for the NCAA plan, while CFA institutions, a controlling majority of Division I-A members, opposed the plan in near unanimity.[4]

Individual institutions began testing the water for instant riches as the NCAA was attempting to reenter the TV arena. Notre Dame, which had watched quietly during the Oklahoma-Georgia court case, surprisingly turned down a $20 million network offer for its own games, deciding instead to stay with its fellow CFA members.[5] Other institutions, such as Oklahoma, Georgia, Nebraska, and Southern California, put their games up for sale, but the results were disappointing. Only Notre Dame could attract a significant national audience and multimillion dollar contracts.

Meanwhile, the CFA was wasting little time reentering the TV sweepstakes. The CFA met at the same time and in the same Chicago hotel at which the NCAA was drawing up its proposed TV plan. That Midwest city may have been picked by the NCAA for more than its central location in the nation. It was Big 10 territory, and the Big 10 and PAC-10 had never seen eye-to-eye with the CFA. Wayne Duke, who had beaten out Chuck Neinas for the prestigious position of Big 10 commissioner a few years before, had bitterly said that the CFA's votes against the proposed NCAA plan were truly votes "against the NCAA, more specifically against Walter Byers, and that's tragic. . . . It was calculated to replace the NCAA with the CFA." The editor of *Football News* called Duke's comments "a classic insult to the president of the CFA." It was "vintage Duke" the CFA organ noted, "at his patronizing best. It was Duke the antique administrator of the cobwebbed Big 10."[6] The tension between the CFA and the Big 10 was unprecedented. Within weeks, the CFA came up with about $35 million worth of contracts with ABC and ESPN for the 1984 season. That came close to the $39 million earned the previous year under the NCAA plan, but it took about twice as many telecasts to bring in $4 million less. That, according to a CFA spokesman, Richard Snider, was still "better than expected."[7]

The Big 10 and PAC-10 again stood alone and contracted with CBS for about $10 million, considerably less than their payment of more than $14 million from the previous NCAA plan. However, the Big 10 and PAC-10 had one plum—the Rose Bowl, the "granddaddy" of the bowl games. That single game was worth a total of $11 million to the two conferences each year.[8]

There were no immediate financial winners among the big-time football institutions after the antitrust ruling.[9] As Jim Litvack, an economics professor at Princeton, stated: "Some colleges learned what we teach in Econ I. Members of a monopoly form that monopoly to make lots and lots of money. . . . You break that monopoly and they no longer make as much money."[10] Litvack was probably tweaking the Division I-A schools, for he was also executive director of the Ivy League, which had only recently been driven out of Division I-A status when the NCAA reorganized. The victors, if there were any, were the television networks and syndicators who could now purchase TV rights at bargain prices.

An immediate mad scramble for big-time football telecasting took place within a month of the Supreme Court ruling. It resulted in a confusion of ten networks and syndicators carrying multiple telecasts through most of the afternoon and evening hours each Fall Saturday. There was little collective concern to preserve gate receipts by limiting telecasting, as the NCAA had claimed was needed in its losing Supreme

Table 6   **Preseason Lineup of 1984 College Football Telecasting**

Network / Syndicator	Licensor	Number of Games
ABC	CFA	20
CBS	Big 10 / PAC-10	15
	Army / Navy	1
	Boston College / Miami	1
ESPN	CFA	15
Jefferson Productions	ACC	12
Katz Communications	Big 8	11–14
	Eastern Independents (Boston College, Pitt, Syracuse, Miami)	15
TCS / Metro Sports	Big Ten	12–15
	Notre Dame	4
	PAC-10	12–15
	Penn State	3
Raycom	SWC	8
SportsTime	Missouri Valley	8–12
WTBS	Mid-American Conference	8–12
	SEC	8–12
PBS	IVY	8

Lineup of 1983 College Football Telecasting

Network	Licensor	Number of Games
ABC	NCAA	35
CBS	NCAA	35
WTBS	NCAA	19

Source: House Subcommittee on Oversights and Investigations of the Committee on Energy and Commerce, Televised College Football, Hearing, 98th Cong., 2d sess., 31 July 1984.

Court defense. The dog-eat-dog world of free enterprise television reigned supreme. Even the Ivy League got involved by choosing the Public Broadcasting System as its network. The PBS sports broadcasts of the Ivies appeared to be more an educational model, something new in the history of Ivy League sports as well as that of intercollegiate athletics in general.[11]

Congress was not to be left out of the television picture. Shortly after the June 1984 Supreme Court decision, Congress began hearings on televised college football in order to determine the consequences of the breakup of a classic cartel and the reinstatement of collegiate Home Rule, or a free market, in television.[12] Would a television free market lead to a collapse of intercollegiate athletics as it was known? Should Congress grant the NCAA a limited exemption from antitrust laws? The NCAA believed that it should once again be given television rights. NCAA president John Toner testified, evoking Justice White's minority opinion, that his organization should control any TV plan because the NCAA was designed to foster the "goal of amateurism [while] reducing the financial incentives toward professionalism . . . so that intercollegiate athletics supplement, rather than inhibit, educational achievement." The PAC-10's Wiles Hallock, citing twenty-one years of NCAA TV experience, told a Congressional committee that the NCAA had done an exemplary job of "preserving the integrity of the great game of college football," and that was "more important than all the money in the world."[13]

Congress, however, did not agree with the NCAA leadership. Congressional leaders were more prone to agree with a Des Moines television executive who testified that "no legislative action is necessary. . . . Congress should not grant the NCAA or any other group a monopoly over college football on television."[14] In not doing so, Congress was being rather consistent in its movement to deregulate American business in the 1970s and 1980s. The decision to leave college football telecasting deregulated was compatible with the deregulation in the telephone industry, airlines, and rail, trucking, and financial organizations, including the ill-fated savings and loan institutions.[15] Colleges would have to learn to compete in the world of free market television, just as they had learned long before to compete on the football field.

At first there were no winners among the universities in the television sweepstakes, with the possible exception of the CFA in general. The CFA, and especially Chuck Neinas, had got what they wanted from the Supreme Court decision. Neinas was not exactly forthright when he told members of a Congressional hearing that the CFA had not been created "to grab more television exposure and revenues."[16] With the Supreme Court decision, Neinas and the CFA, composed of five major conferences and several prominent independents, could replace Walter Byers and the NCAA as the dominant television entity. The NCAA's attempt to recreate a national TV plan following the Supreme Court decision was abandoned when the NCAA Television Committee decided on November 1, 1984 not to pursue an in-season network contract.[17] Had the CFA been successful in getting the Big 10 and the PAC-10 to join in its plan, it could have gained its own monopoly among the big-time institutions. Yet, the Big 10 and PAC-10 presidents were wary of the CFA's motives from the first, and they continued to be skeptical following the return to Home Rule in television.

The CFA immediately came into antitrust conflict over television with the Big 10 and PAC-10, owing to two scheduled "crossover" games between CFA institutions and members of the PAC-10. An early season game between the CFA's Nebraska and the PAC-10's UCLA and a later game between the CFA's Notre Dame and the PAC-10's USC were both PAC-10 home games. As such, they would be telecast by CBS, the network of the Big 10 and PAC-10. However, the CFA refused to allow its institutions to be telecast in so-called crossover games. UCLA and USC had to go to Federal District Court for a ruling that the CFA was violating antitrust laws by refusing to allow CBS to telecast PAC-10 games with the CFA schools.[18] Not content with the ruling, the CFA petitioned an appeals court and lost again, with the court deciding that the CFA was doing what the NCAA had done for the previous thirty years, employing a group boycott and price-fixing.[19] The CFA had learned little from the three years of litigation it had helped fund for its own members, Oklahoma and Georgia.

With a considerable cut in television fees for big-time institutions, the football powers looked for solutions. The animosity among the dominant participants was so great, however, that little could be done. Charles Young, Chancellor of UCLA, called a meeting of fifteen big-time institution presidents toward the conclusion of the first chaotic season under Home Rule. Nine presidents were from CFA institutions, and six were from the Big 10 and PAC-10. Young asked, "How do we get out of the mess we are in?"[20] There were no immediate answers. Two-thirds of a year after the Supreme Court decision, Chuck Neinas lamented that if the NCAA "had responded in a statesmanlike manner, the situation could be entirely different today."[21] Don Canham of Michigan wrote Walter Byers about what he believed could be done with "the football television mess." Byers responded, "I am not convinced progress can be made until everyone is willing to forget the immediate past." Byers said there were "legally permissible answers," but he believed that "those that supported the original lawsuit don't want to consider them."[22] He was right.

Meanwhile Theodore Hesburgh and Edmund Joyce of Notre Dame bided their time within the CFA, waiting for the right moment to create their own network. Notre Dame was in the unique position of being the only "National University" in big-time intercollegiate athletics. As such, it alone commanded recognition by television networks. This had also been true a generation before, when the NCAA had taken away Home Rule rights to television in the 1950s—something Hesburgh and Joyce had clear memories of. Roone Arledge of ABC had reminded the Notre

Dame leaders of their special status in 1977 when he testified at a Congressional hearing. "There is no question," Arledge noted, "that Notre Dame, which is an independent institution and keeps all of the television revenue . . . could do infinitely better selling [its] own schedule to one of the networks and would be a very attractive package."[23] In 1984, Hesburgh and Joyce were still occupying offices in the "Touchdown Jesus" building, the Hesburgh Library, where a mosaic of Jesus is visible through the north goalposts from the floor of the stadium. This time Notre Dame decided to go along with the CFA and its 1984 television contract, even though Notre Dame could have made millions contracting for itself. Six years later, though, Notre Dame finally did what it had wanted to do forty years before.

In early 1990, while Edmund Joyce was involved in negotiating for the CFA's new five-year contract with ABC, Notre Dame secretly withdrew from the CFA television contract and signed a $38 million, five-year contract with NBC. Joyce either had changed his mind or had not been sincere when he had remarked to the CFA's Chuck Neinas that "college football can be preserved and strengthened only by all the major schools acting together."[24] Notre Dame, by acting alone while pretending to cooperate with the CFA, became the first institution since 1950 to have its own football television network. Only Notre Dame could forge such a network agreement, as reflected by an article in *Sports Illustrated* titled "We're Notre Dame and You're Not."[25] The withdrawal was the first major setback to the CFA, and it would not be the last.[26] Once Notre Dame had decided to go its own way, other institutions and, especially, conferences sensed that they, too, might make better deals outside of the CFA.

While independent Notre Dame was mulling over the desire for its own TV network, Penn State, the second most important football independent, began what became a major shift in conference affiliations. With its strong winning tradition as an independent in football, Penn State formally and informally discussed joining conferences throughout the late 1970s and into the 1980s. Penn State officials, especially football coach Joe Paterno, put forth a strong effort to form an all-sports conference in the East that would include football, basketball, and other lesser sports. When the Big East basketball conference was created in 1979, without Penn State, the Eastern all-sports conference idea appeared doomed. Nevertheless, informal discussions continued between leaders at Penn State and Big 10 institutions, including presidents of those schools. Penn State could bring an Eastern presence in television to the

Table 7 **Major Football Television Agreements from 1996**

Conference / Institution	TV Network	Contract Amount	To Year
ACC	ABC / ESPN	$70,000,000	2000
Big East	CBS	65,000,000	2000
Big Ten / PAC-10	ABC	115,000,000	2000
Big 12	ABC / Liberty	100,000,000	2000
SEC	CBS	85,000,000	2000
Notre Dame	NBC	38,000,000	2000

Source: Chronicle of Higher Education, 16 March 1994, A37–38. Amounts are estimates from newspaper accounts, and their accuracy is suspect.

Big 10,[27] while the Big 10 could bring Penn State academic prestige and stronger athletic competition. In December of 1989, without any discussion among athletic directors of the Big 10, Penn State was invited by the presidents to become the eleventh Big 10 member. In less than four years, a football schedule was devised and Penn State was playing football in the Big 10. While the Big 10 had enjoyed a national identity for most of the twentieth century, Penn State gave it an instant television market from the Atlantic Ocean to beyond the Mississippi River.[28] The Big 10 and the PAC-10 now comprised a coast-to-coast television package of twenty-one institutions. Penn State's move was worth millions to the Big 10 Conference, and it excited the imagination of other conferences.

The Big East, a conference created for basketball, was impacted immediately, as a number of Big East institutions also had independent football teams. Having a major university such as Penn State drop such rivals as Boston College, Pittsburgh, Syracuse, and West Virginia from its football schedule would be devastating to big-time Eastern football independents if adequate replacements were not found. The Big East Conference soon included football, when eight big-time football schools—Boston College, Miami, Pittsburgh, Rutgers, Syracuse, Temple, Virginia Tech, and West Virginia—joined together. Miami was vital to the Big East success, as it had won multiple national championships in the previous decade. Immediately the Big East became a recognized power among conferences, one with football TV network potential. The inevitable demise of the CFA TV contract drew closer.

Other conferences began to expand to cover larger areas of the TV marketplace. The Southeastern Conference expanded to twelve teams, drawing Arkansas away from the Southwest Conference. The Atlantic Coast Conference added football power Florida State. The Big 8 drew four members from the Southwest Conference, making it the Big 12. Knowing that the CFA television contract would expire after the 1995 season, the individual conferences made their pitch for TV independence from the CFA in 1993 and produced contracts early in 1994. Beginning in 1996, conferences replaced the CFA in television negotiations as Home Rule encouraged even greater strides back to smaller, but stronger, units negotiating for television money.

Six of the Division I-A conferences and Notre Dame controlled the television market, and Notre Dame was in the lead. Nevertheless, the previous decade of disarray had taken its toll on big-time football institutions. Wayne Duke, former commissioner of the Big 10, reflected: "That was the most debilitating experience I and many others endured in forty years of college administration. . . . It was quite obvious what was going to happen. The idea was there would be overexposure. TV revenue would be down. TV ratings would be down. . . . The conference members would fight each other over TV money. . . . Conference revenue sharing would change . . . and then there would be realignment."[29]

Duke likely also had an opinion about the negative role the CFA and Chuck Neinas had played in the football telecasting mess. Unlike the NCAA, the CFA and Neinas had just about finished their time in the limelight. The NCAA, though driven out of college football for the time being, remained a dominant fixture in intercollegiate athletics. It was able to reign supreme because it still held the annual NCAA Division I basketball tournament. "March Madness," with its closing Final Four basketball extravaganza telecast each year, continued to grow strong under the NCAA even as the NCAA's control of football telecasts was eliminated by the Supreme Court. College basketball came of age on television during the football television turmoil of the 1970s and 1980s.

24 Basketball: From Madison Square Garden to a Televised Final Four

COLLEGE BASKETBALL never reached the popularity of football for most big-time institutions, but since the 1960s it has made remarkable strides to catch up with the gridiron game. From the 1930s, when Ned Irish popularized basketball with nationally visible contests at the Madison Square Garden, the growth of James Naismith's 1891 invention has easily become the second most important college sport, both in game attendance and in television viewing.

The Brooklyn-raised Ned Irish demonstrated entrepreneurial skills in sports from an early age. He was paid to cover school sports as a journalist in New York and continued as a correspondent for New York newspapers while attending the University of Pennsylvania in the mid-1920s. Basketball was his interest. Upon graduation from Penn, he took a position with the New York *World-Telegram*. As the Depression worsened, Irish began working with New York City's flamboyant mayor, Jimmy Walker, who was seeking ways to raise funds for the unemployed. One idea was to hold basketball benefits in the underused Madison Square Garden. In early 1931, the idea was put to the test and a college triple-header filled the arena. When it was decided that regular Madison Square Garden games might be successful, Ned Irish, the young Penn business graduate, stepped into the picture. Backed by New York Giants football owner, Tim Mara, Irish said that he could guarantee the Garden $4,000, the average cost of renting the arena, for each night of college basketball. The 25-year-old sportswriter would schedule games, sell tickets, and create publicity for regular games at the Garden. Early in the 1934 season, Irish scheduled a doubleheader at the Garden that included the feature intersectional contest in which New York University defeated the Irish of Notre Dame, 25-18. With eight doubleheaders in the 1934–35 season, Ned Irish drew nearly 100,000 fans to the Garden. This began a sixteen-year love affair between college basketball fans and Madison Square Garden.[1]

Above all else, it was Ned Irish's promotion of basketball at Madison Square Garden that established college basketball on a national level. One of Irish's games was particularly pivotal in the sports' modernization. Nearly 18,000 fans came out to see Stanford's innovative Hank Luisetti play against coach Clair Bee's Long Island University on December 30, 1936. Only months after basketball had been introduced to the world in the telecasts of the Berlin Olympics, the "best college player ever," Hank Luisetti, brought the western style of play to the communications capital of the world. Luisetti was already a phenomenon in the Pacific Coast Conference when he brought deft ball-handling skills and his one-hand set and running one-hand shots to New York City.[2] His one-hand shots were a marked contrast to the usual two-hand, set-shot style that had been in use since basketball's origin. Luisetti brought excitement to the game as his Pacific Coast Conference champions beat Long Island 45-31 and ended its forty-three-game winning streak. As Luisetti walked off the floor at game's end he received a standing ovation. That season and the next, Luisetti was named Collegiate Player of the Year, and he soon appeared with film star Betty Grable in *Campus Confessions*.[3] Even with no television and little radio coverage to publicize him, Luisetti's name had instant recognition. And while it took over a decade for the one-hand shot to become accepted, Ned Irish had already set the stage for a college basketball national tournament.

With the success of his Madison Square Garden basketball games, Irish decided that a tournament hosted at the Garden could produce a national champion and put money in his pocket. Using the Metropolitan Basketball Writers Association as the sponsoring agent, Irish created the first National Invitational Tournament in 1938. He cultivated great interest both locally and nationally by balancing teams from New York City and other Eastern towns with those from colleges from across the nation. In one semifinal matchup, Colorado defeated New York University 48-47. Colorado's basketball team was led by its all-American football player, Byron "Whizzer" White, who would later, as a Supreme Court justice, side with the NCAA in its telecasting battle. In another semifinal, Temple beat Oklahoma A & M and its successful coach Henry Iba, who much later would become the coach of the first U.S. team to lose in the Olympics in 1972. Temple easily defeated Colorado in the finals, 60-36, and became the first national champion in college basketball.[4]

Interest generated by the Irish's National Invitational Tournament prompted Ohio State coach Harold Olsen to propose a national tournament sponsored by the National Association of Basketball Coaches under the banner of the NCAA. William Owens of Stanford, NCAA president, stated, "The prestige of college basketball should be supported and demonstrated to the nation by the colleges themselves, rather than being left to private promotion and enterprise."[5] Yet the NCAA had no Ned Irish to publicize the event. Conducted just two months before the first sports telecast in America, the finals of the March 1939 NCAA tournament found Oregon defeating Ohio State, 46-33. The site was Evanston, Illinois, on the Northwestern University campus, a far cry from the glamour of New York City's Madison Square Garden. The NCAA recorded a meager $42.54 surplus from the first tourney, one-tenth of the amount the NCAA boxing tournament brought in that year.[6] The NCAA basketball tourney would remain a distant second in national interest to the National Invitational Tournament until the 1950s, when a betting scandal located to a great extent in New York City tarnished the city, Madison Square Garden, and the National Invitational Tournament, driving colleges away from the arena.

The year that the NCAA created its first television plan for football, 1951, was also the year that the greatest scandal in collegiate sport history broke. The ever-present commercialism turned uglier as basketball players found new ways to benefit from the increasingly popular game by accepting payoffs. A college professor from Tulane University spoke out after the scandal broke and asked if it was possible to "dredge [athletics] out of the fetid slough of commercialism in which it is at present sunk."[7] The collegiate sport world had been warned about the selling of games more than a half-century before, when Yale's Walter Camp cautioned colleagues about the commercial-professional spirit surrounding intercollegiate athletics. "A man who begins by selling his skill to a college," the father of American football forewarned, "may someday find himself selling an individual act in a particular contest . . . selling games."[8] That was 1893; it was now 1951 and his words were still appropriate.

The 1951 betting scandal can be traced back to basketball gambling in the 1930s in Madison Square Garden and in the Catskill Mountains. Summer basketball was played as a means of entertainment among resort hotels in the Catskill Mountains north of New York City. The college basketball stars competed in what was snidely dubbed the "Borscht Circuit in the Jewish Alps."[9] The players, often using assumed names, were paid for jobs at the hotels and frequently paid after the games if they won—or if those attending the games won their bets. The gamblers were present and clearly known to the players, who at times were asked to shave points to stay under the point spread or make the final total score end in a nine, a seven, or whatever number a gambler had chosen. Betting pools and thrown games were common.[10]

Gambling was part of the resort college basketball scene during the summers, but the action there was likely more limited than the big-time basketball gambling that went on in New York City, especially at Madison Square Garden contests. According to Kenneth Norton of Manhattan College, "Basketball was not a medium for betting until the intersectional games were started in the Garden. . . . Madison Square Garden . . . created a national game for the people. They created national enthusiasm. It grew and grew and grew."[11] Gambling grew with it. In 1945, the New York City District Attorney's Office tapped the phone of a suspected thief and discovered a basketball fixing plan involving five members of

Brooklyn College's basketball team, each of whom had been paid $1,000 cash. At the same time, Lenny Hassman of City College of New York was dumping, or purposely losing, games under famed coach Nat Holman. On the Pacific Coast, Victor Schmidt, acting commissioner of the Pacific Athletic Conference, warned the conference about the bribing of New York City basketball players.[12] In the Midwest, President Justin Morrill of the University of Minnesota cautioned members of the NCAA that basketball players "will fall an easy prey to the easy-money approaches of unscrupulous gamblers." Morrill warned that "the possibility of a devastating betting scandal hovers like a black Harpy over the big-time intercollegiate athletic scene."[13] On the East Coast, the large Eastern College Athletic Conference discussed the problem of betting odds, tip sheets, and point spreads.[14] Little was done, however, until Frank Hogan of the New York City District Attorney's Office began to uncover and prosecute those involved in the cheating scandal.

In that second year of the U.S. involvement in the Korean War, well before basketball became important on television, District Attorney Hogan discovered thirty-three basketball players from seven institutions, who had been involved in the rigging of at least forty-nine games in nineteen states.[15] Most of the fixed games had revolved around the point spread. Point spreads are used by the gambling industry to increase betting, especially in potentially lopsided games. If a team is predicted to win by a wide margin, say, fifteen points, either a bet on the favored team to win by sixteen or more points or a bet on the underdog to lose by fourteen or fewer points would pay off. The point spread, then, equalized the teams for betting purposes and generally increased the amount of money bet. Gamblers, however, have always preferred a sure bet. Bribing players to keep the score within the point spread does not require a player to intentionally lose a game, only keep the score down if his team is favored by a large margin.

While the scandal appeared to be centered on New York City and Madison Square Garden, it reached out to other parts of the nation as well. Adolph Rupp of Kentucky, the winningest coach in basketball history until Dean Smith, claimed that "gamblers couldn't get to our boys with a ten-foot pole."[16] Lexington was home to both the University of Kentucky and horse racing's Kentucky Derby. According to Phog Allen, who had coached Adolph Rupp at the University of Kansas, Lexington was also the collegiate gambling center of America, well before the University of Kentucky was ever on television. Kentucky had played in featured doubleheaders at the gambling haven, Madison Square Garden, under Rupp since 1935, when it lost to New York University 23-22, and and it continued to play there a number of times before the scandal of 1951 broke.[17] The first known game in which Kentucky players were bought by gamblers was a 1948 game against St. John's in Brooklyn. At first, gamblers asked Kentucky players to go over the point spread, or win by more points than expected, but in later games they were paid to shave points instead. Some Kentucky players, such as the seven-foot Bill Spivey, had played in the Catskill Mountains and had met gamblers there. Though Spivey was innocent except for not reporting having been approached by gamblers, three stars from the 1948 team shaved points, including all-Americans on Rupp's first national champion team, Ralph Beard and Alex Groza. The scandal gave basketball a black eye and caused many to discourage the playing of games outside of university campuses.[18] Kentucky was given the severest sanction by the NCAA following the revelations of the scandal: it was banned from basketball for a year. Basketball was also damaged in New York City, where the National Invitational Tournament came into disrepute. However the game and the NCAA tournament would continue to grow along with the rise of television.

Adolph Rupp's fast-breaking offenses and tight man-for-man defenses at Kentucky generated interest for basketball in the 1940s and 1950s as his teams won three of the first twelve NCAA championships before the tournaments were popularized by television. Kentucky's teams might have won more NCAA championships had they not chosen to participate in the more prestigious National Invitation Tournament. For instance, in 1946, the year the NCAA tournament was first telecast by WCBS in New York City, Kentucky went 28-2 and won the National Invitational Tournament title over Rhode Island. Meanwhile Oklahoma A & M beat North Carolina in the NCAA tourney. The next year, Kentucky was 34-3 and again did not enter the NCAA tournament. In 1947, the Kentucky Wildcats entered the NCAA championships and beat Baylor in the finals, finishing with a 36-3 record. Kentucky repeated in 1949 by defeating Oklahoma A & M and earning a 32-2 record. Rupp's Wildcats returned to the National Invitational Tournament in 1950 and finished 25-5. The next year, after the NCAA tourney had expanded from eight to sixteen teams, Kentucky won the NCAA championship and ended the season 32-2.[19] Kentucky continued in 1952, losing only three games, but was suspended by the NCAA for the 1953 season following the point-shaving revelations.

The scandal rocked the moral sensibilities of intercollegiate athletics, but the NCAA basketball tourney kept expanding as interest in basketball grew. The NCAA brought in four times as much money from attendance at its basketball tourney as it collected from membership dues.[20] Coming back from its year of banishment, Rupp's team went undefeated in 1954, 25-0, but declined entry into the NCAA tournament after three of its players were declared ineligible for the tourney because they were in graduate school. Even though the team had voted 9-3 to go to the NCAA championship tourney, Rupp said no: "If we can't play with our full team, we won't allow a bunch of turds to mar the record established in large measure by our three seniors."[21] That year, 1954, the NCAA finals were telecast nationally for the first time as LaSalle, with the great Tom Gola, beat Bradley University 92-76.

Even with basketball's broadening appeal, it took another decade before there was continuous telecasting of the NCAA finals. But those telecasts would eventually have an influence on black-white relationships and the civil rights movement in America. Unlike NCAA college football, which had begun telecasting on NBC a dozen years before, the 1963 NCAA Final Four was ignored by major TV networks. It was, however, picked up by the Sports Network Incorporated (SNI) and carried by about 120 stations nationally.[22] For six years SNI telecast the basketball finals, paying a mere $200,000 each year for the privilege.[23] The NCAA tournament television revenues were still less than 1 percent of the riches brought in from the football television plan.[24] However, the SNI broadcasts showed the nation the increasing number African American players who began to dominate the game, first in the North and then belatedly in the South. The southern delay was to be expected, for in 1962 it took federal action to allow James Meredith to enroll as the first black student at the University of Mississippi. The following year, Governor George Wallace defied a court order and stood in the door of the University of Alabama to prevent African Americans from attending the state institution. Elsewhere, outstanding black basketball players were starring for their universities. These players included Jerry Harkness of the Loyola of Chicago champions in 1963, Walt Hazzard of the champion UCLA team the following year, Cazzie Russell of Michigan, which lost to UCLA in 1965, and the entire starting team from Texas Western the next year.

The 1966 in NCAA basketball finals were a watershed in black-white sport relations. The Texas Western–Kentucky matchup brought the best-known basketball coach in history, Adolph Rupp, and his "white supremacy theory," together with a Texas Western team composed of five black starters.[25] Rupp had never had a black player on his team in his nearly four decades of coaching at Kentucky. Despite the 1954 Supreme Court decision in *Brown v. Board of Education* and subsequent call to end segregation, Rupp was reluctant to recruit blacks to his state's flagship university. This reluctance was, however, not dissimilar from that of other southern state institutions that still refused to admit African American students, athletes or not, to their universities.

Kentucky was the top-ranked team in the nation, seeking its fifth national championship under Adolph Rupp, when it went up against the underdogs from Texas Western (later the University of Texas–El Paso). The Texas starters came mainly from such inner city locations as New York, Detroit, Houston, and Gary, Indiana. They came to El Paso to play under Don Haskins, a strict disciplinarian who, at age 36, emphasized in practice the hard work of defense. With only one loss for the season, but not having played a team in the national top ten, Texas Western had been able to beat Oklahoma City and Cincinnati before nipping Kansas in two overtimes to reach the Final Four. Though Texas Western had five white players, none of them figured in the defeats of Utah (85-78) or in the championship game with Kentucky (72-65).

Many in the country were surprised that a team of all black starters could beat Kentucky's all-white squad, led by Louie Dampier and Pat Riley, the future prominent pro basketball coach. No one was more surprised than Rupp, who had been convinced that though black athletes had impressive physical skills, they lacked the discipline and intelligence to play his demanding style of game.[26] Haskins received enormous amounts of hate mail after presiding over intercollegiate basketball's version of *Brown v. Board of Education*.[27] Yet the nation had seen firsthand that African Americans could be just as disciplined and intelligent in their approach to basketball as white players. Even the great UCLA coach, John Wooden, appeared surprised at Haskins's success with an all-black group of starters: "To take a bunch of seemingly undisciplined kids and do what Don Haskins did," Wooden stereotypically commented, "is one of the most remarkable coaching jobs I've seen."[28]

Much like Hank Luisetti had helped change basketball from a controlled two-hand, set-shot game to one with more fluid, one-hand shots, African Americans were instrumental in changing the nature of the game by demonstrating a wide variety of improvisational play and individual excellence. Their athletic proficiency and ability to play above the rim increased the lure of basketball as a gate and television attraction. College coaches who were hired to win and fill arenas increasingly needed to recruit talented black players if they wanted to remain in the coaching profession. When, shortly after the Texas Western victory, Vanderbilt University announced that it would accept black athletes, the desegregation of the entire Southeastern Conference followed rapidly. Rupp was reluctant, but three years after his defeat at the hands of Texas Western, and shortly before he retired, he recruited his first African American player, Tom Payne, a seven-foot center.[29] At about the same time basketball in the South was becoming desegregated and interest in telecasting college basketball was on the rise, the NCAA made a proposal for an NCAA television network to include basketball along with football.

Black college basketball players in the 1960s, from Oscar Robertson (player of the year in 1960) to Lou Alcindor, who later changed his name to Kareem Abdul-Jabbar (player of the year in 1969), dominated the game. William Leggett, longtime TV critic for *Sports Illustrated,* pointed out that college basketball became national with the televised Houston-UCLA basketball game in 1968. This was the year of the assassinations of civil rights activist Martin Luther King, Jr., and political liberal Robert Kennedy; the year of the Tet Offensive by the North Vietnamese communists; and the year several black athletic revolts erupted, including the Black Power salutes at the Mexico City Olympics. This was also the year that featured two all-time basketball greats, both African Americans—Houston's Elvin Hayes and UCLA's Lew Alcindor. UCLA came into the game with a forty-seven consecutive-win streak, and Houston had won seventeen straight, undefeated since UCLA had beaten the Houston Cougars in the Final Four championships the previous year. On January 20, 1968, before the largest basketball crowd in history, a standing-room-only audience of 52,693 packed into the Houston Astrodome, 6'9" Elvin Hayes scored thirty-nine points, grabbed fifteen rebounds, blocked eight shots, and handed out four assists, leading his team to a 71-69 victory. Meanwhile, the action was caught by a hastily assembled independent network of 150 stations in forty-nine states.[30] The national audience brought institutional prestige to the competing schools and clearly showed that televised basketball could bring increased revenue to universities. It certainly caught the eyes of athletic administrators, most of whom had heretofore paid attention only to football.

In the early 1970s, the head of the NCAA Television Committee, Forest Evashevski, suggested that an NCAA network should be formed to create a national basketball package to tie in with the football package that had been in existence for two decades. Evashevski, the athletic director at Iowa and its former football coach, told NCAA executive director Walter Byers that Byers was "the one person in whom I have confidence enough to beat [NFL commissioner Pete] Rozelle" and successfully compete with the NFL's three-network package, which at the time included ABC's *Monday Night Football*.[31] Evashevski believed that proceeds from a twenty-six-week series featuring both NCAA football and basketball would meet a financial need in big-time college athletics. In other words, the popularity of televised college basketball could help colleges challenge the NFL's increasing encroachment on the entertainment dollar. Byers agreed that "a national basketball package . . . would indeed be a good tie-in to the football series."[32]

The growing TV market for college basketball was actually already being exploited by conferences within the NCAA. If an NCAA basketball contract was created, either as a tie-in with football or as an independent contract, the NCAA series would come into conflict with conference arrangements. In addition, the networks themselves were not convinced that telecasting college basketball regularly would increase their profits. NBC was only interested in telecasting a few Sunday games immediately preceding the NCAA tournament. CBS thought basketball might meet a Friday-night need on its network but knew that NCAA games would conflict with Friday-night high school basketball. ABC believed that college basketball might fill a niche on Monday nights after *Monday Night Football* was over and also be a good filler for Sunday-afternoon programming. But no network in the mid-1970s saw basketball as truly prime-time programming.[33]

The NCAA Television Committee, nevertheless, promoted the idea of tying a regular-season basketball television series into future basketball championship contracts.[34] The committee knew that the next basketball championship would bring in about $2.5 million from television and that an in-season contract also might be lucrative. The NCAA group recommended such a plan to the NCAA Executive Committee, which approved a schedule of ten basketball games, six to be national telecasts and the other four to receive regional coverage.[35] The membership of the NCAA did not rush to have national controls over basketball as it had for football in 1951. Officials at Indiana University, for instance, replied negatively to an NCAA questionnaire on whether to restrict basketball telecasting, saying, "NCAA basketball television, will have a devastating effect on institutional television."[36] Indiana, with a great basketball tradition, was probably looking enviously across the state at Notre Dame, which already had a national basketball TV network. Big 10 commissioner Wayne Duke told members of the Big 10 that "the NCAA will eventually be involved in controlling basketball telecasts, as it presently controls the television of football games."[37]

Unlike the football plan formulated two decades before, the TV committee's proposal for basketball had nothing to do with protecting gate receipts of the individual institutions—it had only to do with making money. Thus, Walter Byers and the NCAA's legal counsel were aware that the proposed basketball plan might not survive antitrust scrutiny as had football telecasts. Nevertheless, the lure of money kept NCAA officials interested in pursuing a national TV policy on basketball, knowing full well that the 1975 Supreme Court had ruled in *Goldfarb v. Virginia State Bar* that educational institutions were no longer immune from antitrust attack where their activity was of a business nature, such as televised basketball.[38] The NCAA continued proposing possible national basketball television plans until the late 1970s, when NCAA legal counsel, George Gangwere, forcefully addressed the NCAA Television Committee and emphasized that any plan, if taken to court in antitrust action, would have "minimal chances of being successfully defended." The committee finally decided to "abandon any further thought of coordinating a combined tournament and in-season basketball package."[39] That was wise, for the College Football Association was already nipping at the heels of the NCAA football television plan, and pursuit of a profit-driven national basketball network would have further weakened the NCAA's legal position in controlling college football telecasting.

In 1979, the year the NCAA abandoned hope for a national TV plan for basketball, the NCAA basketball championship featured Indiana State's Larry Bird against Michigan State's Earvin "Magic" Johnson. College basketball, unlike college football in the 1960s, was not overshadowed by the professional game. (Ironically, Bird and Johnson would move on to the NBA the next year and help drive professional basketball to unprecedented financial success in the late 1980s.) With these two players, both the college game and the professional game rose to new heights. "March Madness," as the NCAA national basketball championship became known, continued basketball's ascent to challenge football for the number-one place in college athletics.

Whereas big-time college football had no "on the field" championship to create a dynamic climax at the end of the year, college basketball, with its exciting, fast-paced athleticism, particularly that of inner city players, held a showcase event to conclude each season. College football, using its old, conservative bowl game format, could not produce the annual excitement of the spring conclusion to the indoor winter game. Between 1970 and 1975, the basketball championship, featuring greats like Bill Walton of UCLA, Ernie DiGregorio of Providence, David Thompson of North Carolina State, and Kevin Grevey of Kentucky, more than quintupled its TV revenues, while college basketball claimed seven of the top ten basketball telecasts and the pros only three. In another five years, as Butch Lee of Marquette, Jack Givens of Kentucky, Larry Bird, and Magic Johnson displayed their talents, the commercial value of the NCAA championships more than tripled. It tripled again in another five years as Isiah Thomas of Indiana, Patrick Ewing of Georgetown, and Michael Jordan of North Carolina showcased their athletic genius.[40]

The networks, driven by ratings and advertising dollars, raised their bids for the basketball championships just as they had previously done in football. From the late 1960s to the late 1970s, the NCAA basketball tournament as a whole had slightly more than a 10-point television rating compared to more than 12 points for the NCAA football network series. ABC's Roone Arledge took note and campaigned for basketball to become part of the ABC football contract. He told the NCAA in 1967 that outside of football "basketball is the glamour item." Walter Byers and the NCAA knew that, and the TV committee voted unanimously not to combine basketball with the football contract.[41] At the time, the NCAA was being paid less than $200,000 for telecasting the Final Four by SNI.[42] The excitement of the Texas Western victory over Kentucky in 1966 and the beginning of a new era with Lew Alcindor and UCLA the next fall raised the television stakes and opened the eyes of the major networks. At the end of SNI's six-year contract, NBC bought the tourney with a bid more than double the amount SNI had previously paid, making it a million-dollar two-year contract.[43] It was a smart financial decision by NBC, for the 1969 Final Four in Louisville was a sellout, with an excess demand of more than 50,000 ticket requests to see Alcindor and UCLA go for their third consecutive national title under coach John Wooden. The nation was ready to watch, and advertisers were ready to pay the network to hawk their wares. The skyrocketing commercial value of the tournament to colleges and the increased demand for basketball was seen in the number of new arenas built since the 1970s and the dynamic increase in coaching salaries.

There were well-known and well-paid coaches in college basketball before the riches of network telecasting came to the sport in the 1970s and 1980s. Nevertheless, before basketball's surge in popularity there were considerably fewer of them, and nearly all had salaries considerably below those of the big-time football coaches. Walter Meanwell, at the University of Wisconsin from the second decade of the twentieth century to the 1930s, Forrest "Phog" Allen, at the University of Kansas from the 1920s to the 1950s, and the Adolph Rupp, who was at Kentucky for forty years, until the early 1970s, are examples. Yet, basketball coaches' salaries were more in line with university professors' salaries than with company executives, as became case by the end of the century.

Dr. Walter Meanwell, an early exponent of scientific basketball and pattern play, was paid $3,250 in 1916 after winning Big 10 championships in four of the five previous years. At the depths of the Depression, during his last year of coaching, his salary was $6,250.[44] Meanwell's career exemplified commercialism in basketball before radio and television came to be a driving force in intercollegiate athletics. Dr. Meanwell wrote several books on basketball and coauthored a book on athletic training with Knute Rockne, Notre Dame's famed football coach. More importantly, Meanwell endorsed the official Big 10 "Wilson-Meanwell Basketball," the first basketball to have hidden laces and a pressure valve; by doing so, he received a 3 percent royalty on each basketball sold. Meanwell also had a shoe contract with Servus Rubber Company beginning in 1924, from which he received from three to three and a half cents for each pair of shoes sold. His summer basketball coaching clinics further increased his income.[45] Walter Meanwell's business dealings set the tone for the future high-priced shoe contracts, product endorsements, and sports clinics of big-time coaches.

Forrest "Phog" Allen coached college basketball for forty-six years, spending most of his career at the University of Kansas. Just before he retired in 1956 with a leading 591 victories, his salary was $9,500, the highest paid to a coach in the Big 7, which included Missouri, Nebraska, and Oklahoma. Allen was one of the few individuals who was paid as much as the football coach, which was highly unusual then.[46] He coached twenty-four conference championships, successfully conducted a one-man crusade to have basketball included in the Olympics (it first appeared at the 1936 Berlin games), and wrote three books and hundreds of magazine articles. He knew the commercial value of basketball success, but he never had a television contract from which he or his winning teams could benefit financially.

Adolph Rupp's salary, when he began coaching basketball at the University of Kentucky in 1930, was less than half that of Walter Meanwell at Wisconsin. His yearly take of $2,800 included his work as an assistant football coach, a common duty of many if not most basketball coaches then. Rupp previously had played for Phog Allen at Kansas, where Dr.

James Naismith, the inventor of basketball, had spent most of his career. Rupp also spent considerable time visiting the University of Wisconsin and observing Meanwell's screening-type offense. Over the next forty-two years, Rupp, using what he had learned from a number of mentors, set up his own approach, one that was disciplined but still relied on fast breaks. He garnered 874 victories and four NCAA championships, all before television became vital to promoting the game. Because the "Baron of Bluegrass" raised prize beef cattle and choice tobacco, he had his own commercialized income outside of coaching. Not that Rupp was opposed to the commercial aspect of basketball; he was the first to take his basketball teams to Madison Square Garden in 1935. A decade later, his players commercialized themselves when they took bribes to throw games or shave points in the 1940s, leading to the aforementioned betting scandal of 1951.

Rupp appears to have never gotten rich from basketball coaching, contrary to what occurred with regularity after he retired in 1972. By the end of the century, coaches such as Rick Pitino at Kentucky could quickly become millionaires. This was due in part to inflated salaries made possible by increased NCAA tourney TV receipts, but often the windfall came through product endorsements and sums offered by shoe and clothing manufacturers to dress teams in the companies' logos, sometimes in company-sponsored arenas. As an Atlanta Constitution writer anticipated, one might observe the Georgia Tech Nike shoes play against the Clemson Converse shoes in the Georgia Tech McDonald's Center.[47] The logo wars were launched by the companies who profited from the increased commercialization of college sport and are furthered by the successful coaches who can get the company logos on national television—yet these symbols of commercialism are ironically worn by players who are considered amateurs.

Rupp's starting salary of $2,800 is a far cry from the $1 million bonus that Pitino would have received had he coached Kentucky through his 1999–2000 contract.[48] Pitino was considered well worth the salary and bonus promised by Kentucky because he had led Kentucky to a national championship in 1996. In another year, however, Pitino left Kentucky for a ten-year, $70 million contract to coach the professional Boston Celtics.[49] Even Kentucky's television money could not match that offer. Television, however, especially coverage of the highly-rated NCAA basketball tournament, continued to bring in large sums of money, and successful coaches benefitted from it.

The NCAA basketball championship reached new financial heights

Table 8   **TV Ratings: Basketball Championshiop vs. Highest Bowl Rating, 1973–2000**

Year	Basketball Championship	TV Rating	Football Bowl	TV Rating
1973	UCLA–Memphis State	20.5	Rose, USC–Ohio State	30.0
1974	N.C. State–Marquette	19.9	Rose, Ohio State–USC	30.7
1975	UCLA–Kentucky	21.3	Rose, USC–Ohio State	31.3
1976	Indiana–Michigan	20.4	Rose, UCLA–Ohio State	30.6
1977	Marquette–N. Carolina	19.3	Rose, USC-Michigan	26.9
1978	Kentucky-Duke	19.9	Rose, Washington-Michigan	29.2
1979	Michigan St.–Indiana St.	24.1*	Rose, USC-Michigan	23.3
1980	Louisville-UCLA	19.8	Rose, USC–Ohio State	28.6
1981	Indiana–N. Carolina	20.7	Orange, Oklahoma–Florida State	24.1
1982	N. Carolina–Georgetown	21.6	Rose, Washington-Iowa	25.0
1983	N.C. State–Georgetown	22.3	Sugar, Penn State–Georgia	24.4
1984	Georgetown-Houston	19.7	Orange, Miami-Nebraska	23.5
1985	Villanova-Georgetown	23.3	Rose, USC–Ohio State	21.4
1986	Louisville-Duke	20.7	Rose, UCLA-Iowa	22.7
1987	Indiana-Syracuse	19.6	Fiesta, Penn State–Miami	25.1
1988	Kansas-Oklahoma	18.8	Orange, Miami-Oklahoma	20.8
1989	Michigan–Seton Hall	21.3**	Orange, Miami-Nebraska	18.5
1990	U. Nevada Las Vegas–Duke	20.0	Rose, USC-Michigan	14.6
1991	Duke-Kansas	19.4	Orange, Colorado–Notre Dame	18.3
1992	Duke-Michigan	22.7	Rose, Washington-Michigan	15.8
1993	N. Carolina–Michigan	22.2	Sugar, Alabama-Miami	18.2
1994	Arkansas-Duke	21.6	Orange, Florida State–Nebraska	17.8
1995	UCLA-Arkansas	19.3	Rose, Penn State–Oregon	19.6
1996	Kentucky-Syracuse	18.3	Fiesta, Nebraska-Florida	18.8
1997	Arizona-Kentucky	18.9	Sugar, Florida–Florida State	17.9
1998	Kentucky-Utah	17.8	Orange, Nebraska-Tennessee	13.3
1999	Connecticut-Duke	17.2	Fiesta, Tennessee–Florida State	17.2
2000	Michigan State–Florida	14.1	Sugar, Florida State–Virginia Tech	17.5

*First basketball final rated higher than highest bowl game, the Earvin "Magic" Johnson (Michigan State) vs. Larry Bird (Indiana State) contest.
**Basketball finals since 1989 have nearly always rated higher than highest bowl game.

Source: "Report to the NCAA Special Committee to Study a Division I-A Football Championship," 6 May 1994, NCAA Headquarters, B183 and table 7.1; and *Broadcasting and Cable* (1983–2000), passim.

when the NCAA negotiated a $1.725 billion contract with CBS for the 1995–2002 period and a $6 billion agreement for the years 2003–13. Unlike the football bowls, in which networks never knew who would be playing in what game and could not predict ratings from year to year, the NCAA basketball playoffs had consistently high and predictable ratings, an important variable for those willing to spend millions on advertising.

The stability of championship basketball helped it bring in much more money than what football bowl games could offer. From the 1970s on, during every five-year period, the amount of television money generated by March Madness more than doubled. By 1994, the gross revenue from the men's basketball championship had reached $137 million, while all football bowl game receipts were about one-quarter that amount.[50] With the 1995–2002 CBS basketball contract, the $215 million a year from TV alone made for an even greater disparity between the NCAA basketball tourney and football bowls. With an even greater disparity created by the $6 billion contract beginning in 2003, the desire of athletic leaders and television interests to match or exceed the commercial popularity of the NCAA basketball championship led to increased pressure to create a true championship in Division I-A football.

TV's Unfinished Business: The Division I-A Football Championship

AS THE twentieth century came to a close, football telecasting remained a vibrant part of college athletics while bowl games, without a clear-cut Division I national championship, faded like dying stars. They still illuminated the individual institutions that enjoyed the prestige of a winning season, but bowl receipts quickly dwindled.[1] By the end of the century, bowl attendance was declining, TV ratings were dropping, and participating teams were being forced by contract to buy up unpurchased tickets.[2] Nevertheless, corporate sponsorship of bowls, as distracting as it was from the game and as much as it diminished the traditional bowl names with such titles as the Southwestern Bell Cotton Bowl, FedEx Orange Bowl, and Nokia Sugar Bowl, kept the commercialized contests alive for the colleges that still saw value in continuing the tradition.[3]

Like most century-long ideas, the bowl games would not die easily, even though their commercial potential had not kept up with that of March Madness in college basketball or the lure of the playoffs and Super Bowl in professional football. As these traditional bowl games lingered on, the movement toward a true national championship was kept at bay. There were at least five groups who feared a national championship tournament and helped keep the bowl games alive: southern universities, which since the 1930s had gotten more than a fair share of bowl invitations as a way of drawing local supporters to the southern stadiums; most bowl committees, which feared the death of their specific bowls and the subsequent interruption to their way of life; corporate sponsors, who believed in the advertising value of the corporate-named bowls; and many football coaches, who feared a championship that would make losers out of all but one coach, jeopardizing their jobs.[4] The last group, however, was likely more important than these four.

Possibly most influential in keeping the outdated bowls in lieu of a playoff were the college presidents. Though most presidents would never admit it publicly, they feared that football coaches would gain even more power and prestige than they already had if a national championship were promoted. Already at many institutions, the football coach had become far more important than the president in the eyes of the public, the alumni, the students, and, most decidedly, the governing board. Presidents who opposed the playoff system, however, used another justification. They argued that such a playoff would intensify the commercialization of football.

The paradox of a commercial justification by the presidents, however, was as vacuous as it was hypocritical, for presidents were in the forefront of making their entire institutions, not just their athletic departments, commercial ventures rather than principally educational ones. Presidents had been involved in making football a highly commercialized enterprise for a century. They had done this by first allowing the New York City Thanksgiving Day games that began in the 1870s, by hiring coaches and sometimes sharing the gate receipts with them, by building huge stadiums throughout the twentieth century, and by exploiting radio and television for commercial purposes since the 1930s and 1940s.

With this early commercialization, the football coach of a big-time institution was soon in the public eye often more than the president. In 1905, for example, the new 26-year-old Harvard coach, Bill Reid, was paid the enormous salary of $7,000 to lead the Crimson against Yale, a wage nearly equal to that of the best-known educator in America and president of Harvard for over three decades, Charles W. Eliot.[5] Presidents, then and later in the century, were resentful of those who had benefitted most from the commercial intrusions they themselves had made into both university life and their own domain as potentates of institutions of higher learning. Walter Byers, leader of the NCAA for over three decades, was as familiar with the inflated egos of presidents as he was with those of football coaches. He once wrote, "It's hard on the ego of a president to be less admired than his football coach."[6] This was a major reason why presidents blocked a national championship in football, which they felt would further increase the power and prestige of football coaches at their expense.

Television networks, on the other hand, saw a Division I championship playoff as something that, like the Final Four in basketball, could challenge the high TV ratings and advertising dollars of the World Series in professional baseball and the Super Bowl in professional football. Sharp network executives such as Roone Arledge realized the commercial advantage of a playoff not long after television became important to college football. Yet, for all his brilliance, Arledge and ABC could not get NCAA members to move away from the traditional bowl games and produce a true national championship, as had become the norm in each of the other seventy-nine Division I, II, and III sports, including women's athletics, since the 1960s.

Roone Arledge sat down with the NCAA Television Committee in January of 1966 and told members that they would "waste an opportunity if they do not explore nationally the possibility of a bona fide playoff pattern during the three weekends at football season's end to determine a legitimate champion." A playoff, Arledge claimed, "would attract tremendous audiences and big financial returns."[7] At the time, ABC had just recaptured the NCAA football contract, and Arledge clearly saw the immediate advantage to ABC and to himself if his playoff idea were to be accepted. Soon thereafter, the NCAA created a Committee for the Advancement of Intercollegiate Football to "investigate the possibility of an eight-team NCAA championship at season's end in order to lend meaning to each year's competition." This sentence, as well as a statement that the playoff would add "magnetism and excitement" to the football season, were stricken from the final edition of the 1966 NCAA Television Committee Report as a political accommodation to those who opposed creating more commercialism and institutional power among the football leaders, who often dominated other concerns of big-time universities.[8]

A Division I championship was ripe for the picking in the mid-1960s. The NCAA had already created a smaller-college division playoff in football, which was contended at the Grantland Rice Bowl in Murfreesboro, Kentucky, the Camellia Bowl in Sacramento, the Pecan Bowl in Abilene, and the Tangerine Bowl in Orlando. The smaller colleges wanted their championship, the College Division Playoff, to be televised, but the networks were not interested.[9] What the networks were willing to pay for was a big-time championship. ABC, the NCAA carrying network without a professional football contract, could see that the new NFL, with teams from the former American Football League, was about to create a four-division televised playoff. This would add lustre to pro football, likely at the expense of the college game.[10] The pressure from ABC to initiate a college football playoff was resented by some in the NCAA who opposed a championship but favored retaining the familiar bowl games. NCAA Television Committee member Thomas Hamilton compared ABC's promotion of a playoff to the network's urging the year before to carry the famed Notre Dame–Michigan State "championship" game on national TV.[11] Despite the NCAA Television Committee's recommendation to play for a national championship, others at the NCAA resisted both ABC and the committee in the late 1960s.

ABC and Roone Arledge were only the most visible of those calling for a televised national championship in big-time football. As the 1960s came to a close, the nation's involvement in the Vietnam War was causing rapid inflation, hurting athletic departments across the nation. When Management Television Systems (MTS) suggested a two-team, closed-circuit televised national championship in 1971, a number of NCAA leaders listened. The president of MTS, Jesse Brill, claimed that a two-team playoff could gross $15 million. Brill believed that a national, giant-screen, closed-circuit network could bring in several million spectators if some outdoor stadiums were used for the telecasts.[12] Though Walter Byers dismissed the proposal for the time being as illegal for Division I football, it was not a dead issue. Within a couple months, the NCAA Television Committee again voted 8-4 for a single-game championship, but nothing came of the proposal.[13]

Throughout the 1970s, other proposals for a football championship were presented, including one to bring together the two teams with the highest ratings after the bowl games to play for the championship. Still, another plan involved a multiteam playoff. Under this scheme, ABC, the regular-season network, would get the first option to carry the championship games. As expected, the plan drew the wrath of NBC, which believed the championship would detract from the its traditional—and profitable—bowl games, particularly its televised Rose Bowl game.[14]

As the 1970s closed, there seemed little chance that a national championship could be created, for the College Football Association had taken direct aim at destroying the NCAA football TV plan and, possibly, the NCAA itself. Of the CFA coaches present at the 1979 annual CFA

Table 9   **College Football Television Ratings and Fees (1968–1993)**

Year	Network(s)	Neilsen Rating	TV Fees
1968	ABC	12.9	$10,200,000
1969	ABC	13.9	10,200,000
1970	ABC	13.8	12,000,000
1971	ABC	14.0	12,000,000
1972	ABC	13.1	13,500,000
1973	ABC	12.1	13,500,000
1974	ABC	12.0	16,000,000
1975	ABC	12.9	16,000,000
1976	ABC	14.1	18,000,000
1977	ABC	12.4	18,000,000
1978	ABC	12.0	29,000,000
1979	ABC	11.5	29,000,000
1980	ABC	11.3	31,000,000
1981	ABC	12.0	31,000,000
1982	ABC / CBS / TBS	10.7	64,800,000
1983	ABC / CBS / TBS	9.8	74,200,000
1984*	ABC / CBS	7.2	35,300,000
1985	ABC / CBS	7.1	54,600,000
1986	ABC / CBS	7.0	54,600,000
1987	ABC / CBS	6.0	53,200,000
1988	ABC / CBS	6.2	52,700,000
1989	ABC / CBS	6.2	53,200,000
1990	ABC / CBS	5.5	52,700,000
1991	ABC / NBC	6.1	96,500,000
1992	ABC / NBC	6.0	94,500,000
1993	ABC / NBC	6.5	95,300,000

*In 1984 ABC was the network for the CFA, while CBS covered the Big Ten and PAC-10. This was the year after NCAA lost control of football telecasting and the year Chuck Neinas called for a national playoff.

Source: "Report to the NCAA Special Committee to Study a Division I-A Football Championship," 6 May 1994, NCAA Headquarters, B33–34, tables 3.2.1 and 3.2.2.

meeting, only Vince Dooley of Georgia favored a playoff, and only five of about one hundred CFA members present supported such a game.[15] The idea of a playoff would gain significant CFA backing only after the NCAA's TV plan had been defeated by the CFA's subsidized Oklahoma-Georgia lawsuit in the early 1980s.

Almost as soon as the U.S. Supreme Court had rendered its 7-2 judgment that the NCAA's TV plan was illegal, the CFA, led by executive director Chuck Neinas, attempted to take the NCAA's place both in television and in the organization of a playoff. The CFA might have been successful had the Big 10 and the PAC-10 joined the rest of the CFA's big-time powers. When they did not, the result was a glut of football tele-casting, a buyer's market that cut the payouts from networks and cable systems by over 50 percent.[16] This financial plight may have been what spurred Neinas to call for a CFA national championship playoff.

To the consternation of Neinas and the CFA, about a month after the 1984 Supreme Court ruling, U.S. District Judge Burciaga declared that despite the NCAA having its TV monopoly broken up, the NCAA would be allowed to sell its rights to a big-time football championship tourney. Neinas, however, had his own plan to one-up the NCAA.[17] He proposed an eight-team playoff that was projected to deliver more than $50,000,000 to the CFA. The seven games would bring in an estimated $13.5 million from ticket sales and $40 million from TV fees. If the advertising rates were similar to those of the NCAA basketball championship ($185,000 per 30 seconds), over $100 million would be generated from the championship by TV alone. Thirty-second TV advertising rates for the most popular sporting events at the time were $500,000 for the Super Bowl, $250,000 for the World Series, and $225,000 for the Rose Bowl. The highly profitable televised first-round games would be played in the first two weeks in December, the semifinals on New Year's Day, and the championship game two weeks later. The five conference champions of the CFA would get automatic bids, as would the top independent team and two other CFA teams selected by a knowledgeable committee. Each team in the tourney would receive a minimum of $1 million, with the final two receiving $6 million. Each of the sixty-three members of the CFA would also be paid nearly $500,000 as part of the contract.[18] This may have sounded good to some, but Bob Devaney, athletic director at Nebraska, summed up a potential looming battle: "I believe there will be a large amount of opposition from the football coaches . . . and also from the academic community. Certainly there will be opposition from the bowls."[19] Devaney was right; Neinas' CFA proposal never stood a chance.

After the breakup of the NCAA football TV contract, each year brought calls for a tournament to decide the national championship rather than having polls determine the number-one team following the bowl games. Television money often dictated who would play whom in what were considered "championship" games. For instance, Penn State and Miami were both undefeated in the fall of 1986 when, according to Gordon White of the New York Times, in a mid-November commercial coup at a Miami restaurant they agreed to play for the "championship" at the Fiesta Bowl. TV money brought the two teams together for a price of \$2.4 million each. Although it was not be a real championship game, people felt satisfied that a number-one team had been chosen to go up against Penn State. Coached by conservative Joe Paterno, Penn State upset the Miami team, led by Jimmy Johnson, 14-10, in the most-watched game in college history.[20] It wouldn't have mattered greatly if a real championship tourney had been proposed that year, as the consensus of the newly created NCAA Presidents' Commission, composed of forty-four chief executive officers, was opposed to a championship.[21]

Some years there were more voices calling for a tourney than others, but the Presidents' Commission always stood in the way. When the NCAA Football Post Season Subcommittee of the Special Events Committee recommended a one-game championship contest on the Sunday before the Super Bowl, the chairman of the Presidents' Commission, John Slaughter, said that it would serve no purpose but to stroke the ego of the winner (rather than his own or those of other presidents, he might have added). All of the Division I-A presidents on the commission voted against the proposal, including Ed Jennings of Ohio State, Martin Massengale of Nebraska, Joab Thomas of Alabama, and Bernard Slinger of Florida State, each a major football school.[22] Their vote was reconfirmed when the Division I-A schools voted 98-13 to reject the one-game national championship and any future considerations unless there was "compelling evidence" to support such a playoff. About the only schools voting for the profitable venture were the minor schools such as Hawaii, Southwestern Louisiana, and Tulsa, probably because they could see some financial benefits coming their way.[23]

The Presidents' Commission nevertheless did not deter proposals for a national championship in the 1990s. After a bowl coalition had formed in 1992 to create some type of national championship at a bowl site, proposals kept coming in for a real championship. Yet only Notre Dame and six of the ten Division I-A conferences entered into the bowl coalition. Chuck Neinas admitted that "the Bowls realize that the coalition is just an intermediate step" to a playoff.[24] Dick Schultz, outgoing executive director of the NCAA, suggested either a one-game or four-team playoff and predicted a real championship would take place within the decade.[25] At about the same time, Rick Kulis of the Home Shopping Network tried to sponsor a one-game college football national championship.[26] By 1993, a championship for Division I-A had again become a hot topic. Nike, along with the Creative Artists Agency, proposed a championship to the NCAA Post Season Football Subcommittee. Soon after, Jack Lindquist, president of the Walt Disney Company, tried to bring a national

Table 10   **Bowl Game vs. NCAA Basketball Championship Receipts and Ratings, 1985–1994**

Year	All Bowl Games	Highest Nielsen Rating	Basketball Championship	Rating
1985	$47,600,000	21.4	$34,800,000	23.3
1986	50,200,000	22.7	41,200,000	20.7
1987	55,500,000	25.1	49,100,000	19.6
1988	59,500,000	20.8	61,400,000	18.8
1989	65,600,000	18.5	70,400,000	21.3
1990	74,200,000	14.6	76,100,000	20.0
1991	79,800,000	18.3	130,200,000	19.4
1992	81,700,000	15.8	135,400,000	22.7
1993	84,200,000	18.2	148,000,000	22.2
1994	88,400,000	17.8	153,000,000	21.6

Source: "Report to the NCAA Special Committee to Study a Division I-A Football Championship," 6 May 1994, NCAA Headquarters, B12–13, 21.

championship game to Orange County, California, something that Dennis Swanson of ABC believed might generate $50 to 60 million from TV alone and another $40 million from such things as sponsorship fees, payment by cities, and ticket sales.[27] Pressure seemed to be coming from all angles, including the Pasadena Tournament of Roses Association and the Aloha Bowl in Hawaii, to host a postseason championship game.

After the NCAA announced the formation of a research group to study the feasibility of a Division I-A football playoff, hopes were again raised for those who did not believe "Poll Bowls" should determine championships. Television revenues were a major driving force behind the recommendation to have a championship, whether such recommendations consisted of one, four, eight, or twelve games. The lengthy 1994 report turned in by the research group clearly showed that the NCAA basketball championship had drawn higher television ratings in every one of the previous six years than any bowl game, including the four years when bowl games determined an unofficial "national football championship." Furthermore, of the ten Division I-A conferences, all conferences but one had received less income from bowl games than from the men's basketball championship in the 1993–94 season. In that same time, the gross receipts of football bowl games had increased only 33 percent while the men's basketball championship had grown by 120 percent. By 1989, the highest-rated TV bowl game had fallen below the highest-rated NCAA basketball game, a shift that would not be reversed. The disparity between football and basketball ratings was not because the Nielsen audience ratings for basketball had risen dramatically since 1973—they had not—but because the Nielsen ratings for bowl games had been cut in half between the 1970s and the 1990s. The study showed that an eight-team football playoff could produce well over $100 million. The championship game alone would be worth about $33 million, three-quarters of that produced from television revenues.[28] Furthermore, these were probably conservative estimates.

The business-oriented presidents were not convinced that the overwhelming economic value of a Division I-A football playoff outweighed the negatives of giving football increased power within the universities. They voted against the playoff idea, yet, paradoxically, they still got increased commercialism. They allowed the corporate sponsorship of bowl games to move ahead at an accelerating pace. Indeed, they did nothing to prevent the expansion of the illusory Alliance Bowl System that was set up in the early 1990s.

The vigorous corporate sponsorship of bowl games began in 1986 when the Fiesta Bowl Association made an agreement with the Sunkist Citrus Growers Association to officially associate the Sunkist name with the game in exchange for a cash compensation fee. Within a decade almost all bowls had corporate prefixes: the Mazda Gator Bowl, the Sea World Holiday Bowl, the USF&G Sugar Bowl, and so on.[29] If presidents had sincerely wanted to cut back on football commercialism, they could have put a stop to this blatant corporate financial takeover of the bowls. Presidents have not only been reluctant to slow commercialism, but they have fostered it in order to cover athletic costs, which have risen much faster than the rate of inflation. As leaders of the NCAA, presidents have only kept what they considered to be the most negative commercial advertising images from being shown by potential bowl sponsors. Thus, the only businesses prevented from becoming bowl sponsors were those that sold alcohol or tobacco products, organizations that promoted gambling, or professional sports organizations (to protect the image of what was considered to be amateur college athletics).[30]

The Alliance Bowl system was devised by members of the NCAA to continue the traditional bowls with a chance that a championship game based upon ratings could be planned as one of the numerous bowl games. This, however, was a misleading concept from the start. From the 1970s, there was a schism between a majority of the big-time football powers in the CFA and those from the Big 10 and the PAC-10, who had refused to join the CFA. The Big 10 and PAC-10 conferences also claimed the largest bowl bonanza, as they had joined together in 1946 to prevent any other conferences from participating in the Rose Bowl, the most prestigious and lucrative postseason contest. When the Alliance Bowl system was constructed in 1992, the Big 10 and PAC-10 remained aloof.[31]

The multimillion-dollar Rose Bowl contract was too important to both the Big 10 and PAC-10 conferences to give up in hopes of determining a national champion on the field. The television revenues from the Rose Bowl alone had risen to about one-third those from the entire total of eighteen bowl games.[32] When the Alliance Coalition failed to include two of the strongest big-time conferences, the hopes for holding a national championship on a regular basis were eliminated. The bowl coalition, even if it had managed to enlist all the big-time conferences, could never have substituted effectively for a true championship, for it was not based on the direct field competition of an eight-team playoff. Ranking by polling raises interest, but it does not represent true competition in athletics, which demands athletic contests, not the potentially biased results of polls. In its six-year existence, the Alliance Coalition produced only two matchups of the number-one and number-two teams (according to opinion polls): Alabama beat Miami, 34-13, in 1993, and Florida State beat Nebraska, 18-16, in 1994.

In 1998, the Alliance Coalition changed its name and strategy and attempted once again to satisfy both the proponents of traditional bowls and those who desired a national champion. A Bowl Championship Series (BCS) was created, and this time the Big 10 and PAC-10 joined with the other big-time schools. The BCS came closer to achieving an opinion-based national winner but again missed the mark for a true championship, the kind occurring in every other NCAA sport including Division I-AA, II, and III football. A complicated system of win-loss records, computer rankings, opinion polls, and strength of schedules attempted to do what only face-to-face competition could ever accomplish. The manipulated Bowl Championship Series did not satisfy those who wanted a true championship.

With the passing of the twentieth century, still no televised playoff in Division I-A football appeared on the NCAA drawing board for the new millennium. Yet, the history of intercollegiate athletics indicates that one will likely be created in the future, if for no other reason than the impelling commercial interest in the amount of money that a playoff would produce. Intercollegiate athletics had been commercialized since that first railroad-sponsored rowing meet between Harvard and Yale in 1852. There was no diminution of the commercialization of college sports, men's or women's, a century and a half later.

There was a nationalization of contests in the twentieth century, yet, apart from national championships, the greatest interest had remained in regional competitions. Games such as Alabama-Auburn, Florida–Florida State, Michigan–Ohio State, Oklahoma-Texas, and Southern Cal–UCLA still remained the greatest draws for game attendance and television ratings unless there was a potential interregional national "championship" on the line. For over a half-century, the highest Nielsen ratings on TV have consistently been those for regional contests, unless the one "national" football team, Notre Dame, was involved. A national championship grounded in regional interest, not poll numbers, was firmly in the interest of commercialized college football.[33]

A national playoff based upon traditional regional conferences appeared to be an attractive option for those who wanted to keep the commercialization within the institutions of the NCAA rather than spread among the numerous bowl committees and their corporate sponsors. While about 90 percent of the income from the NCAA Division I men's basketball championship remained with the NCAA and its institutions, less than half of the bowl receipts benefited institutions of the NCAA.[34] If the NCAA conducted a playoff system based upon regional conferences, it would almost surely excite tremendous interest, and the income generated would likely increase revenues for the institutions by a factor of two or three. By pooling the television and gate receipts along with other auxiliary income, all of the Division I-A football institutions could benefit enormously from a national playoff. In addition, those institutions that made the playoffs could profit individually from their participation just as those who made the basketball playoffs have done.

The historically rich regional conference systems that first developed in the late nineteenth century could be the focal point for an eight-team playoff at the conclusion of each season. By using traditional conference rivalries in the quarterfinals each year, the NCAA football tournament could build upon the interest that has existed for generations. For example, one quarterfinal game would logically pit the winners of two major Southern conferences, the Southeastern Conference and the Atlantic Coast Conference, against each another. Another logical contest would be between champions of the Big 12 Conference in the West and the newly created Mountain West Conference. The Big 10 winner, as it has for over a half-century, would play the winner of the PAC-10 in a third quarterfinal game. The champion from the Big East, a relatively new conference, would play the the team chosen best among the highest-rated member of one of the previous conferences, the independents, and the other less prestigious Division I-A conferences, Conference USA, Mid-America, and Western Athletic Conference. In this way, regional conferences would play against their closest conference (South-South and West-West) in two of the quarterfinals, while the traditional Big 10–PAC-10 contest would remain. The Big East winner scheduled against the best nonchampion of the six noted conferences, the independents, or the remaining conferences would be the least logical of the quarterfinal matchups. Even then, the possibility of a Big East university such as Miami against the independent Notre Dame would have high appeal.

This eight-team playoff would focus participants and fans on seeing their team win its conference and become eligible for the national championship playoff. This concentration on conferences would tend to strengthen them. In addition, big-time Division I-A institutions would no longer feel the necessity to schedule two or three easy and uninteresting games each year to secure wins and thus become eligible for the national "poll" championship. If Florida, Nebraska, or Penn State were to schedule tough nonleague opponents and lose, it would not hurt their chances for a national championship. Teams would no longer feel obliged to run up the score against inferior opponents simply to raise their standing in the polls. Most important, teams of more equal strength would likely feel that they could play one another in nonconference games without fearing that a loss would drop them in the polls and eliminate them from the national championship or a favored bowl game. The clear result would be greater general interest in big-time football.

To preserve the traditional end-of-the-season bowl sites, the quarterfinals, semifinals, and finals could be played in seven of the bowls themselves. For instance, each year the Orange Bowl could host the Southeastern Conference–Atlantic Coast Conference contest; the Cotton Bowl, the Big 12–Mountain West game; the Rose Bowl, the Big 10–PAC-10 game; and the Sugar Bowl, the game between the Big East champion and the highest-ranked independent or other conference team. The two semifinal games might be take place in the Fiesta Bowl and Citrus Bowl, and the finals could be played in a domed stadium anywhere in America or in an undomed stadium in the southern climes.

Scheduling the three weekends of contests may be problematical because student-athletes generally have final exams in mid-December, but students on football teams, like their counterparts in basketball and other sports, have been playing contests around academic pursuits for well over a century. If the playing season were to begin in early September, there would be twelve playing dates in September, October, and

November. This could accommodate all conference play, including a conference divisional playoff if one were needed, before nearly all Division I-A institutions begin final exams in the first two weeks of December. The championship quarterfinals could be played in the last week of November or the first week of December, but they might more logically be played on New Year's Eve and New Year's Day to attract more spectators. The semifinals could be scheduled on the second Saturday after New Year's Day, prior to the NFL conference championships, while the finals could be played the week before the NFL Super Bowl.

To provide end-of-the-season bowl contests during the traditional holiday season, teams that did not win their conferences could be invited to participate in other traditional bowl games, generally before the NCAA championship quarterfinal games. To increase interest, the number-two conference teams could be paired up (such as the Atlantic Coast Conference versus Southeastern Conference and Big 10 versus PAC-10). Other bowls could invite teams that they thought would be competitive or prove highly popular. As universities for decades have considered a high number of bowl games to be of value, this system would carry on that tradition. Universities could use the games for prestige, football teams could continue to use games as rewards for successful seasons, and the bowls, television networks, and cable systems could go on sponsoring their commercial endeavors as in the past.

On November 30, 1876, Yale University won the first "national championship playoff" when the Intercollegiate Football Association sponsored a New York City contest between the two strongest institutions playing football (then called rugby) in the East. Yale beat Princeton on that first Thanksgiving Day contest by scoring two touchdowns, the first principally with a run by Walter Camp, the "father of American football," followed by a successful kick for goal, then the determining factor in scoring.[35] National championships since then have not always been so clearly determined on the field of play. There have been at least twenty-four various methods of selecting a big-time national football champion in the past. Twelve methods were in use when the "Report to the NCAA Special Committee to Study a Division I-A Football Championship" was released in 1994. By looking to an "on-the-field" championship, as Yale and Princeton did in 1876, the circuit would be completed to a true championship, a tradition begun well over a century before. College football would be no more or less commercialized than it has been over the past century, but the growth in fan interest and television potential would make the financial results skyrocket. Nevertheless there are those, such as Jim Delany, Big 10 commissioner, who opened the twenty-first century with the assertion: "If fans want a play-off, they can get it from the NFL or the NBA."[36] That, indeed, might happen, to the financial detriment of big-time football and college athletics in general.

Radio, TV, and Big-Time College Sport: A Timeline

May 24, 1844	Samuel F. B. Morse begins public use of telegraphy with a message, "What hath God wrought?" sent from Baltimore to Washington, D. C.
August 3, 1852	The first intercollegiate contest, a crew meet between Harvard and Yale held at Lake Winnipesauke, New Hampshire, is commercialized when it is sponsored by a railroad.
July 1, 1859	In the first intercollegiate baseball game, held at Pittsfield, Massachusetts, Amherst beats and Williams, 73-32.
August 27, 1869	Harvard travels to London to meet Oxford in a crew meet, held before an estimated 1 million spectators on the Thames River; Oxford wins.
November 6, 1869	At the first intercollegiate football (soccer) game, Rutgers beats Princeton, 6-4; there is little newspaper reporting, meager interest, and no commercialism.
March 10, 1876	Alexander Graham Bell successfully transmits a message, "Come here, Mister Watson, I want you," on his newly invented telephone.
November 24, 1876	At the first so-called national championship and first Thanksgiving Day football game, Yale beats Princeton at the St. George's Cricket Grounds in Hoboken, New Jersey.
1877	Thomas A. Edison applies for a patent on a speaking machine, the phonograph.
1880	Two Englishmen, William E. Ayrton and John Perry, propose transmitting pictures by light-sensitive cells.
January 1884	Paul G. Nipkow of Berlin, Germany, patents a disc-scanning system for sending pictures via a radio transmitter.
1888	Heinrich Hertz and Oliver Lodge independently identify radio waves as belonging to the same family as light waves.
January 1, 1890	The first football bowl game is played in New Orleans between teams called "Princeton" and "Yale" but consisting of players from a number of colleges.
July 2, 1890	The Sherman Antitrust Act is passed, banning conspiracies or combinations in restraint of trade and preserving freedom of trade and competition.
January 1, 1895	Amos Alonzo Stagg organizes the first indoor bowl game, played on a tanbark floor at Tatterssall's Riding Academy in Chicago; Stagg's Chicago team shuts out Notre Dame before 2,000 spectators.

September 1895	Guglielmo Marconi invents the wireless (radio) at his parent's estate in Bologna, Italy.
1896	Tulane University and Wittenberg College experiment with wireless communication.
July 20, 1897	Marconi incorporates the Wireless Telegraph and Signal Company in England.
July 20, 1898	Marconi's wireless gives a report of the Kingstown Regatta off the coast of Ireland to a Dublin newspaper.
March 3, 1899	Marconi bridges the English Channel between England and France by sending a wireless message over thirty-two miles.
October 3, 1899	Sponsored by the *New York Herald,* Marconi reports the first American sporting event on wireless, an America's Cup match, Shamrock versus Columbia, off Sandy Hook, New Jersey.
January 1, 1902	Michigan beats Stanford, 49-0, at the first Rose Bowl game, played in Pasadena before about 8,000 spectators.
December 17, 1902	Marconi sends the first North American radio message to England from Glace Bay, Nova Scotia.
January 19, 1903	Marconi sends the first U.S. radio message to England from South Wellfleet, Cape Cod.
1904	Telephone wire-photos are sent from Munich to Nuremberg, Germany, by physicist Arthur Korn.
December 28, 1905	The concept of "Home Rule" is created at the first NCAA meeting.
April 17, 1906	NCAA President Palmer E. Pierce of West Point emphasizes Home Rule, stating that an institution joining the Association would not lose its independence.
December 24, 1906	Inventor Reginald Fessenden transmits the first true radio broadcast, including voice transmission, from Brant Rock, Massachusetts.
December 29, 1906	The NCAA constitution reflects Home Rule, stating that eligibility rules are a responsibility of each individual institution.
October 17, 1907	The first commercial wireless-radio service begins, sending messages from Clifden, Ireland to the U.S.
January 2, 1909	NCAA President Pierce reconfirms that the NAA is working on the home rule principle.
December 10, 1909	Marconi wins the Nobel Prize in physics for his wireless.
June 24, 1910	An act is passed requiring wireless equipment and operators to be on board certain U.S. ships.
April 14, 1912	David Sarnoff and other wireless operators in the United States receive radio signals reporting survivors from the SS *Titanic* after it hits an iceberg.
August 13, 1912	The Radio Broadcasting Act is passed, requiring broadcasting licenses and assigning wavelengths and time limits for broadcasting.
fall 1912	The University of Minnesota's experimental radio station,

	9X1-WLB, broadcasts a Minnesota football game using a spark transmitter and regular telegraphic signals.
1915	Arthur Church, founder of KMBC, Kansas City, uses his wireless commercially by merchandising radio parts for ham operators.
February 6, 1915	The Panama-Pacific International Exposition at San Francisco opens with demonstrations of the wireless as a major technological advance.
summer 1916	Frank Conrad, an engineer at Pittsburgh's Westinghouse, is issued a radio license for station 8XK, which begins broadcasting in November 1919 and becomes KDKA.
1917	Station 9XM, later WHA at the University of Wisconsin, begins experimental broadcasts with music.
May 25, 1917	NCAA President Pierce proposes a suggestive but not authoritative national athletic policy during World War I.
1919	Vladimir Zworykin conducts television experiments for Westinghouse.
May 1, 1919	F. W. Marvel of Brown University states that college officials are asked to consider their sports amateur but must finance them as if they were commercial and professional.
October 1, 1919	The federal government lifts its World War I ban on amateur radio stations.
November 20, 1919	American Marconi becomes Radio Corporation of America.
May 1920	WATT, Newark, begins carrying programs for two hours twice a week, and charges a $35 commercial rate per week.
August 20, 1920	WWJ (8MK), Detroit, becomes the first regular commercial broadcasting station.
September 6, 1920	The Jack Dempsey–Billy Miske fight results are broadcast on WWJ, Detroit.
October 5, 1920	The first baseball scores of a World Series are broadcast by WWJ, Detroit.
October 14, 1920	Station WRUC at Union College is created.
October 27, 1920	The Westinghouse station in Pittsburgh, the first commercially licensed station in America, is given its call letters, KDKA.
November 2, 1920	KDKA broadcasts the Harding-Cox presidential election results and receives promotional success.
November 25, 1920	WTAM in College Station, Texas, broadcasts the Texas A & M–Texas football game, erroneously acclaimed to be the first football game broadcast in America (see 1912).
April 11, 1921	KDKA broadcasts a blow-by-blow account of the Johnny Ray–Johnny Dundee fight at Pittsburgh's Motor Square Garden, with sportswriter Florent Gibson as the announcer.
July 2, 1921	With Major J. Andrew White announcing, WJY in Hoboken broadcasts the Jack Dempsey–Georges Carpentier heavy-

	weight fight in Jersey City, an event that fixes the nation's interest on radio.
August 4, 1921	The Davis Cup tennis matches are broadcast by KDKA, Pittsburgh.
August 5, 1921	KDKA and Harold Arlin broadcast the first baseball game, in which Pittsburgh beats Philadelphia.
September 14, 1921	The Jack Dempsey–Luis Firpo fight on radio further stimulates radio broadcasting.
October 5, 1921	WJZ in Newark, New Jersey, begins broadcasting; Tommy Cowan recreates the New York Yankee and Giants World Series game using reports phoned from the game site by Sandy Hunt.
November 5, 1921	KDKA broadcasting pioneer, Harold W. Arlin, announces the Pitt–West Virginia game as a commercially sponsored contest; Pittsburgh wins.
November 11, 1921	President Warren Harding takes part in broadcasting the burial services for the Unknown Soldier from the National Cemetery in Arlington, Virginia, to Madison Square Garden and transcontinentally to the San Francisco Civic Auditorium.
December 1921	AT&T begins allowing broadcasters to lease its telephone lines at a price, a practice called "toll broadcasting."
1922	WHA, a Wisconsin educational station, provides a series of music appreciation programs, without yet giving thought to sports programming.
January 1922	Seventy-two universities and schools are licensed to broadcast in the United States.
March 12, 1922	William Jennings Bryan gives a radio sermon on KDKA in Pittsburgh.
June 11, 1922	A transatlantic radiophoto of Pope Pius XI by German Arthur Korn appears in the *New York World.*
June 26, 1922	Marconi delivers an address using the Pall-photophone pickup—motion picture film with recorded sound—over WGY, Schenectady.
July 25, 1922	WBAY, New York, opens as an experimental commercial station operated by AT&T.
August 28, 1922	Commercialized "toll" broadcasting begins when an aparment owner pays AT&T's WEAF $100 for ten minutes of advertising.
October 1922	WJZ broadcasts the entire World Series, with *New York Herald* writer Grantland Rice announcing.
October 28, 1922	A Princeton-Chicago football game is broadcast from Stagg Field in Chicago to New York by WEAF, using long-distance telephone lines; Princeton wins, 21-18.
November 1922	A Penn-Cornell football game is broadcast by WIP in Philadelphia; by now there are 564 broadcast stations of all types.

November 4, 1922	A Notre Dame–Indiana football game is broadcast in South Bend by WSBT.
November 25, 1922	A Harvard-Yale football game is aired through WGY, Schenectady, with Bill McGeehan, sports editor of the *New York Sun,* as commentator.
May 1923	A Harvard baseball game is broadcast by WNAC, Boston.
May 1923	Graham McNamee begins what will become a long and illustrious career in sports announcing by broadcasting in New York for WEAF.
October 10–15, 1923	WEAF broadcasts the World Series games from Yankee Stadium and the Polo Grounds. Graham McNamee takes over from Grantland Rice when Rice retires during the series.
October 23, 1923	The University of Pennsylvania begins radio broadcasting with the Centre College game.
December 19, 1923	Valdimir Zworykin files a patent application for an Iconoscope (electronic "eye") television system for Westinghouse.
January 1924	The Federal Trade Commission charges RCA, AT&T, GE, and Westinghouse with violations of antitrust laws for restraining radio competition.
May 1924	The Indianapolis 500 auto race is broadcast by WGN, Chicago.
June 10–12, 1924	Graham McNamee announces the Republican National Convention in Cleveland on a network of sixteen stations.
June 24–July 9, 1924	Graham McNamee then announces the Democratic Convention at Madison Square Garden on an eighteen-station network.
fall 1924	WGN, Chicago, broadcasts football games from all Big 10 campuses and covers Nebraska, Pennsylvania, and Southern California games.
September 13, 1924	Ted Husing is first hired by David Sarnoff at WJZ and paid $45 per month.
October 4–10, 1924	WEAF's eight-station network broadcasts the World Series from Washington, D.C.'s American League Park and New York City's Polo Grounds.
December 1924	AT&T creates a coast-to-coast hookup of twenty-six stations.
January 1, 1925	KPSN in Pasadena transmits the first local broadcast of a Rose Bowl game, as Notre Dame beats Stanford, with former USC and Olympic track star Charlie Paddock at the microphone. The game is also broadcast to New York City by WGBS with Sigmund Spaeth announcing.
January 25, 1925	John Logie Baird gives the first public TV demonstration in Selfridge, England.
June 1925	The Kentucky Derby is broadcast by WGN, Chicago.
Summer 1925	The Scopes Trial is broadcast by WGN, Chicago, at a price of $1,000 per day.

February 23, 1926	The Federal Radio Commission is created in an effort to end chaos in radio.
September 9, 1926	The National Broadcasting Corporation is founded as a subsidiary of RCA, with WEAF and WJZ in New York as its key stations.
September 12 1926	The Jack Dempsey–Gene Tunney fight is broadcast from Philadelphia to many parts of the world with Major J. Andrew White announcing from WJZ, New York.
fall 1926	Ted Husing debuts his invention, the annunciator board, in the Princeton–Navy game, allowing him to better identify names with numbers in college football broadcasts.
January 1, 1927	NBC broadcasts the first network-carried Rose Bowl using KFI, Los Angeles; Graham McNamee announces the contest between Alabama and Stanford.
January 7, 1927	Philo T. Farnsworth patents an electronic system for television, which uses a dissector tube to scan images for transmission.
January 27, 1927	Columbia Broadcasting System is created.
February 10, 1927	Station KPO asks for exclusive broadcast rights to Stanford football games, including postseason contests.
February 23, 1927	The Radio Act of 1927 creates the Federal Radio Commission to further delineate licensing and prevent monopoly in radio.
April 7, 1927	In the first U.S. public demonstration of television, Bell Telephone Laboratories uses a wire transmission to carry an image of Herbert Hoover between Washington, D.C., and New York City.
September 18, 1927	CBS goes on the air with a sixteen-station network.
September 23, 1927	John Kieran of the *New York Times* discusses future sports telecasts, predicting that spectators would stay home rather than attending events in person.
September 23, 1927	The "long-count," second defeat of Jack Dempsey by Gene Tunney is broadcast on radio from Chicago.
fall 1927	Philo T. Farnsworth transmits television images using sequences of the filmed Dempsey-Tunney fight.
October 6, 1927	The first "talking" movie, *The Jazz Singer,* opens in theaters.
1928	The DeForest Radio Company becomes the first TV station to transmit both picture and sound.
February 8, 1928	A transatlantic television image from England's John L. Baird is received in Hartsdale, New York, by Mia Howe.
March 19, 1928	Radio's famous *Amos 'n' Andy* show is introduced on WMAQ in Chicago.
April 1928	RCA receives a license to operate an experimental television station, W2XBS, in New York City.

June 8, 1928	A regular television schedule, with programming three times a week, is inaugurated by WGY in Schenectady, New York.
June 21, 1928	The annual Harvard-Yale boat race on the Thames River is broadcast by WTIC in Hartford, Connecticut.
July 12, 1928	Outdoor scenes are televised by Bell Telephone Laboratories without the use of artificial lights.
December 23, 1928	NBC establishes a permanent coast-to-coast radio network.
June 27, 1929	Color television is demonstrated by Bell Telephone Laboratories.
October 24, 1929	The classic *American College Athletics* report of the Carnegie Foundation for the Advancement of Teaching is released. It condemns recruiting and payment of college athletes and commercialization but says little about commercial radio broadcasts.
January 1, 1929	Announcer Bill Munday of NBC calls the infamous "wrong-way" Roy Reigles run in the Rose Bowl on NBC, with Graham McNamee serving as the color man.
November 18, 1929	Vladimir Zworykin demonstrates a noiseless, fully electronic television receiver to the Institute of Radio Engineers.
1930	After having filed a patent in 1927, Philo T. Farnsworth receives a patent for his television, to the consternation of RCA, NBC, AT&T, and Westinghouse.
May 1930	The Department of Justice sues RCA, GE, AT&T, and Westinghouse for creating a radio monopoly.
May 22, 1930	Television is demonstrated on a six-foot screen in Proctor's Theatre, Schenectady, New York, by Ernst F. W. Alexanderson.
November 22, 1930	Harvard beats Yale in a game that is broadcast to England by the British Broadcasting Corporation.
1931	Allen B. Du Mont establishes a laboratory that later develops the cathode-ray television tube.
November 2, 1931	The combination of radio coverage and the Depression threatens football gate receipts in the Pacific Coast Conference, according to a Stanford official.
November 1931	Ted Husing is banned by Harvard from announcing its games after calling the play of Harvard star quarterback Barry Wood "putrid."
December 15, 1931	A California radio station protests the Pacific Coast Conference's possible barring of free radio broadcasts at football games.
1932	Major League baseball owners vote not to ban radio broadcasts but instead allow each individual club to adopt its own broadcast policy.
February 1, 1932	Charles W. Kennedy, NCAA vice president, believes the NCAA might have to set standards for athletic scholarships, thus breaking the NCAA tradition of Home Rule.

June 1932	The Eastern Intercollegiate Association, formed in 1926, votes to ban radio for the 1932 football season.
July 27, 1932	The Pacific Coast Conference votes to broadcast on a conference basis.
July 29, 1932	A special meeting of the NCAA notes restrictions on radio broadcasting by the Eastern Colleges Athletic Conference, the Southern Conference, and the Southwest Conference.
July 29, 1932	At a special meeting, the NCAA discusses but rejects legislative action on radio broadcasting policy, preserving the Home Rule principle.
July 29, 1932	Home Rule continues as the NCAA chooses not to take binding action regarding a new federal admission tax on college sports.
July 29, 1932	In a straw vote, NCAA representatives vote 30-4 that radio hurts, rather than helps, football revenues. Major John L. Griffith, Big 10 commissioner, notes that no one at the NCAA special meeting brought up the question of the future of televised football.
August 24, 1932	A claim is made by a university official that University of Iowa radio is a property right belonging to the state of Iowa and that people of Iowa are entitled to football broadcasts.
fall 1932	Ronald "Dutch" Reagan broadcasts University of Iowa football games for $5 a game.
November 21, 1932	RCA (NBC) ceases monopolistic arrangements with GE and Westinghouse, avoiding antitrust action.
1933	The three Major League baseball teams in New York City ban broadcasting.
March 12, 1933	President Franklin D. Roosevelt gives his first "fireside chat" on radio.
February 24, 1934	The Southern Conference bans regular season football radio broadcasts.
June 19, 1934	The Communications Act of 1934 is passed, creating the Federal Communications Commission but without providing for nonprofit educational, religious, or labor-group stations.
fall 1934	Michigan sells its football broadcasting rights to WWJ for $20,000, with Chevrolet as sponsor.
September 30, 1934	The Mutual Broadcasting System is created as a four-station network.
October 1934	Announcer Ted Husing criticizes World Series umpires and is banned from World Series announcing for life by baseball commissioner Kenesaw Mountain Landis.
May 1935	The Big 10 discusses selling radio rights to its football games for $100,000.
September 30, 1935	John L. Griffith, NCAA president, says the NCAA should remain educative and not become a legislative body.
December 13, 1935	The Southern Conference votes to allow radio football broadcasts.

December 13, 1935	A University of North Carolina official A. W. Hobbs notes that television will likely come to college football in the near future.
December 27, 1935	The NCAA appoints a special committee to study the effect of radio broadcasting on game attendance.
January 1, 1936	The Orange Bowl is paid $500 by CBS for radio broadcast rights. Just as Graham McNamee did for the Rose Bowl, announcer Ted Husing gives the Orange Bowl a national audience.
January 22, 1936	Pressure to do away with Home Rule comes with the Graham (eligibility) Plan of the President of the University of North Carolina.
June 23, 1936	The FCC holds a hearing on the future of TV.
August 1, 1936	The Berlin Olympic Games are broadcast by shortwave over a forty-nation switchboard, by a staff that includes American announcers.
August 1, 1936	The Berlin Olympic Games are telecast on closed-circuit television in Berlin and two other German cities, the first telecast of a sports contest.
September 14, 1936	Yale sells its rights to football radio broadcasts for $20,000.
September 26, 1936	The Duke-Colgate football game becomes the first game broadcast coast-to-coast by two major networks, CBS and NBC.
October 5, 1936	AT&T's coaxial cable first carries TV images from New York to Philadelphia.
November 5, 1936	A National Association of State Universities report indicates that few universities offer athletics as part of educational radio.
December 29, 1936	The Radio Broadcasting of Athletic Events Committee of the NCAA claims radio property rights belong to individual institutions, stating that conferences cannot bind member schools.
December 29, 1936	The NCAA declares that it is entirely ethical to sell broadcast rights to home contests.
December 30, 1936	Hank Luisetti of Stanford plays basketball in Madison Square Garden against Long Island University, bringing national acclaim to his new style of play.
March 26, 1937	Allen B. Du Mont invites a guest to see his all-electronic TV receiver.
May 6, 1937	The German dirigible, *Hindenburg,* crashes at Lakehurst, New Jersey, and an eye-witness description is given on the radio by the emotional Herb Morrison of WLS, Chicago.
June 5, 1937	The proposed $100,000 sale of radio broadcasts of Big 10 Conference football games is vetoed by the University of Illinois.
July 1937	The British Broadcasting Corporation telecasts the Wimbledon tennis tournament.

fall 1937   Walter Cronkite begins broadcasting college football games out of Oklahoma City and WKY.

December 12, 1937   Two mobile television vans are purchased by NBC and RCA to begin experiments in preparation for telecasting outdoor events such as sports.

January 28, 1938   NBC announces that television has attained a high performance level.

April 19, 1938   NBC begins a regular schedule, telecasting five hours of programming a week to about 100 receivers in the New York area.

June 5, 1938   A photograph of a woman's field hockey game being telecast in England by the British Broadcasting Corporation is published in the *New York Times Magazine.*

June 14, 1938   Presidents Conant of Harvard and President Dodds of Princeton are invited to a television demonstration by RCA-NBC.

June 22, 1938   The largest radio audience for a sporting event, the Joe Louis–Max Schmeling boxing match, includes nearly two-thirds of all radios.

June 30, 1938   The FCC reports that TV is not ready for commercial use.

October 18, 1938   Allen B. Du Mont licenses the experimental Du Mont TV station, W2XVT, in Passaic, New Jersey.

October 30, 1938   Orson Welles's classic *War of the Worlds,* an adaptation of H. G. Wells's novel portraying an invasion from Mars, is broadcast on CBS radio.

March 27, 1939   The first NCAA national championship in basketball is held at Northwestern University; Oregon defeats Ohio State, 46-33.

April 30, 1939   RCA's debut of commercial television begins with the 1939 New York World's Fair, as President Roosevelt opens the fair on television.

May 17, 1939   The first intercollegiate telecast, a baseball game between Princeton and Columbia, occurs at Baker Field in New York and is announced by Bill Stern.

May 20, 1939   A six-day bicycle race at Madison Square Garden is telecast by NBC.

May 1939   The Intercollegiate Amateur Athletic Association of America track meet from Randall's Island is telecast by NBC.

May 24, 1939   The English Derby is telecast to capacity crowds who pay $2.50 each in four London theaters and view the event on fifteen-by-twenty-foot screens.

June 1, 1939   The first telecast of a boxing match, Lou Nova–Max Baer, is telecast at Yankee Stadium.

June 6, 1939   The University of Illinois forbids commercially sponsored radio broadcasts, except for football.

August 26, 1939   The first Major League baseball game to be telecast, between the Brooklyn Dodgers and the Cincinnati Reds, is covered by two cameras at Ebbets Field and announced by Red Barber.

September 13, 1939   The first telecast of a football practice, (at Fordham), is conducted by NBC with Bill Stern announcing.

September 30, 1939   The first recognized telecast of intercollegiate football, an NBC-carried game between Fordham and Waynesburg (Pennsylvania) College, takes place in Triborough Stadium, Randall Island, New York; Fordham beats Waynesburg.

October 22, 1939   The first pro football game telecast, showing the Brooklyn Dodgers beating the Philadelphia Eagles, is sent from Ebbets Field, Brooklyn.

January 1, 1940   The Rose Bowl Parade is telecast by Don Lee Television, W6XAO, of Hollywood, California.

February 6, 1940   RCA demonstrates color television to the FCC.

February 25, 1940   The first telecast of a pro hockey game takes place, a matchup between the New York Rangers and Montreal Canadiens.

February 28, 1940   The first telecast of a basketball game, in which Pitt beats Fordham, is carried by W2XBS from Madison Square Garden in New York City.

March 2, 1940   The first indoor track and field telecast, the Intercollegiate Amateur Athletic Association of America meet from Madison Square Garden, is sent out on New York's W2XBS.

April 19, 1940   The Brooklyn Dodgers–New York Giants opening game is telecast from Ebbets Field.

August 29, 1940   CBS transmits color television images from New York City to Washington, D.C., and back.

October 5, 1940   The University of Pennsylvania telecasts its first football game with announcer Bill Slater and arranges to show all home games on W3XE, a tradition that would continue for the next ten years except for one year during World War II.

December 31, 1940   NCAA breaks with Home Rule when it creates an investigative arm to explore alleged violations of the amateur code. World War II, however, delays implementation.

January 1, 1941   The Cotton Bowl begins radio broadcasting.

January 27, 1941   The FCC begins to consider color television systems.

May 9, 1941   Large-screen television is demonstrated by RCA in a New York theater, with a showing of the boxing match between Billy Soose and Ken Overlin at Madison Square Garden.

June 16, 1941   The first advertising rate card for television is issued by NBC, quoting $60 an hour between 8 A.M. and 6 P.M. and $120 an hour between 6 and 11 P.M.

July 1941   NBC receives a commercial television license for operating station WNBT, New York City.

September 26, 1941   The first televised and sponsored night football game, between Temple and Kansas, is carried on WPTZ-TV from Owl Stadium, Philadelphia, and sponsored by Atlantic Refining Company.

November 15, 1941   The FCC rules that monopolistic RCA must divest itself of an NBC radio network.

December 7, 1941	Radio quickly announces Japan's attack on Pearl Harbor, launching America's entry into World War II.
August 1942	There are now eleven commercial TV stations licensed or holding construction permits: WNBT, WCBW, and WABD in New York City; WNBW in Washington, D.C.; WRGB in Schenectady; WPTZ in Philadelphia; WTZR and WBKB in Chicago; WTMJ in Milwaukee; and KTSL and KSEE in Los Angeles.
November 11, 1942	Notre Dame strongly considers selling its football radio network rights exclusively to NBC's Blue Network and changing its longtime stance against network exclusivity.
October 1943	American Broadcasting Company purchases NBC's Blue Network, which included three stations and a 168-affiliate station network, for $8 million.
fall 1943	The Pacific Coast Conference's football radio broadcasts earn a total income of $32,332.
May 2, 1944	The future Du Mont TV Network begins with the establishment of W2XAB in New York City.
May 17, 1944	The FCC rules that only five stations can be owned by a single interest, reducing monopoly possibilities.
June 25, 1945	K. L. "Tug" Wilson, NCAA secretary-treasurer, calls for NCAA enforcement of eligibility rules beyond institutional and conference regulations, challenging Home Rule.
August 6, 1945	Westinghouse discloses its plan for Stratovision, whereby airborne transmitters would relay FM and television signals from planes at 30,000 feet, on the same day the U.S. drops the first atomic bomb on Japan, bringing about the end of World War II.
fall 1945	The first commercial telecast at the University of Pennsylvania begins.
December 1, 1945	The first network telecast of college football, the Army-Navy game, is carried by NBC through four cities, New York, Philadelphia, Washington, D.C., and Schenectady.
March 26, 1946	WCBS in New York City carries the first telecast of the NCAA basketball championship, in which Oklahoma A & M triumphs over North Carolina, 43-40.
April 1946	Coaxial cable laid by AT&T becomes operational between New York City and Washington, D.C., allowing for increased network TV.
April 15, 1946	The first permanent television network, linking New York, Philadelphia, and Washington, D.C., is launched by Du Mont Laboratories in New York City.
June 19, 1946	The first significant post-World War II telecast, the Joe Louis-Billy Conn fight, called "the most important event in the history of television," airs. The fight was also the highest-rated radio program in history.

July 22–23, 1946	NCAA Conference of Conferences meets and drafts a statement of "Principles for the Conduct of Intercollegiate Athletics," the origin of the Sanity Code and defeat of Home Rule.
October 1946	The Army-Duke football game is telecast, probably the first southern game to be televised.
October 1946	The FCC grants Iowa State University the first noncommercial TV license.
September 1947	Eight cities now have TV stations: Chicago, Detroit, Los Angeles, New York, Philadelphia, Schenectady, St. Louis, and Washington D.C.
September 27, 1947	The president of Madison Square Garden, John Kilpatrick, proclaims that "Sports will be to television what music was to radio."
September 30, 1947	The first World Series telecast, the Brooklyn Dodgers versus the New York Yankees, is sponsored by Gillette Safety Razor and Ford Motor companies.
November 19, 1947	NCAA president Karl Leib calls for a national conference to solve sectional problems and bring about national eligibility and recruiting rules, a prelude to the challenge of traditional Home Rule and the introduction of the Sanity Code.
November 20, 1947	Notre Dame University, through WBKB-TV in Chicago, telecasts its game with Tulane to an estimated 165,000 in the Chicago area.
December 1947	Coaxial cable connects Boston, New York City, Schenectady, Philadelphia, and Washington, D.C.
December 17, 1947	Eastern College Athletic Conference athletic directors discuss the financial impact of telecasting football.
January 1, 1948	NBC (Station KTLA) telecasts the Rose Bowl game.
January 10, 1948	The NCAA passes the Sanity Code, reducing institutional and conference control (Home Rule) over amateurism and eligibility by creating a Constitutional Compliance Committee. Nevertheless, the code calls for institutional control of athletics.
February 27, 1948	The Eastern College Athletic Conference asks the NCAA to consider banning telecasting of revenue-producing sports on a national basis.
March 14, 1948	Notre Dame receives $15,000 for radio rights and $6,600 for television rights for its football game with Navy in Baltimore.
June 2, 1948	Notre Dame signs television rights with Television Productions for $350 per game over four games.
August 4, 1948	NBC discusses with Norte Dame the potential for an East coast network to carry Notre Dame football games.
August 17, 1948	The University of Oklahoma sells its football television rights for three years for $10 and a percentage of profits to be determined.
September 30, 1948	The FCC places a freeze on new television stations, to lessen the problem of signal interference and to allow those inter-

	ested in educational television to campaign for reserving television channels for educational use.
October 1948	CBS begins its "Football Roundup," broadcasting six games in a three-hour period and switching to wherever the action is; this type of football telecasting proves to be unsuccessful.
fall 1948	The University of Alabama, broadcasting on a sixty-station network, earns about $10,000.
January 11, 1949	An AT&T coaxial cable linking Philadelphia and Chicago is inaugurated.
January 12, 1949	An antitrust consent judgement is entered to end trade restraints in the television industry.
January 18, 1949	A possible "Southern Revolt" looms, with southern schools threatening to withdraw from the NCAA because institutional control is being lost to the nationally enforced Sanity Code.
April 2, 1949	Coaxial cable links Notre Dame's stadium to both the East and Midwest for the 1949 season, and the Du Mont network estimates it will cost over $18,000 to telecast Notre Dame's four home games.
April 14, 1949	The Big 7 (later 8) decides to boycott Oklahoma if it telecasts its football games live, fearing the TV threat to game attendance.
April 20, 1949	The University of Iowa sends a questionnaire regarding the appointment of an NCAA commissioner and opposes the concept of individual institutional control and Home Rule.
June 6, 1949	The University of Pennsylvania, in cooperation with CBS and Zenith, telecasts a surgical operation in color.
fall 1949	The NFL bans telecasting of its games for the season.
September 29, 1949	UCLA and USC sell the joint rights to telecast their home games in the L.A. Memorial Coliseum for $77,000.
October 1949	The U.S. Justice Department rules that a Major League baseball telecasting policy is not in violation of antitrust laws. Based on this decision, the NCAA assumes the legality of its 1951 TV policy.
October 12, 1949	The NCAA, in cooperation with the National Opinion Research Center, agree to conduct a survey of television's effect on football attendance.
fall 1949	Georgia Tech telecasts its football games, becoming one of few Southern schools to do so.
December 1949	Television network station affiliates number as follows: CBS has fifty-six; NBC, fifty-five; Du Mont, fifty-three; and ABC, fifty-two. There are now about 4 million TV sets in America.
1950–60	The number of U.S. households with television grows to 87 percent by 1960.
January 13, 1950	The Eastern College Athletic Conference calls upon the NCAA to amend its constitution so that television can be properly controlled.

January 14, 1950	The penalty of expulsion for seven violators of the Sanity Code is not upheld by the NCAA, and the Sanity Code, in effect, dies.
February 1950	Iowa State University becomes the first educational institution to own and operate a TV station.
April 8, 1950	Du Mont Television Network agrees to pay $185,000 for exclusive rights to Notre Dame football, outbidding both ABC ($145,000) and NBC ($150,000).
April 16, 1950	The Big 10 agrees to ban all football telecasts for the 1950 season.
August 23, 1950	ABC-TV offers the University of Pennsylvania $75,000 for rights to its home football games for 1950.
January 1951	The college basketball point-shaving scandal breaks, damaging the reputation of the sport, New York City, and Madison Square Garden games.
January 6, 1951	President Gordon Gray of the University of North Carolina calls for the NCAA to return to an advisory capacity, or to Home Rule.
January 12, 1951	The NCAA Television Committee calls for collective action, as opposed to Home Rule, and the NCAA votes 161-7 to restrict football telecasting for the 1951 season to protect gate receipts.
January 12, 1951	The NCAA also votes 65-15 to grant competing institutions 75 percent of gross receipts for bowl games, including radio and television monies.
February 2, 1951	President John Cavanaugh of Notre Dame attempts to create a Super Conference of about fourteen schools that would include a national TV contract in opposition to the new NCAA TV policy.
March 7, 1951	The Du Mont Network offers the University of Pennsylvania a $275,000 TV contract for telecasting eight games in the 1951 season.
March 18, 1951	President Harold Stassen of the University of Pennsylvania states that the NCAA football telecasting policy would violate the Sherman Antitrust Act of 1890.
March 19, 1951	The NCAA Council votes to request institutional resignation from the NCAA for any particular school if a state legislature forces that school to violate NCAA television policy. The Oklahoma State Legislature votes not to demand telecasting of Oklahoma and Oklahoma A & M football games.
March 27, 1951	Vice President Theodore Hesburgh of Notre Dame asks to confer with a Department of Justice representative about the possible antitrust action against the NCAA for its national TV plan.
April 18, 1951	The NCAA Television Committee releases restrictions on football telecasts, which put limits on the number of games

	any team might be put on television and mandate total blackouts on several days.
May 1951	Fritz Crisler, Michigan athletic director, proposes the use of pay-per-view television to recover gate loses from football telecasting.
May 15, 1951	The Georgia Tech Club of New York protests the NCAA monopoly of telecasting intercollegiate football.
June 5, 1951	Columbia University states it will not participate in games against Penn if Penn does not comply with NCAA and ECAC TV legislation.
June 6, 1951	The University of Pennsylvania is given the status of a member not in good standing by the NCAA Council as a result of Penn's plans to telecast football.
June 9, 1951	The NCAA declines the University of Pennsylvania's request for a hearing on TV.
June 12, 1951	Princeton University votes to cancel its game with the University of Pennsylvania if Penn does not agree to abide by the NCAA TV plan.
June 15, 1951	President Cavanaugh of Notre Dame opposes threatened boycotts of institutions that want to telecast their football games.
June 20, 1951	The U.S. Department of Justice tells the NCAA that the NCAA TV plan had not been given approval, formal or informal, but a full investigation is underway.
June 22, 1951	The University of Pennsylvania asks the U.S. Department of Justice to determine if the NCAA TV policy is a violation of the Sherman Antitrust Act.
June 25, 1951	Hugh Willett, NCAA President, states that the NCAA will not penalize any team playing Penn.
July 26, 1951	Westinghouse outbids both Du Mont and NBC for the rights to carry NCAA football in 1951, eventually paying $679,800 in rights fees.
August 18, 1951	The first coast-to-coast microwave radio relay system is used.
fall 1951	The NCAA's experimental TV plan is inagurated, creating in effect a classic cartel. The 1951 Notre Dame–SMU game brings in the greatest income to the NCAA, $15,513.
September 29, 1951	The first football game televised in color, California versus Penn, is broadcast by CBS at Franklin Field, Philadelphia.
October 6, 1951	The first coast-to-coast telecast of football, Illinois defeating Wisconsin, is seen on NBC.
October 9, 1951	The Department of Justice brings suit against the NFL on monopoly charges of restricting radio and TV coverage.
December 15, 1951	Edward Krause, Notre Dame athletic director, states that the proposed NCAA abolishment of spring football practice and bowl games would strengthen its NCAA policy to control football telecasting.

December 17, 1951	The Eastern College Athletic Conference votes to play only against institutions in compliance with the NCAA and ECAC television plans.
January 11, 1952	The NCAA expands its power greatly by voting to allow itself to legislate on issues "of general concern" through majority vote, so that TV issues can more easily be legislated.The NCAA also votes 163-8 to carry on its experimental TV control program.
April 14, 1952	The FCC issues its "Sixth Report and Order," in which 242 TV channels are reserved for noncommercial use. Educators meet at Penn State University in April 1952, but there is no discussion to use educational TV for telecasting football for the benefit of the universities.
September 22, 1952	Pennsylvania asks for and is denied permission from the NCAA to telecast its game with Notre Dame on a noncommercial or charity basis outside of the NCAA plan.
September 23, 23, 1952	The first pay TV sporting event, the Joe Walcot–Rocky Marciano fight at Municipal Stadium in Philadelphia, grosses a total of $500,000.
October 1952	The NCAA negotiates for a $50 million pay-as-you-view TV contract in football, but the deal is not closed.
October 7, 1952	Harvard University president James Conant states that Harvard will not be bound by the NCAA TV plan.
November 14, 1952	Chairman of the FCC, Paul A. Walker, urges the Association of Land Grant Colleges to organize a forty-eight-state Educational Television Network and preserve the 242 educational channels set aside by the FCC.
November 17, 1952	Allen B. Du Mont of the Du Mont Television Network states that the NCAA TV football plan is a "restraint of trade" and represents a hypocritical action of athletic departments relative to college presidents, who favored educational objectives of TV.
December 9, 1952	A proposed code for the Ivy League opposes football coaches signing any radio and TV contracts with commercial stations.
December 23, 1952	The Du Mont Television Network contemplates a suit against the NCAA to break its monopoly in telecasting intercollegiate football.
1953	Television profits first exceed radio profits, $68 to $55 million.
January 5, 1953	Notre Dame chooses not to sue the NCAA over its TV plan, hoping, however, that the Justice Department will see the plan as unconstitutional and take action.
March 13, 1953	Notre Dame believes that the NCAA is investigating violations in its athletic program because of the NCAA's opposition to Notre Dame's TV policy.
May 23, 1953	NCAA members vote 157-12 in favor of a national TV plan.The University of Maryland considers creating an independent TV network to carry football games.

May 25, 1953   The first educational TV station, KUHT, begins operations at the University of Houston.

June 20, 1953   The verdict in *United States v. National Football League,* 116 F. Supp. 319, indicates that overall success of a sports venture depends upon the financial stability of each club, tending to support the NCAA's position on a national TV contract.

fall 1953   The first football pay-per-view contest takes place in Palm Springs, a game between Notre Dame and Southern California. The viewing cost is $1.

November 9, 1953   In *Toolson v. New York Yankees,* the U.S. Supreme Court's 7-2 decision reconfirms professional baseball's exemption from antitrust laws.

November 12, 1953   A federal court in Philadelphia rules that controlled television, normally a restraint of trade, is legal in pro football. The decision eases NCAA concerns about the legality of its TV plan.

February 16, 1954   For the sixth straight year, NCAA members favored the NCAA TV plan, this time by 92 percent.

September 27, 1954   Harvard University considered abandoning the NCAA TV plan and beginning an Ivy League .

fall 1954   The Notre Dame football radio network grows to 115 stations in thirty-one states, Washington, D.C., and Alaska for the 1954 season. ABC loses money after its purchase of the NCAA football telecasting rights.

January 6, 1955   The Big 10 threatens to form its own television network if the number of regional football telecasts is not increased. The NCAA agrees to an increase.

1956   CBS, headed by William Paley, obtains NFL TV rights and competes with the popularity of college football.

January 7, 1958   The NCAA Television Committee establishes a subcommittee to study the effects of fee or closed-circuit TV.

November 1959   NBC drops its long-term Friday Night Fights and, with them, Gillette's advertising. Gillette offers $8 million to ABC if it will telecast the fights. With the money, ABC is able to buy NCAA football telecast rights and soon hires Roone Arledge to produce it.

April 24, 1961   The NFL collectively pools TV rights by signing an agreement with CBS and is soon found in violation of antitrust action.

September 30, 1961   The Sports Broadcasting Act of 1961 is passed, providing antitrust protection for the NFL TV contract while protecting colleges and high schools from pro football telecasting on Friday nights and Saturdays.

January 1, 1962   The first national color telecast of a college football game takes place with the Rose Bowl game.

July 11, 1962   Intercontinental live TV is first broadcast following the launching of the *Telstar 1* satellite.

October 20, 1962	The "Hartford Experiment" in subscription TV shows the first subscription college football game, Cornell at Yale.
March 23, 1963	The NCAA basketball championship is televised nationally on the Sports Network Incorporated, with Loyola of Chicago defeating Cincinnati, 60-58.
February 10, 1964	The NFL announces that individual NFL teams will telecast games on Friday nights in 1964, a violation in spirit, if not in letter, of the Sports Broadcasting Act of 1961.
May 6, 1964	Walter Byers notes the NFL's questions about the legality of the NCAA football TV plan, in particular regarding the NCAA's allowing the federal government's three military academies to be a part of it.
June 9, 1964	The NCAA Television Committee emphatically opposes any mention of pro football on NCAA college football telecasts.
August 19, 1964	John Lujack and Frank Albert are unanimously rejected as TV football announcers by the NCAA Television Committee because of their affiliation with professional football.
fall 1964	The NCAA decides to permit unlimited substitutions in football, allowing college football to better compete with the NFL for fan interest.
January 9, 1965	The NCAA Television Committee votes unanimously to allow an additional two minutes of advertising desired by NBC, despite Walter Byers's concern over commercial football.
March 1, 1965	The NCAA Long-Range Planning Committee suggests considering a TV policy for basketball similar to that in football.
May 26, 1965	The U.S. House of Representatives holds hearings on the right of cable television to use live telecasts of sports events without authorization.
June 29, 1965	NBC's Carl Lindeman suggests possible doubleheader football games for the next NCAA TV pact.
August 25, 1965	The NCAA Television Committee unanimously requests that NBC turn its cameras away from any political demonstration at a football game.
October 19, 1965	The NCAA Television Committee agrees to experiment with football doubleheader telecasts for 1966.
January 9, 1966	Roone Arledge suggests an eight-team, big-time televised football championship and promises it would bring large financial returns.
January 9, 1966	The NCAA Television Committee states that the growth of CATV (Community Antenna Television) puts the NCAA TV plan in jeopardy because TV exclusivity is no longer guaranteed to the network carrying the games.
March 19, 1966	The national telecast of the Texas Western–Kentucky game, a watershed in black-white relations in basketball, shows an all-black starting lineup defeat a all-white Kentucky team, 72-65.

August 26, 1966
Over 25 percent of all NCAA football TV income is expended on supporting sport federations in their fight with the AAU for control of amateur sport. The fight with the AAU has implications for the NCAA, which is looking to control women's sports.

October 8, 1966
The NFL's Pittsburgh-Cleveland game is telecast on a Saturday, hurting college football attendance.

October 13, 1966
Roone Arledge suggests night, prime-time TV for college football. The NCAA TV Committee opposes the idea.

January 31, 1967
The NCAA Television Committee suggests in its final report that a televised NCAA eight-team football playoff would add "magnetism and excitement" to college football. ABC's Roone Arledge asks the NCAA Television Committee not to create a decline in ratings with a doubleheader on Thanksgiving Day against pro football. The committee agrees.

April 4, 1967
Walter Byers, NCAA executive director, voices his concern that pro football's four divisions and playoffs in December will overshadow college football telecasts.

October 11, 1967
ABC's Roone Arledge asks the NCAA Television Committee if it would be willing to allow regular series football games to be televised at night, as he believed prime-time sports could thrive; his request is denied.

October 19, 1967
Tom Harmon of ABC Sports advocates an NCAA football playoff series to determine a national championship.

February 21, 1967
The NCAA Television Committee considers meeting in Mexico City at the time of the Mexico City Olympics but is denied financing.

April 9, 1968
NBC purchases the NCAA National Basketball Championship for two years for a combined $2 million beginning in 1969.

July 17, 1968
Asa Bushnell, NCAA Television Committee chair, states that the NCAA is introducing "exception" telecasts to placate the Justice Department and keep its "benevolent monopoly."

November 14, 1968
The NCAA Television Committee, in a 6-5 vote, concedes to ABC's desire to telecast the Notre Dame–Michigan State game nationally.

December 12, 1968
Subscription TV, or pay TV, is authorized by the FCC.

January 7, 1969
Byron R. "Whizzer" White, U.S. Supreme Court Justice, receives the Theodore Roosevelt Award from the NCAA.

September 1970
The NCAA appeals to both the U.S. Department of Justice and Congress to stop the NFL from telecasting games on Friday nights and Saturday.

September 21, 1970
ABC premieres NFL *Monday Night Football.*

February 3, 1971
ABC's Carl Lindemann suggests telecasting college games on Friday nights, when high school games were played, knowing that it was against the law for the pros to do the same thing.

March 23, 1971	Management Television Systems (MTS) proposes a closed-circuit television football playoff.
April 26, 1971	A proposal for a National Football Foundation Hall of Fame, calling for allotting one-half of 1 percent of football TV revenues over six years to build the hall, meets with resistance.
September 5, 1971	Forest Evashevski, Iowa athletic director, suggests the creation of an NCAA TV network to telecast a twenty-six-week, in-season series of football and men's basketball.
September 20, 1971	Oklahoma Secretary of State John Rogers begins legal action against the NCAA for prohibiting telecasting of Oklahoma football games, one decade before the *Oklahoma v. NCAA* antitrust case.
fall 1971	The first football telecast between historically African American colleges, Grambling and Morgan State, is aired.
December 11, 1971	The NFL telecasts a Baltimore-Miami game in Miami on a Saturday, the same time as the Florida A & M–Kentucky State Orange Blossom Classic, in possible violation of federal law.
January 2, 1972	A ban on cigarette advertising on TV comes into effect the day after bowl games, allowing colleges to benefit from the last cigarette advertising during their bowl games.
January 5, 1972	The NCAA Council votes to use a portion of football television revenues to build a headquarters in Shawnee Mission, Kansas.
January 5, 1973	The NCAA argues against Internal Revenue Service ruling 58-502, which states that radio and television rights are incidental to the purposes of the NCAA and thus taxable.
March 2, 1973	The NCAA Television Committee considers a national championship playoff football game as part of the bowl games.
March 25, 1973	The NCAA Television Committee seeks authority to administer over-the-air and cable TV coverage of all NCAA championship events.
April 30, 1974	The NCAA Television Committee proposes tying a ten-game regular season basketball series with its NCAA championship in basketball.
August 7, 1973	The NCAA creates self-determined Divisions, I, II, and III. However, Division I football is predetermined by the NCAA Football Statistics and Classification Committee in order to limit the number of big-time football institutions.
April 11, 1974	The Internal Revenue Service concludes that the NCAA's income from television rights for football and basketball does not constitute income from unrelated trade or business and is not subject to a tax.
fall 1974	Keith Jackson begins a twenty-five-year career as the chief announcer of college football.
June 3, 1975	The NCAA Television Committee strongly considers televising a spring football game. Don Canham of Michigan says

	that if TV monies are divided more evenly among all institutions, the traditional football powers will leave the NCAA.
June 16, 1975	*Goldfarb v. Virginia State Bar* sets the precedent for professional and nonprofit associations to be subject to antitrust review, an indication that the NCAA business activities do not enjoy immunity from the Sherman Antitrust Act.
July 1975	Commissioners of seven big-time conferences convene informally to discuss the impact of President Horn's proposals to redistribute TV and bowl revenues.
July 11, 1975	President Horn of Long Beach State leads campaign to pass a proposal (the "Robin Hood" plan) to more evenly divide TV football revenues among the three NCAA Divisions.
August 11, 1975	The NCAA denies a request to telecast a series of traditional black university football games.
August 28, 1975	President Horn charges Division I institutions with having a secret plan to form a "super" division either within or outside the NCAA.
October 15, 1975	A group of twenty-five representatives from seven major conferences and independents, a forerunner of the College Football Association, gathers to discuss reorganizing the NCAA to meet concerns of big-time football; representatives form a steering committee.
October 17, 1975	The NCAA responds to the FCC's accusations of antitrust action and racial discrimination stemming from the lack of national network telecasts of football at black colleges.
January 13, 1976	The NCAA Television Committee again proposes a Division I football championship.
January 15, 1976	The NCAA discusses creating a new Division I-A and what impact such a division would have on a TV contract. The increasing size of Division I had been a festering problem since the three-division reorganization of 1973.
January 17, 1976	The NCAA votes to review the advisability of splitting Division I into Divisions I and I-A.
March 1976	The FCC drops charges against the NCAA of discrimination against predominately black college football telecasts.
April 13, 1976	Home Box Office (HBO) offers to cablecast games not shown on ABC for $10,000 a game.
May 4, 1976	Chuck Neinas, member of the NCAA Television Committee and Big 8 commissioner, risks a conflict of interest by inviting ABC affiliates to a Big 8 breakfast in Los Angeles and cocktails and dinner in New York City.
July 7, 1976	An organizing committee comprising major conferences and football independents is created, formally beginning what became the College Football Association.
August 3, 1976	The NCAA Television Committee questions Chuck Neinas for hosting representatives of ABC in an attempt to influence future telecasts of Big 8 football games.

August 21, 1976	The University of Oklahoma Board of Regents takes the NCAA to court in attempt to make it reverse its decision to cut football coaching staffs.
September 27, 1976	The University of Alabama joins Oklahoma and also takes the NCAA to court for limiting the number of coaches.
September 29, 1976	Legal counsel informs the NCAA that educational endeavors might no longer be exempt from antitrust action in light of the 1975 Goldfarb Supreme Court case.
October 2, 1976	ABC uses a beer hall as the backdrop for discussing an up coming Ohio State–UCLA football game, which incenses President Harold Enarson because it depicts Ohio State students as "football-crazy beer drinkers" and tarnishes the image of universities.
November 26, 1976	The telecasting of the Pitt–Penn State game on a Friday brings protest from the National Federation of High School Athletic Associations, as it is a violation of the NCAA's agreement to keep Fridays for high school football only.
fall 1976	College football TV ratings reach a high of 14.1.
December 2, 1976	U.S. District Court, in *Minnesota v. NCAA,* finds that Minnesota has a "property right" requiring due process before removing the opportunity for students to participate in intercollegiate basketball.
December 16, 1976	The Atlantic Coast Conference suggests a second NCAA TV football network to increase regional football coverage.
December 20, 1976	The College Football Association holds its organizational meeting.
1971–1976	The NCAA defends itself in thirty-nine court cases, thirty-two of which are initiated by individuals or institutions within the NCAA.
March 13, 1977	The CFA directors encourage the Big 10 and PAC-8 Conferences to join the CFA.
March 28, 1977	CBS proposes a two-network NCAA TV plan for college football.
April 8, 1977	The NCAA becomes involved as the Internal Revenue Service raises questions about taxing bowl receipts and television revenues from the Cotton Bowl game between Texas Christian and Southern Methodist as unrelated business income.
June 15–16, 1977	The CFA holds its first annual convention.
July 1, 1977	The NCAA is part of an FCC investigation regarding TV networks' restrictive contracts and possible antitrust violations.
September 28, 1977	Walter Byers holds that NCAA property interests in college athletes are protected by law.
November 2, 1977	Walter Byers foresees the NCAA being "blind-sided with antitrust charges" in the future.

November 3, 1977	Roone Arledge says that Notre Dame could do "infinitely better" selling its football games to a network rather than through the NCAA plan.
November 1977	The NCAA becomes upset when ABC chooses to show live coverage of Anwar Sadat's historic arrival on Israeli soil, momentarily interfering with the Michigan–Ohio State game.
January 1978	A *Yale Law Journal* article discusses the NCAA's television plan as a per se violation of the Sherman Act.
January 12, 1978	The NCAA votes to divide Division I into I-A and I-AA for football. Members of the seven big-time conferences vote overwhelmingly 54-5, but the overall vote is 82-73. An Ivy League Amendment allowed schools with twelve sports to remain in Division I-A without football attendance standards.
March 31, 1978	The CFA discusses the desirability of broadening its purpose to include all intercollegiate sports of major schools.
June 30, 1978	The NCAA Television Committee conducts a survey of TV's impact on basketball attendance. Results show that 79 percent of NCAA institutions want some NCAA TV controls over basketball telecasting.
July 20, 1978	Warner Cable Corporation's threatened antitrust suit brings an agreement by ABC and the NCAA to allow Warner to cablecast Ohio State games.
November 19, 1978	The NCAA Negotiations Committee for Television Rights of the Division I Basketball Tournament seriously considers combining regular season games with the NCAA tourney contract.
1979	The Entertainment and Sports Programming Network (ESPN) begins operation.
January 3, 1979	The NCAA is advised by legal counsel that a basketball TV plan similar to the football plan would be a "per se" violation of the Sherman Antitrust Act.
January 6, 1979	The NCAA Negotiations Committee for Television Rights of the Division I Basketball Tournament abandons further consideration of combining its tournament and an in-season basketball package.
January 18, 1979	ABC-TV urges the NCAA to seek federal legislation to protect NCAA college football telecasting from extensive cable telecasting.
June 3, 1979	The CFA straw vote indicates that only about 5 percent favor a football playoff.
June 6, 1979	Walter Byers becomes aware of the property rights issue as a challenge to NCAA power, the rights coming to the fore as a result of two court cases against the NCAA.
June 1979	The CFA board of directors appoints a Television Study Committee to evaluate the NCAA TV plan, examine NCAA finances, and consider future CFA TV plans.

July 2, 1979	The CFA acknowledges the need to create an executive director position to increase communication.
November 29, 1979	The CFA Television Committee is invited to join the NCAA Television Committee meeting but declines.
April 1, 1980	Chuck Neinas is hired as executive director of the CFA.
May 20, 1980	Chuck Neinas warns that President Horn's share-the-wealth idea is still alive.
May 22, 1980	The CFA Television Study Committee recommends considering a two-network television plan.
May 30, 1980	The CFA Television Study Committee is instructed to develop a football TV plan more beneficial to the CFA membership.
July 14, 1980	The U.S. Copyright Royalty Tribunal divides up $12 million in cable royalties, of which 4 percent goes to sports claimants such as the NCAA.
October 30, 1980	Southern Methodist athletic director Russ Potts calls for a new NCAA TV plan to include Monday and Saturday-night contests.
November 21, 1980	The CFA releases its television survey, which reveals that 80 percent of the members favor investigating a two-network plan but only 27 percent strongly support the development of a CFA TV plan.
December 1980	Chuck Neinas meets secretly with network executives to gauge interest in a CFA TV agreement separate from the NCAA plan. NBC, which has just lost the NCAA basketball rights to CBS, shows an interest.
January 1981	Members of the CFA vote 44-12 to reserve broadcast property rights, a direct challenge to NCAA control of football telecasting.
February 2, 1981	The NCAA releases a football TV questionnaire.
February 5, 1981	The CFA Television Study Committee meets with the NCAA Television Committee for the second time.
March 13, 1981	The CFA TV plan is distributed to the CFA membership.
April 10, 1981	The NCAA council queries NCAA member institutions to see if individual institutions can negotiate football TV contracts. CFA institutions argue that their individual institutional property rights allow them to reject an NCAA-controlled football TV contract.
April 17, 1981	The NCAA claims that only it can negotiate football TV contracts.
May 11, 1981	An NCAA news release reports a 97.4 percent (220-6) approval of the NCAA TV plan. Division I-A voted 60-1 with 24 abstentions.
June 7, 1981	The CFA votes 44-12-1 to keep its TV rights, not allowing the NCAA to negotiate a TV contract for its members.

July 6, 1981	CFA executive director Chuck Nienas suggests that NCAA legal action against the CFA would be an invitation for CFA members to withdraw from the NCAA.
July 24, 1981	The NCAA negotiates with ABC and CBS for similar $131,750,000 contracts for 1982–85 football telecasting.
August 8, 1981	The CFA and NBC agree to a $180 million four-year TV contract.
August 13, 1981	An NCAA official warns that members appearing on telecasts not approved by the NCAA face expulsion.
August 21, 1981	The CFA membership ratifies the CFA-NBC TV plan by a vote of 33-20, but retains an opt-out deadline of September 10, later extended to December 14.
September 8, 1981	The CFA-funded, class-action suits against the NCAA to determine TV rights are filed by Oklahoma and Georgia in the Federal District Court of Oklahoma and by Texas in the State Court of Austin.
September 17, 1981	Presidents of the Big 8 Conference institutions agree to delay action on the NCAA TV or the CFA plans until after the NCAA can address plans to reorganize.
September 18, 1981	The Federal Court in Oklahoma orders the NCAA not to penalize the Universities of Oklahoma and Georgia as a result of the CFA TV contract.
September 23, 1981	The CFA states that it wants property rights to be included as a topic of discussion at the special convention in December, but the suggestions is denied.
October 25, 1981	The CFA proposes creating a Division IV of the NCAA to include CFA institutions and the Big 10 and PAC-10.
November 2, 1981	Reorganization of the NCAA Television Committee is undertaken to reflect concerns of big-time football powers and women's athletics.
December 4, 1981	Responding to pressure to change its TV policy, the NCAA holds a special convention and votes 137-94 to restructure Division I-A, eliminating the twelve-sport option for Division I-A membership while retaining the minimum stadium attendance.
December 15, 1981	The CFA membership refuses to accept the CFA-NBC TV contract of August 21.
January 12, 1982	The NCAA convention confirms the council's interpretation of April 17, 1981, that only the NCAA can negotiate TV contracts.
February 4, 1982	The University of Texas asks to combine with Oklahoma and Georgia in their case against the NCAA. Oklahoma does not accept the offer.
March 1982	Oklahoma and Georgia withdraw their motion to have their lawsuit certified as a class-action suit when it becomes clear not all CFA members are supportive.
March 24, 1982	Bill 5949, favored by the NCAA, is introduced in Congress to control cable TV retransmissions of sports contests.

March 29, 1982	Beer and wine advertising on football telecasts expands, increasing income.
June 4, 1982	The CFA calls for a fourth division in the NCAA to accommodate big-time football and basketball programs.
July 22, 1982	ABC pays an incentive fee of $250,000 to institutions to move broadcast times of football games.
August 16, 1982	The case brought by the University of Texas against the NCAA is dismissed when a judge says that Texas must abide by NCAA TV rules.
September 14, 1982	Federal District Court Judge Burciaga rules the NCAA TV contract violates the Sherman Antitrust Act, voiding $281.5 million in contracts. The decision is appealed.
September 24, 1982	The NCAA considers telecasting games on Sundays during the NFL strike.
September 1982	The Big 8, the Southeastern Conference, Clemson, Notre Dame, Penn State, and SMU offer financial help in the Oklahoma-Georgia suit against the NCAA.
January 12, 1983	The NCAA approves a resolution allowing the NCAA council to seek a congressional exemption from antitrust legislation for a TV football plan.
January 18, 1983	The CFA resolves to encourage all Division I-A institutions to join the CFA in developing a football marketing concept.
February 21, 1983	The CFA accuses Walter Byers of the NCAA of using a delaying tactic to prevent the CFA and the Big 10 and PAC-10 from signing TV contracts.
May 12, 1983	The Court of Appeals, in a 2-1 vote and "per se" analysis, upholds Judge Burciaga's decision favoring Oklahoma and Georgia and calls the NCAA plan anticompetitive and coercive, condemning the NCAA for threatening members with expulsion and boycott for opposing the NCAA. The decision is appealed.
July 12, 1983	A Division I-A Ad Hoc Committee on College Football Television calls for a moratorium on TV contracts until January 15, 1984.
July 19, 1983	Leaders in football TV appearances from 1952–1982 are reported: Notre Dame (65); Texas (59); USC (57); Michigan and Ohio State (54); Oklahoma (53); UCLA (52); Navy (47); and Alabama, Army, and Penn State (46).
July 21, 1983	U.S. Supreme Court Justice Byron White grants a stay on the Court of Appeals antitrust decision, pending a review by the Supreme Court.
August 25, 1983	The American Council on Education files an amicus curiae brief in the U.S. Supreme Court, hoping to protect the interests of universities in general.
October 1983	Barry Fey, of Feyline Presents in Denver, offers Nebraska and Texas a total of $3 million plus 25 percent of gross TV rev-

	enue for a national championship game in either the Superdome or the Rose Bowl.
November 10, 1983	The U. S. Department of Justice files an amicus curiae brief in support of Oklahoma and Georgia's legal efforts against the NCAA.
January 4, 1984	The U.S. Court of Appeals for the D.C. Circuit determines that sports teams own copyright interest in telecasts of their games.
March 20, 1984	The Supreme Court hears the Oklahoma-Georgia case against the NCAA.
June 27, 1984	In *NCAA v. Board of Regents of University of Oklahoma,* the Supreme Court votes 7-2 to declare the NCAA television policy to be in violation of the Sherman Antitrust Act, the first antitrust ruling against amateur sport.
June 28, 1984	The NCAA Division I-A Television Committee meets to devise a less restrictive NCAA TV plan, one that is quickly endorsed by the NCAA council.
July 1984	Notre Dame is offered, but declines, a multiyear, $20 million contract by NBC for nationally telecasting its football games.
July 10, 1984	Division I-A institutions vote 66-44 to reject a new NCAA plan for televising football, with the Big 10 and PAC-10 favoring the plan and the CFA opposing.
July 11, 1984	The Big 10 and PAC-10 conferences vote not to join the CFA in a television package.
July 18, 1984	The Big 10 and PAC-10 conferences negotiate a contract with CBS to telecast their football games.
July 20, 1984	The CFA negotiates a football television contract with ABC.
July 31, 1984	The House of Representatives Committee on Energy and Commerce holds a hearing on televised college football. John Toner predicts the eventual formation of a "Super Conference" for football powers.
September 10, 1984	A Federal District Judge rules that the CFA and ABC cannot prevent "crossover" telecasts of CFA football games with PAC-10 UCLA and USC games by CBS.
October 29, 1984	Judge Burciaga issues a "Memorandum Opinion," stating that institutions could assign their TV property rights as they saw fit and that the NCAA could sell rights to its own championship football games.
November 1, 1984	The NCAA decides not to pursue an in-season TV contract for football.
November 6, 1984	UCLA Chancellor Charles Young calls a meeting of big-time college presidents to consider ways to clean up the football telecasting mess.
November 19, 1984	The U.S. Senate holds hearings on college football telecasting.
November 29, 1984	Michigan athletic director Don Canham complains that TV overexposure and low rights fees plague football.

December 5, 1984	Chuck Neinas of the CFA proposes an eight-team playoff that would, he reasons, produce more than $50 million for CFA institutions.
January 14, 1985	The Athletic Coast Conference votes to separate from the CFA TV plan but reconsiders.
January 1, 1986	The trend toward corporate sponsorship of bowl games begins when Sunkist Citrus Growers Association pays the Fiesta Bowl Association to have "Sunkist" added to the bowl name.
November 11, 1986	The Southeastern Conference, which had earlier voted to separate from the CFA TV contract, votes 6-4 to remain with the CFA after gaining concessions from the CFA to telecast more SEC games.
October 1, 1987	The NCAA Presidents' Commission vetoes a proposal of the NCAA Football Post Season Subcommittee for a one-game Division I-A football championship.
November 22, 1989	CBS and the NCAA agree to a $1 billion, seven-year telecasting contract for the basketball tourney.
December 15, 1989	Penn State is invited to join the Big 10, a move that initiates major changes in conference alignments in the 1990s and influences TV markets.
February 5, 1990	Notre Dame signs a multimillion, multiyear TV contract with NBC for national football broadcasts, damaging in the process the CFA's TV contract.
September 5, 1990	The Federal Trade Commission charges the CFA and Capital Cities / ABC-TV with violating antitrust laws, jeopardizing the CFA's five-year TV contract beginning in 1991.
February 5, 1991	The Big East forms a football conference to augment its basketball conference.
July 11, 1991	A bowl alliance is created to help foster the idea of top-ranked teams playing for a national championship at a bowl game.
August 6, 1991	The Federal Trade Commission antitrust violation charges against the CFA and ABC for their television contract are dismissed.
1991–1992	Arkansas and South Carolina join the Southeastern Conference, while Florida State joins the Atlantic Coast Conference, increasing the conferences' TV market value.
December 1, 1992	The Big 10 and PAC-10 announce a multiyear Rose Bowl agreement with ABC worth about $11.5 million a year.
January 13, 1993	NCAA executive director Richard Schultz suggests a possible playoff for Division I-A football as a way to increase TV monies, revenue that would be used to help women's sports and gender equality.
February 11, 1994	The Southeastern Conference decides to leave the CFA TV plan and signs a contract with CBS worth about a $100 million.

February 14, 1994	The Atlantic Coast Conference signs football television contracts with ABC and ESPN for a total of about $70 million.
February 15, 1994	The Big East receives about $65 million for football telecasting with CBS and soon adds Rutgers and West Virginia to its conference.
March 9, 1994	The Big 8 adds four institutions (Baylor, Texas A & M, Texas Tech, and Texas, from the Southwest Conference), forming the Big 12 and a larger TV market, and receives a five-year, $100 million TV deal with ABC and Liberty Sports beginning in 1996.
May 6, 1994	The NCAA releases its massive "Report to the NCAA Special Committee to Study a Division I-A Football Championship," showing five possible playoff formats and projecting potential TV revenues.
December 6, 1994	The NCAA and CBS sign a TV contract worth $1.725 billion for the NCAA basketball tourneys over the years 1995–2002.
September 1, 1997	The NCAA and Host Communications contract for five-year NCAA licensing and radio broadcast rights worth more than $80 million.
May 1998	Eight institutions of the sixteen-member Western Athletic Conference (Brigham Young, Colorado State, San Diego State, Air Force, Nevada Reno, New Mexico, Utah, and Wyoming) announce that they are forming the Mountain West Conference.
June 10, 1998	The NCAA devises a complicated Bowl Championship Series to determine who might play in a Division I-A "championship" bowl game.
January 9, 1999	Division I-A institutions vote to allow a twelfth game in the football season and eliminate preseason games such as the Kickoff Classic and the Pigskin Classic.
February 1999	Notre Dame rejects an invitation from the Big 10 to become its twelfth member. The new Mountain West Conference and ESPN network sign a $48 million TV contract to broadcast both football and basketball.
November 18, 1999	The NCAA and CBS sign a TV contract for the NCAA basketball tournament for a minimum $6 billion over the years 2003 through 2013, which includes TV rights, cable, satellite, digital and home video, marketing, radio, and other rights.
January 6, 2000	Big 10 commissioner Jim Delany states: "If fans want a playoff, they can get it from the NFL and the NBA."

Notes

Introduction

1. Newspaper clipping, ca. August 1975, Walter Byers Papers, vol. 151, Folder "TV: Football, 1975," NCAA Headquarters, Indianapolis, Ind.
2. Stephen Horn to presidents of the National Collegiate Athletic Association member institutions, 11 July 1975, Walter Byers Papers, Box "TV Comm. 1972," Folder "TV Comm. 1976," NCAA Headquarters.
3. NCAA Television Committee minutes, 2–3 June 1975, 4, NCAA Headquarters.
4. Cedric W. Dempsey to Walter Byers, NCAA Executive Director, 21 July 1977, Walter Byers Papers, vol. 152, Folder "TV: Football 7/77–12/77," NCAA Headquarters.
5. Walter Byers, NCAA Executive Director, to Stephen Horn, 20 September 1975, Walter Byers Papers, Box "TV Comm. 1972," Folder "TV Comm. 1976," NCAA Headquarters.
6. For early commercialization of college athletics see Ronald A. Smith, *Sports and Freedom: The Rise of Big-Time College Athletics* (New York: Oxford University Press, 1988).
7. Owen Johnson, *Stover at Yale* (1912; New York: Collier Books, 1968), 192.
8. Charles Baird, Michigan Athletic Association, to James R. H. Wagner, President, Pasadena Tournament of Roses Association, 30 October 1901, Earl H. Rathbun Papers, Folder "Correspondence 1901–02," Michigan Historical Collection, Bentley Historical Library (emphasis added).
9. A. B. Hart, "Evils of Organized Athletics in American Colleges," *Current History* 31 (December 1929): 558.
10. *Chicago Tribune,* 1 February 1940, in Harold H. Swift Papers, Folder 1, Box 116, University of Chicago Archives.
11. John Reed Kilpatrick, quoted in Edward P. Morgan, "Fifty-Mile Bleachers," *Collier's,* 27 September 1947, 32.
12. "An Analysis of the Operations for the Six Years Ended June 30, 1991," Chancellors' Central Files, Box 299, Folder 23, University of Nebraska Archives. Radio income from the 1990 Nebraska football network was $538,000, while income from the College Football Association TV contract was $100,000.
13. F. W. Marvel, quoted by Frank W. Nicolson, Wesleyan, James R. Angell, Chicago, and Thomas A. Storey, CCNY, to President Ray L. Wilbur, Stanford, 1 May 1919, President Wilbur Papers, Box 27, Folder 4, Stanford University Archives.
14. NCAA Constitution, 1.3.1 Basic Purpose, 1998–99 NCAA Division 1 Manual (Overland Park, Kans.: NCAA, 1998), 1.
15. Smith, *Sports and Freedom,* 27–29, 34–37.
16. The institutions that formed the NCAA first met at the end of December 1905 and organized officially in 1906 as the Intercollegiate Athletic Association of the United States. The name was changed to the NCAA in 1910.

1 The Media and Early College Sport

1. *New York Times,* 18 May 1939, 20.
2. Joseph J. Mathews, "The First Harvard-Oxford Boat Race," *New England Quarterly* 33 (March 1960): 74–82.

3. See Ronald A. Smith, *Sports and Freedom: The Rise of Big-Time College Athletics* (New York: Oxford University Press, 1988).

4. *Boston Daily Evening Transcript,* 5 August 1852, 1–2.

5. *New York Herald,* 10 August 1852, 2, and Guy M. Lewis, "America's First Intercollegiate Sport: The Regattas from 1852–1875," *Research Quarterly* 38 (December 1967): 639.

6. *Franklin and Hampshire Gazette,* 1 July 1859, as quoted in "College Beginnings," *American College* 1 (December 1909): 222–24, and *New York Clipper,* 9 July 1859, 95, and 13 August 1859, 132.

7. *Rutgers Targum,* January 1869, 8.

8. Ibid.

9. Paul Hornung, *Woody Hayes: A Reflection* (Champaign, Ill.: Sagamore Publishing, 1991), 205–14.

10. *New York Clipper,* 26 July 1873, 133.

11. *New York World,* 19 July 1874, 1, 4–5.

12. *New York Daily Tribune,* 22 July 1874, 8.

13. John N. Ostrom to Andrew W. White, 17 November 1875, Andrew D. White Papers, Cornell University Archives; and Waterman T. Hewett, *Cornell University* (New York: University Publication Society, 1905), 3:161. A Harvard alumnus wrote: "We, the aristocrats, prefer to race with each other, and not compete with farmers and mechanics." *Harvard Advocate,* 22 October 1875, 31.

14. *Spirit of the Times,* 22 July 1876, 641.

15. Jotham Potter and W. Earle Dodge, Princeton Football Association, to the Football Associations of Harvard, Yale, and Columbia, 7 November 1876, quoted in Parke H. Davis, *Football the American Intercollegiate Game* (New York: Charles Scribner's Sons, 1911), 67. Davis's book remains the best early history of college football.

16. "Original Constitution of the Intercollegiate Football Association," Walter Camp Papers, Box 1, Folder 23, Yale University Archives.

17. Davis, *Football,* 361–62. Camp was called the "father of American football" as early as 1887. See *New York Herald,* 25 November 1887, 6.

18. *New York Herald,* 25 November 1887, 4.

19. *New York Herald,* 27 November 1890, 9.

20. See, for example, *New York Herald,* 25 November 1892, 3, 1 December 1893, 3, and 23 November 1894, 11.

21. Ethelbert D. Warfield, "Are Foot-Ball Games Educative or Brutalizing?" *Forum* 20 (January 1894): 653.

22. W. R. Dudley to Burt Wilder, Cornell University, 20 February 1895, Burt G. Wilder Papers, 14/26/95, Box 1, Cornell University Archives.

23. John R. Betts, "Organized Sport in Industrial America" (Ph.D. diss., Columbia University, 1951), 205, 249.

24. Herbert Hoover, "The First Big Game," in Pete Grothe, ed., *Great Moments in Stanford Sports* (Palo Alto, Calif.: Pacific Books, 1952), 18.

2   Marconi, the Wireless, and Early Sports Broadcasting

1. Eric Barnouw, *Tube of Plenty: The Evolution of American Television* (New York: Oxford University Press, 1975), 6–9.

2. Richard M. Stepleton, "ESPN, Marconi and the America's Cup," *Gannett Center Journal* 1 (fall 1987): 13–15; Susan J. Douglas, *Inventing American Broadcasting, 1899–1922* (Baltimore: Johns Hopkins University Press, 1987), 4–9; and Eric Barnouw, *A Tower in Babel* (New York: Oxford University Press, 1966), 13–15.

3. *New York Herald,* 4 October 1999, 4. As Marconi carried out his wireless broad-

casting, he was charged with infringement of patent rights by Prof. Amos E. Dolbear of Tufts College near Boston. Dolbear had been experimenting with the wireless for several years. See also *New York Herald,* 3 October 1899, 3; 6 October 1899, 5; and 8 October 1899, 8.

4. Barnouw, *Tube of Plenty,* 12–17.

5. Robert Earl Lee, "A History of Radio Broadcasting at the University of Nebraska," (Master's thesis, University of Nebraska, 1952), 7.

6. *South Bend Tribune,* 13 October 1933.

7. Quoted in Gleason L. Archer, *History of Radio to 1926* (New York: American Historical Society, 1938), 112.

8. Undated manuscript, Folder "History of WLB," E. W. Ziebarth Papers, University of Minnesota Archives, and Stuart L. Bailey, "9X1-WLB Experimental Radio and Broadcasting Station of the University of Minnesota," *Minnesota Techno-Log* 6 (April 1926): 216, 238, 242.

9. Patrick Clark, *Sports Firsts* (New York: Facts on File, 1981), 42. Henry C. Dethlott, in *A Centennial History of Texas A&M University, 1876–1976* (College Station: Texas A&M Press, 1975), 510, claimed that the Texas A&M–Texas radio broadcast was on Thanksgiving Day in 1919, not 1920. It was broadcast from a ham radio station 5YA using wireless telegraphy in the Electrical Engineering Building, a station that later became WTAW. On the telegraph, a shortened form of the game was given, in which, for example, "TFP 8 YL" meant Texas attempted a forward pass but the passer was thrown for an eight-yard loss.

10. Barnouw, *Tube of Plenty,* 20.

11. Ibid., 20–24.

12. Ibid., 37–41.

13. *New York Times,* 29 October 1892, 26.

14. WEAF later became WNBC in New York City.

15. William Peck Banning, *Commercial Broadcasting Pioneer: The WEAF Experiment, 1922–1926* (Cambridge: Harvard University Press, 1946), 90–96, and Salloy Bedell Smith, *In All His Glory: The Life of William S. Paley* (New York: Simon and Schuster, 1990), 54.

16. Barnouw, *A Tower in Babel,* 30–36.

17. Karen Buzzard, *Electronic Media Ratings: Turning Audiences into Dollars and Sense* (Boston: Focal Press, 1992), 3–5.

18. Robin Lester, *Stagg's University: The Rise, Decline, and Fall of Big-Time Football at Chicago* (Urbana: University of Illinois Press, 1995), 118.

19. *Chicago Tribune,* 29 October 1922, part 2, 4, and 30 October 1922, 19; *Football Scrapbook* 163 (October–November 1922), A. A. Stagg Papers, University of Chicago Archives; and Banning, *Commercial Broadcasting Pioneer,* 110–11.

3   The Broadcasters

1. Ray Poindexter, *Golden Throats and Silver Tongues: The Radio Announcers* (Conway, Ark.: River Road Press, 1978), 10–12, and Kenneth Bilby, *The General David Sarnoff and the Rise of the Communications Industry* (New York: Harper & Row, 1986), 56–57.

2. Poindexter, *Golden Throats,* 10–11, and Erik Barnouw, *A Tower in Babel* (New York: Oxford University Press, 1966), 80–81.

3. Randy Roberts, *Jack Dempsey: The Manassa Mauler* (Baton Rouge: Louisiana State University Press, 1979), 100–129.

4. This is the conclusion of Huntington Williams in "The News in Network TV Sports," *Gannett Center Journal* 1 (fall 1987): 26. Others have made similar comments.

5. Poindexter, *Golden Throats,* 14–15.

6. Ibid., 16–17.

7. Robert Earl Lee, "A History of Radio Broadcasting at the University of Nebraska," (Master's thesis, University of Nebraska, 1952), 9–10.

8. Ted Husing, *Ten Years Before the Mike* (New York: Farrar & Rinehart, 1935), 55–56. While the story is likely, one cannot place a great deal of authority on its veracity.

9. Poindexter, *Golden Throats and Silver Tongues,* 14–15.

10. Charles Fountain, *Sportswriter: The Life and Times of Grantland Rice* (New York: Oxford University Press, 1993), 195–96; Mark Inabinett, *Grantland Rice and His Heroes: The Sportswriter as Mythmaker in the 1920s* (Knoxville: University of Tennessee Press, 1994), 8–9; and William A. Harper, *How You Played the Game: The Life of Grantland Rice* (Columbia: University of Missouri Press, 1999), 312–13.

11. Barnouw, *A Tower in Babel,* 91.

12. "Radio and Television Retailing, January 1947," Du Mont Laboratories, Box 13, Folder "'C' 1947," Manuscript Division, Library of Congress.

13. For salary information see, for example, "Enter Professional Coach," *Literary Digest,* 29 April 1922, 48; E. G. Mahin, "Science or Athletics?" *Science* 55 (19 May 1922): 527; Dean L. B. R. Briggs, Harvard, to President A. Lawrence Lowell, Harvard, 22 July 1922, President Lowell Papers, 1919–22, Folder 96, Harvard University Archives; Harvard Corporation minutes, 25 September 1922, Harvard University Archives; Harvard Athletic Committee minutes, 7 January 1925, Harvard University Archives; Acting President W. S. Sutton, University of Texas, to President A. L. Lowell, Harvard University, 10 July 1924, President Lowell Papers, 1922–25, Folder 6B, Harvard University Archives; Douglas Anderson, Athletic Committee Chairman, Tulane University, to President William P. Few, Duke University, 8 September 1924, William H. Wannamaker Papers, Box 25, Folder "Applications, 1925," Duke University Archives; and Arnold Eddy, *Troyditionally Yours: Recollections Mostly about Sports 1920s, 1930s, and 1940s* (privately published, 1988), 28.

14. The classic study of intercollegiate athletics, Howard J. Savage et al., *American College Athletics* (New York: Carnegie Foundation for the Advancement of Teaching, 1929), 173, indicates that small colleges paid football coaches about 9 percent more than full professors, while large colleges paid about 8 percent more.

15. Barnouw, *A Tower in Babel,* 4.

16. John W. White, W. S. Chaplin, and A. B. Hart, "Athletic Report," 12 June 1888, HUD 8388.3B, Harvard University Archives.

17. Robin Lester, *Stagg's University: The Rise, Decline, and Fall of Big-Time Football at Chicago* (Urbana: University of Illinois Press, 1995), 53–54.

18. *Northwestern University President's Annual Report, 1904–05,* 19, Northwestern University Archives.

19. Barnouw, *A Tower in Babel,* 283.

20. John M. Carroll, *Red Grange and the Rise of Modern Football* (Urbana: University of Illinois Press, 1999), 1–9.

21. Bill Cusumuano, "'M' Football, WWJ 56-Year Partners," (Michigan State University Program, 1978), 34, and Poindexter, *Golden Throats,* 42–44, 49.

4   Graham McNamee and Ted Husing Dominate the Airwaves

1. "Radio and Television Retailing, January 1947," Du Mont Laboratories, Box 13, Folder "'C' 1947," Manuscript Division, Library of Congress. By the time of the Depression in 1932, there were about 18 million radios in use in America, and there were 56 million by the time the United States entered into World War II.

2. William Peck Banning, *Commercial Broadcasting Pioneer: The WEAF Experiment,*

1922–1926 (Cambridge: Harvard University Press, 1946), 111–12; and Erik Barnouw, *Tube of Plenty: The Evolution of American Television* (New York: Oxford University Press, 1975), 40–47.

3. Ray Poindexter, *Golden Throats and Silver Tongues: The Radio Announcers* (Conway, Ark.: River Road Press, 1978), 61.

4. Graham McNamee, "Tell Us about the Game!" *American Magazine,* May 1928, 155.

5. *Who Was Who in America* (Chicago: Marquis Who's Who, 1943), 2:365.

6. Banning, *Commercial Broadcasting Pioneer,* 142–43.

7. Graham McNamee, *You're on the Air* (New York: Harper & Bros., 1926), 62.

8. Banning, *Commercial Broadcasting Pioneer,* 144, and Poindexter, *Golden Throats,* 29.

9. McNamee, *You're on the Air,* 63, 82. McNamee was the announcer at the famous 1924 Democratic National Convention in Madison Square Garden, which took 103 ballots to nominate John W. Davis.

10. McNamee, *You're on the Air,* 144–45.

11. Red Barber, *The Broadcasters* (New York: Da Capo, 1985), 29; and Heywood Broun, in his foreword to McNamee, *You're on the Air.*

12. Ted Husing, *Ten Years Before the Mike* (New York: Farrar & Rinehart, 1935), 8.

13. *Current Biography* (Bronx, N.Y.: H. W. Wilson Co., 1942), 404; and Julian Bach, Jr., "Hold 'Em Husing!," *Literary Digest,* 6 November 1937, 22–23; and Husing, *Ten Years Before the Mike,* 14.

14. Husing, *Ten Years Before the Mike,* 40–42.

15. Poindexter, *Golden Throats and Silver Tongues,* 63.

16. *New York Herald Tribune,* 21 November 1927, 14.

17. Bach, "Hold 'Em Husing!," 23.

18. William S. Paley, *As It Happened: A Memoir* (Garden City, N.J.: Doubleday, 1979), 39.

19. Husing, *Ten Years Before the Mike,* 42, 65.

20. Ibid., 163–65; and *New York Times,* 13 October 1929, 10:17. Walter Kennedy, a future NBA commissioner, was once also, like Les Quailey, Husing's assistant, for football broadcasts. See Barber, *The Broadcasters,* 30.

21. Bach, "Hold 'Em Husing!" 22–23.

22. Poindexter, *Golden Throats and Silver Tongues,* 97, 144, and *Who Was Who in America,* 5:477.

5 The Radio Threat to College Football Attendance

1. Graham McNamee, *You're on the Air* (New York: Harper & Bros., 1926), 101.

2. W. P. Fuller, Jr., to John C. Macfarland, Los Angeles, 2 November 1931, President Wilbur Papers, Box 77, Folder "Board of Athletic Control," Stanford University Archives.

3. Guy C. Earke, Jr., telegram to President Wilbur, Stanford University, 15 December 1931, Ibid.

4. "Taking Football off the Air," *Literary Digest,* 9 July 1932, 35, and "Does Radio Cut the Football Gate?" *Literary Digest,* 16 July 1932, 32–33.

5. President Charles W. Kennedy, NCAA, to NCAA members, 1 June 1932, President's Correspondence and Papers, 1932, Folder 435, University of California Archives.

6. NCAA *Proceedings,* 29 July 1932, 44, NCAA Headquarters, Indianapolis, Ind.

7. Ibid., 37, 38, 42, 43, 45, 48, 50.

8. Ibid., 43.

9. Richard R. Price, Chair, Radio Broadcasting Committee of the University of Minnesota, memorandum to Radio Broadcasting Committee, 13 January 1932, Box 28,

Folder "Radio Broadcasting, 1932–35," Minnesota University Comptroller Papers, University of Minnesota Archives.

10. NCAA *Proceedings,* 29 July 1932, 37–38, 45, 54, NCAA Headquarters.

11. Ibid., 47.

12. Ibid., 42.

13. Ibid., 48.

14. W. H. Bates, University of Iowa, to J. D. Phillips, University of Wisconsin, and other Big 10 institutions, 24 August 1932, Box 28, Folder "Radio Broadcasting 1932–35," Minnesota University Comptroller Papers, University of Minnesota Archives.

15. Ray Poindexter, *Golden Throats and Silver Tongues: The Radio Announcers* (Conway, Ark.: River Road Press, 1978), 101.

16. Arthur Lincicome, Assistant Comptroller, University of Illinois, to J. D. Phillips, University of Wisconsin, and other Big 10 institutions, 16 August 1932, Box 28, Folder "Radio Broadcasting 1932–35," Minnesota University Comptroller Papers, University of Minnesota Archives.

17. Julius E. Schmidt, Vice President, University of Michigan, to J. D. Phillips, University of Wisconsin, and other Big 10 institutions, 8 August 1932, Box 28, Folder "Radio Broadcasting 1932–35," Minnesota University Comptroller Papers, University of Minnesota Archives.

18. The straw vote showed that thirty of thirty-four members believed that radio had a negative impact on football revenues. NCAA *Proceedings,* 29 July 1932, 54, NCAA Headquarters.

19. Ibid., 54.

20. Ibid., 51.

21. Ibid., 54–59.

22. "Refining Influence," *Time,* 14 September 1936, 43.

23. Ibid., 44.

24. W. T. Middlebrook, University of Minnesota Comptroller, to Alfred W. Peterson, University of Wisconsin Comptroller, 11 October 1934, Box 28, Folder "Radio, Football, 1934–36," Minnesota University Comptroller Papers, University of Minnesota Archives, and "Refining Influence," 43.

25. William F. Humphrey, Mackay Radio, San Francisco, telegram to President John F. O'Harra, Notre Dame, 7 December 1934, UPOH, Box 68, Folder 25, University of Notre Dame Archives.

26. President Lotus Caufman, University of Minnesota, to Committee on Intercollegiate Athletics and Committee on Radio Broadcasting, 26 September 1935, Box 28, Folder "Radio Football, 1934–35," Minnesota University Comptroller Papers, University of Minnesota Archives; and "Memorandum," ca. 1936, Vice President's Records, 1934–46," UVOC, Box 6, Folder 52, "Radio Broadcasts, 1934–37," University of Notre Dame Archives. The Big 10 survey in 1936 showed the conference was split both on whether there should be a unified Big 10 policy and on whether income should be split equally among all members. See "Report of Committee on Radio Broadcasting of Athletic Events," 25 February 1936, Michigan University Board in Control of Intercollegiate Athletics, Box 36, Folder "Radio Broadcasting 1935," Michigan Historical Collections, Bentley Historical Library.

27. "Radio Broadcasts of 1937 Football Games at Ann Arbor," Board in Control of Intercollegiate Athletics, Box 21, Folder "Papers 1937 March 1," Michigan Historical Collection, Bentley Historical Library. An undated memorandum, Vice President's Records, 1934–46, UVOC, Box 6, Folder 52, "Radio Broadcasts, 1934–37," University of Notre Dame Archives, indicates that Michigan received $21,500, but it is likely in error. Michigan received only $4,000 in 1935 and $8,000 the following year.

28. C. E. Bowen, Athletic Business Manager, Illinois, to President A. C. Willard, 5 March 1937, President Willard General Correspondence, Box 16, Folder "Athletic Association," University of Illinois Archives.

29. "Refining Influence," 43.

30. Ibid.

31. University of Pennsylvania Executive Board of Trustees minutes, 21 July 1936, University of Pennsylvania Archives.

32. Princeton Board of Trustees minutes, 22 October 1936, Princeton University Archives.

33. Harvard Athletic Committee minutes, 22 November 1937, Harvard University Archives.

34. Bingham to Conant, 1 December 1937; Conant to President H. W. Dodds, Princeton, 10 December 1937; Conant to Dodds, 3 January 1938; Dodds to Conant, 6 January 1938; Conant to Dodds, 7 January 1938; and Conant to Dodds, 18 March 1938, President Conant Papers, 1937–38, Box 3, Folder "Athletic Association," Harvard University Archives.

35. Conant, to Lenox R. Lohr, NBC, 14 June 1938, and Dodds to Lohr, 8 April 1938, ibid.

6   In the Image of Rockne

1. *South Bend News-Times,* 6 June 1937.

2. Murray Sperber, *Shake Down the Thunder: The Creation of Notre Dame Football* (New York: Henry Holt, 1993), 167. Sperber's book is well researched and one of the few unglorified accounts of Notre Dame football.

3. Knute Rockne to W. G. Hay, WGN, Chicago, 3 September 1926, UADR, Box 13, Folder 47, University of Notre Dame Archives.

4. Sperber, *Shake Down the Thunder,* 320.

5. John H. Murphy, Notre Dame Chair, Faculty Board in Control of Athletics, to Dan D. Halpin, Manager, Television Receiver Sales, RCA, Camden, N.J., 9 June 1948, Vice President John Murphy Papers, UVMR, Box 4, Folder "TV," University of Notre Dame Archives.

6. William F. Humphrey, Mackay Radio, San Francisco, telegram to President John F. O'Harra, Notre Dame, 7 December 1934, UPOH, Box 68, Folder 25, University of Notre Dame Archives.

7. Transcript of "Broadcast of Harold Anson Bruce over Station WHN," 8 October 1934, UPOH, Box 68, Folder 25, University of Notre Dame Archives.

8. Paley to O'Donnell 20 November 1936, Vice President's Records, 1934–46, UVOC, Box 6, Folder 52, "Radio Broadcasts, 1934–1937," University of Notre Dame Archives.

9. Brown to McCarthy 5 February 1937, UVOC, Box 6, Folder 53, University of Notre Dame Archives.

10. Ward to McCarthy, 10 February 1937, ibid.

11. L. E. McGivena, New York City, to McCarthy, 24 February 1937, ibid.

12. M. H. Miller to McCarthy, 10 March 1937, ibid.

13. Jim Cleary to McCarthy, 11 February 1937, UVOC, Box 6, Folder 52, University of Notre Dame Archives.

14. McCarthy to Francis C. Barton, Jr., H. W. Ayer & Sons Advertising Agency, New York City, 24 May 1937, ibid.

15. Vice President Hugh O'Donnell, Notre Dame, to Sidney N. Strotz, NBC, 9 October 1939, ibid.

16. Joe Petritz, Sports Publicity Director, Notre Dame, to Vice President John J. Cavanaugh, Notre Dame, 10 September 1941, ibid.

17. Cavanaugh to President Niles Trammel, NBC, 7 August 1941 and 27 August 1941, and Proposed Press Release, 14 September 1941, ibid.
18. Notre Dame believed Michigan's radio income was $12,000. Joseph Petritz, Notre Dame Sports Publicity Director, to Cavanaugh, 8 April 1942, Vice President's Records, 1934–46, UVOC, Box 6, Folder 57, University of Notre Dame Archives.
19. Cavanaugh to Trammell, 7 August 1941, "Statement of 1943 Notre Dame Football Broadcasting and Revenues," 16 September 1944, Petritz to Cavanaugh, 8 April 1942, Walter Kennedy, Notre Dame Department of Publicity, to Cavanaugh, ca. September 1944, and "Statement of 1944 Notre Dame Football Broadcasting and Revenues," 12 January 1945, ibid.
20. Dan Halpin, Camden, New Jersey, to H. E. Jones, Notre Dame Business Manager, 30 April 1948, UVMR, Box 4, Folder "TV," University of Notre Dame Archives.
21. Murphy to Frank P. Schreiber, WGN, Chicago, 17 June 1948, ibid.
22. "Notre Dame Football," PNDP, 3021–02, University of Notre Dame Archives.
23. Murphy to Paul J. Pfohl, RCA, Chicago, 24 May 1949, Vice President John Murphy Papers, UVMR, Box 4, Folder "TV," University of Notre Dame Archives.
24. Proposed TV Contract by RCA Victor, ca. spring 1949, Vice President John Murphy Papers, ibid.
25. Hesburgh to Robert Dunne, 20 October 1949, President Hesburgh Papers, UVHS, Box 3, Folder "TV-September 1949," University of Notre Dame Archives. At the time, Hesburgh was particularly interested in telecasting football on large screens in movie theaters.

7   Radio Goes "Bowling"

1. Graham to Robertson Griswold, Jr., Baltimore, 25 November 1936, President Graham Files, 2/2/3, Box 20, Folder "Football: Broadcasts, 1935–41," University of North Carolina Archives.
2. *New York Times,* 29 December 1936, 24.
3. "Memorandum," ca. 1936, UVOC, Box 6, Folder 52, University of Notre Dame Archives; and O. M. Solem, University of Iowa Athletic Director, to Richard R. Price, University of Minnesota, 10 June 1936, Box 28, Folder "Radio Football, 1934–36," Minnesota University Comptroller Papers, University of Minnesota Archives.
4. Dale A. Somers, *The Rise of Sports in New Orleans, 1850–1900* (Baton Rouge: Louisiana State University Press, 1972), 252, and Albert B. Crawford, ed., *Yale Football Y Men, 1872–1919* (New Haven: Yale University, 1962), 47.
5. *Chicago Tribune,* 2 January 1894, 12; and Amos Alonzo Stagg and Wesley W. Stout, *Touchdown!* (New York: Longmans, Green, 1927), 181–82.
6. Richard J. Storr, *Harper's University: The Beginnings* (Chicago: University of Chicago Press, 1966), 179.
7. Jack F. Sheehan and Louis Honig, *The Games of California and Stanford* (San Francisco: Commercial Publishing Co., 1900), 88.
8. Herb Michelson and Dave Newhouse, *Rose Bowl Football Since 1902* (New York: Stein & Day, 1977), 17–18.
9. James R. H. Wagner, President, Pasadena Tournament of Roses Association, to Charles Baird, Michigan Athletic Association, 1 November 1901, 13 November 1901, 18 November 1901, 27 November 1901, 11 December 1901, and 12 December 1901, and Baird to Wagner, 20 October 1901, 18 November 1901, and 2 December 1901, Earl H. Rathbun Papers, Folder "Correspondence 1901–02," Michigan Historical Collection, Bentley Historical Library.
10. "Pasadena New Year's Day Tournament of Roses Notes," Earl H. Rathbun Papers,

Folder "Notes and Articles about Rose Bowl, 1902," Michigan Historical Collection, Bentley Historical Library; and Michelson and Newhouse, *Rose Bowl Football*, 34, 37.

11. Thomas A. Storey, NCAA chairman of the Committee on Extension of the Influence of the NCAA, to President A. L. Lowell, Harvard, 25 May 1920, President Lowell Papers, 1919–22, Folder 96, Harvard University Archives.

12. William Thomas, San Francisco, telegrams to President A. Lawrence Lowell, 26 November 1919 and 19 November 1919, ibid.

13. Briggs to President A. Lawrence Lowell, Harvard, 8 December 1919, ibid.

14. Harvard Athletic Committee minutes, 2 December 1919, Harvard University Archives.

15. P. V. K. Johnson, President, Harvard Club of Southern California, telegram to Lowell, 8 December 1919, and Stephenson telegrams to Lowell, 8 and 9 December 1919, Lowell Papers, 1919–20, Folder 96, Harvard University Archives.

16. *Cambridge to Pasadena and Return* (1920; rpt. Cambridge: Harvard Varsity Club, 1994), 46.

17. "Rules and Regulations of the Committee on Athletic Sports (1925)," in Lowell Papers, 1922–1925, Folder 563, Harvard University Archives. The agreement was passed in 1923.

18. William H. Barrow, Chairman, Faculty Committee on Athletics, Athletics Report, in President's Report (1923), 195, Stanford University Archives.

19. President R. L. Wilbur, Stanford, to Glenn Warner, 26 January 1922, President Wilbur Papers, Box 51, Folder 13, Stanford University Archives. Warner was hired away from Pittsburgh in 1922 with the understanding that Warner would not leave Pittsburgh until 1924.

20. Ray Poindexter, *Golden Throats and Silver Tongues: The Radio Announcers* (Conway, Ark.: River Road Press, 1978), 49.

21. "Contract of Employment," 25 March 1924, President Matthew Walsh General Correspondence, UPWL, Box 53, Folder "Rockne-Columbia," University of Notre Dame Archives.

22. Michelson and Newhouse, *Rose Bowl Football*, 54–65.

23. A. D. McDonald, New Orleans, to President Matthew Walsh, Notre Dame, 11 January 1925, Vice President M. A. Mulcaire Records, UVMU, Box 2, Folder "Athletic Correspondence," University of Notre Dame Archives.

24. Vice President M. A. Mulcaire, Notre Dame, to L. B. Henry, Rose Bowl Chairman, 18 December 1929, Mulcaire Records, UVMU, Box 2, Folder "Henry, Leslie B.," University of Notre Dame Archives. Mulcaire wrote: "We felt it would not be fair to him to keep him under the nervous strain which such an event would cause in view of the fact that he has suffered so much and so long during the past football season."

25. Author interview with Father Joyce, Notre Dame, 14 September 1988.

26. Bruce Corrie, "A History of the Atlantic Coast Conference," (P.E.D. diss., Department of Physical Education, Indiana University, 1970), 75.

27. Suzanne Rau Wolf, *The University of Alabama* (University: University of Alabama Press, 1983), 148.

28. Graham McNamee, "Behind the Mike," *American Magazine*, April 1928, 189.

29. Michelson and Newhouse, *Rose Bowl Football*, 74–75.

30. Coffman to Governor Theodore Christianson, St. Paul, 3 November 1930, President's Papers, Box 42, Folder "Post-Season Games for Charity," University of Minnesota Archives.

31. Poindexter, *Golden Throats and Silver Tongues*, 220, and William O. Johnson, Jr., *Super Spectator and the Electric Lilliputians* (Boston: Little, Brown, 1971), 50.

32. Ted Husing, *Ten Years Before the Mike* (New York: Farrar & Rinehart, 1935), 170. Red

Barber, in *The Broadcasters* (New York: Da Capo, 1985), 21–35, tells of Husing's general arrogance and the day that he criticized umpiring in the 1934 World Series, after which he never again broadcast a World Series.

33. Bingham to President Conant, 6 January 1937, President Conant Papers, 1936–37, Box 2, Folder "Athletic Board of Review," Harvard University Archives.

34. O. F. Long to F. E. Reichart, Former chairman of the Big 10, 25 October 1938, Senate Athletic Committee Chairman and Faculty Representative's File, 1907–1968, Box 2, Folder "Western Conference, 38–39," University of Illinois Archives.

35. Dennis W. Brogan, *The American Character* (New York: Knopf, 1944), 143.

36. *Washington Post,* 9 December 1941, 26.

8   Sport and the New Medium of Television

1. *New York Times,* 23 September 1927, 20; "Du Mont Memo," Du Mont Laboratories, Box 71, Folder "T.V. Education, 1952," Manuscript Division, Library of Congress; Erik Barnouw, *Tube of Plenty* (New York: Oxford University Press, 1973), 17; Erik Barnouw, *A Tower in Babel* (New York: Oxford University Press, 1966), 154, 211, 232; Francis Wheen, *Television: A History* (London: Century Publishing, 1985), 11; and *Pennsylvania Gazette,* January 1941, 127.

2. William Uricchio, "Television as History: Representations of German Television Broadcasting, 1935–1944," in Bruce A. Murray and Christopher J. Wickham, eds., *Framing the Past: The Historiography of German Cinema and Television* (Carbondale: Southern Illinois University Press, 1992), 193.

3. Though Jesse Owens won four gold medals in the 1936 Summer Olympics, the Germans easily outdistanced the United States in gold medals, 33 to 24, and in total medals, 89 to 56. Italy came in a distant third.

4. *New York Times Magazine,* 5 June 1938, 6, and Dave Berkman, "Long Before Arledge . . . Sports and Television: The Earliest Years: 1937–1947—as Seen by the Popular Press," *Journal of Popular Culture* 22 (fall 1988): 49–62.

5. U. S. Federal Communications Commission, *Fourth Annual Report,* 30 June 1938 (Washington, D.C.: U.S. Government Printing Office, 1939), 65.

6. Erik Barnouw, *The Golden Web* (New York: Oxford University Press, 1968), 127.

7. *New York Times,* 26 February 1939, 9:10; and Orrin E. Dunlap, Jr., *The Future of Television* (New York: Harper & Bros., 1942), 1, 5.

8. Ray Poindexter, *Golden Throats and Silver Tongues: The Radio Announcers* (Conway, Ark.: River Road Press, 1978), 117.

9. *New York Times,* 18 May 1939, 29.

10. William O. Johnson, Jr., *Super Spectator and the Electric Lilliputians* (Boston: Little, Brown, 1971), 36; *Philadelphia Inquirer,* 18 May 1939, 25; and *New York Times,* 18 May 1939, 29.

11. *New York Times,* 18 May 1939, 29.

12. Johnson, *Super Spectator,* 36.

13. Philip Kerby, *The Victory of Television* (New York: Harper & Bros., 1939), 63.

14. *New York Times,* 17 May 1939, 19.

15. Dunlap, *Future of Television,* 11.

16. The President of Madison Square Garden, John Reed Kilpatrick, made this analogy in 1947. See Berkman, "Long Before Arledge," 57.

17. *Radio Daily,* 7 October 1941, 7.

18. *New York Times,* 27 August 1939, 5:4, 3 September 1939, 9:10, and 4 September 1939, 10:10; and Red Barber, *The Broadcasters* (New York: Da Capo, 1985), 120, 133.

19. Barber, *The Broadcasters,* 134.

20. *New York Times,* 14 September 1939, 31, 24 September 1939, 9:10, 29 September 1939, and 1 October 1939, 5:1; and Johnson, *Super Spectator,* 44.
21. Richard Whittingham, *What a Game They Played* (New York: Harper & Row, 1984), 193–94; and Phil Patton, *Razzle-Dazzle: The Curious Marriage of Television and Professional Football* (Garden City, N.Y.: Dial Press, 1984), 7–10.
22. *New York Herald Tribune,* 8 August 1950.
23. *Daily Pennsylvanian,* 4 October 1940, 1.
24. *Pennsylvania Gazette,* January 1941, 127. University of Pennsylvania leadership in television included research by Prof. Herbert E. Ives, a Penn graduate who had helped conduct the first American public demonstration of TV, transmitting Herbert Hoover's likeness between Washington, D.C., and New York in April 1927, and also participated in the first demonstration of color TV, in June 1947, from Pennsylvania's University Hospital. See "University of Pennsylvania 'Firsts,'" 2 December 1977, University of Pennsylvania Archives.
25. *Daily Pennsylvanian,* 4 October 1940, 1, and 7 October 1940, 1; *Pennsylvania Gazette,* January 1941, 127; and *New York Times,* 22 September 1940, 9:10.
26. Herb Michelson and Dave Newhouse, *Rose Bowl Football Since 1902* (New York: Stein & Day, 1977), 22. Michelson and Newhouse incorrectly note that the first television coverage of the parade was in 1947 (29).
27. Du Mont Laboratories, Box 14, Folder "Don Lee Television, 1939–40," Manuscript Division, Library of Congress.

9   Networks, Coaxial Cable, Commercialism, and Concern

1. Coaxial cable is a sort of pipe in which wire is supported by insulators that prevent it from touching the inner walls. Coaxial cable can carry hundreds of signals simultaneously without interference, allowing television images to be transmitted. As early as August 1940, CBS sent color TV images over coaxial cable from New York City to Washington, D.C., and back. See "Press Release, 30 August 1940," Du Mont Laboratories, Box 12, Folder "C.B.S., 1940–46," Manuscript Division, Library of Congress.
2. Ernest A. Marx, memorandum to Allen B. Du Mont, 21 June 1946, Du Mont Laboratories, Box 33, Folder "Marx, Ernest A., 1946," Manuscript Division, Library of Congress; and Ed Papazin, *Medium Rare: The Evolutionary Worship and Impact of Commercial Television* (New York: Media Dynamics, 1989), 1.
3. "Sports, Early Diet of Radio, Nourish Television," *Business Week,* 29 June 1946, 18; and Sterling Quinlan, *Inside ABC: American Broadcasting Company's Rise to Power* (New York: Hastings House, 1979), 21. The Hooper radio rating was 67.2, the highest commercial rating ever and only outdone by three President Franklin Roosevelt broadcasts.
4. A. Robert Ginsburgh, Executive Assistant to Secretary of War, Washington, D.C., to Allen B. Du Mont, Passaic, N.J., 28 October 1946, Du Mont Laboratories, Box 13, Folder "Complimentary Letters, 1946," Manuscript Division, Library of Congress; and *New York Times,* 5 December 1946, 33.
5. Edward P. Morgan, "Fifty-Mile Bleachers," *Collier's,* 27 September 1947, 30.
6. *New York Times,* 12 October 1947, 56.
7. Murphy to William Fay, 16 February 1948, Vice President John Murphy Papers, UVMR, Box 4, Folder "TV," University of Notre Dame Archives.
8. Dan Halpin, TV Sales Manager, to President John J. Cavanaugh, Notre Dame, 28 October 1947, and Thomas J. McMahon, N. W. Ayer & Sons, Philadelphia, to Vice President John Murphy, 29 October 1947, Vice President John Murphy Papers, UVMR,

Box 4, Folder "TV," University of Notre Dame Archives; and "Television Contract" (1947), UDIS, Box 25, Folder "Television, 1955–58," University of Notre Dame Archives.

9. F. C. O'Keefe, New York City, to Vice President John Murphy, Notre Dame, 4 June 1948, Vice President John Murphy Papers, UVMR, Box 4, Folder "TV," University of Notre Dame Archives.

10. Dan Halpin, RCA manager, Camden, New Jersey, to H. E. Jones, Business Manager, Notre Dame, 30 April 1948, and W. C. Eddy, WBKB, Director of TV, to John Murphy, 2 June 1948, ibid. For comparison, Ohio State was offered $100 per game by the Crosley Broadcasting Corporation of Cincinnati to televise its home games in 1948. See Dwight W. Martin, Crosley Broadcasting Corporation, to Richard C. Larkins, Ohio State Athletic Director, 19 March 1948, Director of Athletics Papers, 9/3–1/20, "Television, 1947–50," Ohio State University Archives.

11. W. C. Eddy, Director of WBKB-TV, Chicago, to John Murphy, 2 June 1948, Vice President John Murphy Papers, UVMR, Box 4, Folder "TV," University of Notre Dame Archives.

12. Vice President John Murphy to Dan Halpin, RCA, Camden, N.J., 14 March 1949, ibid.

13. RCA television proposal and J. K. West, RCA Vice-President, to John H. Murphy, 16 May 1949, ibid; and Stanley Frank, "Main Event: TV vs. SRO," *Nations Business,* March 1949, 46–48, 84.

14. "Du Mont Television Network Proposal," Vice President John Murphy Papers, UVMR, Box 4, Folder "TV," University of Notre Dame Archives.

15. Paul Fogarty, WGN-TV, to John Murphy, 6 June 1949, ibid.

16. John Murphy to Theodore Hesburgh, Notre Dame, 9 November 1949, Hesburgh Papers, UVHS, Box 3, Folder "TV-September 1949," University of Notre Dame Archives.

17. Leslie Arries, Du Mont Television Network, to Vice President Theodore Hesburgh, Notre Dame, 29 December 1949, ibid.

18. Though there was no official Ivy League in the 1940s, the press generally called the group of schools led by Harvard, Yale, and Princeton the "Ivy League" well before the official formation in the 1950s.

19. Francis Murray, University of Pennsylvania Athletic Director, to Acting President William DuBarry, Penn, 8 April 1952, Papers of the Office of the President, 1950–55, Box 53, Folder "Intercollegiate Athletics 9," University of Pennsylvania Archives.

20. NCAA *Proceedings* (1950), 109, NCAA Headquarters, Indianapolis, Ind.

21. President Robert E. Kintner, ABC, telegram to President Harold E. Stassen, University of Pennsylvania, 23 August 1950, Papers of the Office of the President, 1950–55, Box 54, Folder "Intercollegiate Athletics TV 1," University of Pennsylvania Archives.

22. "Attendance Figures in Major Conferences for 1950," Papers of the Office of the President, 1950–55, Box 53, Folder "Intercollegiate Athletics, TV 2," University of Pennsylvania Archives.

23. NCAA *Proceedings* (1948), 118–38, NCAA Headquarters.

24. Ibid., 118, 119, 124.

25. Ibid., 128.

26. Ibid. 130–35.

27. Ibid., 136.

28. Ibid., 188–96. The NCAA institutions as a whole would vote on any ousting of NCAA members.

29. Eastern College Athletic Conference minutes, 17 December 1947, 64, 71, ECAC Headquarters, Centreville, Mass. The ECAC had been formed in 1938.

30. NCAA *Proceedings* (1949), 149–57, NCAA Headquarters.

31. *New York World-Telegram,* 7 September 1949.

32. Eastern College Athletic Conference minutes, 9 December 1949, ECAC Headquarters.

33. NCAA *Proceedings* (1949), 117, NCAA Headquarters.

10   Notre Dame Chooses Commercial TV

1. Bill Fay, "Inside Sports," *Collier's,* 19 February 1949, 56. Fay was right on other counts. For instance, 1949 was the high point for minor league baseball, with 464 teams and attendance of 42 million. By 1952, attendance had been cut in half.

2. NCAA *Proceedings* (1950), 116, NCAA Headquarters, Indianapolis, Ind.

3. Ibid., 118.

4. Ibid., 122.

5. John Murphy, memorandum to Theodore Hesburgh, 9 November 1949, President Hesburgh Papers, UVHS, Box 3, Folder "TV-September 1949," University of Notre Dame Archives. An acquaintance of Notre Dame coach Frank Leahy was told that "the Church—and Notre Dame—thrive on persecution." Bert Dunne, San Francisco, to Frank Leahy, 5 October 1949, ibid.

6. See for instance Murphy, memorandum to Hesburgh, 9 November 1949; Edward J. McCrossin, memorandum to C. J. Witting, 14 November 1949, and N. L. Halpern, TV Consultant, New York City, to Leslie Arries, Du Mont, Director of Sports, 17 November 1949, Du Mont Laboratories, Box 36, Folder "Witting, Christian, 1949–50," Manuscripts Division, Library of Congress; and Edgar Kobak, President, Mutual Broadcasting System, to Theodore Hesburgh, 28 November 1949, President Hesburgh Papers, UVHS, Box 3, Folder "TV-September 1949," University of Notre Dame Archives.

7. Robert V. Dunne, San Francisco, to Theodore Hesburgh, 5 October 1949, President Hesburgh Papers, UVHS, Box 3, Folder "TV-September 1949," University of Notre Dame Archives.

8. Ibid.

9. Hesburgh to Dunne, 20 October 1949, ibid.

10. Dunne, to Hesburgh, 5 October 1949, ibid.

11. Kenneth L. Wilson to Theodore Hesburgh, 31 March 1950, and Hesburgh to Leslie Arries, Du Mont TV Network, 27 January 1950, President Hesburgh Papers, UVHS, Box 3, Folder "TV September 1949 # 2" University of Notre Dame Archives.

12. NCAA *Proceedings* (1950), 122, NCAA Headquarters.

13. Hesburgh to Arries, 27 January 1950, President Hesburgh Papers, UVHS, Box 3, Folder "TV September 1949 #2," University of Notre Dame Archives.

14. Kobak to Hesburgh, 24 January 1950, President Hesburgh Papers, UVHS, Box 3, Folder "TV-September 1949," University of Notre Dame Archives; and Robert E. Kintner, President, ABC, to Harold E. Stassen, President, Penn, 23 August 1950, Papers of the Office of the President, 1950–55, Box 54, Folder "Intercollegiate Athletics TV 1," University of Pennsylvania Archives.

15. Hesburgh to Kobak, 27 January 1950, President Hesburgh Papers, UVHS, Box 3, Folder "TV-September 1949 #2," University of Notre Dame Archives.

16. Joseph McConnell, President, NBC, to Hesburgh, 27 March 1950, Dan D. Halpin, Manager, RCA, to Hesburgh, 31 March 1950, and Hesburgh, telegram to Dan Halpin, 10 April 1950, President Hesburgh Papers, UVHS, Box 3, Folder "TV-September 1949 #2," University of Notre Dame Archives. Hesburgh thanked Halpin and NBC for making a supplementary bid.

17. Thomas Velotta, ABC, to Hesburgh, 5 April 1950, and Robert Kintner, ABC, to John Cavanaugh, President, Notre Dame, 11 April 1950, ibid.

18. Hesburgh to Arries, 8 April 1950, ibid.

19. K. L. Wilson to Hesburgh, 31 March 1950, ibid.
20. "Television Policy of the Big 10 Conference, 18 April 1950," Director of Athletics Papers, 9/3–1/20, Folder "Television, 1947–50," Ohio State University Archives.
21. *The New Haven Journal-Courier,* 12 September 1950, in President Miller Papers, Box 17, Folder "Athletics-Intercollegiate Conference," Northwestern University Archives; newspaper clipping, ca. August 1950, President Hesburgh Papers, UVHS, Box 3, Folder "TV-September 1949, #3," University of Notre Dame Archives; and *Advertising Age,* 4 September 1950, 12.
22. Cavanaugh to President G. L. Cross, University of Oklahoma, 2 February 1951, President Cavanaugh Papers, UPCC, Box 6, Folder 7, University of Notre Dame Archives. Included among the original recipients of the letter were the presidents of Indiana, Iowa State, Michigan State, Navy, North Carolina, Oklahoma, Pennsylvania, Pittsburgh, Southern Methodist, Texas, UCLA, Southern California, West Point, and Yale. Minnesota and possibly other big-time institutions received similar letters a few days later. See Cavanaugh Papers, Box 6, Folder 22, University of Notre Dame Archives.
23. Texas Tech appears to have been the first major football team to travel by plane when it visited Detroit University in 1937. *National Association of Collegiate Directors of Athletics, 1893–1993: The Centennial Celebration of Our Profession* (Cleveland, Ohio: NACDA, 1983), 80.
24. See letters in Vice President Hesburgh Papers, UVHS, Box 3, Folder "Athletics-Fr. Cavanaugh's Inquiry," University of Notre Dame Archives.
25. Ibid.
26. G. A. Farabaugh to Hesburgh, 27 April 1951, Vice President Hesburgh Papers, UPHS, Box 94, University of Notre Dame Archives.
27. Farabaugh, Chapleau & Roper, South Bend law firm, "Memorandum Brief," to Vice President Hesburgh, 28 April 1951, ibid. Emphasis is mine. A New York law firm agreed with the South Bend lawyers that the NCAA's experimental TV plan was unconstitutional, in violation of both the Sherman Antitrust Act (1890) and the Clayton Act (1914). See Gale, Bernays, Falk and Eisner, New York City, to G. A. Farabaugh, South Bend, Indiana, 1 May 1951, ibid.
28. President Cavanaugh said that he did not believe in "blindly acquiescing . . . under threat of boycott." "Statement of John J. Cavanaugh, President of Notre Dame," President Cross Papers, Box 77, Folder "Football, Television, 1950," University of Oklahoma Archives.

11 Penn Challenges the NCAA and the Ivy League

1. *Springfield* [Massachusetts] *Republican,* 29 December 1905, 3.
2. Quoted in Arthur S. Link, ed., *The Papers of Woodrow Wilson* (Princeton: Princeton University Press, 1973), 16:370.
3. NCAA *Proceedings* (1947), 188–96, NCAA Headquarters, Indianapolis, Ind. The new Sanity Code was destined to last only two years before it was voted out by the NCAA as unworkable, but the Home Rule tradition had been broken. New national collective eligibility rules would soon return to the NCAA.
4. Ibid. (1950), 203.
5. Ibid., 117.
6. Ibid. (1951), 207. There was irony in the movement for collective NCAA action in television, for the legislation that the NCAA voted on after national TV controls was to do away with the Sanity Code, returning once again to Home Rule.
7. *New York Herald Tribune,* 8 August 1950.
8. *Philadelphia Inquirer,* 2 September 1950, clipping in UPF8.5 News Bureau—Sub-

ject Files, Box 33, Folder 5, University of Pennsylvania Archives; and Robert E. Kintner, President, ABC, telegram to President Harold E. Stassen, 23 August 1950, Stassen to Kintner, 28 August 1950, and James H. Carmine, Philco Vice-President, telegram to Stassen, 24 August 1950, Papers of the Office of the President, 1950–55, Box 54, Folder "Intercollegiate Athletics, TV 1," University of Pennsylvania Archives.

9. George L. Cross, *Presidents Can't Punt* (Norman: University of Oklahoma Press, 1977), 154.

10. *New York Herald Tribune,* 8 August 1950.

11. Herbert A. Knight, Oak Park, Ill., to the President of the Pennsylvania Board of Trustees, 19 January 1951, Papers of the Office of the President, 1950–55, Box 53, Folder "Intercollegiate Athletics-Ivy 1," University of Pennsylvania Archives.

12. President Harold Stassen, University of Pennsylvania, to President Harold Dodds, Princeton, 22 January 1951, ibid.

13. Les Arries, Du Mont Laboratories, memorandum to Father Hesburgh, Vice President, Notre Dame, 18 January 1951, President Hesburgh Papers, UVHS, Box 3, Folder "TV, January 1951," University of Notre Dame Archives.

14. Hesburgh to Arries, 22 January 1951, President Hesburgh Papers, UVHS, Box 3, Folder "TV, January 1951," University of Notre Dame Archives; and Francis T. Murray, to Kurt Peiser, University of Pennsylvania Development Office, 1 February 1951, Papers of the Office of the President, Box 53, Folder "Intercollegiate Athletics, TV-2," University of Pennsylvania Archives. The Du Mont offer of $38,375 per game was later withdrawn, and a contract with ABC was signed on June 6, 1951, for $260,000. Penn would be paid $30,000 for each of six games and $40,000 each for the Army and Navy games. See contract and Stassen to William DuBarry, Francis Murray, and Kurt Peiser, 29 May 1951, in Papers of the Office of the President, 1950–55, Box 54, Folder "Intercollegiate Athletics, TV-3," University of Pennsylvania Archives.

15. Hesburgh, memorandum to President John Cavanaugh, Notre Dame, 10 May 1951, President Hesburgh Papers, UVHS, Box 3, Folder "Athletics: NCAA TV," University of Notre Dame Archives.

16. Murray, to Peiser, 1 February 1951, and Mortimer W. Loewi, Director, Allen B. Du Mont Laboratories, to Murray, 7 March 1951, Papers of the Office of the President, 1950–55, Box 53, Folder "Intercollegiate Athletics, TV 2," University of Pennsylvania Archives.

17. Eastern College Athletic Conference minutes, 24 January 1951, ECAC Archives, Centrevillo, Mass.

18. Ibid., 13 March 1951.

19. Ibid.

20. Ibid., 7 June 1951.

21. Stassen, draft of a letter to Hugh Willett, President, NCAA, 18 March 1951, Papers of the Office of the President, 1950–55, Box 53, Folder "Intercollegiate Athletics, TV-3," University of Pennsylvania Archives.

22. Willett, telegram to Stassen, 6 June 1951, Papers of the Office of the President, Box 54, Folder "Intercollegiate Athletics, TV-4," University of Pennsylvania Archives.

23. University of Pennsylvania Board of Trustees minutes, 5 April, 25 May, 26 June, and 22 October 1951, University of Pennsylvania Archives.

24. *New York Times,* 15 June 1951.

25. President Harold Dodds, Princeton, to President Stassen, 12 June 1951, President John Dickey, Dartmouth, to Stassen, 21 June 1951, and Brutas Hamilton, California Athletic Director, telegram to Murray, 19 June 1951, Papers of the Office of the President, Box 54, Folder "Intercollegiate Athletics, TV-7," University of Pennsylvania

Archives; Robert B. Meigs, Secretary, Board of Trustees, Cornell, to Murray, 11 June 1951, Box 53, Folder "Intercollegiate Athletics," University of Pennsylvania Archives; and *Time,* 18 June 1951, 69.

26. President John J. Cavanaugh, Notre Dame, to Edgar Kobak, New York City, 7 March 1951, President Cavanaugh Papers, UPCC, Box 10, Folder 6, University of Notre Dame Archives; and Fred L. Steers, Chicago, to Theodore Hesburgh, 15 June 1951, President Hesburgh Papers, UVHS, Box 3, Folder "TV, January 1951," University of Notre Dame Archives.

27. University of Pennsylvania Board of Trustees minutes, 22 October 1951. The withdrawal of the policy came at the end of June, 1951.

28. Robert T. McC—, Chair, Board of Trustees, to Rev. Elwood F. Reeves, Duncannon, Penn., 12 June 1951, Papers of the Office of the President, Box 54, Folder "Intercollegiate Athletics, TV-5," University of Pennsylvania Archives.

29. John A. Brown, Philadelphia, to Stassen, 22 June 1951, ibid., Folder "Intercollegiate Athletics, TV-9," University of Pennsylvania Archives.

30. Sanford Winters, Wolcott, Conn., to President Harold Stassen, University of Pennsylvania, 15 June 1951, ibid., Folder "Intercollegiate Athletics, TV-6," University of Pennsylvania Archives.

31. University of Pennsylvania, draft of telegram to Hugh C. Willett, President, NCAA, 14 June 1951, ibid., Folder "Intercollegiate Athletics, TV-5."

32. Morison to Murray, 26 June 1951, and Morison to Joseph L. Rauh, Jr., NCAA Counsel, Washington, D.C., 20 June 1951, President Hesburgh Papers, UVHS, Box 3, Folder "Athletics: NCAA TV," University of Notre Dame Archives.

33. "Sports and TV: What Next?" *Business Week,* 16 June 1951, 24.

34. Stassen, memorandum to Murray 2 July 1951, Papers of the Office of the President, Box 54, Folder "Intercollegiate Athletics, TV-5" University of Pennsylvania Archives; Murray to Willett, 11 July 1951, Murray, telegram to Willett, 13 July 1951, and Murray to Ralph Furey, NCAA TV Committee, 19 July 1951, Box 54, Folder "Intercollegiate Athletics, TV-10," University of Pennsylvania Archives; and "Draft of Television Plan," Murray to Hesburgh, 3 July 1951, President Hesburgh Papers, UVHS, Box 3, Folder "Athletics: NCAA TV," University of Notre Dame Archives.

35. Hesburgh to William Hunter, USC Athletic Director, 10 August 1951, President Hesburgh Papers, UVHS, Box 3, Folder "TV, January 1951"; President John J. Cavanaugh to Galvin Hudson, Memphis, Tennessee, 14 September 1951, President Cavanaugh Papers, UPCC, Box 10, Folder 6, University of Notre Dame Archives; and *New York Times,* 29 April 1951.

36. Robert E. Kintner, President, ABC, to Francis T. Murray, University of Pennsylvania Athletic Director, 31 August 1951, and Kintner to President Harold E. Stassen, University of Pennsylvania, 19 September 1951, Papers of the Office of the President, Box 54, Folder "Intercollegiate Athletics, TV-11," University of Pennsylvania Archives.

37. Francis T. Murray, "Address to ECAC Membership, 12-14-51," Eastern College Athletic Conference minutes, ECAC Headquarters, Centreville, Mass.

38. Murray to Stassen, 21 December 1951, Papers of the Office of the President, 1950–55, Box 54, Folder "Ivy Group Presidents," University of Pennsylvania Archives.

39. Murray to Asa S. Bushnell, ECAC Executive Director, 12 November 1951, Papers of the Office of the President, Box 54, Folder "Intercollegiate Athletics, TV-12," University of Pennsylvania Archives; Murray to Stassen, 21 December 1951, Papers of the Office of the President, Box 54, Folder "Ivy Group Presidents," University of Pennsylvania Archives; and Murray, "Address to ECAC Membership 12-14-51," in Eastern College Athletic Conference minutes, ECAC Headquarters.

12 The NCAA Experimental Year

1. For instance, President Frederick L. Hovde of Purdue noted his interest in educational TV in a letter to President John C. Cavanaugh of Notre Dame about Cavanaugh's Super Conference idea and control of TV. Yet, Hovde never suggested football could contribute to the growth of educational TV. This is just one more example of educators not thinking of athletics as educational. See Hovde to Cavanaugh, 10 March 1951, President Hesburgh Papers, UVHS, Box 3, Folder "Athletics-Father Cavanaugh's Inquiry," University of Notre Dame Archives. Iowa State station WOI-TV became the first regularly licensed TV station owned and operated by an educational institution when it began telecasting in February 1950. By 1952 it was carrying telecasts of NCAA football. See Ned Disque, "Nation's First Educational TV Station," *Nation's Schools* (November 1952): 92. The first meeting of a group of educators to discuss the use of educational TV occurred on 16 October 1950. A month later, educators appeared before the Federal Communications Commission on behalf of educational TV. On 14 April 1952, the FCC gave its famous "Sixth Report and Order," in which 242 channels were reserved for noncommercial use. See *Television in Education* (Report of Educational Television Programs Institute—April 1952), President Holt Papers, Folder "Television 1951-July 1955," University of Tennessee Archives.

   FCC began an effort for educational TV in 1950 by forming a Joint Committee on Educational Television. In 1952, the Ford Foundation made a grant to establish a program for education, which became known as National Educational Television. Telecasting college football was never part of the scheme. See Erik Barnouw, *Tube of Plenty* (New York: Oxford University Press, 1975), 140, 202. The same year, 1952, Paul Walker, Chairman of the FCC, urged the Association of Land Grant Colleges to organize a forty-eight-state Educational Television Network on coaxial cable. He believed the colleges should preserve the 242 education channels set aside for them by the FCC. Here was a chance for universities to use educational TV and, if they wished, to have a network for telecasting college football as part of educational television. College presidents lost an opportunity to bring college football under greater educational control. See *New York Times*, 14 November 1952, L29. The FCC defined educational television as any program put on by an educational institution. See Allen B. Du Mont, Speech at Penn State College, 21 April 1952, Du Mont Laboratories, Box 71, Folder "TV Education, 1952," Manuscripts Division, Library of Congress.

2. *NCAA Proceedings* (1952), 154, NCAA Headquarters, Indianapolis, Ind.

3. Ronald A. Smith, "Television, Antitrust Laws, and the Conflict between Home Rule and a National NCAA Policy, 1939–1994," Report to the NCAA, 1994, 79–80; "NCAA Television Committee Report to the Forty-Sixth Annual Convention," 10–12 January 1952, Du Mont Laboratories, Box 19, Folder "NCAA, 1952," Manuscript Division, Library of Congress; William Boddy, *Fifties Television: The Industry and Its Critics* (Urbana: University of Illinois Press, 1990), 49; and *New York Times*, 26 July 1951, C29.

4. "NCAA Television Plan for 1951," ca. July 1951, Papers of the Office of the President, Box 54, Folder "Intercollegiate Athletics, TV-10," University of Pennsylvania Archives; Thomas J. Hamilton, Chair, NCAA Television Committee, to NCAA member institutions, 17 May 1951, President Brehm Papers, Box 2, Folder "Television & Athletics," University of Tennessee Archives; "The Effects of Television on College Football Attendance, Report No. 3," 22 April 1952, Series 5/21/7, Box 1, University of Wisconsin Archives; and "TV . . . Caught in Its Own Network," *Senior Scholastic* 59 (10 October 1951): 14. See "TV Disrupts Sports Business," *Business Week*, 27 January 1951, 49–52.

5. "Statement by John J. Cavanaugh, President of Notre Dame," 15 June 1951, President Cross Papers, Box 77, Folder "Football, Television 1950," University of Oklahoma Archives; and Theodore Hesburgh, Vice President, Notre Dame, to Edward Krause, Notre Dame Athletic Director, 5 July 1951, President Cavanaugh Papers, UPCC, Box 6, Folder 22, University of Notre Dame Archives.

6. Krause to Tug Wilson, NCAA Television Committee, 20 November 1951, President Cavanaugh Papers, UPCC, Box 6, Folder 23, University of Notre Dame Archives. Krause's letter had been composed by Vice President Theodore Hesburgh a couple weeks earlier. See President Hesburgh Papers, UVHS, Box 3, Folder "Athletics: NCAA," University of Notre Dame Archives.

7. Miskovsky to Oscar White, President, Oklahoma Board of Regents, 26 August 1952, President Cross Papers, Box 100, Folder "Football General," University of Oklahoma Archives.

8. George Lynn Cross, *Presidents Can't Punt* (Norman: University of Oklahoma Press, 1977), 154–58; and Walter Kraft, President, NCAA, to President G. L. Cross, Oklahoma, President Cross Papers, Box 77, Folder "Football, Television, 1950," University of Oklahoma Archives.

9. President G. L. Cross, Oklahoma, to Kenneth Ferris, Athletic Business Manager, 9 August 1951, President Cross Papers, Box 88, Folder "Football 1951," University of Oklahoma Archives.

10. Warren O. Thompson, Chair, Colorado Faculty Committee on Athletics, to President Robert L. Stearns, Colorado, 6 March 1951, President's Office, Series 1, Box 29, Folder "Athletics, 1927–53," Archives, University of Colorado at Boulder Libraries; and "Legislative Resolution 3," Legislature of Nebraska, 26 February 1951, President Cross Papers, Box 77, Folder "Football, Television, 1950," University of Oklahoma Archives.

11. *Variety,* 31 January 1951, 23.

12. Robert McAuliffe to Theodore Hesburgh, 7 November 1951, President Hesburgh Papers, UVHS, Box 3, Folder "TV-January 1951," University of Notre Dame Archives.

13. Hesburgh to Robert McAuliffe, 12 November 1951, President Hesburgh Papers, UVHS, Box 3, Folder "TV-January 1951," University of Notre Dame Archives.

14. *Chicago Tribune,* 9 November 1951, 4:1. The previous week, NBC in Chicago had experienced transmission difficulties with two games, Michigan-Illinois and Army–South Carolina.

15. Eastern College Athletic Conference minutes, 14 December 1951, ECAC Headquarters, Centreville, Mass.

16. *Chicago Tribune,* 10 November 1951, 3:1.

17. The NCAA hired an experienced Washington, D.C., lawyer in the communications business, Joseph Rauh, as special counsel on the question of antitrust violations. Rauh was a former law clerk for Justice Felix Frankfurter, as well as an assistant general counsel at the Federal Communications Commission and a prominent advisor to the Democrat Party.

18. Eastern College Athletic Conference minutes, 14 December 1951, ECAC Headquarters.

19. "Football Blackout," *Time,* 3 December 1951, 101.

20. Robert W. Peterson, *Pigskin: The Early Years of Pro Football* (New York: Oxford University Press, 1997), 198; and Walter Byers, NCAA Executive Secretary, memorandum to NCAA Council, Executive Committee and Television Committee, 23 October 1951, President Hesburgh Papers, UVHS, Box 3, Folder "Athletics: NCAA TV," University of Notre Dame Archives.

21. Allen B. Du Mont, of Du Mont Laboratories and the Du Mont Television Network, noted that there were about 4 million sets in 1949; by 1951 that number had grown

to more than 16 million, and 23,000 miles of coaxial cable tied networks together. Allen B. Du Mont, Speech at Penn State College, 21 April 1952, Du Mont Laboratories, Box 71, Folder "TV Education, 1952," Manuscript Division, Library of Congress.

22. "NCAA Television Questionnaire," 8 December 1951, President E. B. Fred Correspondence Files, 1951–52, Series 4/15/1, Box 162, Folder "Athletics," University of Wisconsin Archives.

23. "NCAA Experimental Television Program: Preliminary Financial Report," 11 January 1952, Series 5/21/7, Box 1, University of Wisconsin Archives.

24. NCAA *Proceedings* (1952), 161, NCAA Headquarters.

25. *Chicago Tribune,* 9 November 1951, 4:1.

13   Networks

1. Allen B. Du Mont to Ralph Bather, Hollis, N.Y., 26 March 1937, Du Mont Laboratories, Box 14, Folder "Allen B. Du Mont, 1936–37," and Du Mont to *Radio Daily,* 30 November 1938, Du Mont Laboratories, Box 14, Folder "Du Mont, Allen B., 1938," Manuscripts Division, Library of Congress; Gary N. Hess, *An Historical Study of the Du Mont Television Network* (New York: Arno Press, 1979), 43–49; and *Facts on File* (New York: Facts on File, 1940), 127.

2. Hess, *Du Mont Television Network,* 49.

3. *New York Times,* 5 December 1946, 33.

4. Hess, *Du Mont Television Network,* 54.

5. John J. Burke, interoffice memorandum, to Vice President John Murphy, Notre Dame, Vice President John Murphy Papers, UVMR, Box 4, Folder "TV," University of Notre Dame Archives.

6. "Leslie Arries's Du Mont Television Network Bid for Five 1949 Notre Dame Games," undated, ibid.; M. W. Loewi, memorandum to A. B. Du Mont, 11 July 1949, Du Mont Laboratories, Box 32, Folder "Loewi, Mortimer, 1946–52," Manuscript Division, Library of Congress; and Edward J. McCrossin, memorandum to C. J. Witting, 14 November 1949, and N. L. Halpern, TV consultant, New York City, to Leslie Arries, Du Mont Director of Sports, 17 November 1949, Du Mont Laboratories, Box 36, Folder "Witting, Christian, 1949–50," Manuscript Division, Library of Congress.

7. David Harris, *The League: The Rise and Decline of the NFL* (New York: Bantam Books, 1986), 13.

8. Edgar Kobak, New York City, to Vice President Theodore N. Hesburgh, Notre Dame, 24 January 1950, Hesburgh Papers, UVHS, Box 3, Folder "TV-September 1949," University of Notre Dame Archives. The World Series TV rights in 1950 were worth $800,000.

9. Hess, *Du Mont Television Network,* 200.

10. Hesburgh to Leslie Arries, Du Mont Television Network, 27 January 1950, Hesburgh Papers, UVHS, Box 3, Folder "TV, September 1949 #2," University of Notre Dame Archives.

11. Mortimer W. Loewi, memorandum to Allen B. Du Mont, 19 February 1951, quoted in Hess, *Du Mont Television Network,* 201.

12. Broadcasting Magazine, *The First 50 Years of Broadcasting* (Washington, D.C.: Broadcasting Publications, 1982), 91, 102; and Lewis J. Paper, *Empire: William S. Paley and the Making of CBS* (New York: St. Martin's Press, 1987), 177.

13. Hesburgh to Leslie G. Arries, Du Mont, 22 January 1951, President Hesburgh Papers, UVHS, Box 3, Folder "TV, January 1951," University of Notre Dame Archives.

14. NCAA Television Committee, "Report to the Forty-Sixth Annual Convention of the National Collegiate Athletic Association," 10–12 January 1952, Du Mont Laboratories, Box 19, Folder "NCAA, 1952," Manuscript Division, Library of Congress.

15. Quoted by Keeton Arnett, memorandum to Chris J. Whitting and Dan Halpin, Du Mont, 3 November 1952; and Arnett to Allen B. Du Mont, 11 November 1952, ibid.

16. Allen B. Du Mont, "The Public's Stake in the NCAA's Plan for Television Football," 17 November 1952, Du Mont Laboratories, Box 28, Folder "Arnett, Keaton, 1951–53," Manuscript Division, Library of Congress.

17. William A. Roberts, Washington, D.C., to Allen B. Du Mont, ca. 23 December 1952, Du Mont Laboratories, Box 19, Folder "NCAA, 1953," Manuscript Division, Library of Congress.

18. *Business Week,* 26 September 1953, 52, 54; "Touchdowns, TV, and the Law," *Business Week,* 21 November 1953, 32; and Press Release, 28 October 1953, Du Mont Laboratories, Box 11, Folder "B 1953," Manuscript Division, Library of Congress.

19. *United States v National Football League,* 116 F. Supp. 319 (1953). Judge Alan K. Grim's decision, however, did not restrict telecasting of outside games in home territories when the home team was playing away, it did not restrict radio of outside games in home territories, and it did not give the NFL commissioner power to prevent all television and radio broadcasts.

20. Gerald Lyons, memorandum to Chris Witting, Tom McMahon, and Keeton Arnett, Du Mont Laboratories, 23 May 1953, Du Mont Laboratories, Box 28, Folder "Arnett, Keeton, 1951–53," Manuscript Division, Library of Congress.

21. Notre Dame Press Release, 3 January 1953, President Hesburgh Papers, UPHS, Box 94, University of Notre Dame Archives.

22. Harvard Athletic Committee minutes, 1 December 1952, Harvard University Archives. Conant's message to the Athletic Committee was somewhat more harsh. He told the Harvard athletic officials to tell the NCAA that "Harvard does not intend to be bound by the policy or to associate itself with it." The Athletic Committee believed that Conant's point "could be stated more tactfully." Harvard Athletic Committee minutes, 3 November 1952.

23. Gerald Lyons, memorandum to Chris Witting, Tom McMahon, and Keeton Arnett, 23 May 1953, Du Mont Laboratories, Box 28, Folder "Arnett, Keeton, 1951–53, Manuscript Division, Library of Congress.

24. FCC Network Study Staff, "Prospects for a Fourth Network in Television," *Journal of Broadcasting* 2 (winter 1957–58): 11; Sterling Quinlan, *Inside ABC: American Broadcasting Company's Rise to Power* (New York: Hastings House, 1979), 46–47; and Hess, *Du Mont Television Network,* 113. It is quite likely that the FCC would not have allowed the merger, for ABC was merged with United Paramount Theatres and Paramount Pictures had a significant holding of Du Mont stock. (Because of antitrust violations, in 1950 Paramount Pictures had been broken up United Paramount Theatres and Paramount Pictures.)

14 Regional Conferences Challenge a National Policy

1. "Report of the NCAA 1955 Television Committee to the Fiftieth Annual Convention of the NCAA," 10–11 January 1956, Records of the Office of the President, 1949–1966, Box 16, Folder "NCAA Television Plan, 1954–55," Georgia Tech Archives. The National Opinion Research Center (NORC) reported after the 1951 experimental season that there was little difference in gate attendance between regional and national games, though it was expected that there would be a greater negative effect on regional games. The college leaders apparently knew differently. See NORC Report no. 3, "The Effects of Television on College Football Attendance," 22 April 1952, President Brehm Papers, Box 2, Folder "Television & Athletics," University of Tennessee Archives.

2. Edward W. Krause, Notre Dame Athletic Director, to President John J. Cavanaugh,

Notre Dame, 4 June 1952, President Theodore Hesburgh Papers, Box 3, Folder "Athletics: NCAA TV," University of Notre Dame Archives; and Jack Falla, *NCAA: The Voice of College Sports* (Mission, Kans.: NCAA, 1981), 106–7.

3. Lindsey Nelson, *Hello Everybody, I'm Lindsey Nelson* (New York: William Morrow, 1985), 176.

4. Thomas J. Hamilton to the NCAA membership, 21 May 1951, President Brehm Papers, Box 2, Folder "Television & Athletics," University of Tennessee Archives.

5. NCAA Television Committee, "Report to the Forty-Sixth Annual Convention of the National Collegiate Athletic Association," 10–12 January 1952, Du Mont Laboratories, Box 19, Folder "NCAA, 1952," Manuscript Division, Library of Congress.

6. One could note the hypocrisy involved with an institution such as Yale over division of receipts. In 1936, when Yale was a significant football power and received a $20,000 contract for its radio rights, there was apparently no discussion of dividing the receipts with other Ivy institutions. By 1951, after Yale had deteriorated as a big-time power, Yale's athletic director, Robert Hall, proposed that colleges unite to divide TV revenues. Hall stated: "It's high time that our colleges adopted a point of view that is unselfish and do what is best for the common good." *New York Times,* 29 April 1951, in Papers of the Office of the President, 1950–55, Box 54, Folder "Intercollegiate Athletics, TV-3, University of Pennsylvania Archives. The Robin Hood" proposals in the 1950s were raised to a high pitch in the mid-1970s, leading opponents to create the College Football Association, a group of big-time football schools that spearheaded breaking up the NCAA TV monopoly in the early 1980s and threatened the existence of the NCAA.

7. Based on football attendance in 1950, the Southeast Conference, with 1,765,000, was second, behind the Big 10, with 2,223,000, and just ahead of the Pacific Coast Conference, with 1,557,000. See "Attendance Figures in Major Conferences for 1950," Papers of the Office of the President, 1950–55, Box 53, Folder "Intercollegiate Athletics, TV-2," University of Pennsylvania Archives.

8. "Television Policy of the Big 10 Conference, 18 April 1950," Director of Athletics Papers, 9/3–1/20, Folder "Television, 1947–50," Ohio State University Archives. While banning TV, the Big 10 allowed a major theatrical chain to show big games in Detroit and Chicago, with a broadcast delay of thirty seconds. The Big 10 did so, almost certainly, to counter Notre Dame, who was telecasting into these two close metropolitan areas. It was evidently part of the Big 10 strategy to isolate Notre Dame, as Michigan and Northwestern, among others, refused to schedule games with Notre Dame. See newspaper clipping, ca. August 1950, President Theodore Hesburgh Papers, Box 3, Folder "TV Sept. 1949, # 3," University of Notre Dame Archives.

9. Asa S. Bushnell, NCAA Television Committee Chair, to Albert B. Moore, NCAA President, 20 April 1953, President Brehm Papers, Box 2, Folder "Television & Athletics," University of Tennessee Archives.

10. NCAA *Proceedings* (1954), 207, NCAA Headquarters, Indianapolis, Ind.

11. Ibid., 235.

12. Ibid., 219.

13. "The Effects of Television on College Football Attendance," Report no. 5, prepared for the NCAA by the National Opinion Research Center, 22 April 1954, Records of the Office of the President, 1949–1966, Box 16, Folder "NCAA TV Plan, 1954–55," Georgia Tech Archives.

14. Big 10 memorandum, 29 March 1954, Board in Control of Intercollegiate Athletics, Box 35, Folder "Walter Byers 1952–54," Michigan Historical Collections, Bentley Historical Library.

15. "Membership Voting Record on NCAA Football Television Plan," ca. 1975, Walter Byers Papers, vol. 151, Folder "TV: Football, 1975," NCAA Headquarters.

16. NCAA *Proceedings* (1955), 201, NCAA Headquarters. Fritz Crisler of Michigan gave a short history of the Big 10's move toward regionalism.

17. "The Effects of Television on College Football Attendance," Report No. 5, NCAA, 22 April 1954, President Brehm Papers, Box 2, Folder "Television & Athletics," University of Tennessee Archives.

18. "Report of the Liaison Officer of the 1953 NCAA Television Committee," ca. January 1954, Box "Television," NCAA Headquarters.

19. Robert J. Kane, Cornell Athletic Director, to Dean A. B. Moore, University of Alabama and President of the NCAA, 12 April 1954, Unprocessed Athletic Department Papers, Folder "Committee on Federal Admissions Tax—NCAA," University of Alabama Archives.

20. See chapter 5 for discussion of Yale's radio contract.

21. NCAA *Proceedings* (1955), 200–201, NCAA Headquarters.

22. E. L. Romney, NCAA Television Committee Chair, to C. P. Houston, NCAA President, 9 March 1955, President Brehm Papers, Box 2, Folder "Television & Athletics," University of Tennessee Archives.

23. *New York Times,* 3 March 1955, 33. See also "Football: Calling a 'Bluff,'" *Newsweek,* 17 January 1955, 79.

24. Bernie Moore, Southeastern Conference Commissioner, to O. C. Aderheld, President, Southeastern Conference, 16 February 1955, President Brehm Papers, Box 2, Folder "Television," University of Tennessee Archives.

25. N. W. Dougherty, University of Tennessee Faculty Representative, to Clarence P. Houston, Tufts College, 3 February 1955, N. W. Dougherty Collection, Box 20, Folder 7, University of Tennessee Archives.

26. N. W. Dougherty, University of Tennessee faculty representative, to President C. E. Brehm, University of Tennessee, 15 March 1955, President Brehm Papers, Box 2, Folder "Television & Athletics," University of Tennessee Archives.

27. "A Joint Meeting of the Southern, Southeastern and Southwest Conferences, May 28, 1949," memorandum, Records of the Office of the President, 1949–1966, Box 16, Folder "NCAA Regional Conference, May 28, 1949," Georgia Tech Archives; and Athletic Advisory Committee minutes, 18 January 1949, President Rufus C. Harris Papers, Box 1, Folder "Athletic Advisory Committee," Tulane University Archives.

28. Moore to Byers, 22 May 1955, Unprocessed Athletic Department Papers, Folder "Walter Byers Correspondence, 1954," University of Alabama Archives.

29. *New York Times,* 4 December 1955, 5:2. Notre Dame athletic director Moose Krause predicted that unrestricted football telecasts would exist within a year or two once the 1955 regional compromise had been achieved. See *New York Times,* 16 March 1955, 48.

15 TV and the Threat of Professional Football

1. For example, college football admissions brought in ten times as much as professional football in 1948. See Jerry N. Jordan, "The Long Range Effect of Television and Other Factors on Sports Attendance," 7 June 1950, President Brehm Papers, Box 2, Folder "Television & Athletics," University of Tennessee Archives.

2. NCAA *Proceedings* (1954), 203, NCAA Headquarters, Indianapolis, Ind.; and Benjamin G. Rader, *In Its Own Image: How Television Has Transformed Sports* (New York: Free Press, 1984), 45, 52.

3. David S. Neft et al., *The Sports Encyclopedia: Pro Football* (New York: Grosset & Dunlap, 1974), 17–31, 105.

4. Ibid., 156.

5. Don Giesy, memorandum to A. B. Du Mont, Du Mont Laboratories, Box 132, Folder

"Photography," Manuscript Division, Library of Congress; Box 11, Folder B, Manuscript Division, Library of Congress; and Neft, *The Sports Encyclopedia: Pro Football,* 116.

6. Sterling Quinlan, *Inside ABC: American Broadcasting Company's Rise to Power* (New York: Hastings House, 1979), 54–58, and William S. Paley, *As It Happened: A Memoir* (Garden City, N.Y.: Doubleday, 1979), 274. ABC, the network associated with NCAA football from the 1960s on, first purchased the rights in 1954, after NBC had owned them for two years. Once General Motors, which had advertised with NBC, decided not to advertise with ABC, other advertisers stayed away and ABC lost $1.8 million after having paid $2.5 million for the rights. Quinlan called ABC's acquisition "a program triumph and a financial disaster." NBC then obtained the rights for the next five years.

7. Quoted in William O. Johnson, Jr., *Super Spectators and the Electric Lilliputians* (Boston: Little, Brown, 1971), 118–19.

8. *New York Times,* 28 December 1921, 13, and NCAA *Proceedings* (1921), 62, NCAA Headquarters. Charles D. Daly of West Point (and a Harvard graduate) was elected president; John Heisman of the University of Pennsylvania became vice president; J. W. Wilce of Ohio State became secretary-treasurer; and Fielding H. Yost of Michigan and Robert Fisher of Harvard were named trustees of the AFCA.

9. *New York Times,* 25 November 1925, 18.

10. Ibid., 20 November 1925, 25. Grange was accused of signing a pro contract before his last game against Ohio State. He denied this, saying: "I have not received a penny. I have not signed a contract."

11. Robert W. Peterson, *Pigskin: The Early Years of Pro Football* (New York: Oxford University Press, 1997), 88.

12. "From a Graduate Window," *Harvard Graduates' Magazine* 34 (March 1926): 403.

13. NCAA *Proceedings* (1954), 212, NCAA Headquarters.

14. Theodore Hesburgh to Frank Reichstein, *Beloit Daily News,* Wisconsin, 8 January 1953, President Hesburgh Files, UPHS, Box 94, University of Notre Dame Archives.

15. NCAA *Proceedings* (1955), 202, NCAA Headquarters; and "Proceedings of NCAA-Sponsored 'Conference of Conferences,'" 13–14 June 1954, Unprocessed Athletic Department Papers, Folder "Conference of Conferences," University of Alabama Archives. The five NFL teams in the area were the Chicago Bears, the Chicago Cardinals, the Cleveland Browns, the Detroit Lions, and the Green Bay Packers.

16. Peterson, *Pigskin,* 202–3, and Jim Spence, *Up Close and Personal: The Inside Story of Network Television Sports* (New York: Atheneum, 1988), 63–64.

17. *New York Times,* 14 November 1959, 15.

18. *United States v. National Football League,* 196 F. Supp. 445 (E.D. Pa. 1961).

19. Lionel S. Sobel, *Professional Sports and the Law* (New York: Law-Arts Publishers, 1977), 583–88, and David Harris, *The League: The Rise and Decline of the NFL* (New York: Bantam Books, 1986), 14–16.

20. Eastern College Athletic Conference Executive Council minutes, 7 December 1961, ECAC Headquarters, Centreville, Mass.

21. In 1966, when the NFL and AFL merged, the Sports Broadcasting Act of 1961 was extended to include the protection of high schools from professional football telecasting. Sobel, *Professional Sports and the Law,* 588.

22. As the 1961 act was written, the proposed broadcasts would technically not be in violation of the law since individual clubs, rather than the league, would sell their rights to the games. See Law Offices of Swanson, Midgley, Jones, Blackmar, & Edgar to Walter Byers, NCAA Executive Director, 7 May 1964, Unorganized Walter Byers Papers, Folder "T.V.," NCAA Headquarters. The NCAA had been concerned almost a decade before, when the NFL was telecasting on Saturday nights. A member of the

NCAA Television Committee at the 1954 annual convention condemned the NFL for "moving in on a day which we think belongs to college football." NCAA *Proceedings* (1954), 235, NCAA Headquarters.

23. Walter Byers to Emanuel Celler, 24 February 1964, Unorganized Walter Byers Papers, Folder "T.V.," NCAA Headquarters.

24. The athletic director of the University of California, Santa Barbara, said that if the big-time schools begin telecasting on Friday nights, "they will kill us." *New York Times,* 11 January 1956, 38; and Clifford B. Fagan, National Federation of State High School Athletic Associations Executive Secretary, to Walter Byers, NCAA Executive Director, 30 November 1966, Unorganized Walter Byers Papers, Folder "T.V.," NCAA Headquarters.

25. "Background Information on Football TV Legislation," memorandum, ca. 3 March 1964, Rep. Emanuel Celler to Everett D. Barnes, Colgate University, 17 March 1964, and Walter Byers, telegram to fifteen senators, 14 February 1964, Box "TV: Legislation, 1965–1968," Folder "Television: Legislation 1964," Walter Byers Papers, NCAA Headquarters; and *Congressional Record,* 3 March 1964, 3988–89.

26. NCAA Television Committee minutes, 9–10 June 1964, NCAA Headquarters.

27. Kenneth E. Midgley, attorney, Kansas City, to Charles M. Neinas, NCAA Headquarters, 4 May 1964, and Walter Byers, NCAA Executive Secretary, to William R. Reed, Big 10 Commissioner, 6 May 1964, Walter Byers Papers, Box "TV: Legislation, 1965, 68," Folder "TV: Legislation 1964," NCAA Headquarters.

28. NCAA Television Committee minutes, 15–17 March 1965, NCAA Headquarters.

29. As quoted in Johnson, *Super Spectator and the Electric Lilliputians,* 155. Lindemann also may have irritated the NCAA by calling for greater flexibility in choosing more attractive football games, in order to achieve higher TV ratings, to possibly telecast doubleheaders to sell more advertising, and to telecast more regional dates if NBC could select the participating teams. NCAA Television Committee minutes, 29–30 June and 1 July 1965, NCAA Headquarters.

30. Lindsey Nelson, *Hello Everybody, I'm Lindsey Nelson* (New York: William Morrow, 1985), 299.

31. William R. Reed, Big 10 Commissioner, to Walter Byers, NCAA Executive Director, 1 July 1964, Walter Byers Papers, Box "T.V.: Leg., 1965–68," Folder "T.V.: Leg., 1964"; Reed to Pete Rozelle, NFL Commissioner, 1 October 1964, Walter Byers Papers, Box "T.V.: Leg., 1965–68," Folder "T.V.: Leg., 1964"; Reed to Senator Philip A. Hart, 10 June 1965, Walter Byers Papers, Box "T.V.: Leg., 1965–68," Folder "T.V.: Leg., 1965–1968"; and NCAA Television Committee minutes, 29–30 June and 1 July 1965, NCAA Headquarters.

32. David M. Nelson, *The Anatomy of a Game: Football, the Rules, and the Men Who Made the Game* (Newark: University of Delaware Press, 1994), 218–20.

33. Ibid., 226–27.

34. "Resolution of NCAA Council," (1952). Penn State athletic director Ernest B. McCoy wrote Crisler on 17 January 1953, saying that "the new rules will aid our particular institution from an economic standpoint." Fritz Crisler Papers, Box 4, Folder "Correspondence 1953," Michigan Historical Collections, Bentley Historical Library; and Nelson, *Anatomy of a Game,* 260–63.

35. Nelson, *Anatomy of a Game,* 298.

36. College Football Association minutes, 16–17 June 1978, Chancellors' Central Files, Box 227, Folder "CFA 1977–80," University of Nebraska Archives.

37. NCAA Television Committee minutes, 7 January 1968 and 1–2 September 1970, and "Recommended NCAA Football Television Plan for 1968 and 1969," Walter Byers Papers, vol. 48, Folder "TV: General 8/67–9/67," NCAA Headquarters.

38. NCAA Television Committee minutes, 29–30 June 1967, NCAA Headquarters.

39. Carroll H. "Beno" Cook, ABC, to E. M Cameron, Duke Athletic Director, ca. January 1967, E. M. Cameron Papers, Box 4, Folder "Television, 1963–70," Duke University Archives.

40. "TV Committee's Straw Votes—March 11 and 12, 1969," Walter Byers Papers, vol. 47, Folder "TV: General 1/69–4/69," NCAA Headquarters.

41. Cook to Cameron, ca. January 1967.

42. NCAA Television Committee minutes, 19 August 1964, NCAA Headquarters.

43. Ibid., 31 January–1 February 1967.

44. For insight into Roone Arledge, see Randy Roberts and James Olson, "The Roone Revolution," *Winning Is the Only Thing: Sports in America Since 1945* (Baltimore: Johns Hopkins University Press, 1989), 113–31.

45. Bushnell to Byers, 11 November 1968, Walter Byers Papers, vol. 47, Folder "TV: General 9/68–12/68," NCAA Headquarters.

46. Byers to William Flynn, Boston College, 7 November 1968, Walter Byers Papers, ibid.

47. NCAA Television Committee minutes, 1–2 September 1970, NCAA Headquarters.

48. Arledge to Byers, 24 November 1970, and Arledge to William J. Flynn, Chairman of NCAA Television Committee, 1 December 1970, Walter Byers Papers, vol. 149, Folder "TV: Football, 10/70–12/70," NCAA Headquarters.

49. "Tentative Proposal to Athletic Directors for National Football Foundation," 26 April 1971, Walter Byers Papers, vol. 149, Folder "TV: Football, 1/71–6/71," NCAA Headquarters.

50. Thomas Hansen, NCAA, memorandum to Byers, 3 May 1971, ibid. The Rutgers Hall was never built. The first College Football Hall of Fame was built on an island on the Ohio River near Cincinnati. It failed financially within a few years. In the 1990s, a new Hall was built in South Bend, Indiana, near the hallowed football grounds of the University of Notre Dame. The very first intercollegiate football game, held at Rutgers in 1869, was really a soccer game, as running with the ball was not permitted. See Ronald A. Smith, "Rutgers vs. Princeton: A Football First," in *Sports and Freedom: The Rise of Big-Time College Athletics* (New York: Oxford University Press, 1988), 69–72.

51. Thomas Hansen, memorandum to Byers, 3 May 1971, Walter Byers Papers, vol. 149, Folder "TV: Football, 1/71–6/71," NCAA Headquarters.

52. James H. Decker, Chairman, NCAA Television Committee, memorandum to NCAA Council, 1 October 1971, Walter Byers Papers, vol. 150, Folder "TV: Football, 10/71–12/71, NCAA Headquarters.

53. *Centre (Penn.) Daily Times,* 27 October 1993, 4D. Schultz had only recently resigned as head of the NCAA over allegations of wrongdoing in the athletic program at the University of Virginia, where he had been athletic director. Schultz favored a four-team playoff in football to boost interest in and increase earnings for college football.

16   Roone Arledge and the Influence of ABC-TV

1. Ronald A. Smith, "Television, Antitrust Laws, and the Conflict between Home Rule and a National NCAA Policy, 1939–1994," Report to the NCAA, fall 1994, 79–80, NCAA Headquarters, Indianapolis, Ind.

2. Bert R. Sugar, *"The Thrill of Victory": The Inside Story of ABC Sports* (New York: Hawthorn Books, 1978), 46–47.

3. *New York Times,* 17 March 1960, 40; William O. Johnson, Jr., *Super Spectator and the Electric Lilliputians* (Boston: Little, Brown, 1971), 151; and Benjamin G. Rader, *In Its Own Image: How Television Has Transformed Sports* (New York: Free Press, 1984), 102–3.

4. Walter Byers, *Unsportsmanlike Conduct: Exploiting College Athletes* (Ann Arbor: University of Michigan Press, 1995), 85.

5. Sugar, *"The Thrill of Victory,"* 47–54; Jim Spence, *Up Close and Personal: The Inside Story of Network Television Sports* (New York: Atheneum, 1988), 51–52; Byers, *Unsportsmanlike Conduct,* 86; Ron Powers, *Supertube: The Rise of Television Sports* (New York: Coward-McCann, 1984), 110–15; and Rader, *In Its Own Image,* 103. Howard Cosell, ABC's controversial sports announcer, remarked that Scherick "knew how to negotiate rights." Howard Cosell, *Cosell* (Chicago: Playboy Press, 1973), 136.

6. Sugar, *"The Thrill of Victory,"* 50.

7. Spence, *Up Close and Personal,* 52. Spence became senior vice president of ABC Sports; Howard became a top producer for ABC Sports for over two decades; and Simmons moved on to NBC, then became head of ESPN, and later was named the first commissioner of the United States Football League.

8. As quoted in Marc Gunther, *The House that Roone Built: The Inside Story of ABC News* (Boston: Little, Brown, 1994), 34.

9. Walter Byers to William R. Reed, Big 10 Commissioner, 4 September 1954, Unprocessed Athletic Department Papers, Folder "Walter Byers Correspondence 1954," University of Alabama Archives.

10. Quoted in Gunther, *The House That Roone Built,* 17–18.

11. Ibid., 18.

12. *Wide World of Sports* came within hours of being canceled before the first episode. College football saved it. Few advertisers were interested in *Wide World,* and ABC offered one-quarter of its valued college football advertising to anyone would who buy one-quarter of the show. This enticed Reynold's Tobacco to buy into *Wide World.* Martin Mayer, *About Television* (New York: Harper & Row, 1972), 186.

13. College football as "T & A," that is, tits and ass, was symbolic of its role as entertainment, rather than part of "A & S," the traditional arts and sciences in higher education. ABC became known for its "T & A" under Arledge as it moved to become the number-one network in sports coverage.

14. Gunther, *The House That Roone Built,* 17. After CBS's ratings dropped rapidly in 1976–77, CBS began to use ABC's "T & A" policy to increase ratings. See Salloy Bedel Smith, *In All His Glory: The Life of William S. Paley* (New York: Simon & Schuster, 1990), 516.

15. For Arledge's innovations, see "Playboy Interview: Roone Arledge," *Playboy,* October 1976, 63–86; Powers, *Supertube,* 125–38; Gunther, *The House That Roone Built,* 8–29; Randy Roberts and James Olson, *Winning Is the Only Thing: Sports in America Since 1945* (Baltimore: Johns Hopkins University Press, 1989), 113–31; Richard O. Davies, *America's Obsession: Sports and Society Since 1945* (Fort Worth, Tex.: Harcourt Brace, 1994), 89–93; Spence, *Up Close and Personal,* 51–91.

16. Phil Patton, *Razzle-Dazzle: The Curious Marriage of Television and Professional Football* (Garden City, N.Y.: Dial Press, 1984), 65–67. The first truly "instant" replay occurred in the Army-Navy game, 7 December 1963, telecast by CBS, two weeks after a famous instant replay of Jack Ruby shooting Lee Harvey Oswald, John F. Kennedy's assassin.

17. "Playboy Interview: Roone Arledge," 66.

18. Beano Cook to Walter Byers, ca. 1 June 1969, Walter Byers Papers, Box "TV: Legislation, 1965–68," Folder "TV: General 5/69–6/69, NCAA Headquarters.

19. "NCAA Television Program Financial Report," 6 November 1974, Walter Byers Papers, vol. 149, Folder "TV, ABC, 1974," NCAA Headquarters.

20. "Changes in Appearance Rules in the NCAA Television Plan," Walter Byers Papers, vol. 150, Folder "TV: Football, 1973," NCAA Headquarters.

21. *Wall Street Journal,* 18 November 1966.
22. NCAA Television Committee minutes, 16 November 1966, NCAA Headquarters.
23. Ibid., 31 January and 1 February 1967. An estimated 33 million watched the contest on TV. See John Durant and Les Etter, *Highlights of College Football* (New York: Hastings House, 1970), 191.
24. Carroll H. Cook to Walter Byers, 13 March 1973, Walter Byers Papers, vol. 148, Folder "TV, ABC, 1972–73, NCAA Headquarters.
25. See, for instance, NCAA Television Committee minutes, 31 January and 1 February 1967, NCAA Headquarters.
26. William J. Flynn to Arthur L. Guepe, Commissioner, Ohio Valley Conference, 14 April 1969, Walter Byers Papers, vol. 97, Folder "TV: General 1/69–4/69," NCAA Headquarters.
27. "TV Committee's Straw Votes—March 11 and 12, 1969," ibid. For numerous restrictions, see NCAA Television Committee minutes, passim, NCAA Headquarters.
28. Sugar, *"The Thrill of Victory,"* 273, and NCAA Television Committee minutes, 11–12 October 1967, NCAA Headquarters.
29. NCAA Television Committee minutes, 11–12 October 1967, NCAA Headquarters.
30. Byers to William Flynn, 7 November 1968, Walter Byers Papers, vol. 97, Folder "TV: General 9/68–12/68," NCAA Headquarters.
31. Byers to Asa Bushnell, NCAA TV Program Director, 27 June 1969, Walter Byers Papers, Box "TV: Legislation, 1965–68," Folder "General 5/69–6/69," NCAA Headquarters; and Sugar, *"The Thrill of Victory,"* 276–78.
32. Carl Lindemann, Jr., to Walter Byers, 17 April 1969, Walter Byers Papers, vol. 97, Folder "TV: General 1/69–4/69," NCAA Headquarters.
33. Sugar, *"The Thrill of Victory,"* 278.
34. Jim Spence of ABC claimed that Byers was "the most powerful man in American sports." See Spence, *Up Close and Personal,* 128.
35. Ibid., 129. The emphasis is Spence's.
36. NCAA Television Committee minutes, 1–2 September 1970, NCAA Headquarters.
37. Arlodge testified in Congress that ABC carried NCAA football for business reasons but not for profit. "I think you know it is pretty well widespread we lose a lot of money on college football." Hearings of the House Communications Subcommittee Regarding Sports Event Telecasting, 3 November 1977, Walter Byers Papers, vol. 152, Folder "TV Football, 7/77–12/77, NCAA Headquarters.
38. Quoted in Johnson, *Super Spectator and the Electric Lilliputians,* 159–60.
39. Beano Cook, ABC, to "Comrades," including Walter Byers, ca. 10 June 1969, Walter Byers Papers, Box "T.V." Leg., 1965–68," Folder "TV: General 5/69–6/69," NCAA Headquarters.
40. Byers, *Unsportsmanlike Conduct,* 144–45.
41. Spence, *Up Close and Personal,* 129.
42. Ibid., 128–29, and Byers, *Unsportsmanlike Conduct,* 264–66.
43. Spence, *Up Close and Personal,* 130–31, and Byers, *Unsportsmanlike Conduct,* 266.
44. Spence, *Up Close and Personal,* 132; and Byers, *Unsportsmanlike Conduct,* 267.

17   Advertising, Image versus Money, and the Beer Hall Incident

1. Ronald A. Smith, *Sports and Freedom: The Rise of Big-Time College Athletics* (New York: Oxford University Press, 1988), 27–29. Harry A. Scott of Columbia University spoke at the NCAA convention in 1955, condemning the historical aspects of college athletic commercialism. He considered the 1852 Harvard-Yale crew meet the beginning of an educational-commercial "dilemma of major proportions in institutions of higher learning in the United States." He condemned educators for not in-

tegrating athletics into the curriculum as an integral part of physical education and general education. NCAA *Proceedings* (1955), 227–28, NCAA Headquarters, Indianapolis, Ind.

2. Smith, *Sports and Freedom,* 44, 78–82.

3. See, for instance, the list of products banned from NCAA football telecasts in "Recommended NCAA Football Television Plan for 1968 and 1969," Office of the President Records, 1961, 1971, Box 17, Folder 34, Georgia Tech University Archives.

4. Proposed Press Release, 14 September 1941, Vice President's Records, 1934–46, UVOC, Box 6, Folder 58 "Radio Broadcasts, 1941–4," University of Notre Dame Archives; and Wendell S. Wilson, Illinois Athletic Director, to Frank E. Schooley, Station WILL, 24 April 1939, President Willard General Correspondence, Box 38, Folder "Radio Broadcast," University of Illinois Archives.

5. A. W. Hobbs, Chair, "Sub-Committee of the Advisory Committee Recommendations," ca. August 1940, President Graham Files, 2/2/3, Box 20, Folder "Football: Broadcasts, 1935–41," University of North Carolina Archives.

6. Addison Pennfield Papers, Box 1, Folder 11, Duke University Archives.

7. "NCAA Television Committee Report—1956," President Brehm Papers, Box 2, Folder "Television," University of Tennessee Archives.

8. As early as 1957, NBC asked a researcher to discuss his findings linking cigarette smoking and cancer, but the tobacco industry apparently put pressure on NBC, and the show was canceled. See Erik Barnouw, *The Image Empire* (New York: Oxford University Press, 1970), 73–74.

9. NCAA Television Committee minutes, 4–5 April, 7–8 June, and 29–30 June 1967, NCAA Headquarters. The first attempt to ban cigarette advertising ended in a 6-6 vote. The 8-2 defeat came less than a month later.

10. Donald Ewen, American Cancer Society, to Walter Byers, 27 November 1967, Senator Robert Kennedy, telegram to Marcus Plant, NCAA President, 16 November 1967, and Marcus Plant to Senator Robert Kennedy, 22 November 1967, Walter Byers Papers, vol. 47, Folder "TV: General 10/67–12/67," NCAA Headquarters.

11. NCAA Television Committee minutes, 7 January and 25–26 March 1968, NCAA Headquarters.

12. Ibid., 1–2 September 1970.

13. *New York Times,* 6 September 1936, 2:1.

14. "Refining Influence," *Time,* 14 September 1936, 43.

15. Carl J. Friedrich and Evelyn Sternberg, "Congress and the Control of Radio-Broadcasting, 1," *American Political Science Review* 37 (October 1943): 815.

16. Red Barber, *The Broadcasters* (New York: Da Capo, 1985), 182.

17. "Excerpt from the 1951 Football Broadcasting Policy of the University of Notre Dame," President Cross Papers, Box 88, Folder "Football 1951," University of Oklahoma Archives; Proposed Press Release, 14 September 1941, Vice President's Records, 1934–46, UVOC, Box 6, Folder 58, "Radio Broadcasts, 1941–44," University of Notre Dame Archives; and President Harold E. Stassen, University of Pennsylvania, draft of letter to President Hugh C. Willet, NCAA, 6 November 1952, Papers of the Office of the President, Box 54, Folder "Intercollegiate Athletics, TV-15," University of Pennsylvania Archives. As early as 1948, Notre Dame had a TV policy of prohibiting beer, wine, liquor, tobacco, laxative, or patent medicine advertising. "Contract between Notre Dame and Television Productions, Inc., September 1948," Vice President John Murphy Papers, UVMR, Box 4, Folder "TV," University of Notre Dame Archives.

18. Francis T. Murray, Pennsylvania Athletic Director, to President Harold E. Stassen, University of Pennsylvania, 30 July 1951, Papers of the Office of the President, Box 54, Folder "Intercollegiate Athletics, TV-8," University of Pennsylvania Archives;

NCAA Television Committee, "Report to the Forty-Sixth Annual Convention of the NCAA," 10–12 January 1952, Du Mont Laboratories, Box 19, Folder "NCAA, 1952," Manuscript Division, Library of Congress; and Ronald A. Smith, "Television, Antitrust Laws, and the Conflict Between Home Rule and a National NCAA Policy, 1939–1994," Report to the NCAA, fall 1994, 79.

19. NCAA Television Committee minutes, 27 July 1966, NCAA Headquarters.

20. Ibid., 29–30 June 1967.

21. "Recommended NCAA Football Television Plan for 1968 and 1969," Walter Byers Papers, vol. 48, Folder "TV: General 8/67–9/67," NCAA Headquarters. Other banned products were feminine hygiene products, habit-forming drugs, patent medicines, laxatives, political organizations, and other "controversial" organizations.

22. "Recommended NCAA Football Television Plan for 1968 and 1969," Office of the President Records, 1961, 1971, Box 17, Folder 34, Georgia Tech University Archives.

23. Raymond H. Thornton, University of California, Irvine Athletic Director, to Marcus Plant, NCAA President, 14 November 1968, Walter Byers Papers, Box "TV: Legislation, 1965–68," Folder "TV: Legislation, 1965–68," NCAA Headquarters.

24. Asa Bushnell, TV Program Director, to Roone Arledge, ABC, 15 May 1968, Walter Byers Papers, vol. 47, Folder "TV: General 5/68–8/68," NCAA Headquarters.

25. Plant to Byers, 4 September 1968, Walter Byers Papers, vol. 47, Folder "TV: General 9/69–12/68," NCAA Headquarters.

26. NCAA Television Committee minutes, 11–12 March 1969, Walter Byers Papers, Box "TV: Leg., 1965–1968," NCAA Headquarters.

27. Ibid., 29–30 June 1967; and Byers to William Flynn, NCAA Television Committee chair, 7 November 1968, Walter Byers Papers, vol. 47, Folder "TV: General 9/68–12/68," NCAA Headquarters.

28. "Paris-Mutuels Tonic Puts New Life in Race Season," *Literary Digest,* 29 July 1933, 27; Dixon Wecter, *The Age of the Great Depression, 1929–1941* (Chicago: Quadrangle Books, 1971), 243; Similarly, Pennsylvania Blue Laws had been abandoned in 1933 so that professional baseball and football could be played on Sunday and taxed. See J. Thomas Jable, "Sports, Amusements, and Pennsylvania Blue Laws, 1682–1973," (Ph.D. diss., Penn State University, 1974), 150–70; and John A. Lucas, "The Unholy Experiment—Professional Baseball's Struggle against Pennsylvania Sunday Blue Laws 1926–1934," *Pennsylvania History* 38 (April 1971): 173.

29. Asa S. Bushnell to ABC Sports, 4 June 1969, Walter Byers Papers, Box "TV: Leg., 1965–1968," Folder "TV: General 5/69–6/69," NCAA Headquarters.

30. NCAA Television Committee minutes, 1–2 September 1970, NCAA Headquarters. The vote was 9-0, with two abstentions.

31. NCAA Television Committee Administrative Committee minutes, 26 May 1972, NCAA Headquarters.

32. NCAA Television Committee minutes, 18–19 May 1977, NCAA Headquarters.

33. Walter Byers to Lou Holtz, Arkansas football coach, 26 April 1982, Walter Byers Papers, Box "TV, Football, 1986," Folder "TV, Football, 1/82–6/82," NCAA Headquarters.

34. Holtz to Byers, 22 March 1982, ibid.

35. President Leslie S. Wright, Samford University, to President Harold L. Enarson, Ohio State University, 25 November 1975, President Enarson Papers, 3/j/27/8, Folder "NCAA Correspondence: 1973–80," Ohio State University Archives.

36. NCAA Television Committee minutes, 28–29 March 1976, NCAA Headquarters.

37. "Recommended NCAA Football Television Plan for 1968 and 1969," Walter Byers Papers, vol. 48, Folder "TV: General 8/67–9/67," NCAA Headquarters.

38. Bert R. Sugar, *"The Thrill of Victory": The Inside Story of ABC Sports* (New York: Hawthorn Books, 1978), 160–61.

39. Roone Arledge, ABC Sports, to Harold Enarson, Ohio State University, 15 November 1976, Walter Byers Papers, Box "TV Committee 1976," Folder "TV Committee 1976," NCAA Headquarters.

40. Enarson to Elton Rule, 18 October 1976, Walter Byers Papers, Box "TV Committee 1976," Folder "TV Committee 1976," NCAA Headquarters. Enarson stated that ABC had done a disservice to students, missed the significant stories on his campus, and eroded public confidence in higher education. He asked ABC to "stop using football telecasts as a vehicle for feeding the public distorted stereotypes which malign most students and degrade universities." If Enarson had been truly honest about his feelings about what ABC was doing to college football telecasts, he could have complained about the "jiggle" factor, commonly called "T & A" (tits and ass), that ABC was noted for. According to Salloy Bedell Smith, in a biography of CBS's William S. Paley, CBS considered using the ABC's T & A formula to attain success. It was easy to see the T & A factor—namely, the focus on cheerleaders—in ABC's NCAA football series following timeouts or touchdowns. See Salloy Smith, *In All His Glory: The Life of Williams S. Paley* (New York: Simon & Schuster, 1990), 516. Lampley's 1975 UCLA game feature showed a twenty-five-second clip on the beach at Santa Monica and a twenty-three-second clip on the UCLA campus, replete with a number of attractive females. See Arledge to Enarson, 15 November 1976, President Enarson Papers, 3/j/16/15, Folder "Council of Ten: ABC, 1976–78," Ohio State University Archives.

41. Arledge to Enarson, 15 November 1976, President Enarson Papers, 3/j/16/15, Folder "Council of Ten: ABC, 1976–78," Ohio State University Archives.

42. Roone Arledge of ABC eventually agreed to Enarson's demands that "there will be no more beer hall or comparable 'scenes' shown relative to the NCAA football telecasts," according to Seaver Peters, chair of the NCAA Television Committee. Peters to Edwin M. Crawford, Vice President, Ohio State University, 15 April 1977, President Enarson Papers, 3/j/16/15, Folder "Council of Ten: ABC, 1976–78," Ohio State University Archives.

43. NCAA *Proceedings* (1978), A89–90, NCAA Headquarters.

44. Ibid., 193.

45. For a lengthy discussion of television, football, and antitrust actions, see Smith, "Television, Antitrust Laws."

46. NCAA Football TV Committee minutes, 28–29 March 1982, NCAA Headquarters; and "1982–1985 NCAA Football Television Plan," June 1982, NCAA Headquarters.

47. While this account shows the hypocrisy among presidents, especially Enarson, on other fronts, one could praise Enarson for his leadership. When he was president of Cleveland State University in 1966, he and his governing board selected John McLendon as the first black basketball coach hired by a predominately white institution. McLendon had coached in the first integrated college basketball game, which at the time was illegal in North Carolina, twenty-one years before the Atlantic Coast Conference broke the racial barriers. When McLendon's North Carolina Central College all-black team played the Duke Navy Medical School all-white team in 1944 during World War II, the contest was played as a "secret" game. McLendon's team defeated the Medical School students, and the event was not made public until 1995. See "NACDA Announces the John McLendon Minority Postgraduate Scholarship Awards," *Athletics Administration* 33 (December 1998): 16–23.

48. Alexander Wolff, "Dean Smith Unplugged," *Sports Illustrated,* 22 December 1997, 56.

18   The Television Announcer's Role in Football Promotion

1. Ray Poindexter, *Golden Throats and Silver Tongues: The Radio Announcers* (Conway, Ark.: River Road Press, 1978), 117.
2. *New York Times,* 13 September 1939, 31, and 29 September 1939, 28.
3. Ibid., 15 October 1939, 9:12.
4. Poindexter, *Golden Throats and Silver Tongues,* 147.
5. Mary C. O'Connell, ed., *Connections: Reflections of Sixty Years of Broadcasting* (New York: National Broadcasting Co., 1986), 9.
6. Ibid.
7. James W. Harper, "Stern, William 'Bill,'" in David L. Porter, ed., *Biographical Dictionary of American Sports: Outdoor Sports* (Westport, Conn.: Greenwood Press, 1988), 99.
8. *Life* magazine claimed that Stern was the "country's most popular football broadcaster." "Life Goes to a Football Broadcast," *Life,* 14 October 1946, 131.
9. O'Connell, *Connections,* 232.
10. Lindsey Nelson, *Hello Everybody, I'm Lindsey Nelson* (New York: William Morrow, 1985), 21–22.
11. Ibid., 55, 61, 65–66.
12. Ibid., 41–42, 136.
13. James W. Harper, "McLendon, Gordon Barton," in Porter, ed., *Biographical Dictionary of American Sports,* 77–78.
14. Nelson, *Hello Everybody,* 175–76.
15. Ibid., 176, 182.
16. Ibid., 181.
17. Ibid., 206.
18. Ibid., 218–19.
19. John M. Carroll, *Red Grange and the Rise of Modern Football* (Urbana: University of Illinois Press, 1999), 183–90.
20. Nelson, *Hello Everybody,* 219.
21. Ibid., 226.
22. *New York Times,* 13 April 1960, 47. Red Smith of the *New York Herald Tribune* was honored as the top sportswriter.
23. NCAA Television Committee minutes, 9–10 March 1966, NCAA Headquarters, Indianapolis, Ind.
24. Nelson, *Hello Everybody,* 289, 299–301.
25. William Taaffe, "Final Score: ABC 14, CBS 3," *Sports Illustrated,* 6 December 1982, 91.
26. Marc Gunther, *The House That Roone Built: The Inside Story of ABC News* (Boston: Little, Brown, 1994), 25; "Spotlight," *Sports Illustrated,* 9 February 1987, 54; and Leonard H. Goldenson, *Beating the Odds: The Untold Story Behind the Rise of ABC* (New York: Charles Scribner's Sons, 1991), 208.
27. Stan Issacs, "No Armageddon Bowls for Him," *Sports Illustrated,* 1 October 1979, 56.
28. "Spotlight," *Sports Illustrated,* 9 February 1987, 54.
29. Paul Hornung, *Woody Hayes: A Reflection* (Champaign, Ill.: Sagamore Publishing, 1991), 54, 77–78, 164; and NCAA Television Committee minutes, 21 November 1977, NCAA Headquarters.
30. Hornung, *Woody Hayes,* 197–98.
31. Jerry Crowe, "Big Man on Campus," *Sporting News,* 21 August 1995, S10.
32. Ibid., S9.

33. Hornung, *Woody Hayes,* 199.
34. For instance, see the NCAA Television Committee minutes, 19 August 1964, NCAA Headquarters.
35. Ibid., 1–2 September 1970, NCAA Headquarters.
36. Sterling Quinlan, *Inside ABC: American Broadcasting Company's Rise to Power* (New York: Hastings House, 1979), 172; and Huntington Williams, *Beyond Control: ABC and the Fate of Networks* (New York: Atheneum, 1989), 52.
37. *Variety,* 7 July 1971, in Walter Byers Papers, vol. 143, Folder "TV, ABC, 1971," NCAA Headquarters.
38. Jerry Izenberg, *How Many Miles to Camelot? The All-American Sport Myth* (New York: Holt, Rinehart, & Winston, 1972), 184–86.
39. NCAA Television Committee minutes, 25 August 1965, NCAA Headquarters.
40. George H. Gangwere to Walter Byers, NCAA Executive Director, 9 December 1969, Walter Byers Papers, Box "TV: Legislation, 1965–68," Folder "TV: General 7/69–8/69," NCAA Headquarters.
41. William S. Paley, head of CBS, discussed an analogous situation in 1954 when he pondered backing Edward R. Murrow's efforts to expose the demagogue Joseph Mc-Carthy, who was unethically using the communist issue in the early 1950s to further his political cause. Paley, in this case, chose the truth over economic expediency and allowed Murrow to telecast his condemnation of McCarthy on 9 March 1954, which helped to lead to the downfall of McCarthy and McCarthyism. See Lewis J. Paper, *Empire: William S. Paley and the Making of CBS* (New York: St. Martin's Press, 1987), 173.
42. Walter Byers to Roone Arledge, 19 December 1977, Walter Byers Papers, Box "TV Communication 1978," Folder "TV Communication 1978," NCAA Headquarters.
43. Walter Byers, *Unsportsmanlike Conduct: Exploiting College Athletes* (Ann Arbor: University of Michigan Press, 1995), 140–41.

19   The Cable Television Dilemma

1. Patrick R. Parsons and Robert M. Frieden, *The Cable and Satellite Television Industries* (Boston: Allyn & Bacon, 1998), 29–30; Timothy Hollins, *Beyond Broadcasting: Into the Cable Age* (London, England: BFI Publishing, 1984), 114; and Ralph M. Negrine, ed., *Cable Television and the Future of Broadcasting* (New York: St. Martin's Press, 1985), 16.
2. Hollins, *Beyond Broadcasting,* 121; and Negrine, ed., *Cable Television,* 18.
3. Howard J. Blumenthal and Oliver R. Goodenough, *This Business of Television* (New York: Billboard Books, 1991), 49.
4. "Football Fortune," *Business Week,* 18 October 1952, 34.
5. NCAA *Proceedings* (1954), 209, NCAA Headquarters, Indianapolis, Ind. Leahy's Notre Dame record was 107-13-9 (.864%), with five national championships from 1941–43 and 1946–53, while Knute Rockne was 105-12-5 (.881%), with six national championships from 1918–30.
6. Ibid., 224.
7. *New York Times,* 11 January 1956, 38, and *Philadelphia Inquirer,* 26 July 1955, 1.
8. Hollins, *Beyond Broadcasting,* 121; and *Warner AMEX Cable Communications v. A.B.C.,* Affidavit in Opposition to Preliminary Injunction, 30 July 1980, Walter Byers Papers, Box "TV Negotiations, 1980," Folder "TV Negotiations, 1980," NCAA Headquarters.
9. Asa Bushnell, NCAA Television Committee, to Philip Brown, NCAA Counsel, 17 July 1968, Walter Byers Papers, vol. 47, Folder "TV: General 5/68–8/68," NCAA Headquarters.

10. Ibid., and Blumenthal and Goodenough, *This Business of Television,* 119.
11. Don Canham, NCAA Television Committee, to Asa S. Bushnell, NCAA TV Project Director, 14 October 1970, and Canham to Walter Byers, 5 October 1970, Walter Byers Papers, vol. 149, Folder "TV: Football, 10/70–12/70, NCAA Headquarters.
12. "1971 NCAA Closed Circuit Television Regulations," adopted by the NCAA Television Committee, 20 July 1971, Walter Byers Papers, vol. 150, Folder "TV: Football 7/71–9/71," NCAA Headquarters.
13. Jesse M. Brill, President, MTS Sports, to Walter Byers, 23 March 1971, ibid.
14. Walter Byers, NCAA Executive Director, to Asa S. Bushnell, NCAA TV Consultant, 14 September 1971, ibid.
15. Bushnell to James Decker, Syracuse University Athletic Director, 10 May 1971, ibid.
16. Bushnell to Decker, ibid.; and Walter Byers to Jesse M. Brill, President, MTS Sports, 15 July 1971, ibid.
17. Parsons and Frieden, *The Cable and Satellite Television Industries,* 1; Hollins, *Beyond Broadcasting,* 122; and Huntington Williams, *Beyond Control: ABC and the Fate of the Networks* (New York: Atheneum, 1989), 111.
18. Home Box Office Proposal for National Collegiate Athletic Association, NCAA Headquarters; Don Canham, Michigan, to Walter Byers, 21 April 1976 and 27 April 1976, and Walter Byers to Seaver Peters, NCAA Television Committee, 13 April 1976, Walter Byers Papers, vol. 152, Folder "TV Football, 1976," NCAA Headquarters.
19. NCAA Television Committee minutes, 20–21 February 1977, NCAA Headquarters.
20. See Ritchie Thomas, NCAA Counsel, to Dean Burch, Federal Communications Commission, Chair, 1 February 1974, Walter Byers Papers, vol. 151, Folder "TV: 1975," NCAA Headquarters.
21. Walter Byers to Edmund Joyce, Executive Vice President, Notre Dame, 10 October 1974, and Joyce to Byers, 19 September 1974 and 18 October 1974, Walter Byers Papers, vol. 151, Folder "TV: Football, 7/74–12/74," NCAA Headquarters.
22. This is not to downplay the Notre Dame threat. In 1977 at the Congressional Hearing Regarding Sports Telecasting Arrangement, Roone Arledge of ABC testified that Notre Dame officials "could do infinitely better selling their own school to one of the networks and would be a very attractive package." Hearings transcript attached to Ritchie T. Thomas, NCAA legal counsel, to Thomas C. Hansen, NCAA Assistant Executive Director, 8 November 1977, Walter Byers Papers, vol. 152, Folder "TV: Football 7/77–12/77," NCAA Headquarters.
23. "1978–1981 NCAA Football Television Plan," 18 June 1977, Walter Byers Papers, vol. 119, Folder "Legal, 1978," NCAA Headquarters.
24. NCAA Television Committee minutes, 10 January 1977, NCAA Headquarters.
25. Hearings of the House Communications Subcommittee Regarding Sports Event Telecasting, 3 November 1977; and Ritchie T. Thomas, NCAA legal counsel, to Thomas C. Hansen, NCAA Assistant Executive Director, 8 November 1977, Walter Byers Papers, vol. 152, Folder "TV Football, 7/77–12/77," NCAA Headquarters.
26. NCAA Television Committee minutes, 21 September 1977, NCAA Headquarters.
27. Ritchie T. Thomas, NCAA Counsel, Washington, D.C., to Walter Byers, 1 July 1977, Walter Byers Papers, vol. 144, Folder "TV, ABC, 1977," NCAA Headquarters.
28. "Settlement Agreement between Warner Cable and ABC and NCAA," 20 July 1978, Walter Byers Papers, vol. 119, Folder "Legal, 1978," NCAA Headquarters. QUBE would cablecast six home and four away games, paying $5,000 per game, 60 percent of which would go to Ohio State and 40 percent to the NCAA. See NCAA Television Committee minutes, 24 July 1978 and 20 September 1978, NCAA Headquarters.
29. Two pages of handwritten notes about concerns with the Warner, ABC, NCAA Settlement, July 1978, Walter Byers Papers, vol. 119, Folder "Legal, 1978," NCAA Headquarters.

30. NCAA Television Committee minutes, 9 January 1979, NCAA Headquarters.

31. ESPN Information Packet, Walter Byers Papers, vol. 153, Folder "TV: Negotiations Cable, 1979," NCAA Headquarters; and Leonard H. Goldenson and Marvin J. Wolf, *Beating the Odds: The Untold Story Behind the Rise of ABC* (New York: Charles Scribner's Sons, 1991), 434–39.

32. James R. Spence, Jr., to Byers, 18 January 1979, and Byers to Spence, 27 January 1979, Walter Byers Papers, vol. 144, Folder "TV, ABC, 1979," NCAA Headquarters.

33. *Warner Amex Cable v. American Broadcasting Companies, Inc.,* 499 F. Supp. 537 (S.D. Ohio 1980); Glenn M. Wong, *Essentials of Amateur Sports Law* (Dover, Mass.: Auburn House, 1988), 508; Robert C. Berry and Glenn M. Wong, *Law and Business of the Sports Industries* (Dover, Mass.: Auburn House, 1986), 2:535–36; and Gary A. Uberstine, ed., *Law of Professional and Amateur Sport* (New York: Clark Boardman Company, 1988), Chap. 18, 35.

34. NCAA Television Committee minutes, 29–30 June, 1 July 1965, NCAA Headquarters; and "Questions and Answers Concerning the College Football Association," 10 November 1976, Chancellors' Central Files, Box 227, Folder "CFA 1977–1980," University of Nebraska Archives.

35. Council of Ten minutes, 8 May 1978, President Enarson Papers, 3/j/16/18, "Council of Ten: Minutes and Reports: 1977–80," Ohio State University Archives.

36. The CFA TV committee was comprised of Stan Bates, Western Athletic Conference; Ed Czekaj, Penn State University; Eugene Corrigan, University of Virginia; Charley Scott, University of Alabama; Cliff Speegle, Southwest Athletic Conference; and Charles Neinas, Big 8 Conference. Neinas would become the first executive director of the CFA in 1980. See "Chronology of CFA Involvement in the Area of Football Television," Memorandum, 15 December 1981, President Banowsky Papers, Box 92, Folder 13, University of Oklahoma Archives.

37. NCAA Television Committee minutes, 16 December 1976, Walter Byers Papers, Box "TV Comm 1972," Folder "TV Comm 1976"; "CBS Sports Proposal to the NCAA Television Committee, March 1977," Walter Byers Papers, Box "TV Comm 1977," Folder "TV Comm 1977"; and "Results of NCAA Television Committee Membership Survey," NCAA Television Committee minutes, 12–13 April 1977," NCAA Headquarters.

38. NCAA *Proceedings* (1979), 90, NCAA Headquarters; and Captain J. O. Coppedge, "Report of Television Committee to Opening Session of 1979 NCAA Convention," Walter Byers Papers, Box "TV Comm 1978," Folder "TV Comm 1979 Jan–Feb," NCAA Headquarters.

39. In December 1981, The NCAA held a special convention to tighten Division I-A entry and to grant greater power to big-time football powers over television policy. See NCAA *Special Convention Proceedings,* 3–4 December 1981.

40. Charles Standford, ABC, to George Gangwere, NCAA counsel, 13 April 1982, Walter Byers Papers, Box "TV, Cable, 1983," Folder "TV: CBS 1982–1984," NCAA Headquarters.

41. See *Cox Broadcasting and ABC v. NCAA and TBS,* Appellants Brief, 27 August 1982, Walter Byers Papers, Box "TV Negotiations 1981," Folder "TV Negotiations 1982"; Charles Stanford, ABC, to George Gangwere, NCAA Legal Counsel, n.d., Walter Byers Papers, Box "TV Negotiations, 1983," Folder "TV Supplementary Series, Football 1982," NCAA Headquarters; and Berry and Wong, *Law and the Business of the Sports Industries,* 515.

20 TV Money, Robin Hood, and the Birth of the CFA

1. See NCAA *Proceedings* (1951–80), NCAA Headquarters, Indianapolis, Ind.
2. The NCAA Executive Committee voted to channel football TV receipts into the general budget beginning in the fall of 1972. Ibid. (1972), 36.
3. In 1941, the NCAA and competing teams split $9,043.92 after the NCAA had taken 10 percent from the net receipts. Ibid. (1941), 156–57.
4. Ibid., 247; ibid. (1962), 336; and "Financial Analysis, National Collegiate Division I Men's Basketball Championship," Walter Byers Papers, Box "TV Negotiations, 1985," NCAA Headquarters.
5. Thomas J. Hamilton, Chair, NCAA Television Committee, to the NCAA membership, 21 May 1951, President Brehm Papers, Box 2, Folder "Television & Athletics," University of Tennessee Archives.
6. *New York Times,* 29 April 1951, in the Papers of the Office of the President, 1950–55, Box 54, Folder "Intercollegiate Athletics TV-3," University of Pennsylvania Archives.
7. Theodore Hesburgh to Douglas Mills, Illinois Athletic Director, 6 October 1952, President Theodore Hesburgh Files, UPHS, Box 94, University of Notre Dame Archives; and NCAA *Proceedings* (1953), 231, NCAA Headquarters.
8. See chapter 10 for more information on Notre Dame and the Super Conference.
9. NCAA Television Committee minutes, 1–2 April 1963, NCAA Headquarters.
10. NCAA *Proceedings* (1964), 71, NCAA Headquarters.
11. NCAA Television Committee minutes, 9–10 June 1964, 19 October 1965, and 7–8 June 1967, NCAA Headquarters.
12. See NCAA *Proceedings* (1965–69), passim, NCAA Headquarters; Charles Neinas, memorandum to Walter Byers, 11 May 1965, unprocessed Walter Byers Papers, Folder "Officers," and Executive Committee minutes, 15–17 August 1968, Walter Byers Papers, vol. 149, Folder "TV: Football, 1/71–6/71," NCAA Headquarters.
13. NCAA Television Committee minutes, 20–21 March 1970, and Executive Committee minutes, 17–18 August 1970, Walter Byers Papers, vol. 149, Folder "TV: Football 1/71–6/71," NCAA Headquarters.
14. Don Canham to Walter Byers, 24 October 1974, Walter Byers Papers, Box "TV Committee 1972," Folder "TV Committee 1974," and "Television's Contributions to NCAA Division II and Division II," 13 November 1974, Walter Byers Papers, vol. 154, Folder "TV, ABC, 1974," NCAA Headquarters.
15. *Who's Who in America,* 55th ed., (New Providence, N.J.: Marquis Who'sWho, 2001), 2449.
16. Don Yaeger, *Undue Process: The NCAA's Injustice for All* (Champaign, Ill.: Sagamore Publishing, 1991), 201; and Walter Byers, *Unsportsmanlike Conduct: Exploiting College Athletes* (Ann Arbor: University of Michigan Press, 1995), 197–99. Long Beach was cited for providing illegal payments to players, free airline trips for basketball players, jobs for athletes' parents, and fraudulent test scores for athletes, among other violations. As Horn was well versed in politics, both academically and through direct involvement, it is somewhat difficult to believe that he was naive about the problems and politics of athletics at Long Beach when he became president in 1970. After researching in about sixty college archives and looking at the papers of roughly 200 college presidents, I have yet to find a college president who was naive relative to athletics. Horn may be that exception, but it's not likely.
17. NCAA *Proceedings* (1974), 226, NCAA Headquarters.
18. Stephen Horn to President Harold L. Enarson, Ohio State University, 22 February 1974, President Enarson Papers, 3/j/27/8, "NCAA Correspondence: 1973–80," Ohio State University Archives.

19. NCAA *Proceedings* (1973), A21–24, NCAA Headquarters.

20. Ibid. (Special Convention, 14–15 August 1975), 59.

21. Stephen Horn, memorandum to presidents of NCAA Member Institutions, 11 July 1975, Walter Byers Papers, Box "TV Committee 1972," Folder "TV Committee 1976," NCAA Headquarters.

22. "Interim Report of the Commissioner to the Council of Ten," 24 July 1975, President Enarson Papers, 3/j/16/17, Folder "Council of Ten, 1973–76," Ohio State University Archives; and "Questions and Answers Concerning the College Football Association," 10 November 1976, Chancellors' Central Files, Box 227, Folder "CFA 1977–80," University of Nebraska Archives.

23. NCAA Television Committee minutes, 2–3 June 1975, 4, NCAA Headquarters.

24. Byers to Horn, 20 September 1975, Walter Byers Papers, Box "TV Committee 1972," Folder "TV Committee 1976," NCAA Headquarters.

25. Robert C. James to Byers, 5 September 1975, Walter Byers Papers, vol. 151, Folder "TV: Football, 1975," NCAA Headquarters.

26. Horn to Byers, 28 August 1975, Marcus Plant Papers, Box 6, Folder 6–16, Michigan Historical Collection, Bentley Historical Library.

27. Byers to Horn, 20 September 1975, ibid.; and Marcus L. Plant, "Draft Remarks" No. 1, ca. August 1975, ibid.

28. "Transcript of Special Meeting," Walter Byers Papers, vol. 151, Folder "TV: Football, 1975," NCAA Headquarters.

29. NCAA *Proceedings* (1976), 40–48, NCAA Headquarters.

30. Plant, "Draft Remarks" No. 1, ca. August 1975, Marcus Plant Papers, Box 6, Folder 6–16, Michigan Historical Collection, Bentley Historical Library.

31. Byers to John A. Fuzak, NCAA President, 7 August 1975, vol. 151, Folder "TV: Football, 1975," NCAA Headquarters.

32. "Questions and Answers Concerning the College Football Association," 10 November 1976, Chancellors' Central Files, Box 227, Folder "CFA 1977–80," University of Nebraska Archives.

33. Charles M. Neinas, Executive Director of the CFA, testimony, House Subcommittee on Oversights and Investigations of the Committee on Energy and Commerce, *Televised College Football,* Hearing, 98th Cong., 2d sess., July 31, 1984.

34. "Articles of the College Football Association," adopted 20 December 1976, Chancellors' Central Files, Box 227, Folder "CFA, 1977–80," University of Nebraska Archives.

35. Robert C. James, Chair, CFA Organizing Committee, to CEOs, Faculty Representatives, and Athletic Directors of Selected Institutions, 29 September 1976, Chancellors' Central Files, Box 227, Folder "CFA 1977–80," University of Nebraska Archives; and President Fred C. Davison, Chair, CFA Board of Directors, "History of College Football Association," 11 June 1980, President Banowsky Papers, Box 74, Folder 13, University of Oklahoma Archives. The steering committee consisted of Chair Robert James, ACC; Edward Czekaj, Penn State; Wayne Duke, Big 10; Wiles Hallock, PAC-8; Carl James, Duke; Edmund P. Joyce, Notre Dame; Henry T. Lowe, SEC; and Albert M. Witte, SWC.

36. Fred C. Davison, "History of College Football Association," 11 June 1980, President Banowsky Papers, Box 74, Folder 13, University of Oklahoma Archives.

37. Ibid. Emphasis is mine.

38. Harold Shechter, Ohio State Faculty Representative, to President Harold L. Enarson, Ohio State University, 8 August 1978, President Enarson Papers, 3/j/16/16, Folder "Council of Ten: 1978," Ohio State University Archives.

39. Edmund P. Joyce, Vice President, Notre Dame, to President Arthur G. Hansen, Purdue, 18 April 1978, President Davison Papers, Box 19, Folder "CFA," University of

Georgia Archives; Robben W. Fleming, President, Michigan, to President Fred Davison, Georgia, President Davison Papers, Box 19, Folder "CFA, June 16–18, 1978," University of Georgia Archives; and "Report to the Council of Ten, 5 May 1980," President Enarson Papers, 3/j/27/10, Folder "NCAA Minutes and Reports: 1979–80," Ohio State University Archives.

40. NCAA *Proceedings* (1978), 111, A15–18, NCAA Headquarters.

41. "Contract for Employment" for Chuck Neinas, 30 May 1980, President Davison Papers, Box 18, Folder "CFA," University of Georgia Archives. In addition to the salary, Neinas also received an automobile, $50,000 term insurance, disability, hospitalization, and major medical insurance comparable to his Big 8 commissioner's insurance.

42. Walter Byers, *Unsportsmanlike Conduct: Exploiting College Athletes* (Ann Arbor: University of Michigan Press, 1995), 175–76; and Seaver Peters, Chair, NCAA Television Committee, to Charles Neinas, 13 August 1976, Neinas to Peters, 18 August 1976, NCAA Television Committee minutes, 9 September 1976, and Byers to Peters, 8 September 1976, Walter Byers Papers, Box "TV Committee 1972," Folder "TV Committee 1976," NCAA Headquarters.

43. Byers, *Unsportsmanlike Conduct,* 176.

21   TV Property Rights and a CFA Challenge to the NCAA

1. *Washington Post,* 17 September 1976, D4.

2. Walter Byers to Marcus L. Plant, University of Michigan, 4 January 1977, Walter Byers Papers, vol. 119, Folder "Legal: 1/77–6/77, NCAA Headquarters, Indianapolis, Ind.

3. "Motion to Dismiss of NCAA, Oklahoma Television Sports v. NCAA," 12 August 1974, Walter Byers Papers, vol. 117, Folder "Legal: 1974," NCAA Headquarters.

4. *Oklahoma Journal,* 21 August 1976, 1–2; and *Daily Oklahoman,* 24 August 1976, 1.

5. *Hennessey v. National Collegiate Athletic Association,* 564 F.2d 1136, 1146–47 (5th Cir. 1977); and Robert C. Berry and Glenn M. Wong, *Law and Business of the Sports Industries* (Westport, Conn.: Praeger, 1993) 2:782–83.

6. George Gangwere to Walter Byers, 29 September 1976, Walter Byers Papers, vol. 118, Folder "Legal: 6/76–12/76," NCAA Headquarters.

7. *Behagan v. Intercollegiate Conference of Faculty Representatives,* 346 F. Supp. 602 (D. Minn. 1972) and Berry and Wong, *Law and Business of the Sports Industries,* 2:88–90.

8. John W. Johnson, "Minnesota Gopher Basketball: Problems on the Court and in the Courts," in Charles E. Quirk, ed., *Sports and the Law: Major Legal Cases* (New York: Garland, 1996), 205–14, esp. 211.

9. Berry and Wong, *Law and Business of the Sports Industries,* 2:229–231.

10. Carl L. Reisner, "Tackling Intercollegiate Athletics: An Antitrust Analysis," *Yale Law Review* 77 (January 1978): 658.

11. Gangwere to Byers, 29 September 1976, Walter Byers Papers, vol. 118, Folder "Legal: 6/76–12/76," NCAA Headquarters. Four years later, Gangwere wrote: "Prior to 1975 the NCAA could, with considerable justification from the cases, argue that it was immune from the anti-trust law because it was an educational organization without commercial objectives." Gangwere to Byers, 3 January 1979, Walter Byers Papers, vol. 153, Folder "TV: Negotiations Committee, 1979," NCAA Headquarters.

12. "What Is the College Football Association?" President Davison Papers, Box 18, Folder "CFA-7," University of Georgia Archives.

13. The predicted 1.6 grade point average for incoming freshmen was eliminated by the NCAA in 1973. Aside from the inability to equitably monitor the rule, there is strong

evidence that the national movement in the 1960s and 1970s to remove academic restrictions and lower academic standards for minority groups and those disadvantaged by a lack of academic preparations was vital in removing standards for college athletic eligibility. See, for instance, Vincent J. Dooley, "Response to Subjects Raised During Jan Kemp vs. Leroy Ervin-Virginia Trotter Court Case," 31 January 1986, Ralph Beaird Papers, Box "1968–87," University of Georgia Archives; and Walter Byers, *Unsportsmanlike Conduct: Exploiting College Athletes* (Ann Arbor: University of Michigan Press, 1995), 339–40.

14. CFA Board of Directors minutes, 16 June 1977, President Davison Papers, Box 19, Folder "CFA, June 15–16, 1977," University of Georgia Archives.

15. Fred Davison to Joe Paterno, 13 April 1977, ibid.

16. Council of Ten minutes, 8 May 1978, President Enarson Papers, 3/j/16/18, Folder "Council of Ten: Minutes and Reports: 1977–80," Ohio State University Archives. President James Zumberge of the University of Southern California also chided the CFA for its "pious pronouncements on academic standards" and stated: "If I could be convinced that the CFA really could improve the academic standards and enforce them without an investigative army, I would work hard to bring the PAC-10 into the club." Zumberge to Charles M. Neinas, CFA Executive Director, 26 November 1980, President Davison Papers, Box 19, Folder "CFA," University of Georgia Archives.

17. Tom Osborne to Barry Switzer, Oklahoma football coach, and other Big 8 coaches, 19 June 1978, Chancellors' Central Files, Box 227, Folder "CFA 1977–80," University of Nebraska Archives. Osborne said that thirteen players of the 1976 and 1977 All Big 8 teams would not have qualified for scholarships under the triple option plan.

18. Chuck M. Neinas, Big 8 Commissioner, to President Fred C. Davison, CFA Board of Directors Chair, and Henry T. Lowe, CFA Secretary-Treasurer, 21 February 1979, President Davison Papers, Box 19, Folder "CFA," University of Georgia Archives.

19. "Report of CFA TV Study Committee," 22 May 1980, President Banowsky Papers, Box 74, Folder 13, University of Oklahoma Archives.

20. Ibid.

21. Richie T. Thomas, NCAA Counsel, Washington, D.C., to Walter Byers, 1 July 1977, Walter Byers Papers, vol. 144, Folder "TV, ABC, 1977," NCAA Headquarters; Charles M. Neinas, CFA Executive Director, to Fred C. Davison, President, University of Georgia, and Henry T. Lowe, School of Law, University of Missouri, 22 October 1980, President Davison Papers, Box 19, Folder "CFA-2," University of Georgia Archives; and College Football Association minutes, 7 June 1981.

22. Byers to William J. Flynn, NCAA Television Committee, and President James Frank, Lincoln University and NCAA president, 8 February 1979, Walter Byers Papers, vol. 153, Folder "TV: Negotiations Committee, 1979," NCAA Headquarters.

23. NCAA Negotiations Committee for Television Rights of the Division I Basketball Tournament minutes, 6 January 1979, NCAA Headquarters; and George Gangwere to Walter Byers, 3 January 1979, Walter Byers Papers, vol. 153, Folder "TV: Negotiations Committee, 1979," NCAA Headquarters.

24. Byers to Richard F. Pfizenmayer, NCAA Legal Counsel, Washington, D.C., 2 November 1977, Walter Byers Papers, vol. 119, Folder "Legal: 7/77–12/77," NCAA Headquarters.

25. Charles M. Neinas, memorandum to CFA TV Study Committee, 30 April 1980, President Banowsky Papers, Box 74, Folder 13, University of Oklahoma Archives.

26. NCAA Television Committee minutes, 18–20 July 1980, Walter Byers Papers, Box "TV Negotiations 1980," Folder "TV Negotiations 1980," NCAA Headquarters.

27. Chuck Neinas, memorandum to CFA institutions, 21 November 1980, President Banowsky Papers, Box 74, Folder 13, University of Oklahoma Archives.

28. Edgar Kobak, President, Georgia Tech Club of New York, to Col. Blake R. Van Leer,

President, Georgia Tech, 22 May 1951, President Theodore Hesburgh Papers, UVHS, Box 3, Folder "TV, January 1951," University of Notre Dame Archives.

29. Fred C. Davison, memorandum to CFA members, 13 March 1981, President Banowsky Papers, Box 119, Folder 33, University of Oklahoma Archives.

30. Larry Thompson and Philip R. Hochberg, CFA Legal Counsel, memorandum to Charles Neinas, ca. April 1981, President Davison Papers, Box 18, Folder "CFA-6," University of Georgia Archives.

31. "Institutional Control of Institutional Property: An Essential Principle for a Healthy NCAA," CFA Position Paper, ca. May 1981, President Davison Papers, Box 18, Folder "CFA Meeting, Dallas," University of Georgia Archives.

32. NCAA News Release, 11 May 1981, and President James Frank, NCAA, to CEOs of Certain Members of the NCAA, 18 April 1981, Walter Byers Papers, Box "TV, Football, 1980," Folder "TV, Football 1/81–6/81," NCAA Headquarters.

33. President James Frank, NCAA, to NCAA CEOs, 23 June 1981, President Banowsky Papers, Box 119, Folder 33, University of Oklahoma Archives.

34. "National Collegiate Basketball Championships Agreement," Draft 2, Walter Byers Papers, Box "TV Contracts, 1981–82," Folder "TV Contracts, 1981–82," NCAA Headquarters.

35. Walter Byers described the power struggle and animosity in "The Pursuit of Power and Money," in his *Unsportsmanlike Conduct,* 253–72.

36. College Football Association minutes, 7 June 1981.

37. Byers, *Unsportsmanlike Conduct,* 264.

38. See, for instance Carl C. James, Big 8 Commissioner, memorandum to Big 8 members, 13 August 1981, President Banowsky Papers, Box 119, Folder 33, University of Oklahoma Archives; and Walter Byers's notes attached to "Memorandum," ca. fall 1981, Walter Byers Papers, Box "TV Negotiations '1980,'" Folder "TV Negotiations '1980,'" NCAA Headquarters.

39. Daniel G. Gibbens, Oklahoma Faculty Representative, memorandum to President William S. Banowsky, University of Oklahoma, 10 September 1981, President Banowsky Papers, Box 119, Folder 33, University of Oklahoma Archives.

40. Special Meeting of the Chief Executive Officers, Faculty Representatives, and Athletic Directors of the Big 8 Conference minutes, 2 September 1981, Central Administration, President's Office, Series 1, Box 171, Folder 1, "Big 8 Conference 1981–82," University of Colorado Archives; and C. James, Commissioner, Big 8, to Walter Byers, 3 September 1981, Walter Byers Papers, Box "TV Communications," Folder "TV, Football, 1982," NCAA Headquarters.

41. Quoted in John Underwood, "To-Do Over What to Do," *Sports Illustrated,* 21 September 1981, 38.

42. Francis W. Bonner to President James Frank, NCAA, 10 September 1981," Walter Byers Papers, Box "Special Convention," Folder "Special Convention, 1981," NCAA Headquarters.

43. See James Frank and John Toner, NCAA officers, memorandum to CEOs, Faculty Athletic Representatives, ADs, and Primary Women Athletic Administrators of NCAA member institutions, 18 September 1981, and Fred Davison, President, University of Georgia, to President James Frank, NCAA, 23 September 1981, Walter Byers Papers, Box "Special Convention," Folder "Special Convention, 1981," NCAA Headquarters.

44. William S. Banowsky to President James Frank, NCAA, 22 September 1981, President Banowsky Papers, Box 119, Folder 33, University of Oklahoma Archives.

45. "Official Notice and Program of the 4th Special Convention of the NCAA," St. Louis, Missouri, 3–4 December 1981, NCAA Headquarters.

46. NCAA Special Convention *Proceedings* (3–4 December 1981), A-5-7.

22   Oklahoma and Georgia Carry the TV Ball for the CFA Team

1. R. Gerald Turner, Executive Assistant to Oklahoma President, note to President Banowsky, Oklahoma, ca. 10 July 1981, President Banowsky Papers, Box 92, Folder 13, University of Oklahoma Archives. The concern was raised by Oklahoma's faculty representative to the NCAA, Daniel Gibbens, a lawyer and member of the CFA television negotiating team. Others on the committee included Carl James, commissioner of the Big 8 Conference, W. H. McLellan, athletic director of Clemson University, Joseph Paterno, athletic director and head football coach at Penn State University, and Charles Neinas, executive director of the CFA.

2. Ned Joyce to Chuck Neinas, 15 August 1981, President Davison Papers, Box 18, Folder "CFA," University of Georgia Archives.

3. Stanley M. Ward, Chief Legal Counsel, University of Oklahoma, to College Football Association, Boulder, Colo., 21 October 1981, President Banowsky Papers, Box 92, Folder 13, University of Oklahoma Archives.

4. Andy Coats, CFA Counsel, to Charles M. Neinas, Fred C. Davison, CFA President of the Board, and Stan Ward, Chief Legal Counsel, University of Oklahoma, 24 December 1981, Ralph Beaird Papers, Box "U. of OK and GA v. NCAA," University of Georgia Archives.

5. See Wilford Bailey, Faculty Representative, Auburn University, and Secretary, SEC, to William S. Banowsky, Oklahoma, 6 December 1981, President Banowsky Papers, Box 92, Folder 13, University of Oklahoma Archives; and "Board of Regents v. NCAA, Deposition of William S. Banowsky, U.S. District Court for the Western District of Oklahoma, 21 December 1981," President Banowsky Papers, Box 156, Folder 9, University of Oklahoma Archives.

6. Chuck Neinas of the CFA told Banowsky: "Without your courage, and that of Fred Davison, it is unlikely that the NCAA would have been challenged in the Courts and the major universities would continue to be dominated by the NCAA hierarchy." Neinas to Banowsky, 28 October 1982, President Banowsky Papers, Box 1, Folder 26, University of Oklahoma Archives.

7. Neinas to Andy Coats, University of Oklahoma, 23 April 1982, President Banowsky Papers, Box 156, Folder 8, University of Oklahoma Archives.

8. Neinas to Coats, 28 April 1982, ibid.

9. For a discussion of legal fees, see Charles Neinas to President Fred Davison, Georgia, and Daniel Gibbens, Oklahoma, 20 August 1982, President Banowsky Papers, Box 119, Folder 26, University of Oklahoma Archives.

10. See "College Football Association Financial Statement and Accountants' Report," 30 June 1982, President Banowsky Papers, Box 119, Folder 26, University of Oklahoma Archives.

11. Neinas to Davison and Gibbens, 4 May 1982, President Davison Papers, Box 18, Folder "CFA," University of Georgia Archives.

12. "June Trial Date Probable in Football Television Litigation," *NCAA News* clipping, 15 March 1982, President Banowsky Papers, Box 156, Folder 8, University of Oklahoma Archives. The issue of property rights in sports broadcasting had first been addressed in 1938 by the courts in *Pittsburgh Athletic Company v. KQV Broadcasting Company,* No. 3415, 24 F. Supp. 490 (W.D. PA 1938). The Pittsburgh Pirates play-by-play rights were sold exclusively to General Mills to be broadcast by NBC over stations KDKA and WWSW. General Mills believed it was losing advertising revenue because a Pittsburgh station, KQV, had broadcasters at Forbes Field without permission and carried the game to its listeners. The court decided that the property right of broadcasting belonged to the club solely. The case permanently changed the nature of property rights in the sport setting. See Michele Murphy, "Sports Broad-

casting: Who Owns the Property Rights?" in Charles E. Quirk, ed., *Sports and the Law: Major Legal Cases* (New York: Garland, 1996), 215–31.

13. "Declaration of Judgement and Permanent Injunction," *University of Oklahoma and University of Georgia v. NCAA,* 14 September 1982, President Davison Papers, Box 18, Folder "College Football Association," University of Georgia Archives; "The Sherman Antitrust Act, July 2, 1890," in Richard B. Morris, *Basic Documents in American History* (Princeton, N.J.: D. Van Nostrand, 1956), 135; and *Board of Regents of the University of Oklahoma v. NCAA,* 546 F. Supp. 1276 (W.D. Okla. 1982). A month earlier, the University of Texas's case against the NCAA had been dismissed by the Texas State Court, preventing Texas from telecasting its own games. See "Court Rejects Challenge to NCAA's Sway Over TV," *Chronicle of Higher Education,* 1 September 1982.

14. See this argument in Carl L. Reisner, "Tackling Intercollegiate Athletics: An Antitrust Analysis," *Yale Law Journal* 88 (January 1978): 658.

15. Ironically, the NCAA was negotiating for Sunday and Monday-night football telecasts for the duration of the NFL football strike of 1982. This, at the same time it was claiming protection of gate receipts and the need to limit telecasts. See "News Release," 24 September 1982, Walter Byers Papers, Box "TV, Football, 1986," Folder "TV, Football, 7/82–12/82," NCAA Headquarters, Indianapolis, Ind.

16. "University of Oklahoma v. NCAA: Notice of Appeal, 17 September 1982," President Banowsky Papers, Box 156, Folder 8, University of Oklahoma Archives.

17. United States Court of Appeals 10th Circuit No. 8202148, filed 12 May 1983, President Banowsky Papers, Box 156, Folder 7, University of Oklahoma Archives.

18. Ibid.

19. Justice White, 10th Circuit Justice, "NCAA v. University of Oklahoma on Application for Stay," No. A-24, received 21 July 1983, Officer of the Clerk Supreme Court, U.S., President Davison Papers, Box 38, Folder "NCAA," University of Georgia Archives.

20. The American Council on Education had taken stances on athletics three decades earlier, when it supported a "Presidents' Report" in 1952 after the athletic scandals of 1951, and again in 1974, when it sponsored the Study of Intercollegiate Athletics under George Hanford. See John R. Thelin, *Games Colleges Play: Scandals and Reform in Intercollegiate Athletics* (Baltimore: Johns Hopkins University Press, 1994).

21. Sheldon Elliot Steinbach, ACE General Counsel, to ACE Executive Committee, 25 August 1983, Ralph Beaird Papers, Box "U. of OK & U. of GA v. NCAA," University of Georgia Archives.

22. "Brief of the American Council on Education, as Amicus Curiae, in Support of the Petition for Certiorari," October 1983, President Banowsky Papers, Box 156, Folder 7, University of Oklahoma Archives.

23. Neinas to Philip Hochberg, CFA Counsel, 9 December 1983, President Davison Papers, Box 18, Folder "CFA-4," University of Georgia Archives; James Ponsoldt to Philip Hochberg, 12 December 1983, Ralph Beaird Papers, Box 30/67, "B," University of Georgia Archives; and Philip Hochberg Interest of Amicus Curiae Draft for CFA, 23 December 1983, Ralph Beaird Papers, Box 30/67, "A," University of Georgia Archives.

24. Proposed "Interest of Amicus Curiae," ca. October 1983, President Davison Papers, Box 18, Folder "CFA," University of Georgia Archives. In December 1983, Neinas wrote to CFA counsel Philip Hochberg that "the television issue should be considered under a Rule of Reason analysis and not as a per se violation." Neinas to Hochberg, 9 December 1983, President Davison Papers, Box 18, Folder "CFA-4," University of Georgia Archives.

25. The "Interest of Amicus Curiae on Behalf of the CFA" Hochberg submitted on 3 January 1984 stated: "Price fixing and other restrictive practices become even more anticompetitive . . . and mandate a per se analysis of the NCAA's behavior." See Ralph Beaird Papers, Box 30/67, "B," University of Georgia Archives.

26. Ibid.

27. Banowsky to Honorable Don Nickles, 3 December 1982, President Banowsky Papers, Box 156, Folder 8, University of Oklahoma Archives.

28. NCAA *Proceedings* (1983), 192, A87–88, NCAA Headquarters; and Neinas to Davison and Gibbens, 31 January 1983, President Davison Papers, Box 18, Folder "CFA," University of Georgia Archives. The resolution was presented by PAC-10 commissioner Wiles Hallock.

29. Robert Atwell, ACE Executive Vice President, to ACE Committee on Division I Intercollegiate Athletics, 10 March 1983, J. W. Peltason, ACE, to Byers, 19 April 1983, and Byers to John L. Toner, University of Connecticut, Athletic Director, 13 May 1983, Walter Byers Papers, Box "Special Convention," Folder "Select Committee on Athletic Concerns in Education," NCAA Headquarters.

30. Sheldon Elliot Steinbach, ACE General Counsel, to ACE Executive Committee, 25 August 1983, Ralph Beaird Papers, Box "U. of OK & U. of GA v. NCAA," University of Georgia Archives.

31. Clyde Muchmore, CFA Counsel, to Dean Ralph Beaird, University of Georgia School of Law, 31 August 1983, Ralph Beaird Papers, Box 30/67, "B," University of Georgia Archives.

32. Senator Strom Thurmond assured Oklahoma and the CFA that if an antitrust exemption was awarded to the NCAA it would apply to conferences as well. Thurmond said that the Judiciary Committee would not meet on college football telecasting until after a Supreme Court ruling. See Neinas to Andy Coats, Oklahoma Counsel, President Banowsky Papers, Box 156, Folder 7, University of Oklahoma Archives.

33. For a shortened version of the majority and dissenting opinions, see Paul C. Weiler and Gary R. Roberts, *Sports and the Law: Text, Cases, Problems* (St. Paul, Minn.: West Group, 1998), 750–63. The well-known lawyers conclude that the Board of Regents case is "among the most important . . . the most complex and confounding in all of the law of sports." They, too, see the conflict between "academic and amateur values and commercial market values" (763).

34. *Board of Regents v. NCAA*, 104 Sup. Ct. 1984 (1984). For another analysis of the Supreme Court decision, see Eric A. Seiken, "The NCAA and the Courts: College Football on Television," in Quirk, ed., *Sports and the Law*, 56–62.

35. Seiken, "The NCAA and the Courts," 56–62.

36. Ibid.

37. Philip Hochberg, the prevailing counsel, congratulated himself for his legal handling of the "nonsubstantive aspects of the case almost as well as Andy [Coats] and Clyde [Muchmore] handled the substantive aspects." Hochberg believed that retaining Dean Griswold, the former Harvard Law School dean "working with the Justice Department for well over a year, bringing in the Association of Independent Television Stations, and, finally, squelching the proposed ACE brief" gave impetus to their case and led to victory. Philip R. Hochberg to President Fred C. Davison, University of Georgia, 16 July 1984, Ralph Beaird Papers, Box "U. of OK & GA v. NCAA," University of Georgia Archives. Griswold was paid $225 per hour for his services.

38. Quoted in House Subcommittee on Oversights and Investigations of the Committee on Energy and Commerce, *Televised College Football,* Hearing, 98th Cong., 2d sess., July 31, 1984.

23   TV, Home Rule Anarchy, and Conference Realignments

1. Andy M. Coats, Clyde A. Muchmore, and Harvey D. Ellis, legal counsel, Oklahoma City, memorandum in John D. Swofford, NCAA Television Committee chair, memorandum to NCAA Executive Officers of Division I-A, 28 June 1984, Ralph Beaird Papers, Box "U. of OK & GA v. NCAA," University of Georgia Archives.
2. Board of Regents, "University of Oklahoma v. NCAA 'Plaintiffs' Response to NCAA's Motion to Modify Judgment," 9 July 1984, filed in the U. S. District Court for the Western District of Oklahoma, Ralph Beaird Papers, Box "U. of OK & GA v. NCAA," University of Georgia Archives; "Recommended NCAA Football Television Plan for 1984," Ralph Beaird Papers, Box 20/67, "B," University of Georgia Archives.
3. House Subcommittee on Oversights and Investigations of the Committee on Energy and Commerce, *Televised College Football,* Hearing, 98th Cong., 2d sess., 31 July 1984.
4. Affidavit of David E. Cawood, NCAA, Assistant Executive Director, in *Board of Regents of the University of Oklahoma, et al., v. NCAA,* 10 August 1984. Chuck Neinas of the CFA claimed that USC of the PAC-10 and Michigan State of the Big 10 had voted against the NCAA TV proposal. See Charles M. Neinas, CFA Executive Director, to Andy Coats, CFA Counsel, 22 August 1984, Ralph Beaird Papers, Box "U. of OK & GA v. NCAA," University of Georgia Archives. Apparently the University of Pittsburgh was the sole CFA member to vote for the NCAA plan. See *New York Times,* 11 July 1984, B5.
5. "Taking Away the N.C.A.A.'s Ball," *Time,* 9 July 1984, 77.
6. *Football News,* 4 September 1984, 28.
7. Senate Committee on the Judiciary of the U. S. Senate, *The Supreme Court Decision in NCAA v. University of Oklahoma,* 98th Cong., 2d sess., 19 November 1984.
8. *Football News,* 4 September 1984, 28.
9. One study showed that in 1983, the year before the antitrust breakup of the NCAA contract, there were a total of eighty-nine televised games with revenues of $69 million. A year later, after the breakup, there were 195 televised games producing $45 million, including income from regional and local syndication. See Matthew C. McKinnon et al., *Sports Law* (Lancing, Mich.: Lupus Publications, 1996), chap. 3, 29.
10. Quoted in the *New York Times,* 26 August 1984, 5:9. Litvack was also executive director of the Ivy League.
11. *New York Times,* 17 July 1984, B10. The Ivy League is often portrayed as having high athletic standards within an educational model. Its history tells a different story. More so than any other group of colleges, Ivy League institutions, led by Harvard, Yale, and Princeton, were the first to participate in highly commercialized and professionalized athletics. In the twentieth century, the rest of America's big-time institutions essentially cloned what the Ivy institutions had created in the nineteenth century. See Ronald A. Smith, *Sports and Freedom: The Rise of Big-Time Intercollegiate Athletics* (New York: Oxford University Press, 1988).
12. Senate Committee on the Judiciary, *The Supreme Court Decision in 'NCAA v. University of Oklahoma,'* Hearing, 98th cong., 2d sess., 19 November 1984; and House Subcommittee on Oversights and Investigations of the Committee on Energy and Commerce, *Televised College Football,* Hearing, 98th Cong., 2d sess., 31 July 1984.
13. House Subcommittee, *Televised College Football,* 31 July 1984, 68.
14. Senate Committee, *The Supreme Court Decision,* 19 November 1984, 4.
15. Roger E. Meiners, *Regulations and the Reagan Era: Politics, Bureaucracy and the Public Interest* (New York: Holmes & Meier, 1989), 6.
16. House Subcommittee, *Televised College Football,* 31 July 1984.

17. Senate Committee, *The Supreme Court Decision,* 19 November 1984. Judge Burciaga had cleared the NCAA to sell TV rights on 29 October 1984, but the NCAA by then showed little interest in pursuing the option.

18. Testimony of Robert J. Wussler, TBS, House Subcommittee, *Televised College Football,* 31 July 1984; Charles M. Neinas, to Andy Coats, CFA Counsel, 22 August 1984, Ralph Beaird Papers, Box "U of OK & GA v. NCAA," University of Georgia Archives; and *New York Times,* 11 September 1984, B13.

19. Senate Committee, *The Supreme Court Decision,* 19 November 1984; and Robert C. Berry and Glenn M. Wong, *Law and Business of Sports Industries* (Westport, Conn.: Praeger, 1993), 2:761.

20. Charles E. Young, Chancellor, UCLA, mailgram to William Banowsky, President, University of Oklahoma, and fourteen other Division I presidents, 6 November 1984, President Banowsky Papers, Box 156, Folder 5, University of Oklahoma Archives. Other presidents invited included Otis Singletary of Kentucky, Bryce Jordan of Penn State, Martin Massengale of Nebraska, Don Shields of Southern Methodist, Ed Jennings of Ohio State, Bill Gerberding of Washington, Michael Heyman of California, Wes Postvar of Pittsburgh, Tad Foote of Miami, Jim Friedman of Iowa, John Ryan of Indiana, Chris Fordham of North Carolina, Chapel Hill, Bill Banowsky of Oklahoma, Peter Magrath of Minnesota, and Theodore Hesburgh of Notre Dame.

21. Neinas to Fred Davison, President, University of Georgia, and Dan Gibbens, University of Oklahoma, 27 February 1985, President Davison Papers, Box 18, Folder "CFA," University of Georgia Archives.

22. Walter Byers, NCAA Executive Director, to Donald B. Canham, Michigan Athletic Director, 30 October 1985, Walter Byers Papers, Box "TV: Football, 1986," Folder "TV, Football, 1985," NCAA Headquarters, Indianapolis, Ind.

23. House Communications Subcommittee Regarding Sports Event Telecasting, Hearing, 3 November 1977, as quoted in Ritchie T. Thomas, NCAA legal counsel, to Thomas C. Hansen, NCAA Assistant Executive Director, 8 November 1977, Walter Byers Papers, vol. 152, Folder "TV Football, 7/77–12/77," NCAA Headquarters.

24. Ned Joyce to Chuck Neinas, 15 August 1981, President Davison Papers, Box 18, Folder "CFA," University of Georgia Archives.

25. William F. Reid, "We're Notre Dame and You're Not," *Sports Illustrated,* 19 February 1990, 56–60.

26. Notre Dame's withdrawal meant a reduction of about $35 million in the CFA's five-year television contracts with ABC and ESPN. *New York Times,* 9 February 1990, D5.

27. Soon after the 1984 Supreme Court decision, the *Daily Oklahoman Times,* 12 July 1984, 22, suggested that the Big 10 and PAC-10 could make more money staying out of a CFA TV contract, and in the future the Big 10 might wish to enlist Penn State to get into the Eastern TV market.

28. *New York Times,* 16 December 1989, A47; and Austin Murphy, "Out of Their League?" *Sports Illustrated,* 7 May 1990, 46–49. There was such an uproar among Big 10 athletic officials against Penn State joining the conference that the presidents postponed "official" action. On June 4, 1990, the presidents voted 7-3 to admit Penn State. Since a two-thirds vote was needed, a change of one president's vote would have defeated Penn State's entry.

29. Quoted in *NCAA News,* 15 June 1994, 4.

24   Basketball

1. Jerry Jaye Wright, "Irish, Edward Simmons 'Ned,'" in David L. Porter, ed., *Biographical Dictionary of American Sports: Basketball and Other Indoor Sports* (Westport, Conn.: Greenwood Press, 1989), 140–42; Charles Rosen, *Scandals of '51* (New

York: Holt, Rinehart, & Winston, 1978), 20–21; and John D. McCallum, *College Basketball, U.S.A. since 1892* (New York: Stein and Day, 1978), 54–55.

2. Luisetti did not invent the running one-hander or the jump shot. They were developments of long standing. See John Christgau, *The Origins of the Jump Shot: Eight Men Who Shook the World of Basketball* (Lincoln: University of Nebraska Press, 1999), 13–15.

3. Jay Langhammer, "Luisetti, Angelo Joseph 'Hank'" in Porter, ed., *Biographical Dictionary of American Sports,* 187–88; Larry Fox, *Illustrated History of Basketball* (New York: Grosset & Dunlap, 1974), 61–67; Robert W. Peterson, *Cages to Jump Shots: Pro Basketball's Early Years* (New York: Oxford University Press, 1990), 108–10; and Neil D. Isaacs, *All the Moves: A History of College Basketball* (Philadelphia: J. B. Lippincott, 1975), 111–15.

4. Fox, *Illustrated History of Basketball,* 68–69.

5. Quoted in Jack Falla, *NCAA: The Voice of College Sports* (Mission, Kans.: National Collegiate Athletic Association, 1981), 186.

6. NCAA *Proceedings* (1939), 117, NCAA Headquarters, Indianapolis, Ind.

7. Herndon Thomson, Tulane School of Architecture, to President Rufus C. Harris, Tulane, 2 December 1951, President Rufus C. Harris Papers, Box 1, Folder "Athletics-New Policy," Tulane University Archives.

8. Walter Camp, "Undergraduate Limitation in College Sports," *Harper's Weekly,* 11 February 1893, 143.

9. See comments in Charley Rosen, *Barney Polan's Game: A Novel of the 1951 College Basketball Scandal* (New York: Seven Stories Press, 1998), 41; and Asa Bushnell, Eastern College Athletic Conference Executive Director, memorandum to ECAC Member Colleges, 30 July 1951, ECAC minutes, ECAC Headquarters, Centreville, Mass.

10. Bushnell, memorandum to ECAC member institutions, 30 July 1951, ECAC minutes, ECAC Headquarters; and Rosen, *Scandals of '51,* 42–43.

11. Quoted in ECAC minutes, 21 June 1961, ECAC Headquarters.

12. "Pacific Coast Conference Report of Acting Commissioner," June 1945, President Wilbur Papers, Box 135, Folder "Pacific Coast Athletic Conference," Stanford University Archives.

13. J. L. Morrill, "Address at NCAA," 7 January 1947, Box 5 Supplement, Folder "J. L. Morrill-President," Department of Intercollegiate Athletic Papers, University of Minnesota Archives; and Chicago *Daily News,* 7 January 1947, 1.

14. ECAC minutes, 11 December 1948, ECAC Headquarters.

15. Rosen, *Scandals of '51,* 215.

16. Russell Rice, *The Wildcat Legacy* (Virginia Beach, Va.: JCP Corp. of Virginia, 1982), 85; and Russell Rice, *Kentucky Basketball's Big Blue Machine* (Huntsville, Ala.: Strode Publishers, 1976), 217.

17. Rice, *Kentucky Basketball's Big Blue Machine,* 111, 227.

18. Ibid., 85

19. The number of teams entering the NCAA basketball championship are as follows: 8 in 1939–51; 16 in 1952; 22–25 in 1953–74; 40 in 1979; 48 in 1980–82; 52 in 1983; 53 in 1984; 64 in 1985–present.

20. NCAA *Proceedings* (1954), 313, NCAA Headquarters. The basketball tourney netted $130,000, while dues brought in less than $35,000 in 1952.

21. Quoted in Rice, *Kentucky Basketball's Big Blue Machine,* 247–48.

22. NCAA *Proceedings* (1964), 180, NCAA Headquarters; and Gwilym S. Brown, "The Maitre D' of Sports TV," *Sports Illustrated,* 8 November 1965, 54.

23. William Hyland, SNI, to Walter Byers, 27 May 1968, Walter Byers Papers, vol. 47, Folder "TV: General 5/68–8/68, NCAA Headquarters.

24. Gene Duffy, NCAA, memorandum to Walter Byers, 13 December 1966, Walter Byers Papers, vol. 48, Folder "TV: General 1965–66," NCAA Headquarters. In 1966, the receipts were $180,000 from basketball and $21,500,000 from football.

25. A writer for the *Los Angeles Times,* 13 March 1997, C1, described Rupp as a "White Supremist" when comparing him to Kentucky's black coach, "Tubby" Smith, who led his Kentucky team to the Final Four in 1997.

26. Richard O. Davies, *America's Obsession: Sports and Society since 1945* (Fort Worth, Tex.: Harcourt Brace, 1994), 47–49.

27. Alexander Wolff, "The Bear in Winter," *Sports Illustrated,* 1 March 1999, 58, 64.

28. Joe Gergen, *The Final Four: An Illustrated History of College Basketball's Showcase Event* (St. Louis: The Sporting News, 1987), 137–41.

29. Rice, *Kentucky Basketball's Big Blue Machine,* 346.

30. William Leggett, "NBC and the New College Try," *Sports Illustrated,* 2 July 1975, 52.

31. Forest Evashevski to Walter Byers, 5 September 1971, Walter Byers Papers, vol. 150, Folder "TV: Football, 10/71–12/71," NCAA Headquarters.

32. Byers to Evashevski, 3 November 1971, ibid.

33. NCAA Television Committee minutes, 7 February 1974, Walter Byers Papers, vol. 153, Folder "TV: Negotiations Committee, 1979," NCAA Headquarters.

34. Ibid.

35. Appendix AA to the 1974 NCAA Television Committee minutes, 30 April 1974, Walter Byers Papers, vol. 153, Folder "TV: Negotiations Committee, 1979," NCAA Headquarters.

36. "Report on Basketball Television Questionnaire," 30 April 1974, Walter Byers Papers, Box "TV Committee 1972," Folder "TV Committee 1974," NCAA Headquarters.

37. Big 10 Directors of Athletics minutes, 1–3 December 1975, President Enarson Papers, 3/j/27/9, Folder "NCAA Minutes and Reports: 1975–76," Ohio State University Archives.

38. George Gangwere, NCAA Counsel to Walter Byers, 3 January 1979, Walter Byers Papers, vol. 153, Folder "TV: Negotiations Committee, 1979," NCAA Headquarters; and John C. Weistart and Cym H. Lowell, *The Law of Sports* (Indianapolis: Bobbs-Merrill, 1979), 765.

39. NCAA Negotiations Committee for Television Rights of the Division I Basketball Tournament minutes, 6 January 1979, NCAA Headquarters.

40. "Financial Analysis of National Collegiate Division I Men's Basketball Championship," Walter Byers Papers, Box "TV Negotiations, 1983," Folder "TV, Other Sports 1982–1985"; and "1980–1987 Basketball Television Contracts," Walter Byers Papers, Box "TV Committee," Folder "TV Committee, General, 1982–87," NCAA Headquarters; and William Leggett, "NBC and the New College Try," *Sports Illustrated,* 2 June 1975, 52.

41. NCAA Television Committee minutes, 11–12 October 1967, NCAA Headquarters.

42. Gene Duffy, memorandum to Walter Byers, 13 December 1966, Walter Byers Papers, vol. 48, Folder "TV: General 1965–66," NCAA Headquarters.

43. Carl Lindemann, Jr., NBC, to NCAA Basketball Television Committee, 9 April 1968, Walter Byers Papers, vol. 48, Folder "TV: Basketball Championship," NCAA Headquarters.

44. "Report of the Regents Committee on Physical Education, 29 March 1916," Chancellors of the University, Misc. Files, B Series, Series 4/0/1, Box 1, University of Wisconsin-Madison Archives; and Board of Regents minutes, 4 August 1933, University of Wisconsin-Madison Archives.

45. "Athletic Equipment Purchases, 1925–26 through December 23, 1935," memorandum in Folder "Athletic Situation," and Walter E. Meanwell to Harold M. Wilkie, President, Board of Regents, 13 January 1936, Folder "Statements from Dr. Mean-

well," Series 4/14/1, Box 2, George Sellery Papers, University of Wisconsin-Madison Archives.

46. "Big 7 Intercollegiate Athletic Departments Salaries of Key Positions, 1954–55," President's Office, Series 1, Box 29, Folder "Athletics 1954–59," University of Colorado at Boulder Archives.

47. *Atlanta Constitution,* 2 March 1997, E1.

48. *Chronicle of Higher Education,* 16 June 1993, A35.

49. *New York Times,* 1 April 1997, B11.

50. "Report to the NCAA Special Committee to Study Division I-A Football Championship," 9 May 1994, A7–A8, NCAA Headquarters.

25   TV's Unfinished Business

1. As an example, the University of Nebraska went to six consecutive bowl games from 1986 to 1991 (three Fiesta Bowls and one Citrus, Sugar, and Orange Bowl). Trip expenses exceeded income in three of the six, so the average bowl profit was about $1,000 per year. "An Analysis of the Operations for the Six Years Ended June 30, 1991," Chancellors' Central Files, Box 299, Folder 23, University of Nebraska Archives.

2. For instance, in the period 1975–84 only 5 percent of the January 1 bowl games had Nielsen ratings below 10; from 1985–1994, 48 percent had ratings below 10. The highest rating scored by a January 1 bowl game in the period from 1975–79 was 28.3; in the 1990–94 period it was 16.9. The Rose Bowl rating dropped from 28.6 in 1980 to 11.3 in 1994. See "Report to the NCAA Special Committee to Study a Division I-A Football Championship," 6 May 1994, A5, B14, 16, 160, and chart 7.1+, NCAA Headquarters, Indianapolis, Ind.

3. For an insightful account of bowl game illogic, see Michael MacCambridge, "End the Tug of War," *Inside Sports* 20 (January 1998), 66–74.

4. Ohio State faculty representative Edwin Crawford advised in 1978 that "southern schools don't want [a championship playoff] because there are so many Bowls located in the South that a playoff series would prevent a number of southern schools from going to a Bowl and gaining the TV and Bowl money they now are accustomed to receiving." Crawford, memorandum to President Harold L. Enarson, Ohio State University, 3 August 1978, President Enarson Papers, 3/j/16/18, Folder "Council of Ten: Minutes and Reports: 1977–80," Ohio State University Archives.

5. Ronald A. Smith, ed., *Big-Time Football at Harvard, 1905: The Diary of Coach Bill Reid* (Urbana: University of Illinois Press, 1994), xv.

6. Walter Byers, *Unsportsmanlike Conduct: Exploiting College Athletes* (Ann Arbor: University of Michigan Press, 1995), 138.

7. NCAA Television Committee minutes, 9–10 January 1966, NCAA Headquarters.

8. Ibid., 31 January–1 February 1967.

9. Ibid., 29–30 June 1967.

10. Ibid., 4–5 April 1967.

11. Thomas Hamilton, Athletic Association of Western Universities Conference, to Roone Arledge, ABC, 19 October 1967, Walter Byers Papers, vol. 47, Folder "TV: General 10/67–12/67," NCAA Headquarters.

12. Jesse M. Brill to Walter Byers, 23 March 1971, Walter Byers Papers, vol. 150, Folder "TV: Football 7/71–9/71," NCAA Headquarters.

13. Byers to Brill, 15 July 1971, and Byers to Asa S. Bushnell, NCAA TV consultant, 14 September 1971, Walter Byers Papers, vol. 150, Folder "TV: Football 7/71–9/71," NCAA Headquarters.

14. NCAA Television Committee minutes, 1–2 March 1971, NCAA Headquarters; J. O. Coppedge, NCAA Television Committee, to CEOs of the Southern Conference, 13

April 1978, Walter Byers Papers, Box "TV Committee, 1978," Folder "TV Committee 1978," NCAA Headquarters; and Chester R. Simmons, NBC, to Walter Byers, 27 April 1979, Walter Byers Papers, Box 152, Folder "TV: Football, 1/79–7/79," NCAA Headquarters.

15. College Football Association minutes, 2–3 June 1979.

16. "Report to the NCAA Special Committee to Study a Division I-A Football Championship," 6 May 1994, NCAA Headquarters, B33.

17. "Oklahoma v. NCAA Memorandum Opinion of Judge Burciaga," 29 October 1984, President Davison Papers, Box 18, Folder "CFA," University of Georgia Archives.

18. Charles M. Neinas to CFA Television Committee, 5 December 1984, Chancellors' Central Files, Box 218, Folder "Athletics 1984–85," University of Nebraska Archives.

19. Bob Devaney to Martin Massengale, Chancellor, University of Nebraska, 14 December 1984, ibid.

20. *New York Times,* 6 January 1987, B11.

21. Gordon S. White, Jr., "NCAA Opposes Playoff," *New York Times,* 9 January 1987, A23.

22. "NCAA Panel Wants Playoff," *New York Times,* 3 March 1987, A25; and "Presidents Veto Playoffs," *New York Times,* 1 October 1987, B12.

23. "NCAA Rejects 1-A Football Playoffs," *New York Times,* 13 January 1988, B11; and "Report to the NCAA Special Committee to Study a Division I-A Football Championship," 6 May 1994, B4, NCAA Headquarters.

24. *USA Today,* 31 December 1991, A8. The participating conferences were the ACC, Big East, Big 8, PAC-10, SEC, and SWC.

25. Keith Dunnavant, "One Game Closer to a College Superbowl?" *Business Week,* 28 September 1992, 130.

26. *USA Today,* 4 December 1991, C3.

27. "Report to the NCAA Special Committee to Study a Division I-A Football Championship," 9 May 1994, B4–B5, NCAA Headquarters; Bill Byrne, Nebraska Athletic Director, to Chancellor Graham Spanier, Nebraska, 15 December 1993, Chancellors' Central Files, Box 299, Folder 27, University of Nebraska Archives; and *Los Angeles Times,* 19 November 1993, C1.

28. "Report to the NCAA Special Committee to Study a Division I-A Football Championship, 6 May 1994, A4–A6, B206, table 7.1, and C10; and *USA Today,* 12 May 1994, C1.

29. The USF&G paid more than $10 million over five years to have its name attached to the Sugar Bowl. See Richard W. Stevenson, "Renaming Bowl Games," *New York Times,* 31 December 1986, D9.

30. "Report to the NCAA Special Committee to Study a Division I-A Football Championship," 6 May 1994, B112.

31. Ibid., B53.

32. Ibid., B107.

33. In the summer of 1995, I presented a report to the NCAA titled "NCAA Division I-A Football Playoff: A Timeline." This eleven-page report concluded with a proposed eight-team playoff based upon regional conference representation. That eight-team proposal differs only slightly from the one below.

34. "Report to the NCAA Special Committee to Study a Division I-A Football Championship," 6 May 1994, B33.

35. See Parke H. Davis, *Football the American Intercollegiate Game* (New York: Charles Scribner's Sons, 1911), 69–70; L. H. Baker, *Football: Facts and Figures* (New York: Farrar & Rinehart, 1945), 538; and Ronald A. Smith, *Sports and Freedom: The Rise of Big-Time College Athletics* (New York: Oxford University Press, 1988), 77–78.

36. Quoted by Howard Bloom, *Sports Business News,* 6 January 2000.

Bibliographical Essay

Archives

The most important material used in the writing of this volume was garnered from about fifty archives searched across the nation. University archives often have huge collections of sport material, and I have used them extensively. Generally I begin my searches with the institution's presidential papers. Nearly every significant action or problem in intercollegiate athletics is reflected in presidential correspondence. Those who believe that reforms led by college presidents are needed to combat the intense commercialization and increased professionalism in American intercollegiate "amateur" sport will do well to consider how presidents have behaved in the past. Materials found in presidential papers lead one to question presidential leadership of intercollegiate athletics. In the papers I perused of several hundred presidents, I found they were well informed about intercollegiate athletics issues. When problems existed, a number of presidents did nothing, some launched cover-ups to protect the institutions or themselves, and a minority took the honorable stance and acted with integrity. Likewise, no archival information suggests that problems associated with cashing in on broadcasting and other commercial activities can easily be reformed, if that is even desired. My conclusions have been reinforced by my probes into governing board actions, faculty athletic committee minutes, athletic directors' papers, athletic association records, coaches' documents, conference commissioners' correspondence and reports, alumni records, and student diaries and reminiscences. My experience in searching primary sources shows that conducting ethical intercollegiate athletics this past century is as difficult as it is with any important human activity.

The institutions whose archives have been significant, sometimes vital, to the writing of this book include: Alabama, Arizona State, Brown, Butler, California, Chicago, Clemson, Colorado, Columbia, Cornell, Dartmouth, Drake, Duke, Georgetown, Georgia, Georgia Tech, Harvard, Illinois, Maryland, Michigan, Minnesota, Nebraska, North Carolina, Northwestern, Notre Dame, Ohio State, Oklahoma, Penn State, Pennsylvania, Princeton, Rutgers, Southern California, Stanford, Tennessee, Tulane, United States Military Academy, West Point, United States Naval Academy, Annapolis, Virginia, William and Mary, Wisconsin, and Yale. Probably the five schools whose archives have been most important to this study for understanding the radio and television influence are the University of Georgia, the University of Michigan, the University of Notre Dame, the University of Oklahoma, and the University of Pennsylvania.

Nonuniversity repositories have been important as well. Most notable are the National Collegiate Athletic Association Archives, which include the Walter Byers Papers and the NCAA Television Committee minutes. A valuable primary source containing verbatim discussions from the first convention in 1906, the NCAA *Proceedings,* is also housed in the NCAA Archives. The Manuscript Division of the Library of Congress holds a number of relevant collections. Among these, the Du Mont Laboratories Collection revealed the background for the Du Mont Television Network and was crucial in forming aspects of this study. Information from several athletic conferences was helpful, including that from the Atlantic Coast Conference Collection and the Eastern College Athletic Conference Archives. Material in the Los Angeles Amateur Athletic Foundation was also useful.

General Works on Sport, Radio, and Television

A group of sport history survey works discuss the media's impact on sport, especially that of radio and television. A number are written by historians. Two volumes by Benjamin G. Rader bring major issues to the front: *From the Age of Folk Games to the Age of Televised Sport,* 4th ed. (Englewood Cliffs, N.J.: Prentice Hall, 1999) and *In Its Own Image: How Television Has Transformed Sport* (New York: Free Press, 1984). In the latter, Rader tries to show that television has negatively transformed sport by reducing its ability to bind communities together, damaging the capacity of sporting activity to create rituals that promote society's traditional values. He includes material on college sports, somewhat thin on primary sources, in his condemnation that TV deluded the "true sports fan into being satisfied with an endless array of crude forms of sensationalism" (116). Joan Chandler, in *Television and National Sport: The United States and Britain* (Urbana: University of Illinois Press, 1988), challenges Rader's belief in the transforming effect of TV by maintaining that televised sports represents cultural continuity, not cultural change. Randy Roberts and James Olson, in *Winning is the Only Thing: Sports in America Since 1945* (Baltimore: Johns Hopkins University Press, 1989), include two chapters devoted to television and sport, one of which is an especially fine look at the influence of Roone Arledge. Well over a quarter of Richard O. Davies's *America's Obsession: Sports and Society Since 1945* (Fort Worth, Tex.: Harcourt Brace, 1994) is given to television and to college sport. Elliott J. Gorn and Warren Goldstein's *A Brief History of American Sports* (New York: Hill and Wang, 1993) is a nicely written history, but the authors confuse the impact of television in colleges during the 1940s and 1950s, treating the subject as if television were creating great wealth for big-time schools as it did a generation later.

Two earlier histories, Foster Rhea Dulles, *A History of Recreation: America Learns to Play* (New York: Appleton-Century-Crofts, 1965) and John R. Betts, *America's Sporting Heritage: 1850–1900* (Reading, Mass.: Addison-Wesley, 1974) show the influence of radio and television on American culture. The "nefarious" impact of television on college sport is noted by Allen Guttmann in *Sport Spectators* (New York: Columbia University Press, 1986). Steven A. Riess's important work, *City Games: The Evolution of American Urban Society and the Rise of Sport* (Urbana: University of Illinois Press, 1989), points out the impact of radio and TV on urban society. An important early work on American sport should not be forgotten: Frederick W. Cozens and Florence S. Stumpf, in *Sports in American Life* (Chicago: University of Chicago Press, 1953), discuss the place of radio and television in the life of American colleges. Scholars should also look at the volume by Ted Vincent, *The Rise and Fall of American Sport: Mudville's Revenge* (Lincoln: University of Nebraska Press, 1994). It is not Vincent's analysis of the role of the electronic media in sport that should be noted but his interesting point of view that "the media hype of 'the biggest' and 'the most spectacular' may not be for the best" (3).

Among the works by journalists and members of the electronic media who provide an inside look at radio and television influences on sport, the following are significant. An early discussion of TV and sport can be found in William O. Johnson's *Super Spectator and the Electric Lilliputians* (New York: Basic Books, 1976). Ron Powers, in *Supertube: The Rise of Television Sports* (New York: Coward-McCann, 1984), provides back-scene drama in television network dealings with NCAA football. David A. Klatell and Marcus Norman, in *Sports for Sale: Television, Money, and the Fans* (New York: Oxford University Press, 1988), demonstrate keen insights into the impact of cable TV on American sport. Terry O'Neil's *The Game Behind the Game: High Stakes, High Pressure in Television Sports* (New York: Harper & Row, 1984) looks at the inside of CBS Sports, including college football and the telecasting of the NCAA basketball tourney. Phil Patton's *Razzle-Dazzle: The Curious Marriage of Television and Professional Football* (Garden City, N.Y.: Dial Press, 1984), while emphasizing professional football, shows the interconnectedness of televised pro football and the college game. Bert Sugar's *The Thrill of Victory: The Inside Story of ABC Sports* (New York: Hawthorn Books, 1978) is particularly good in showing ABC's impact on college sport in the 1960s and 1970s. Jim Spence, in *Up Close and Personal: The Inside Story of Network Television Sports* (New York: Atheneum, 1988), provides an insightful chapter on Walter Byers and the NCAA football TV package. The anthology edited by Lawrence A. Wenner, *Media, Sports, and Society* (Newbury Park, Calif.: Sage Publications, 1989) emphasizes the impact of TV on sport.

Intercollegiate Athletics

There is a growing scholarly body of knowledge about the place of intercollegiate athletics and the influence of the media on their development in American society. Walter Byers's *Unsportsmanlike Conduct: Exploiting College Athletes* (Ann Arbor: University of Michigan Press, 1995) is a must-read. Byers, longtime executive director of the NCAA, offers a lengthy inside discussion of the ABC, CBS, and NBC television contracts and the players who participated in those negotiations, such as Roone Arledge of ABC, Chuck Neinas of the CFA, and Father Ned Joyce of Notre Dame. Jack Falla devotes a chapter of his *NCAA: The Voice of College Sports, A Diamond Anniversary History, 1906–1981* (Mission, Kans.: NCAA, 1981) to "the electronic free ticket." John

M. Carroll's award winning biography, *Red Grange and the Rise of Modern Football* (Urbana: University of Illinois Press, 1999), incorporates Grange's radio and television announcing profession into his more popular life in amateur and professional football. Robin Lester's *Stagg's University: The Rise, Decline, and Fall of Big-Time Football at Chicago* (Urbana: University of Illinois Press, 1995) does not devote much time to radio, but this superior institutional history of intercollegiate athletics places the University of Chicago and intercollegiate athletics in general in the commercial setting that college athletics had secured in the second half of the nineteenth century.

An insider's look at an institution and its athletic policy, including policy on radio and television, is provided by the president of the University of Oklahoma, George L. Cross. His *President's Can't Punt* (Norman: University of Oklahoma Press, 1977) acknowledges the commercial impact of football and the electronic media on his university during the time of coach Bud Wilkinson. There are a number of useful public documents, but transcripts from the *Televised College Football,* Hearings, Subcommittee on Oversights and Investigations of the Committee on Energy and Commerce, House of Representatives, 98th Congress, Second Session, 31 July 1984, is particularly valuable for understanding the deregulation of college football telecasting. A book-length report, "Report to the NCAA Special Committee to Study a Division I-A Football Championship," May 6, 1994, NCAA Archives, offers a well-designed study on the value of a Division I-A championship playoff. My earlier books, *Sports and Freedom: The Rise of Big-Time College Athletics* (New York: Oxford University Press, 1988) and *Big-Time Football at Harvard 1905: The Diary of Coach Bill Reid* (Urbana: University of Illinois Press, 1994) accentuate the commercial emphasis of men's intercollegiate athletics from its early beginnings, before radio and television.

Specific histories of college football are important to understanding the place of the electronic media in the development of intercollegiate athletics. The most complete history of intercollegiate football is John S. Watterson's *College Football: History, Spectacle, Controversy* (Baltimore: Johns Hopkins University Press, 2000). Watterson does a nice job of summarizing the NCAA television controversy of the 1970s and 1980s. Until this was written, the best book on college football was Parke H. Davis's early history, *Football the American Intercollegiate Game* (New York: Charles Scribner's Sons, 1911). David M. Nelson's *The Anatomy of a Game: Football, the Rules, and the Men Who Made the Game* (Newark: University of Delaware Press, 1994) contains a wealth of material on football developments, including television's role as an unreasonable intrusion into the game in the eyes of the rules committee. Two additional books rich in factual material are L. H. Baker, *Football: Facts and Figures* (New York: Farrar & Rinehart, 1945), and Tom Perrin, *Football: A College History* (Jefferson, N.C.: McFarland, 1987).

A chapter in Frederick Rudolph, *The American College and University: A History* (New York: Vintage Books, 1962) places the development of college football within the larger nineteenth-century institution, though not without a number of inaccuracies. Amos Alonzo Stagg and Wesley W. Stout's *Touchdown!* (New York: Longmans, Green, 1927) is beneficial for better understanding early college football. Robert W. Peterson's *Pigskin: The Early Years of Pro Football* (New York: Oxford University Press, 1997) should be consulted for references to the college game and for his chapter on the television era. Michael Oriard's *Reading Football: How the Popular Press Created an American Spectacle* (Chapel Hill: University of North Carolina Press, 1993) should be read not as a history but as a study on how the print media "created," using Oriard's word, football as a popular spectacle in the latter years of the nineteenth century and early twentieth century. Two often-cited football histories should be noted, though their veracity is somewhat suspect: Alexander M. Weyand, *The Saga of American Football* (New York: Macmillan, 1955) and Allison Danzig, *The History of American Football* (Englewood Cliffs, N.J.: Prentice-Hall, 1955). For biographical data, I would suggest David L. Porter, ed. *Biographical Dictionary of American Sports,* 6 vols. (Westport, Conn.: Greenwood Press, 1988–1995).

For background on basketball, consult Morin Bishop, *100 Years of Hoops* (New York: Bishop Books, 1991); Joe Gergen, *The Final Four: An Illustrated History of College Basketball's Showcase Event* (St. Louis: Sporting News, 1987); Neil D. Isaacs, *All the Moves: A History of College Basketball* (Philadelphia: J. B. Lippincott, 1975); John D. McCallum, *College Basketball, U.S.A. Since 1892* (New York: Stein and Day, 1978); Robert W. Peterson, *Cages to Jump Shots: Pro Basketball's Early Years* (New York: Oxford University Press, 1990); and Charles Rosen, *The Scandals of '51: How Gamblers Almost Killed College Basketball* (New York: Holt, Rinehart, and Winston, 1978) and *Barney Polan's Game: A Novel of the 1951 College Basketball Scandal* (New York: Seven Stories Press, 1998). Joseph Durso's *Madison Square Garden: 100 Years of History* (New York: Simon and Schuster, 1979) provides insight into the importance of the Garden to the development of college basketball in the 1930s and 1940s. There is no book on intercollegiate basketball comparable to that of John Watterson on college football.

Several books help readers understand specific events in college sport history and the place of radio and television. Jerry N. Jordan's *The Long Range Effect of Television and Other Factors on Sports Attendance* (Washington, D.C.: Radio-Television Manufacturers Association, 1950) helped fan the flames of controversy over whether college football should be telecast in the early 1950s. Joe Hendrickson's *Tournament of Roses: The First 100 Years* (Los Angeles: Knapp Press, 1989) and Herb Michelson and Dave Newhouse's *Rose Bowl Football Since 1902* (New York: Stein and Day, 1977) furnish insights into the oldest and most lucrative bowl game.

Radio and Television

For an understanding of radio and television, a logical place to begin is Erik Barnouw's classic three-volume *History of Broadcasting in the United States* (New York: Oxford University Press, 1966–70). The volumes were later condensed in his *Tube of Plenty: The Evolution of American Television* (New York: Oxford University Press, 1975). For radio specifically, one should consult Susan J. Douglas, *Inventing American Broadcasting, 1899–1922* (Baltimore: Johns Hopkins University Press, 1987); Gleason L. Archer, *Big Business and Radio* (New York: American Historical Company, 1939) and *History of Radio to 1926* (New York: American Historical Society, 1938); William P. Banning, *Commercial Broadcasting Pioneer: The WEAF Experiment, 1922–1926* (Cambridge: Harvard University, 1946); Broadcast Magazine, *The First 50 Years of Broadcasting* (New York: Broadcasting Publications, 1982); Frank Buxton and Bill Owen, *The Big Broadcast, 1920–1950* (New York: Viking, 1972); Karen Buzzard, *Electronic Ratings: Turning Audiences into Dollars and Sense* (Boston: Focal Press, 1992); Orin E. Dunlap, Jr., *Marconi, the Man and His Wireless* (New York: Arno Press, 1971) and *Radio and Television Almanac* (New York: Harper, 1951); Sydney W. Head, *Broadcasting in America* (Boston: Houghton Mifflin, 1956); Robert L. Hilliard and Michael C. Keith, *The Broadcast Century: A Biography of American Broadcasting* (Boston: Focal Press, 1992); Frank J. Kahn, ed., *Documents of American Broadcasting* (Englewood Cliffs, N.J.: Prentice-Hall, 1984); J. Fred MacDonald, *Don't Touch That Dial!: Radio Programming in American Life from 1920–1960* (Chicago: Nelson-Hall, 1979); W. Rupert MacLaurin, *Invention and Innovation in the Radio Industry* (New York: Macmillan, 1949); Leonard Maltin, *The Great American Broadcast* (New York: Dutton, 1997); Dugua Marconi, *My Father Marconi* (New York: McGraw-Hill, 1962); Mary C. O'Connell, ed., *Connections: Reflections of Sixty Years of Broadcasting* (New York: National Broadcasting Company, 1986); E. P. J. Shurick, *The First Quarter-Century of American Broadcasting* (Kansas City: Midland Publishing, 1946); Anthony Slide, *Great Radio Personalities in Historic Photographs* (New York: Dover, 1982); Susan Smulyan, *The Commercialism of American Broadcasting, 1920–1934* (Washington, D.C.: Smithsonian Institution Press, 1996); and Llewellyn White, *The American Radio* (Chicago: University of Chicago Press, 1947).

Several autobiographies and biographies illuminate the place of radio broadcasters in college sport. Two early sportscasters, Graham McNamee and Ted Husing, have told their own stories: Graham McNamee's *You're on the Air* (New York: Harper & Bros., 1926) and Ted Husing, *Ten Years Before the Mike* (New York: Farrar & Rinehart, 1935). Red Barber's *The Broadcasters* (New York: Da Capo, 1985) recounts not only his own story but also that of other sports broadcasters before him. Lindsey Nelson describes his early college football broadcasting in his *Hello Everybody, I'm Lindsey Nelson* (New York: William Morrow, 1985). Ernie Harwell, in *Tuned to Baseball* (South Bend, Ind.: Diamond Communications, 1985), gives an interesting account of early Rose Bowl announcers. Ray Poindexter provides a great deal of information on important figures and events in *Golden Throats and Silver Tongues: The Radio Announcers* (New York: Oxford University Press, 1966). David J. Halberstam, in *Sports on New York Radio: A Play-by-Play History* (Chicago: Masters Press, 1999), devotes an entire chapter to college football broadcasting from the early 1920s to the 1970s. On a national level, Curt Smith's *Voices of the Game* (South Bend, Ind.: Diamond Communications, 1987) emphasizes baseball but also touches on college sport, Notre Dame, and the NCAA. Similarly, Curt Smith's *Of Mikes and Men from Ray Scott to Curt Gowdy* (South Bend, Ind.: Diamond Communications, 1998) offers interesting anecdotes on such particulars as the Du Mont Television Network, Notre Dame, Lindsay Nelson, and Red Grange. William A. Harper's *How You Played the Game: The Life of Grantland Rice* (Columbia: University of Missouri Press, 1999), Charles Fountain's *Sportswriter: The Life and Times of Grantland Rice* (New York: Oxford University Press, 1993), and Mark Inabinett's *Grantland Rice and His Heroes* (Knoxville: University of Tennessee Press, 1994) discuss Rice's short-lived broadcasting life.

In addition to Erik Barnouw's influential works, there are a number of histories of television one can consult. Albert Abramson, in *The History of Television, 1880–1941* (Jefferson, N.C.: McFarland, 1987), provides facts on the background leading up to the development of commercial television. Philip Kirby, in *The Victory of Television* (New York: Harper & Bros., 1939), and Orrin E. Dunlap, Jr., in *The Future of Television* (New York: Harper & Bros., 1942), provide the reader with insight into the development of TV. William Boddy's *Fifties Television: The Industry and Its Critics* (Champaign: University of Illinois Press, 1990) offers glimpses into the early growth of television. Gary N. Hess, in *An Historical Study of the Du Mont Television Network* (New York: Arno Press, 1979), is a sound account of the generally forgotten 1940s and 1950s network that provided much of the early telecasting of sports events before it folded. Michael Winship's *Television* (New York: Random House, 1988) is a worthy account of TV, with insights into the early place of sport. James Zigerell's *The Uses of Television in American Higher Education* (New York: Praeger, 1991) confirms the notion that institutions of higher education have given little thought to placing college sport in the model of educational television.

There are a number of network histories and biographies and autobiographies of television insiders. One in particular that sheds significant light on the telecasting of intercollegiate athletics is Marc Gunther's *The House That Roone Built: The Inside Story of ABC News* (Boston: Little, Brown, 1994), which recounts Arledge's early leadership at ABC in sports telecasting. Others that are helpful include: Ken Auletta, *Three Blind Mice: How the TV Networks Lost Their Way* (New York: Random House 1991); Kenneth Bilby, *The General: David Sarnoff and the Rise of the Communications Industry* (New York: Harper & Row, 1986); Peter J. Boyer, *Who Killed CBS?* (New York: Random House, 1988); Leonard H. Goldenson and Marvin J. Wolf, *Beating the Odds: The Untold Story Behind the Rise of ABC* (New York: Charles Scribner's Sons, 1991); William S. Paley, *As It Happened: A Memoir* (Garden City, N.J.: Doubleday, 1979); Lewis J. Paper, *Empire: William S. Paley and the Making of CBS* (New York: St. Martin's Press, 1987); Sterling Quinlan, *Inside ABC: American Broadcasting Company's Rise to Power* (New York: Hastings House,

1979); Salloy Bedell Smith, *In All His Glory: The Life of William S. Paley* (New York: Simon and Schuster, 1990); and Huntington Williams, *Beyond Control: ABC and the Fate of the Networks* (New York: Atheneum, 1989).

Other historical sources on TV that proved useful for this study include Steven Barnett, *Games and Sets: The Changing Face of Sport on Television* (London: British Film Institute, 1990); Howard J. Blumenthal and Oliver R. Goodenough, *This Business of Television* (New York: Billboard Books, 1991); Philip S. Cook, Douglas Gomery, and Lawrence W. Lichty, eds., *The Future of News: Television, Newspapers, Wire Services, Newsmagazines* (Baltimore: Johns Hopkins University Press, 1992); Edward V. Dolan, *TV or CATV? A Struggle for Power* (Port Washington, N.Y.: National University Publications Associated Faculty Press, 1984); Marc Eliot, *American Television: The Official Art of the Artificial* (New York: Anchor Press, 1968); Ralph Engleman, *Public Radio and Television in America* (Thousand Oaks, Calif.: Sage Publications, 1996); Norm Goldstein, *Associated Press History of Television* (Avenal, N.J.: Outlook Book Company, 1991); Tim Hollis, *Forty Magical Years in Television* (Adamsville, Ala.: Campbell's Publishing, 1991); Andrew F. Inglis, *A History of Broadcasting: Technology and Business* (Stonham, Mass.: Focal Press, 1990); Frank Lovece, *The Television Yearbook* (New York: Perigee Books, 1992); Martin Mayer, *About Television* (New York: Harper & Row, 1972); Newton N. Minow, *How Vast the Wasteland Now* (New York: Gannett Foundation Media Center, 1991); Curtis Mitchell, *Cavalcade of Broadcasting* (Chicago: Follett, 1970); Ed Papazin, *Medium Rare: The Evolution, Workings and Impact of Commercial Television* (New York: Media Dynamics, 1991); Anthony Slide, *The Television Industry: A Historical Dictionary* (Westport, Conn.: Greenwood Press, 1991); Steven D. Stark, *Telenation: The Television Shows and Events That Made Us Who We Are* (New York: Free Press, 1997); Neil Sullivan, *The Captain Video Book: The Du Mont Television Network Story* (Washington, D.C.: Loosestrife Press, 1990); Joseph H. Udelson, *The Great Television Race: A History of the American Television Industry, 1925–1941* (Tuscalossa: University of Alabama Press, 1982); U.S. Federal Communications Commission, *Fourth Annual Report,* 30 June 1938 (Washington, D.C.: U. S. Government Printing Office, 1939); Mary Ann Watson, *Defining Visions: Television and the American Experience since 1945* (Ft. Worth, Tex.: Harcourt Brace, 1998) and *Expanding Vista: American Television in the Kennedy Years* (New York: Oxford University Press, 1990); and Francis Wheen, *Television, A History* (London: Century Publishing, 1985).

For history of cable television, consult Partrick R. Parsons and Robert M. Frieden's *The Cable and Satellite Television Industries* (Boston: Allyn and Bacon, 1998). Other helpful studies include Ralph Engleman, *The Origins of Public Access Cable Television: 1966–1972* (Columbia, S.C.: Journalism Monographs, October 1900, Number 123); Dantia Gould, *The Pay-Per-View Explosion* (York, Maine: QV Publishing, 1991); Thomas W. Hazlett and Matthew L. Spitzer, *Public Policy toward Cable Television: The Economics of Rate Controls* (Cambridge: MIT Press, 1997); Timothy Hollins, *Beyond Broadcasting:*

Into the Cable Age (London: BFI Publishing, 1984); Leland L. Johnson, *Toward Competition in Cable Television* (Cambridge: MIT Press, 1994); and Ralph M. Negrine, ed., *Cable Television and the Future of Broadcasting* (New York: St Martin's Press, 1985).

Criticism of Intercollegiate Athletics

There has been no lack of criticism aimed at intercollegiate athletics and its commercialism and professionalism. The classical study is Howard Savage and others, *American College Athletics* (New York: Carnegie Foundation for the Advancement of Teaching, 1929). The Carnegie Report only noted the emerging force of radio in passing as it denounced commercialized athletics that "affect the educational quality of an institution." Over sixty years later, following two failed reform efforts, the Knight Foundation Commission on Intercollegiate Athletics published *Keeping Faith with the Student-Athlete: A New Model for Intercollegiate Athletics* (1991), in which it states that "presidents should control their institution's involvement with commercial television" (14). Of course, as I have argued, presidents have been major contributors to the commercialization and professionalization of college athletics for well over a century. Thus it seems highly unlikely that successful reform might come from the ex-presidents who head the Knight Commission, Father Theodore Hesburgh and William Friday. Educational historian John Thelin begins his study of college sport with the Carnegie Report in his *Games Colleges Play: Scandal and Reform in Intercollegiate Athletics* (Baltimore: Johns Hopkins University Press, 1994). Thelin looks at four failed reform movements in college athletics, including that of the Carnegie and Knight Commissions. Strangely, neither Thelin nor the reform movements themselves, with the possible exception of the Knight commission's, have looked at the media as a major problem facing successful intercollegiate athletic reform.

Allen L. Sack and Ellen J. Staurowsky's *College Athletes for Hire: The Evolution and Legacy of the NCAA's Amateur Myth* (Westport, Conn.: Praeger, 1998) notes the commercializing impact of radio and TV, but the authors do not devote any narrative to considering radio or TV's role in the attempt to return college athletics to the amateur model they favor. For a simple and interesting reform solution, if impractical in America, see Allen Guttmann's "The Anomaly of Intercollegiate Athletics," in Judith Andre and David N. James, eds., *Rethinking College Athletics* (Philadelphia: Temple University Press, 1991), 17–20. Guttmann proposes abandoning intercollegiate athletics as they are known and substituting a German system of private clubs operated outside of the educational institutions. Eliminating two centuries of American college sport, however, might prove to be somewhat difficult.

Several economists have looked at intercollegiate athletics and called for an educational reform. Economist Andrew Zimbalist, in *Unpaid Professionals: Commercialism and Conflict in Big-Time College Sports* (Princeton, N.J.: Princeton University Press, 1999), views sport using an economic analysis, coming to the conclusion that reform is needed among big-time institutions.

He chooses the issues of equal opportunity for athletes, equal pay for coaches, gender equity, and commercial concerns, including television. However, not one of his ten reform proposals has to do with radio or television, the biggest commercializers of big-time colleges since World War II. Another economist, Paul R. Lawrence, in *Unsportsmanlike Conduct: The National Collegiate Athletic Association and the Business of College Football* (New York: Praeger, 1987), devotes two chapters to the NCAA's control of television and bowl games. In them, Lawrence uses the cartel theory, effectively showing the impact of the NCAA television policy in dividing the football marketplace and limiting competition. Another economic history of the NCAA is Arthur A. Fleisher, III, Brian L. Goff, and Robert D. Tollison, *The National Collegiate Athletic Association: A Study in Cartel Behavior* (Chicago: University of Chicago Press, 1992). In it, the authors show how many aspects of the NCAA, including its television policies, represent cartel behavior. Most intercollegiate reforms, they claim, have been used to strengthen the power of the NCAA cartel.

Murray Sperber, a professor in American Studies and Literature at Indiana University, has written three books condemning big-time intercollegiate athletics, *College Sports, Inc.: The Athletic Department vs. the University* (New York: Henry Holt, 1990), *Shake Down the Thunder: The Creation of Notre Dame Football* (New York: Henry Holt, 1993), and *Onward to Victory: The Crises That Shaped College Sport* (New York: Henry Holt, 1998). In the last book, Sperber offers two lengthy chapters on the telecasting of Notre Dame football, but a polemical style and lack of primary sources outside of the University of Notre Dame Archives limit the value of his generalizing to the larger world of intercollegiate athletics. He marshals his facts to conclude that at many big-time institutions, "beer and circus" football have become substitutes for meaningful education—reform has been unsuccessful. Edwin H. Cady, in *The Big Game: College Sports and American Life* (Knoxville: University of Tennessee Press, 1978), calls for reform from his position as a professor of humanities and faculty representative at Duke University. With knowledge of the media influence on big-time sport, Cady concludes his ethereal study of college sport by stating that the Big Game "needs to be liberated from the 'gate' and made independent of the things for which the media and show biz hate themselves" (233). So much for reform.

Legal and Governmental Issues

Intercollegiate athletics are often driven by legal issues, especially those dealing with the electronic media. Several books analyze the legal issues in college sport. John C. Weistart and Cym H. Lowell's *The Law of Sports* (Indianapolis: Bobbs-Merrill, 1979) and *The Law of Sports: 1985 Supplement* (Charlottesville, Va.: Michie Company, 1985) are particularly useful. So, too, are Paul C. Weiler and Gary R. Roberts, *Sports and the Law: Text, Cases, Problems* (St. Paul, Minn.: West Group, 1998); Gary A. Uberstine, ed., *Law of Professional and Amateur Sports* (New York: Clark Boardman Company, 1988); Robert Alan Garrett and Philip R. Hochberg, *Sports Broadcasting and Law* (St.

Paul, Minn.: West Law, 1984); Glenn M. Wong, *Essentials of Amateur Sports Law,* 2d ed. (Dover, Mass.: Auburn House, 1994); and Robert C. Berry and Glenn M. Wong, *Law and Business of the Sports Industries,* 2 vols. (Dover, Mass.: Auburn House, 1986). Other helpful works include: Martin J. Greenberg, *Sports Law Practice* (Charlottesville, Va.: Michie Company, 1993), Matthew C. McKinnon, Robert A. McCormick, and Darryl C. Wilson, *Sports Law* (Lansing, Mich.: Lupus Publications, 1999), Charles E. Quirk, ed., *Sport and the Law: Major Legal Cases* (New York: Garland, 1996), Lionel S. Sobel, *Professional Sports and the Law* (New York: Law-Arts Publishers, 1977), and Steven C. Wade and Robert D. Hay, *Sports Law for Educational Institutions* (New York: Quorum Books, 1988).

Governmental issues clarifying sports broadcasting can be found in several publications. Roger Noll's *Government and the Sports Business* (Washington, D.C.: Brookings Institution, 1974) is an early study in this field, and includes a chapter titled "Sports Broadcasting." Roger E. Meiners's *Regulators and the Reagan Era: Politics, Bureaucracy and the Public Interest* (New York: Holmes & Meier, 1989) is solid on the government's deregulation of the economy in the 1970s and 1980s as it relates to football telecasting. See also Roger Noll and Bruce M. Owen, *The Political Economy of Deregulation* (Washington, D.C.: American Enterprise Institute, 1983) and Robert H. Bork, *The Antitrust Paradox* (New York: Basic Books, 1978).

Periodical Literature and Journal-length Articles

There is a plethora of periodical articles dealing with college sport and the impact of radio and television, many of which are cited in the footnotes. I will only note a few of the most helpful here. Stuart L. Bailey's, "9X1-WLB Experimental Radio and Broadcasting Station of the University of Minnesota," *Minnesota Techno-Log* 6 (April 1926): 216–38, 242, clearly shows the first known college football radio broadcast was in 1912 at Minnesota. Graham McNamee's "Behind the Mike," *American Magazine* 105 (April 1928): 26–27, 187–91, and Julian Bach, Jr., "Hold 'Em Husing!," *Literary Digest,* 6 November 1937, 22–23, provide an inside look at two major sports announcers and college football. Roone Arledge's "It's Sport . . . It's Money . . . It's TV," *Sports Illustrated,* 25 April 1966, 92–100 gives an insider's view of TV's impact on sport. Dave Berkman, "Long Before Arledge . . . Sports and Television: The Earliest Years: 1937–1947—as Seen by the Contemporary Press," *Journal of Popular Culture* 22 (fall 1988): 49–62 effectively summarizes the early years of television and sport. Monkia Elsner, Thomas Muller, and Peter M. Spangenberg, "The Early History of German Television: The Slow Development of a Fast Medium," *Historical Journal of Film, Radio, and Television* 10 (1900): 193–219 clarifies the early German entry into telecasting, including Germany's coverage of the 1936 Olympics. Philip R. Hochberg and Ira Horowitz, "Broadcasting and CATV: The Beauty and Bane of Major College Football," *Law and Contemporary Problems* 112 (winter–spring 1973): 112–28, brings a broadcasting-oriented point of view to problems of telecasting college football.

Michael MacCambridge, "End the Tug of War," *Inside Sports* 20 (January 1998): 66–74, offers logical suggestions for ending bowl games and creating a Division I-A football playoff. Patricia L. Pacey and Elizabeth D. Wichkam, "College Football Telecasts: Where Are They Going?" *Economic Inquiry* 23 (January 1985): 93–113 supplies an economic analysis following the breakup of the NCAA monopoly of football telecasting in 1984. "Playboy Interview: Roone Arledge," *Playboy,* October 1976, 63–86, provides possibly the best view of the Arledge influence on sports telecasting. William F. Reed, "We're Notre Dame and You're Not," *Sports Illustrated,* 19 February 1990, 56–60, shows how, among individual institutions, only Notre Dame could receive a television network contract for college football. Carl L. Reisner, "Tackling Intercollegiate Athletics: An Antitrust Analysis," *Yale Law Review* 77 (January 1978): 655–79, furnishes the legal case against the NCAA TV monopoly, unnerving NCAA officials, including Walter Byers. Eric A. Seiken, "The NCAA and the Courts: College Football and Television," in Charles E. Quirk, ed., *Sports and the Law: Major Legal Cases* (New York: Garland, 1996), 56–62, has a succinct account of the key *NCAA v. Oklahoma* 1984 Supreme Court case. William Uricchio, "Television as History: Representations of German Television Broadcasting 1935–1944," in Bruce A. Murray and Christopher J. Wickham, eds., *Framing the Past: The Historiography of German Cinema and Television* (Carbondale: Southern Illinois University Press, 1972), 167–198, contributes a solid history of early television with a sport motif.

Index